FROMMER'S

Easy

TO

France

By

Margie Rynn, Mary Novakovich, Lily Heise, Kathryn Tomasetti & Tristan Rutherford

Easy Guides are ✦ Quick To Read ✦ Light To Carry
✦ For Expert Advice ✦ In All Price Ranges

FrommerMedia LLC

Published by

FROMMER MEDIA LLC

ISBN 978-1-62887-176-0 (paper), 978-1-62887-177-7 (e-book)

Editorial Director: Pauline Frommer
Editor: Karen Fitzpatrick
Production Editor: Heather Wilcox
Cartographer: Elizabeth Puhl

For information on our other products or services, see www.frommers.com. Frommer Media LLC also publishes its books in a variety of electronic formats.

Manufactured in the United States of America

5 4 3 2 1

HOW TO CONTACT US

In researching this book, we discovered many wonderful places—hotels, restaurants, shops, and more. We're sure you'll find others. Please tell us about them, so we can share the information with your fellow travelers in upcoming editions. If you were disappointed with a recommendation, we'd love to know that, too. Please write to: Support@FrommerMedia.com

FROMMER'S STAR RATINGS SYSTEM

Every hotel, restaurant and attraction listed in this guide has been ranked for quality and value. Here's what the stars mean:

★   Recommended
★★ Highly Recommended
★★★ A must! Don't miss!

AN IMPORTANT NOTE

The world is a dynamic place. Hotels change ownership, restaurants hike their prices, museums alter their opening hours, and buses and trains change their routings. And all of this can occur in the several months after our authors have visited, inspected, and written about these hotels, restaurants, museums and transportation services. Though we have made valiant efforts to keep all our information fresh and up-to-date, some few changes can inevitably occur in the periods before a revised edition of this guidebook is published. So please bear with us if a tiny number of the details in this book have changed. Please also note that we have no responsibility or liability for any inaccuracy or errors or omissions, or for inconvenience, loss, damage, or expenses suffered by anyone as a result of assertions in this guide.

CONTENTS

ABOUT THE AUTHOR

Margie Rynn has been living in and writing about France for more than 15 years. The author of "Pauline Frommer's Paris," she has also written features for numerous magazines. Margie is married to a kind and understanding Frenchman, and they have a lovely 13-year-old son. She lives in Paris.

Mary Novakovich is an award-winning journalist and member of the British Guild of Travel Writers. She has been writing extensively about France and other countries for more than 15 years for "The Independent," "The Guardian," "Sunday Times Travel Magazine," "The Daily Telegraph," the BBC, "France Magazine," and CNN, among others. She is based in Hertfordshire, England.

Lily Heise went to Paris as an exchange student in 2000 and fell in love with the country. She contributes to various publications, both in print and online. She lives in Montmartre and spends her free time exploring off-beat Paris in addition to villages and vineyards around the country.

Kathryn Tomasetti is U.S.-born and Italian-raised. She writes travel and food features for a variety of publications, including "The Guardian" and "The Times." Her travel photos have been published by "National Geographic" and "Time Out." Kathryn resides in Nice, France.

Tristan Rutherford has been a freelance writer for more than a decade. His first assignment took him to Nice, and he has been based there ever since. He has visited more than 60 countries and written about 20 of them for "The Independent" and the "Sunday New York Times Travel Magazine." Tristan also lectures on travel journalism at London's Central Saint Martins.

ABOUT THE FROMMER'S TRAVEL GUIDES

For most of the past 50 years, Frommer's has been the leading series of travel guides in North America, accounting for as many as 24% of all guidebooks sold. I think I know why.

Although we hope our books are entertaining, we nevertheless deal with travel in a serious fashion. Our guidebooks have never looked on such journeys as a mere recreation, but as a far more important human function, a time of learning and introspection, an essential part of a civilized life. We stress the culture, lifestyle, history, and beliefs of the destinations we cover and urge our readers to seek out people and new ideas as the chief rewards of travel.

We have never shied from controversy. We have, from the beginning, encouraged our authors to be intensely judgmental, critical—both pro and con—in their comments, and wholly independent. Our only clients are our readers, and we have triggered the ire of countless prominent sorts, from a tourist newspaper we called "practically worthless" (it unsuccessfully sued us) to the many rip-offs we've condemned.

And because we believe that travel should be available to everyone regardless of their incomes, we have always been cost-conscious at every level of expenditure. Although we have broadened our recommendations beyond the budget category, we insist that every lodging we include be sensibly priced. We use every form of media to assist our readers and are particularly proud of our feisty daily website, the award-winning Frommers.com.

I have high hopes for the future of Frommer's. May these guidebooks, in all the years ahead, continue to reflect the joy of travel and the freedom that travel represents. May they always pursue a cost-conscious path, so that people of all incomes can enjoy the rewards of travel. And may they create, for both the traveler and the persons among whom we travel, a community of friends, where all human beings live in harmony and peace.

Arthur Frommer

THE BEST OF FRANCE

France presents visitors with an embarrassment of riches—you may be overwhelmed by all the choices. Here we've compiled a list of our favorite experiences and discoveries.

FRANCE'S best AUTHENTIC EXPERIENCES

o **Sipping Pastis in Provence:** This anise-flavored liquor is sipped at sundown on every town square, from Arles to the Italian border. Beware: The Provençal are seriously brand-conscious. Order a "51" if you want to look like a local, or a "Janot" for the region's latest organic offering. See chapter 7.

o **Breaking the Bank at Monte-Carlo:** The **Casino de Monte-Carlo** has been the most opulent place to have a flutter for more than 150 years. Its creation turned the tables for Monaco, transforming a provincial port into a world-class tourist destination. See p. 297.

o **Ogling the Pomp of the Popes' Medieval Party Pad:** Avignon's **Palais des Papes,** or Popes' Palace, is a moneyed medley of Gothic architecture, vast banqueting halls, and frescoed suites. The Châteauneuf-du-Pape papal vineyards just north of Avignon still produce some of the most noted wine in France. See p. 198.

o **Buying Your Daily Bread:** Cute little boulangeries are everywhere. The daily baguette run is a ritual for many French people. Get your coins ready (1€, give or take 10 centimes) and join the queue.

o **Shopping on a Market Day:** We recommend the open-air market in **Arles,** one of Provence's most authentic destinations. On Wednesday and Saturday mornings, a colorful line of vendors sells olives, fresh bread, cheese, and local ham underneath the city ramparts, a few blocks from the town's Roman amphitheater. See p. 213. Alternatively, French covered markets are time machines—visiting one is like taking a trip back through the centuries. Both Avignon's **Les Halles** (p. 199) and Cannes' **Marché Forville** (p. 250) offer high-quality artisanal treats to take home, such as olive *tapenade,* as well as great things to snack on while you shop, such as vegetable-stuffed *fougasse* bread, Mara des Bois strawberries, and wedges of Cavaillon melon.

o **Whiling Away an Afternoon in a Parisian Cafe:** There is something quintessentially Parisian about doing nothing in a public space, especially when that space is a cafe. No one will bother you, even if you sit there for hours.

o **Strolling Along the Seine:** The Seine is at the center of Paris's history. Just about every major monument can be seen from here, including the Eiffel Tower, Notre-Dame, and the Louvre. And now that many of the Seine's embankments have been rendered car-free and beautified, strolling them is a pedestrian delight.

o **Chateau-Hopping Through the Loire Valley:** An excursion to the châteaux dotting the valley's rich fields and forests will familiarize you with the French Renaissance's architectural aesthetics. Visit the main castles, such as **Chambord** or **Chenonceau,** and then stop in at some lesser-visited ones, like **Chaumont** or **Valencay.** See chapter 6.

o **Sampling the Best of Chinon's Cellars:** The area around Chinon is a treasure trove of vineyards where you can experience winemaking firsthand—and, of course, taste delicious *vins.* See chapter 6.

FRANCE'S best RESTAURANTS

o **La Couronne,** Rouen (Normandy): A bustling *auberge* in business for more than 6 centuries—and pulling in plenty of celebrity diners along the way—La Couronne makes the most of this region's hearty produce. See p. 131.

ABOVE: **Food street market in Paris.** RIGHT: **Young, romantic couple by the Seine with the Eiffel Tower in the background.**

o **Marché aux Poissons,** Trouville (Normandy): This fish market's dozen seafood stalls perch on the banks of the Touques River. Each one will happily plate up your own unique *plateau de fruits de mer* (seafood platter). Be sure to order a glass of Normandy's famous cider *(cidre),* a delicate, fermented version of apple juice that is a refreshing alcoholic tipple. See p. 141.

o **Oustau de Baumanière,** Les Baux (Provence): The isolated, cinematic setting of the ancient fortress of Les Baux had troubadours singing in its streets during the Middle Ages. Today it is no less romantic. Tucked into the hills surrounding the village, this double-Michelin-starred gem is housed in a 16th-century farmhouse. See p. 209.

o **Le Louis XV,** Monaco (Riviera): Superchef Alain Ducasse oversees this iconic restaurant—regularly rated one of the finest in the world—located in Monte-Carlo's Hôtel de Paris. Dining is extravagant, with fare steeped in lavish ingredients, from white truffles to foie gras, and served in an ornate, golden dining room. Yet many dishes of elegant simplicity are equally magnificent. Best for serious epicureans. See p. 295.

o **Le Grand Véfour** (Paris): There aren't many restaurants where you can both savor an exquisite meal and eat it in a room where Napoléon Bonaparte once dined. Tucked under an arcade at the Palais Royal, Le Grand Véfour has fed everyone from Cocteau to Colette amid magnificent 18th-century decor—now it's your turn. See p. 60.

o **Bistrot Paul Bert** (Paris): When you think bistro, you probably imagine a little place like this: Dark wood furniture, cream-colored walls, and vintage lighting fixtures all evoke a timeless ambience. The menu here is equally classic, and what's more, the kitchen is one of the best in town. See p. 66.

o **Le Domaine des Hauts de Loire,** between Blois and Amboise (Loire): For more than 20 years, Rémy Giraud has been wowing locals and weary chateau-hoppers at his double-Michelin-starred restaurant. The menu showcases seasonal and regional ingredients, such as Aquitaine caviar on pecan shortbread or crispy Gatinais quail with celery cream. See p. 173.

o **La Roche le Roy,** Tours (Loire): The finest in Touraine cuisine is delicately prepared at this award-winning 18th-century manor. See p. 177.

FRANCE'S best HOTELS

o **La Cabro d'Or,** Les Baux (Provence): Spilling out from an original 18th-century farmhouse, La Cabro d'Or makes a luxurious Provençal bolthole. The labyrinthine grounds are undoubtedly some of the loveliest in France. Expect to stumble across walled gardens, bubbling fountains, and flower-strewn courtyards. See p. 209.

o **Hotel Barrière,** Deauville (Normandy): A vision of crushed red velvet, this sumptuous hotel welcomes Hollywood superstars every autumn during the Deauville Festival of American Film. But its glamour endures year-round, with chic guest rooms, private beach, and its Restaurant L'Etrier. See p. 139.

o **Mama Shelter,** Marseille (Provence): The work of legendary designer Philippe Starck, this contemporary hotel is located in the hip cours Julien neighborhood. On the ground floor, there's a courtyard pastis bar, perfect for sampling the city's favorite aperitif. See p. 226.

o **Château Saint-Martin,** Vence (Riviera): Perched on a hilltop just 20 minutes from Nice, Château Saint-Martin is one of the Riviera's most splendid hotels. The gardens are sprinkled with wildflowers. The infinity pool quite literally goes on forever. And a truly exquisite spa is onsite. Lucky guests can gaze at the Mediterranean from bed.

o **Hôtel Belles-Rives,** Juan-les-Pins (Riviera): Once a vacation villa to Zelda and F. Scott Fitzgerald, the Hôtel Belles-Rives still maintains a flamboyant, 1920s feel. Sip a sundowner on the hotel's sea-facing terrace, or try water-skiing at the hotel's aquatic club, the very spot where the sport was invented almost a century ago. See p. 256.

o **Nice Pebbles** (Riviera): Want to live like a local? Nice Pebbles manages around 100 top-quality vacation apartments dotted throughout Nice and along the Riviera's nearby coast. Accommodation is boutique-hotel standard—but at just a fraction of regular hotel rates. See p. 275.

o **Hôtel Caron de Beaumarchais** (Paris): This adorable inn re-creates the ambience of 18th-century Paris, when the hotel's namesake, the author of "The Barber of Seville," was cavorting in the neighborhood. Rooms are covered in fine reproductions of period fabrics and furnished with authentic antique writing tables, ceiling fixtures, and paintings—a bit of Old France right in the middle of the trendy Marais. See p. 47.

o **Relais St-Germain** (Paris): A luxurious mix of past and present makes this hotel a romantic and modern haven, just steps from the bustle of Boulevard St-Germain. Run by the same management as the famous restaurant Le Comptoir du Relais (downstairs), this beautiful spot makes the perfect gourmet getaway. See p. 57.

o **Château d'Artigny,** south of Tours (Loire): Complete your castle experience by staying at one of the Loire's most regal château-hotels. You really will feel like a king, bedding down in Louis XV–style rooms and relaxing in the hotel's luxurious spa. See p. 177.

o **Le Manoir Les Minimes,** Amboise (Loire): Regional charm and character shine through at this reasonably priced manor, a perfect base for exploring the château country. Tucked behind its high walls, it has many rooms facing the river, while others offer glimpses of the royal château of Amboise. See p. 169.

secret **FRANCE**

o **Cycling in the Countryside:** The country that hosts the Tour de France offers thousands of options for bike trips. You're even welcome to take your bike aboard most trains in France, free of charge. For cycling through Provence's vineyards and past pretty hilltop villages, check out **Vélo Loisir en Luberon**'s downloadable routes. See p. 203.

- **Hunting for Antiques:** The 18th- and 19th-century French aesthetic was gloriously different from that of England and North America, and many objects bear designs with mythological references to the French experience. France has some 13,000-plus antiques shops throughout the country. Stop where you see the sign ANTIQUAIRE or BROCANTE.

- **Staking Out a Private Stretch of Sand on the Iles de Lérins** (Riviera): The Iles de Lérins may lie a 20-minute ferry ride from Cannes, but these two car-free islands attract just a fraction of the visitors. Take a picnic lunch and a good book, and leave the crowds back on the coast. See p. 251.

- **Touring Marseille's Waterfront** (Provence): Following extensive urban regeneration during the city's role as European Capital of Culture 2013, much of Marseille now boasts a fresh new appearance. Head down to the city's J4 Esplanade for unbeatable views over the Vieux Port, 12th-century Fort Saint-Jean, and Rudy Ricciotti's ultra-contemporary MuCEM. See chapter 7.

- **Traveling First Class:** France's TGV rail network is the world's fastest. Yet these trains are not just high-speed. When routes are booked in advance, they're wallet-friendly too. Throw in decor by Christian Lacroix and Play-Station Portables available to rent, and you're looking at the classiest public transport in the world. See chapter 9.

- **Cruising France's Rivers:** Floating slowly down one of France's major rivers is a superb way to see hidden corners of the countryside. Most luxury barge cruises offer daily excursions, elegant dinners on deck, and bicycles for solitary exploration. See chapter 9.

- **Reveling in St-Etienne-du-Mont:** This stunning church that sits atop the highest point in the Latin Quarter is often left off the tourist itinerary. A delightful mix of late-Gothic and Renaissance styles, the church has a 16th-century chancel boasting the city's only rood screen, a magnificent work with decorations inspired by the Italian Renaissance. See p. 101.

St-Etienne-du-Mont, Paris.

- **Going Underground at Touraine's Troglodyte Caves:** Admire art, sample regional wine, and even stay the night underground in the Touraine region, home to France's largest area of Troglodyte caves. See p. 184.

- **Returning to the Time of the Crusades:** See the history behind the Crusades at the 12th-century **Abbey of Fontevraud,** one of the largest medieval monasteries in Europe and the final resting place of most of the Plantagenets. See p. 190.

FRANCE'S best FOR FAMILIES

o **Climbing the Heights of Mont-St-Michel** (Normandy): Straddling the tidal flats between Normandy and Brittany, this Gothic marvel is the most spectacular fortress in northern Europe. Said to be protected by the archangel Michael, much of it stands as it did in the 1200s. A pedestrian bridge connects the visitor center and car park to Mont-St-Michel. You can stroll, bike, or trot (in a horse-drawn carriage) across the fortress. See chapter 7.

o **Getting Medieval in the Hilltop Town of Les Baux** (Provence): The age-old hilltown of **Les Baux** has views over Provençal countryside. Kids will love its car-free medieval streets and awesome views, not to mention the daily display of a siege engine catapult. See chapter 8.

o **Making the Most of Modern Art in Antibes** (French Riviera): The **Musée Picasso** (Picasso Museum) in Antibes highlights some of the most accessible art in France. The Spanish painter set up shop in the atmospheric old quarter of Antibes's Chateau Grimaldi some 70 years ago. Children can appreciate the color, vibrancy, and playfulness that made Picasso one of the greats of the 20th century. The far-out sculptures and sunny views of the surrounding coastline will please non-art fans, too. See p. 262.

o **Joining the Cowboys in the Camargue** (Provence): Riding a sturdy Camarguais horse and with a local cowboy to guide you, make your way through the marshes of these beautiful, remote wetlands. Spot pink flamingos and watch the *gardians* with their large felt hats rounding up black bulls bred for the bullrings of the south. If the children don't horse ride, slow boat, bicycle, or Jeep make great alternatives. See chapter 8.

o **Exploring the Calanques** (Provence): In 2013 the Parc National des Calanques became France's newest national park. This stunning series of limestone cliffs and tumbling fjords stretch along the coast for 20km (12 miles) southeast of Marseille. Serious hikers can trek the Calanques' rocky promontories. Families can take in the coastline from aboard one of the many tour boats that depart from Marseille's port. See p. 228.

Cowboys in the Camargue.

Jardin des Plantes, Paris.

o **Learning about History and Fallen Heroes on Normandy's D-Day Beaches:** On June 6, 1944, the largest armada ever assembled departed on rough seas and in dense fog from southern England. Today the entire family can immerse itself in the past with superb interactive exhibits, such as the personal tales detailed at the **Normandy American Visitor Center.** Kids can then run wild on the windswept sands below. See p. 152.

o **Playing in the Jardin des Plantes** (Paris): A splendid place for a picnic, this historic botanical garden is a quiet oasis in the Latin Quarter, where families can relax and tiny travelers can enjoy the playground, hothouses, and green spaces. When playtime is over, everyone can wander over to the small zoo or the adjoining natural-history museum. See p. 99.

o **Walking through a Real Fairy Tale** (Loire): The Loire offers kids the chance to live out their fairy-tale fantasies. Step right into a storybook at the **Château d'Ussé,** the inspiration for "Sleeping Beauty." See p. 189.

FRANCE'S best BEACHES

o **Plage de Deauville** (Normandy): Coco Chanel used the chic resort of Deauville to propel herself to stardom and then added greatly to the town's sense of glamour. Revel in the sun-kissed sense of style with a stroll along the elegant Les Planches boardwalk, which skirts the edge of Deauville's silky, sandy, parasol-dotted *plage* for 2km (1¼ miles). See p. 140.

o **Plage de Pampelonne,** St-Tropez (French Riviera): Any blonde feels like Brigitte Bardot in sunny St-Tropez. And the scantily clad satyrs and nymphs splashing in the summertime surf at Plage de Pampelonne can perk up the most sluggish libido. See p. 240.

o **Hi-Beach,** Nice (French Riviera): A day along the Riviera seaside may be a little different from home: Most beaches here feature private clubs with mattresses, parasols, and chilled Champagne on demand. Nice's Hi-Beach certainly offers all of the above. Yet its contemporary design, organic restaurant, and stellar cocktails set it apart from the crowd. See p. 281.

o **Paloma Plage,** Cap Ferrat (French Riviera): Tucked into one of Cap Ferrat's sheltered bays, petite Paloma Plage is part restaurant/chic beach club and part family-friendly stretch of pebbly shoreline. In the afternoon, fragrant Aleppo pines shade much of the beach. And Brad and Angelina have been known to stop by for dinner. See p. 287.

o **Plage d'Arromanches-les-Bains** (Normandy): This immense beach is dotted with the mammoth, otherworldly remains of Winston, a prefabricated port essential during the D-Day landings. At low tide, the sandy expanse is firm (you can push a stroller or cycle along it!) and truly vast, making it popular with families. See p. 152.

o **The beaches of Juan-les-Pins** (French Riviera): In the resort that invented waterskiing, it's little surprise that all the summertime action centers around Juan-les-Pins'

View of Villefranche-sur-Mer, French Riviera.

golden shores. Spread your towel on central **Plage de Juan-les-Pins.** Or follow the locals to the unnamed sandy suntrap of beach pinched between the Hôtel Belles-Rives and Port Gallice. See p. 258.

o **Calanque d'En Vau** (Provence): Nestled into the heart of Parc National des Calanques, Calanque d'En Vau wouldn't look out of place in the tropics: Imagine an ice-white pairing of pebbly sands and transparent turquoise waters. Sitting at the base of limestone cliffs, it's accessible only on foot (for experienced hikers) or by boat. See p. 228.

o **Plage des Marinières,** Villefranche-sur-Mer (French Riviera): A perfect, seemingly endless sweep of honey-hued sand, this popular beach sits at the base of a wide bay. It's perfect for families, as the sea shelves slowly and waves are seldom seen. See p. 284.

FRANCE IN CONTEXT

The civilization and culture of France make it the most visited country in the world, which in size covers an area smaller than Texas. Yet despite France's size, each region is so intriguing and varied that you may immerse yourself in one province so deeply that you'll never have time to see what's on the other side. Perhaps more than any other country in the world, France is a land to be savored. Ideally, France is discovered slowly by car or along the country's magnificent rail network.

This guide is meant to help you decide where to go in France, but ultimately the most gratifying experience will be your own serendipitous discoveries—sunflowers, a picnic in a poppy field, an hour spent chatting with a small winemaker—whatever it is that stays in your memory for years to come.

FRANCE TODAY

Although not large by North American standards (about the size of Britain and Germany combined), France is densely packed with attractions, both cultural and recreational, and is known for its *joie de vivre.*

Newcomers have commented (often adversely) on the cultural arrogance of the French. But despite its linguistic and cultural rigidity (and an increased popularity in far-right politics), France has received more immigrants and political exiles than any other European country. Part of this derives from France's status as one of Europe's least densely populated nations per square mile, and part of it from the tendency of the French to let others be until their actions become dangerous or obnoxious, not necessarily in that order.

If you're a first-timer, everything in France, of course, is new. But if you've been away for a long time, expect changes. Taxi drivers in Paris may no longer correct your fractured French, but address you in English—and that's tantamount to a revolution. Part of this derives from the county's interest in music, culture, and films from foreign countries, and part from France's growing awareness of its role as a leader of a united Europe.

Chateau and church in Aiguines with St Croix Lake in the background.

Yet France has never been more concerned about the loss of its unique identity within a landscape that has attracted an increasing number of immigrants from its former colonies. Many worry that France will continue to lose the battle to keep its language strong, distinct, and unadulterated by foreign slang or catchwords (and good luck with banning such terms as *l'email* and *le week-end*). But as the country moves deeper into the millennium, foreign tourists spending much-needed cash are no longer perceived as foes or antagonists. *Au contraire:* France welcomes the world to its palaces, parks, beaches, and UNESCO World Heritage sites. And if those tens of millions of guests spend a few euros—and soak up a little local culture while they're here—that's all to the good.

THE HISTORY OF FRANCE

EARLY GAUL When the ancient Romans considered France part of their empire, their boundaries extended deep into the forests of the Paris basin and up to the edges of the Rhine. Part of Julius Caesar's early reputation came from his defeat of King Vercingetorix at Alésia in 52 B.C., a victory he was quick to publicize in one of the ancient world's literary masterpieces, "The Gallic Wars." In that year, the Roman colony of Lutetia (Paris) was established on an island in the Seine (Ile de la Cité).

As the Roman Empire declined, its armies retreated to the flourishing colonies that had been established along a strip of the Mediterranean coast—among others, these included Orange, Arles, Antibes, and Marseille, which today retain some of the best Roman monuments in Europe.

THE CAROLINGIANS From the wreckage of the early first millennium emerged a new dynasty: the Carolingians. One of their leaders, Charles

Martel, halted a Muslim invasion of northern Europe at Tours in 743 and left a much-expanded kingdom to his son, Pepin. The Carolingian empire eventually stretched from the Pyrénées to a point deep in the German forests, encompassing much of modern France, Germany, and northern Italy. The heir to this vast land was Charlemagne. Crowned emperor in Rome on Christmas Day in 800, he returned to his capital at Aix-la-Chapelle (Aachen) and created the Holy Roman Empire. Charlemagne's rule saw a revived interest in scholarship, art, and classical texts, defined by scholars as the Carolingian Renaissance.

THE MIDDLE AGES When the Carolingian dynasty died out in 987, the hectic, migratory Middle Ages officially began. Invasion by Hungarians, Vikings, and the English (who ruled half the country) lent France a cosmopolitan, if fractured, air. Politically driven marriages among the ruling families more than doubled the size of the territory controlled from Paris, a city that was increasingly recognized as the country's capital. Philippe II (reigned 1179–1223) infiltrated more prominent families with his genes than anyone else in France, successfully marrying members of his family into the Valois, Artois, and Vermandois. He also managed to win Normandy and Anjou back from the English. Louis IX (St. Louis) emerged as the 13th century's most memorable king, though he ceded most of the hard-earned military conquests of his predecessors back to the English.

France's burgeoning wealth and power was checked by the Black Death, which began in the summer of 1348. The rat-borne plague killed an estimated 33% of Europe's population, decimating the population of Paris and setting the stage for the exodus of the French monarchs to safer climes in such places as the Loire Valley. A financial crisis, coupled with a series of ruinous harvests, almost bankrupted the nation.

During the Hundred Years' War, the English made sweeping inroads into France in an attempt to grab the throne. At their most powerful, they controlled almost all the north (Picardy and Normandy), Champagne, and parts of the Loire Valley. The peasant-born charismatic visionary Joan of Arc rallied the dispirited French troops as well as the timid dauphin (crown prince), whom she managed to have crowned as Charles VII. As threatening to the Catholic Church as she was to the English, she was declared a heretic and

Roman Arch of Triumph, Orange.

burned at the stake in Rouen in 1431. The place of her demise is now sited in the city's marketplace.

THE RISING POWER By the early 17th century, France was a modern state. Few vestiges of feudalism remained. In 1624, Louis XIII appointed a Catholic cardinal, the duc de Richelieu, as his chief minister. Amassing enormous power, Richelieu virtually ruled the country until his death in 1642.

Although he ascended the throne when he was only 9, Louis XIV was the most powerful monarch Europe had seen since the Roman emperors. The estimated population of France at this time was 20 million, as opposed to 8 million in England and 6 million in Spain. French colonies in Canada, the West Indies, and America (Louisiana) were stronger than ever. The mercantilism that Louis's brilliant finance minister, Colbert, implemented was one of the era's most important fiscal policies, hugely increasing France's power and wealth. The arts flourished, as did a sense of aristocratic style that's remembered with a bittersweet nostalgia today. Louis's palace of Versailles is the perfect monument to the most flamboyantly consumptive era in French history.

THE REVOLUTION & THE RISE OF NAPOLEON Meanwhile, the Enlightenment was training a new generation of thinkers for the struggle against absolutism, religious fanaticism, and superstition. On August 10, 1792, troops from Marseille, aided by a Parisian mob, threw the dimwitted Louis XVI and his tactless Austrian-born queen, Marie Antoinette, into prison. After months of bloodshed and bickering among violently competing factions, the two thoroughly humiliated monarchs were executed.

France's problems got worse before they got better. In the ensuing bloodbaths, both moderates and radicals were guillotined in full view of a bloodthirsty crowd. Only the militaristic fervor of Napoleon Bonaparte could reunite France and bring an end to the revolutionary chaos. A political and military genius who appeared on the landscape at a time when the French were thoroughly sickened by the anarchy following their revolution, he restored a national pride that had been severely tarnished. He also established

Outside view of the famous palace of Versailles.

a bureaucracy and a code of law that has been emulated in other legal systems around the world.

Alas, Napoleon's victories made him overconfident—and made the rest of Europe clamor for his demise. Just as he was poised on the verge of conquering the entire continent, Napoleon's famous retreat from Moscow during the winter of 1812 reduced his formerly invincible army to tatters. Napoleon was then decisively beaten at Waterloo by the combined armies of the English, Dutch, and Prussians. Exiled to the British-held island of St. Helena in the South Atlantic, he died in 1821.

THE BOURBONS & THE SECOND EMPIRE   In 1814, following the destruction of Napoleon and his dream of empire, the Congress of Vienna redefined the map of Europe. The Bourbon monarchy was reestablished, with reduced powers for Louis XVIII, an archconservative. After a few stable decades, Napoleon I's nephew, Napoleon III, was elected president in 1848. Appealing to the property-protecting instinct of a nation that hadn't forgotten the violent upheavals of less than a century before, he initiated a repressive right-wing government in which he was awarded the totalitarian status of emperor in 1851.

As ever, intra-European conflict knocked France off its pedestal once again. In 1870, the Prussians—a rising power in the German east—defeated Napoleon III at Sedan and held him prisoner with 100,000 of his soldiers. Paris was besieged and occupied, an inglorious state for the world's greatest city. After the Prussians withdrew, a violent revolt ushered in the Third Republic and its elected president, Marshal MacMahon, in 1873. Peace and prosperity slowly returned.

THE WORLD WARS   International rivalries, lost colonial ambitions, and conflicting alliances led to World War I, which, after decisive German victories for 2 years, degenerated into the mud-slogged horror of trench warfare. Mourning between 4 and 5 million casualties, Europe was inflicted with psychological scars that never healed. In 1917, the United States broke the European deadlock by entering the war.

After the Allied victory, grave economic problems, plus the demoralization stemming from years of fighting, encouraged the growth of socialism and communism. The French government demanded every centime of reparations it could wring from a crushed Germany, humiliating the country into a vengeful spiral that would have repercussions 2 decades later.

The worldwide Great Depression from 1929 devastated France. Poverty and widespread bankruptcies weakened the Third Republic to the point where successive coalition governments rose and fell. The crises reached a crescendo on June 14, 1940, when Hitler's armies arrogantly marched down the Champs-Elysées, and newsreel cameras recorded French people openly weeping. Under the terms of the armistice, the north of France was occupied by the Nazis, and a puppet French government was established at Vichy under the authority of Marshal Pétain.

Pétain and his regime cooperated with the Nazis in unbearably shameful ways. Not the least of their errors included the deportation of more than 75,000 French Jews to German work camps. Pockets of resistance fighters *(le maquis)* waged small-scale guerrilla attacks against the Nazis throughout the course of the war. Charles de Gaulle, the irascible giant whose personality is forever associated with the politics of his era, established himself as the head of the French government-in-exile.

The scenario was radically altered on June 6, 1944, when the largest armada in history—a combination of American, British, and Canadian troops—successfully established a beachhead on the shores of Normandy. Paris rose in rebellion even before the Allied armies arrived. On August 26, 1944, Charles de Gaulle entered the capital as head of the Fourth Republic.

THE POSTWAR YEARS Plagued by the bitter residue of colonial policies that France had established during the 18th and 19th centuries, the Fourth Republic witnessed the rise and fall of 22 governments and 17 premiers. Many French soldiers died on foreign battlefields as once-profitable colonies in North Africa and Indochina rebelled. After suffering a bitter defeat in 1954, France ended its occupation of Vietnam and freed its former colony. It also granted internal self-rule to Tunisia and Morocco.

Algeria was to remain a greater problem. The advent of the 1958 Algerian revolution signaled the end of the much-maligned Fourth Republic. De Gaulle was called back from retirement to initiate a new constitution, the Fifth Republic, with a stronger set of executive controls. To nearly everyone's dissatisfaction, de Gaulle ended the Algerian war in 1962 by granting the country full independence. The sun had finally set on most of France's far-flung empire.

In 1968, major social unrest and a violent coalition hastily formed between the nation's students and blue-collar workers eventually led to the collapse of the government. De Gaulle resigned when his attempts to placate some of the marchers were defeated. The reins of power passed to his second-in-command, Georges Pompidou, and his successor, Valérie Giscard d'Estaing, both of whom continued de Gaulle's policies emphasizing economic development and protection of France as a cultural resource to the world.

La Défense business district of Paris.

In 1981, François Mitterrand was elected the first Socialist president of France since World War II. During his two terms, he spent billions of francs on his *grands projets* (including the Louvre pyramid, Opéra Bastille, Cité de la Musique, and Grande Arche de La Défense), although unemployment and endemic corruption remained.

On his third try, on May 7, 1995, Chirac won the presidency with 52% of the vote and immediately declared war on unemployment. But his popularity soon faded in the wake of unrest caused by an 11.5% unemployment rate and a stressed economy struggling to meet entry requirements for the European Union that France had signed up for 3 years before.

Financial crisis or not, in May 1996 thousands of Parisian workers took to the streets, disrupting passenger train service to demand a workweek shorter than the usual 39 hours. Most French now work a 35-hour week and retire at 60 years old.

In 1999, France joined with other European countries in adopting the euro as its standard of currency. The new currency accelerated the creation of a single economy comprising over 500 million Europeans, although the ability of several fiscally wayward states to borrow at preferential rates has led to a sovereign debt crisis that remains today. Nonetheless, the European Union now boasts a combined gross national product approaching 19€ trillion, a shade larger than that of the United States and China.

Although Chirac steadied the ship—and most French today think he ran a decent presidency—in 2005 a rotten core was exposed. Decades of pent-up resentment felt by the children of African immigrants exploded into an orgy of violence and vandalism. Riots began in the suburbs of Paris and spread around the country. Throughout France, gangs of youths battled the French police, torching schools, cars, and businesses. Rioting followed in such cities as Dijon, Marseille, and Rouen. Most of the rioters were the sons of Arab and black African immigrants, Muslims living in a mostly Catholic country. The reason for the protests? Leaders of the riots claimed they live "like second-class citizens," even though they are French citizens. Unemployment is 30% higher in the ethnic ghettos of France.

Against a backdrop of discontent regarding issues of unemployment, immigration, and healthcare, the charismatic Nicolas Sarkozy swept into the presidential office in May 2007. Sarkozy, the combative son of a Hungarian immigrant, promised to reinvigorate ties with France's traditional ally, the United States.

Outside of politics, the French looked at Sarkozy's personal life with ridicule. His marriage to Bruni and his holidays with the rich and famous earned him the title of the "bling bling president." In a show of how divided France was over his administration, he lost the 2012 presidential election to socialist challenger François Hollande by a whisker.

Hollande promised a government of hard-working technocrats. Alas, "Monsieur Normal" proved anything but. A series of gaffes—including employing a minister with a secret Swiss bank account to superintend France's endemic tax evasion—made him the least popular president since polling began, with a disapproval rating of 75%. Not content with family ties to his first girlfriend, Ségolène Royale, or his mistress-turned-First Lady, Valérie Trierweiler, he embarked on an ongoing relationship with actress Julie Gayet. His method of courting Miss Gayet (which essentially involved turning up at her apartment on the back of his bodyguard's scooter) was deemed tacky by the French press. As France's non-tourist economy maintains only anemic growth, locals look forward to the 2017 presidential elections with baited breath. Not least as Hollande's recently announced challenger will be … Nicolas Sarkozy.

Alas, January 9, 2015 was a divisive day for French society, not politics. On a chilly winter morning in Paris, two masked gunmen assaulted the office of the satirical magazine "Charlie Hebdo." They killed 11 and injured another 11. While the weekly journal took freedom of speech to the very limits, with equal scorn poured upon Islamic theology as upon France's right-wing National Front, the terrorist outrage was seen as an attack on universal French values. Politicians from around the globe flew in to fly the "Je suis Charlie" banner on Paris's Place de la République alongside their allies. It's hoped that the June–July 2016 UEFA Euro soccer championships—held across eight cities in France—will bring the nation together in a manner not seen since France's multiethnic "rainbow warrior" team hosted—and won—the 1998 World Cup.

ART

Visitors taking pictures of da Vinci's "Mona Lisa" at Paris's Louvre.

France's manifold art treasures range from Rodin's "The Thinker" to Monet's Impressionist "Water Lilies"; its architecture encompasses Roman ruins and Gothic cathedrals as well as Renaissance châteaux and post-modern buildings like the Centre Pompidou. This brief overview is designed to help you make sense of it all.

A fine place to start is Paris's **Louvre.** The world's greatest museum abounds with Renaissance works by Italian, Flemish, and German masters, including **Michelangelo** (1475–1564) and **Leonardo da Vinci** (1452–1519). Da Vinci's **"Mona Lisa"** (1503–05), the most famous painting on the planet, hangs here.

Back in early 19th century, the **romantics** felt that both the ancients and the Renaissance had gotten it wrong and that the Middle Ages was the place to be. They idealized romantic tales of chivalry and the nobility of peasantry. Some great artists and movements of the era, all with examples in the **Louvre,** include **Theodore Géricault** (1791–1824), who painted "The Raft of the Medusa" (1819), which served as a model for the movement; and **Eugène Delacroix** (1798–1863), whose "Liberty Leading the People" (1830) was painted in the romantic style.

Decades later, the **Impressionists** adopted a free, open style, seeking to capture the *impression* light made as it reflected off objects. They painted deceptively loose compositions, using swift, visible brushwork and often light colors. For subject matter, they turned to landscapes and scenes of modern life. You'll find some of the best examples of their works in the **Musée d'Orsay.**

Impressionist greats include **Edouard Manet** (1832–83), whose groundbreaking "Picnic on the Grass" (1863) and "Olympia" (1863) helped inspire the movement with their harsh realism, visible brush strokes, and thick outlines; **Claude Monet** (1840–1926), who launched the movement officially in an 1874 exhibition in which he exhibited his Turner-inspired "Impression, Sunrise" (1874), now in the **Musée Marmottan; Pierre-Auguste Renoir** (1841–1919), known for his figures' ivory skin and chubby pink cheeks; **Edgar Degas** (1834–1917), an accomplished painter, sculptor, and draftsman—his pastels of dancers and bathers are particularly memorable; and **Auguste Rodin** (1840–1917), the greatest Impressionist-era sculptor, who crafted remarkably expressive bronzes. The **Musée Rodin,** Rodin's former Paris studio, contains, among other works, his "Burghers of Calais" (1886), "The Kiss" (1886–98), and "The Thinker" (1880).

The smaller movements or styles of Impressionism are usually lumped together as "post-Impressionism." Again, the best examples of these turn-of-the-20th-century works are exhibited at the **Musée d'Orsay,** though you'll find pieces by Matisse, Chagall, and the cubists, including Picasso, in the **Centre Pompidou** and the key museums of Nice, Rouen, Avignon, and Marseille. Important post-Impressionists include **Paul Cézanne** (1839–1906), who adopted the short brush strokes, love of landscape, and light color palette of his Impressionist friends; **Henri de Toulouse-Lautrec** (1864–1901), who created paintings and posters of wispy, fluid lines anticipating Art Nouveau and often depicting the bohemian life of Paris's dance halls and cafes; **Vincent van Gogh** (1853–90), who combined a touch of crazy Japanese influence with thick, short strokes; **Henri Matisse** (1869–1954), who created **fauvism** (a critic described those who used the style as *fauves,* meaning "wild beasts"); and **Pablo Picasso** (1881–1973), a Málaga-born artist who painted objects from all points of view at once, rather than using such optical tricks as perspective to fool viewers into seeing "cubist" three dimensions.

FRANCE IN POPULAR CULTURE
Books

For a taste of French culture before you travel, we recommend you load a half-dozen titles on your iPad or Kindle. Simon Schama's "Citizens" is the pick of the bunch for a history of the French Revolution. Moving into the 20th century, "Paris Was Yesterday, 1925–1939," is a fascinating collection of excerpts from Janet Flanner's "Letters from Paris" column in the "New Yorker," while "On Paris" comprises a newly bound series of essays by Ernest Hemingway, written for the "Toronto Star" between 1920 and 1924. Two unusual approaches to French history are Rudolph Chleminski's "The French at Table," a funny and honest history of why the French know how to eat better than anyone and how they go about it; and "Parisians: An Adventure History of Paris" by Graham Robb, entertaining historical snippets that range from the French Revolution through the 1968 riots.

Representing the city's most fabulous era are "A Moveable Feast," Ernest Hemingway's recollections of Paris during the 1920s, and Morley Callaghan's "That Summer in Paris: Memories of Tangled Friendships with Hemingway, Fitzgerald and Some Others," an anecdotal account of the same period. Another great read is "The Autobiography of Alice B. Toklas," by Gertrude Stein.

For a fictional tour of the 19th century, pick up "Madame Bovary," by Gustave Flaubert. The carefully wrought characters, setting, and plot attest to Flaubert's genius in presenting the tragedy of Emma Bovary; Victor Hugo's "Les Misérables," a classic tale of social oppression and human courage set in the era of Napoleon I; and "Selected Stories," by the master of the genre, Guy de Maupassant.

For a beguiling literary history of the French Riviera, look no further than "The French Riviera: A Literary Guide for Travellers," edited by Ted Jones. In a similar genre, "The Riviera Set: From Queen Victoria to Princess Grace," by Lita-Rose Betcherman (Kindle only), charts coastal fashions and passions by way of F. Scott Fitzgerald and Brigitte Bardot. "Chasing Matisse," by James Morgan, follows in the footsteps of the Riviera's greatest painter, from St. Tropez to Corsica to Nice.

The olive groves, lavender fields, and rolling hills of Provence are deftly described in "The Man Who Planted Trees," by Jean Giono, a children's book with an adult theme. "The Count of Monte Cristo," by Alexandre Dumas, describes the same magnificent countryside, albeit with a brief incarceration on Marseille's **Château d'If,** a former prison island now on many visitors' itineraries. Marseille's rough and ready underworld is highlighted in "Total Chaos," by Jean-Claude Izzo, along with several other locally set novels.

The pleasures, and pitfalls, of actually living in France's bucolic countryside are catalogued with charm and candor in "The Olive Farm," by Carol Drinkwater, and "A Year in Provence," by Peter Mayle. And regional French cuisine is best indulged by "At Home in Provence," by Patricia Wells, an American chef who also runs a cooking school in the area.

Films

The world's first movie was shown in Paris on December 28, 1895. Its makers were the Lumière brothers, who scared an audience to death with images of a train moving towards the audience seats. Later, Charles Pathé and Léon Gaumont were the first to exploit filmmaking on a grand scale.

The golden age of the French silent screen on both sides of the Atlantic was 1927 to 1929. Actors were directed with more sophistication, and technical abilities reached an all-time high. The film "Hugo" (2011), directed by Martin Scorsese, is a heart-warming tale set against the film industry's transformation during this period. And despite its mind-numbing length, Abel Gance's masterpiece "Napoleon" (1927) is also sweepingly evocative. Its grisly battle scenes are easily as chilling as any war film made today.

In 1936, the Cinémathèque Française was established to find and preserve old (usually silent) French films. By that time, an average of 130 films a year were made in France, by (among others) Jean Renoir, Charles Spaak, and Marcel Carne. This era also brought such French luminaries as Claudette Colbert and Maurice Chevalier to Hollywood.

After World War II, two strong traditions—*film noir* and French comedy—offered viewers new kinds of genre, like Jacques Tati's sidesplitting "Les Vacances du Monsieur Hulot" ("Mr. Hulot's Holiday"). By the mid-1950s, French filmmaking ushered in the era of enormous budgets and the creation of such frothy potboilers as director Roger Vadim's "And God Created Woman," which helped make Brigitte Bardot a celebrity around the world, contributing greatly to the image in America of France as a kingdom of sexual liberation.

By the late 1950s, counterculture was flourishing on both sides of the Atlantic. François Truffaut, widely publicizing his auteur theories, rebelled with a series of short films (like "The 400 Blows" in 1959). Other contemporary directors included Jean-Luc Godard ("A Bout de Souffle"), Alain Resnais ("Muriel"), Agnès Varda ("Le Bonheur"), Jacques Demy ("Les Parapluies de Cherbourg"), and Marguerite Duras ("Detruire, Dit-elle").

Many American and foreign films were filmed in Paris (or else used sets to simulate Paris). Notable ones have included the classic "An American in Paris," starring Gene Kelly, and "Moulin Rouge," starring Ewan McGregor as a Parisian artist. "Last Tango in Paris," with Marlon Brando, was one of the most controversial films set in Paris. Woody Allen's acclaimed "Midnight in Paris" is one of the most recent films to celebrate the City of Light. The film features beautiful shots of the city and includes cameos of iconic figures who lived in Paris in the 1920s.

Many French films have been equally popular around the world. Jean-Pierre Jeunet's "Amélie," with its beautiful scenes shot in Montmartre, continues to enchant. More recently, "La Vie en Rose" earned Marion Cotillard an Oscar in 2008 for her performance as "The Little Sparrow," Edith Piaf.

As France's second city, Marseille has formed the backdrop for several hit movies. Gérard Pirès's "Taxi" in 1998 is a blazing road movie written by Luc

Besson. The 2002 locally filmed action flick "The Transporter," starring muscle-bound Englishman Jason Statham, was also penned by Besson.

Provence was custom-made to be captured on celluloid. From Marcel Pagnol's "La Femme du Boulanger" to Claude Berri's "Manon des Sources," it's one long bucolic playground. Foreign-funded movies sum up the region in similar grand style. Lawrence Kasdan's "French Kiss" pairs uptight American Meg Ryan with devious Frenchie Kevin Kline. The Lubéron's natural charms are showcased in Ridley Scott's "A Good Year" starring Russell Crowe and Marion Cotillard.

The big French-filmed movie of 2014 was another Woody Allen number, "Magic in the Moonlight." This romantic comedy stars Colin Firth and Emma Stone against the sun-kissed backdrop of the French Riviera. Also in 2014, "Grace of Monaco," starring Nicole Kidman, shone a light on the marriage of American actress Grace Kelly into Monaco's Grimaldi family. Viewers flocked to "The Price of Desire", an arty love story featuring Irish designer Eileen Gray and Swiss architect Le Corbusier, in late 2015. It was both filmed and set on Cap Martin near Monaco.

EATING & DRINKING IN FRANCE

As any French person will attest, French food is the best in the world. That's as true today as it was during the 19th-century heyday of the master chef Escoffier. A demanding patriarch who codified the rules of French cooking, he ruled the kitchens of the Ritz in Paris, standardizing the complicated preparation and presentation of *haute cuisine*.

However, at the foundation of virtually every culinary theory ever developed in France is a deep-seated respect for the *cuisine des provinces* (also known as *cuisine campagnarde*). Ingredients usually included only what was produced locally, and the rich and hearty result was gradually developed over several generations of *mères cuisinières*. Springing from an agrarian society with a vivid sense of nature's cycles, the cuisine provided appropriate nourishment for bodies that had toiled through a day in the open air. The movement is alive and well today with a tradition for eating locally produced—or *zero km*—foods.

Gourmets, not just beach lovers, should go to the Riviera. Bouillabaisse, an exquisite fish soup (said to have been invented by Venus) is Marseille's best-known dish. Riviera specialties include *daube* (slow-cooked beef stew), *soupe au pistou* (vegetable soup with basil), and *salade Niçoise* (traditionally made with tomatoes, olives, radishes, scallions, peppers, and tuna or anchovies). All are best served with a glass of ice-cold *rosé* in the afternoon sun.

And Paris? At the center of the country's gastronomic crossroads, it tops the lot. The city literally has thousands of restaurants to choose from. The best of them are listed in this book, or discussed on websites likes **Chowhound** (www.chow.com), **Paris by Mouth** (www.parisbymouth.com), and **Time Out** (www.timeout.fr). Beef from Lyon, lamb from the Auvergne, crêpes from Brittany, and *cassoulet* from southwest France are served up in abundance. This city of 10 million gastronomes has also become a mecca for creative foreign fare. Until you've eaten sashimi, bibimbap, ceviche, and gourmet burgers in Paris, you haven't lived.

> ## Impressions
>
> The French will only be united under the threat of danger. Nobody can simply bring together a country that has 265 kinds of cheese.
>
> —Charles de Gaulle

To accompany such cuisine, let your own good taste—and your wallet—determine your choice of wine. Most wine stewards, called *sommeliers,* are there to help you in your choice, and only in the most dishonest of restaurants will they push you toward the most expensive selections. Of course, if you prefer only bottled water, or perhaps a beer, or even a cider in Normandy, then be firm and order your choice without embarrassment. Some restaurants include a beverage in their menu rates *(boisson compris),* either as part of a set tasting menu in ritzy restaurants or as part of a fixed-price formula in cheaper establishments. Some of the most satisfying wines we've drunk in France came from unlabeled house bottles or carafes, called a *vin de la maison.*

WHEN TO GO

The best time to visit France is in the spring (Apr–June) or fall (Sept–Nov): Métro seats are easier to come by and waiters are good-tempered. The weather is temperate year-round. July and August are the worst for crowds but best for beaches. That's when Parisians desert their city, leaving it to the tourists.

France's weather varies from region to region. Despite its latitude, Paris never gets very cold. Normandy is a little fresher—and foggier—but the Med boasts one long summer, with the French Riviera having 300 days of sun per year. Provence dreads *le mistral* (an unrelenting wind), which most often blows in the winter for bouts of a few days at a time, but can also last up to 2 weeks.

Paris's Average Daytime Temperature & Rainfall

	JAN	FEB	MAR	APR	MAY	JUNE	JULY	AUG	SEPT	OCT	NOV	DEC
TEMP. °F	38	39	46	51	58	64	66	66	61	53	45	40
TEMP. °C	3	4	8	11	14	18	19	19	16	12	7	4
RAINFALL (IN.)	3.2	2.9	2.4	2.7	3.2	3.5	3.3	3.7	3.3	3.0	3.5	3.1

France Calendar of Events

JANUARY

Monte Carlo Motor Rally (Le Rallye de Monte Carlo). The world's most venerable car race. Mid-January. www.acm.mc.

FEBRUARY

Carnival of Nice. Parades, music, fireworks, and "Les Batailles des Fleurs" (Battles of the Flowers) are all part of this celebration. The climax is the burning the Carnival king effigy. Late February to early March. www.nice carnaval.com.

Salon de l'Agriculture. Paris Expo Porte de Versailles, 15e, Paris. A gargantuan hymn to all that is edible, including food, agricultural exhibits, and fabulous farm animals. Late February–early March. www.salon-agriculture.com.

MARCH

Paris Fashion Week. Multiple sites around Paris. See what you'll be wearing next season. Early March; also held at end of September. www.modeaparis.com.

Le Paris-Nice, French Riviera. The nation's second-most-important cycle race is a precursor to the Tour de France. The route runs through the Provence countryside and finishes on Nice's promenade des Anglais. Mid-March. www.letour.com.

Foire du Trône, on the Reuilly Lawn of the Bois de Vincennes, 12e, Paris. This mammoth fun fair operates daily from noon to midnight. Late March to end of May. www.foiredutrone.com.

APRIL

International Garden Festival, Château de Chaumont, Amboise (Loire). An international competition showcasing the best in garden design. Late April to early November. www.domaine-chaumont.fr.

International Marathon of Paris. Runners from around the world compete along the Champs-Elysées. Mid-April. www.paris marathon.com.

MAY

Cannes Film Festival (Festival International du Film). Movie madness transforms this Mediterranean town into a media circus. Admission to films and parties is by invitation. Other films play 24 hours a day. Mid-May. www.festival-cannes.com.

Monaco Formula 1 Grand Prix. The world's most high-tech cars race through Monaco's narrow streets in a blizzard of hot metal and ritzy architecture. Late May. www.formula1.com.

European Night of Museums. For 1 marvelous night, hundreds of museums are open until 1am and free of charge all over France (and in other European countries). In Paris, nighttime rambles are enhanced with performances and lightshows. Mid-May. www.nuitdesmusees.culture.fr.

French Open Tennis Championship, Stade Roland-Garros, 16e, Paris. The French Open features 2 weeks of men's, women's, and doubles tennis on hot, red, dusty clay courts. Late May to early June. www.roland garros.com.

JUNE

Prix du Jockey Club and **Prix Diane-Longines,** Hippodrome de Chantilly. Thoroughbreds from as far away as Kentucky and Dubai compete in this race. On race days, dozens of trains depart from Paris's Gare du Nord for Chantilly, where racegoers take free shuttle buses to the track. Early to mid-June. www.france-galop.com.

Paris Air Show. France's military-industrial complex shows off its high-tech hardware. Fans, competitors, and industrial spies mob Le Bourget Airport. Every 2 years; next event mid-June 2017. www.paris-air-show.com.

Les 24 Heures du Mans Voitures. Racing cars blast around the clock at this venerable circuit. Also hosts the huge September motorcycle rally. Mid-June. www.24h-lemans.com.

Festival Chopin, Paris. Everything you've ever wanted to hear by the Polish exile, who lived most of his life in Paris. Piano recitals take place in the Orangerie du Parc de Bagatelle, 16e. Mid-June to mid-July. www.frederic-chopin.com.

Fête de la Musique, across France. Nationwide festival of sound on the longest evening of the year. Expect drummers and DJs on every street corner. June 21.

Gay Pride Parade, 25 French cities, but the biggest is in Paris, place du 18 Juin 1940 to place de la Bastille. A week of expositions and parties climaxes in a parade patterned after those in New York and San Francisco. Late June. www.gaypride.fr.

Solidays, Paris. Youth, music, and solidarity—those are the catch words at this 2-day mega-concert in the Bois de Boulogne that

Visitors can purchase tickets for almost every music festival, soccer game, or cultural event in France online. Try the official website first, or log onto **FNAC** (www.fnactickets.com), France's largest music chain, which offers a digital reservation service as well as in-store ticket booths.

raises millions for the fight against AIDS. End of June. www.solidays.org

JULY

Les Chorégies d'Orange, Orange. One of southern France's most important lyric festivals presents oratorios, operas, and choral works in France's best-preserved Roman amphitheater. Early July to early August. www.choregies.fr.

Les Nocturnes du Mont-St-Michel. This sound-and-light tour meanders through the stairways and corridors of one of Europe's most impressive medieval monuments. Early July to late August, Monday to Saturday. www.ot-montsaintmichel.com.

Tour de France. The world's most hotly contested bicycle race sends crews of wind-tunnel-tested athletes along an itinerary that detours deep into the Pyrénées, Alps, Provence, and Normandy. The finish line is on the Champs-Elysées. First 3 weeks of July. www.letour.fr.

Festival d'Avignon. This world-class festival has a reputation for exposing new talent to critical scrutiny and acclaim. The focus is usually on avant-garde works in theater, dance, and music. Many of the performances take place in the 14th-century courtyard of the Palais des Pâpes. Last 3 weeks of July. www.festival-avignon.com.

Bastille Day. Celebrating the birth of modern-day France, the nation's festivities reach their peak with country-wide street fairs, fireworks, and feasts. In Paris, the day begins with a parade down the Champs-Elysées and ends with fireworks at Montmartre. July 14. www.parisinfo.com.

Paris Quartier d'Eté. For 4 weeks, music rules sounds around the city. Two dozen French and international performances take place at a variety of locales, including Musée du Quai Branly, the Place de la République, and the Parc de Belleville. Mid-July to mid-August. www.quartierdete.com.

Nice Jazz Festival. The most prestigious jazz festival in Europe. Concerts begin in the afternoon and go on until late at night (sometimes all night) in place Masséna and the Jardin Albert 1er, overlooking Nice's promenade des Anglais. Mid-July. www.nicejazzfestival.fr.

Festival d'Aix-en-Provence. A musical event *par excellence*, with everything from Gregorian chants to operas composed on synthesizers. Recitals are in the medieval cloister of the Cathédrale St-Sauveur. Expect heat, crowds, and loud sounds. July. www.festival-aix.com.

Réncontre d'Arles. The prettiest town in Provence hosts a city-wide photography festival. Prepare to be wowed. July to September. www.rencontres-arles.com.

SEPTEMBER

Deauville American Film Festival. The likes of Clooney, Pitt, and Travolta jet in for a yearly celebration of movies, glitz, and glamour. Early to mid-September. www.festival-deauville.com.

La Villette Jazz Festival. Some 50 concerts are held in various concert spaces in the Parc de la Villette, Paris 19e. Past festivals have included Maceo Parker, Avishai Cohen, and other international artists. Early to mid-September. www.jazzalavillette.com.

Festival d'Automne, Paris. One of France's most famous festivals is also one of its most eclectic, focusing mainly on modern music, ballet, theater, and art. Mid-September to mid-January. www.festival-automne.com.

Festival de la Loire, Orléans (Loire). The Loire River and its banks come alive with sails, music, and food during the largest boat festival in Europe. Late September. www.orleans.fr.

OCTOBER

Les Voiles de St-Tropez. The largest and most glamorous of the French Riviera's classic sailing regattas. Watch tens of millions of euros of sails compete in the confines of the Bay of St-Tropez. Early October. www.lesvoilesdesaint-tropez.fr.

Paris Auto Show, Parc des Expositions, Porte de Versailles, 15e, Paris. This showcase for European car design comes complete with glitzy attendees, lots of hype, and the latest models. Usually first 2 weeks of October (dates vary). www.mondial-auto mobile.com.

Prix de l'Arc de Triomphe, Hippodrome de Longchamp, 16e, Paris. France's answer to England's Ascot is the country's most prestigious horse race, culminating the equine

season in Europe. Early October. www.prix arcdetriomphe.com.

NOVEMBER

Armistice Day, nationwide. In Paris, the signing of the document that ended World War I is celebrated with a military parade from the Arc de Triomphe to the Hôtel des Invalides. November 11.

DECEMBER

Boat Fair (Le Salon Nautique de Paris). Europe's major exposition of what's afloat, at the Parc des Expositions, Porte de Versailles. 1 week in early December. www.salon nautiqueparis.com.

Fête de St-Sylvestre (New Year's Eve), nationwide. In Paris, this holiday is most boisterously celebrated in the Quartier Latin. At midnight, the city explodes. Strangers kiss, and boulevard St-Michel and the Champs-Elysées become virtual pedestrian malls. December 31.

RESPONSIBLE TRAVEL

From pioneering eco-friendly car- and bicycle-sharing programs to an unabashed enthusiasm for *biodynamique* wines, the French have embraced sustainability. In an age when environmental, ethical, and social concerns are becoming ever more important, France's focus on green principles—whether through traditional markets, carbon-neutral public transport, or all-natural outdoor adventure—offers plenty in the way of sustainable tourism.

In order to crisscross France's vast countryside, many French ditch their cars and opt instead for travel on a **TGV** (www.tgv-europe.com). TGVs run from Paris's hub to cities throughout the country, including Nantes, Rouen, Avignon, Aix-en-Provence, Nice, and Marseille.

Many hotels in France have taken measures to preserve the environment; those that have are awarded with a green label. Look for hotels with the title of *La Clef Verte* (Green Key; www.laclefverte.org) or the **EU Ecolabel** (http:// ecolabel.defra.gov.uk). Even if you don't stay at a green hotel, you can still do your bit: Turn off the air-conditioning when you leave the room, request that your sheets aren't changed every day, and use your towels more than once. Laundry makes up around 40% of an average hotel's energy use.

Responsible tourism also means leaving a place in the same condition you found it. You can do this by not dropping litter and respecting the color-coded garbage bin system. Support the local economy by shopping in small neighborhood stores and open-air markets for local, often organic produce.

SUGGESTED ITINERARIES IN FRANCE

3

When the Frommer's guidebooks were first launched, founder Arthur Frommer cautioned his readers, "You can get lost in France." It's still an apt warning—and promise—today.

For those with unlimited time, one of the world's great pleasures is getting "lost" in France, wandering at random, making new discoveries off the beaten path. Few of us have this luxury, however, and so here we present 1- and 2-week itineraries to help you make the most of your time.

France is so treasure-filled that you could barely do more than skim the surface in a week. So relax and savor Paris, Mont-St-Michel, Arles, or Cannes—among other allurements—saving the rest for another day. You might also review chapter 1, "The Best of France," to find out what experiences or sights have special appeal to you and then adjust your itineraries to suit your particular travel plans.

The itineraries that follow take you to some major attractions and some charming off-the-beaten-track towns. The pace may be a bit breathless for some visitors, so skip a town or sight occasionally to give yourself some chill-out time. You're on vacation, after all. Of course, you may also use these itineraries merely as a jumping-off point to develop your own custom-made trip.

THE REGIONS IN BRIEF

Although France's 547,030 sq. km (211,209 sq. miles) make it slightly smaller than the American state of Texas, no other country has such a diversity of sights and scenery in such a compact area. A visitor can travel through the north's flat, fertile lands; the Loire Valley's green hills; or along the southeast's Mediterranean coast. Even more noteworthy are the cultural and historical differences that define each region. To help you decide where best to spend your time, this guide is focused on Paris, plus the country's four most popular regions: Normandy, the Loire, Provence, and the Riviera.

Destinations in France are within easy reach from Paris and each other. **French National Railroads (SNCF)** offers fast service to and from Paris. For example, the highlights of Normandy and the Loire Valley (the château country) are just 1 or 2 hours away from Paris by train. You can travel from Paris to Cannes on the Riviera in 5 hours—or fly down to the Riviera in 45 minutes.

You can motor along nearly 71,000km (about 44,020 miles) of French roads, including a good number of well-maintained superhighways. But do your best to drive the secondary roads too: Nearly all of France's scenic splendors are along these routes.

A "grand tour" of France is nearly impossible for the visitor who doesn't have a lifetime to explore. If you want to get to know a province, try to devote at least a week to a specific region. Note that you'll probably have a more rewarding trip if you concentrate on getting to know two or three areas at a leisurely pace, rather than racing around trying to see everything!

PARIS   France was born in the temperate basin of the Ile de France, where the attractions include **Paris, Versailles, Fontainebleau, Notre-Dame de Chartres,** and **Giverny.** For more information, see chapter 4.

NORMANDY   This region will forever be linked to the 1944 D-Day invasion. Some readers consider a visit to the D-Day beaches the most emotionally worthwhile part of their trip. Normandy boasts 599km (371 miles) of coastline and a maritime tradition. It's a popular weekend getaway from Paris, and many hotels and restaurants thrive here, especially around the casino town of **Deauville.** Normandy's great attractions include the **Rouen** cathedral and medieval **Bayeux.** For more information, see chapter 5.

THE LOIRE VALLEY   This area includes two ancient provinces, Touraine (centered on Tours) and Anjou (centered on Angers). It was beloved by royalty and nobility until Henry IV moved his court to Paris. Head here to see the most magnificent castles in France. Irrigated by the Loire River and its many tributaries, the valley produces many superb wines. For more information, see chapter 6.

PROVENCE   One of France's most popular destinations stretches from the southern Rhone River to the Italian border. Long frequented by starving artists, *la bourgeoisie,* and the downright rich and famous, its premier cities are **Aix-en-Provence,** associated with Cézanne; **Arles,** famous for bullfighting and Van Gogh; **Avignon,** the 14th-century capital of Christendom; and **Marseille,** a port city established by the Phoenicians that today is the melting pot of France. Quieter and more romantic are villages such as **St-Rémy-de-Provence, Les Baux,** and **Gordes.** For more information, see chapter 7.

THE FRENCH RIVIERA (CÔTE D'AZUR)   The resorts of the fabled Côte d'Azur (Azure Coast) still evoke glamour: **Cannes, St-Tropez, Cap d'Antibes,** and **Juan-les-Pins.** July and August are the most buzzing months, while spring and fall are still sunny but way more laid-back. **Nice** is the biggest city and most convenient base for exploring the area. The Principality of **Monaco** occupies only about 2 sq. km (¾ sq. mile) but has enough sights, restaurants, and opulence to go around. Along the coast are some sandy beaches, but many are pebbly. Topless bathing is common, especially in St-Tropez, and some of the restaurants are citadels of conspicuous consumption. Dozens of artists and their patrons have littered the landscape with world-class galleries and art museums. For more information, see chapter 8.

1 WEEK IN PARIS & NORMANDY

If you budget your days carefully, 1 week provides enough time to visit the major attractions of Paris, such as the **Musée du Louvre** (the world's greatest art gallery), the **Eiffel Tower,** and **Notre-Dame.** After 2 days in Paris, head for the former royal stomping grounds of **Versailles,** followed by Normandy (an easy commute from Paris), visiting such highlights as the **D-Day beaches,** the cathedral city of **Rouen** (where Joan of Arc was burned at the stake), the tapestry of **Bayeux,** and the incredible monastery of **Mont-St-Michel.**

Days 1 & 2: Arrive in Paris ★★★

Take a flight that arrives in Paris as early as possible on Day 1. Check into your hotel and hit the nearest cafe for a pick-me-up *café au lait* and a croissant before sightseeing. Take the Métro to the Palais Royal–Musée du Louvre for a visit to the **Musée du Louvre** (p. 81). Spend at least 2 hours here viewing world-class masterpieces such as Leonardo da Vinci's "Mona Lisa." After leaving the Louvre, walk south toward the

Tourists at Sacré-Couer in Montmartre.

Quays of the Seine, spending an hour taking in the tree-shaded banks and panoramic vistas of Paris. Head for **Ile de la Cité** to explore its attractions, including **Ste-Chapelle** (p. 84) and the monumental **Notre-Dame** (p. 75) and its gargoyles. As the evening fades, head for the **Eiffel Tower** for the greatest cityscape in Europe.

On Day 2, begin at the **place de la Concorde** (p. 94) and its Egyptian obelisk, then stroll up the 1.8km (1-mile) avenue of French grandeur, the **Champs-Elysées,** until you reach the **Arc de Triomphe** (p. 90), which you can scale for another panoramic view of Paris. Afterward, head for the **Marais,** a neighborhood that is both hip and historic, where you can stroll by 17th-century mansions, browse the boutiques, or just lunch and lounge in one of the many cafes and bistros lining the narrow streets.

After lunch in one of those snug bistros, visit the **Musée d'Orsay** (p. 107), home to the world's greatest collection of Impressionist paintings. As the afternoon fades, head for **Basilique du Sacré-Coeur** (p. 96) for a crowning view of Paris as the sun sets. Have a final dinner in a Montmartre cafe.

Day 3: A Day Trip to Versailles ★★★

Having survived 2 days in the capital of France, bid *adieu* and take the RER Line C to the **Versailles/Rive Gauche station.** You can spend a full day at Versailles—and then some—or else see the highlights in 3 hours, including the Grands and Petits Appartements, the glittering Hall of Mirrors, Gabriel's Opera House, the Royal Chapel, and the Gardens of Versailles.

Day 4: Normandy's Capital of Rouen ★★

Take an early train to Rouen and check in to one of the city's great hotels. Spend at least 2 hours exploring the city's ancient core, especially its **Cathédrale Notre-Dame** (p. 75), immortalized in paintings by Monet. Stand at the **place du Vieux Marché** (p. 131), where Joan of Arc was executed for heresy in 1431, and visit the **Eglise St-Maclou** (p. 132), a 1432 church in the Flamboyant Gothic style. After lunch, rent a car for the rest of your trip and drive to **Giverny**—it's only 60km (37 miles) southeast of Rouen. At Giverny, visit the **Claude Monet Foundation,** returning to your hotel in Rouen for the night.

Day 5: Bayeux ★★ & Caen ★

Even after a leisurely breakfast, you can easily be in the city of Caen by late morning, with plenty of time to visit **Abbaye aux Hommes** (p. 144), founded by William the Conqueror. After a hearty Norman lunch in Caen, continue west to the city of **Bayeux** to view the celebrated **Musée de la Tapisserie de Bayeux** (p. 150). Stay overnight in Bayeux.

Day 6: The D-Day Beaches ★★★

Reserve this day for exploring the D-Day beaches, where Allied forces launched "the Longest Day," the mammoth invasion of Normandy in June 1944 that signaled the beginning of the end of Hitler's Third Reich.

Your voyage of discovery can begin at the seaside resort of Arromanches-les-Bains, where you can visit the **Musée du Débarquement** (p. 152) before heading to **Omaha Beach** (p. 151), the moving **Normandy American Visitor Center** (p. 152), and the **Overlord Museum** (p. 152), with an easy roadside lunch en route.

That evening, drive to **Mont-St-Michel** (less than 2 hr. away) and stay overnight in the pedestrianized village on "the Rock," giving you plenty

France in 1 Week ①–⑦
Day 1 Arrive in Paris
Day 2 Paris
Day 3 Day Trip to Versailles
Day 4 Rouen: Normandy's Capital
Day 5 Bayeux & Caen
Day 6 The D-Day Beaches
Day 7 Mont-St-Michel

France in 2 Weeks ①–⑭
Day 8 Orléans
Day 9 Amboise & Chenonceau
Day 10 Avignon
Day 11 Avignon to St-Tropez
Day 12 Cannes
Day 13 Nice
Day 14 Nice to Menton

France for Families ●
Days 1 & 2 Paris
Day 3 Versailles
Days 4 & 5 Disneyland Paris
Day 6 Nice
Day 7 Monaco

An Art Lover's Tour of France ●
Days 1 & 2 Paris
Day 3 Aix-en-Provence
Day 4 St-Tropez
Day 5 Antibes & Vallauris
Days 6 & 7 Nice

of time for an early-morning—and relatively tourist-free—visit to this popular UNESCO-protected attraction.

Day 7: Mont-St-Michel ★★★

Allow around 3 hours to explore **Mont-St-Michel** (p. 146). Taking an English-language tour is one of the best ways to enjoy its great abbey, founded in 966. After lunch, return your car to Rouen, where you'll find frequent train services back to Paris, and catch your flight home the following day.

A 1-WEEK EXTENSION TO THE LOIRE VALLEY & THE CÔTE D'AZUR

If you have 2 weeks to explore France, you'll have time to visit several regions—not only Paris, but also the best of the Loire Valley châteaux, the most history-rich town of Provence (Avignon), and several resorts on the Riviera, taking in the beaches, art galleries, and even the Principality of Monaco.

For days 1 through 7, follow the "1 Week in Paris & Normandy" itinerary, above.

Day 8: Orléans, Gateway to the Loire Valley ★

Leave Paris on an early train to **Orléans** (trip time: 1 hr., 15 min.). Rent a car here and drive west to the **Château de Chambord** (p. 165), the largest château in the Loire Valley. Allow 2 hours for a visit. Back on the road again, continue southwest to the **Château de Blois** (p. 164), called "the Versailles of the Renaissance" and a virtual illustrated storybook of French architecture. Stay overnight in Blois.

Interior in Clos-Lucé, the Leonardo da Vinci museum in Amboise.

Day 9: Amboise ★★ & Chenonceau ★★★

In the morning, continue southeast from Blois to **Amboise,** where you can check into a hotel for the night. Visit the 15th-century **Château d'Amboise** (p. 170), in the Italian Renaissance style, and also **Clos-Lucé** (p. 171), last residence of Leonardo da Vinci. In the afternoon, drive southeast to the **Château de Chenonceau** (p. 172), famous for the French dames who have occupied its precincts, including Diane de Poitiers (mistress of the king) and Catherine de Médici (the jealous queen). You can spend a couple of hours at the château before driving back to Amboise for the night.

Day 10: Avignon, Gateway to Provence ★★★

From Amboise, get an early start and drive east to Orléans to return your rental car. Then take an early train from Orléans to Paris's Gare d'Austerlitz, then the Métro or a taxi to the Gare de Lyon, and hop on a TGV bound for Avignon (2½ hr.).

Check into a hotel in **Avignon,** one of Europe's most beautiful medieval cities. Before the day fades, you should have time to wander through the old city to get your bearings, shop for Provençal souvenirs, and see one of the smaller sights, such as the **Pont St-Bénézet.** See p. 197.

Day 11: Avignon to St-Tropez ★★★

In the morning, spend 2 hours touring the **Palais des Papes** (p. 198), the capital of Christendom during the 14th century. After lunch in one of Avignon's cozy bistros or cobblestoned outdoor cafes, rent a car and drive to **St-Tropez** (p. 236). Spend a good part of the early evening in one

Palais des Papes, Avignon.

Scenic view of the Mediterranean coastline from the town of Eze on the French Riviera.

of the cafes along the harbor, indulging in that favorite French pastime of people-watching.

Day 12: Chic Cannes ★★★

Before leaving St-Tropez in the morning, check out the Impressionist paintings at **Musée de l'Annonciade** (p. 239). Drive 50km (31 miles) east along the coast until you reach Cannes.

Assuming it's summer, get in some time at the beach, notably at **Plage de la Croisette** (p. 247), and feel free to wear your most revealing swimwear. In the afternoon, take the ferry to **Ile Ste-Marguerite** (p. 251), where the "Man in the Iron Mask" was imprisoned.

Day 13: Nice, Capital of the Riviera ★★★

It's only a 32km (20-mile) drive east from Cannes to **Nice,** the Riviera's largest city. After checking in to a hotel (the most affordable along the Riviera), stroll through **Vieille Ville** (p. 277), the Old Town. Enjoy a snack of *socca,* a round crepe made with chickpea flour that vendors sell steaming hot in the cours Saleya market. Then amble along the **promenade des Anglais** (p. 277), the wide boulevard along the waterfront. In the afternoon, head for the famed hill town of **St-Paul-de-Vence,** only 20km (12 miles) to the north. You can wander its ramparts in about 30 minutes before descending to the greatest modern-art museum in the Riviera, the **Fondation Maeght** (p. 266).

Continue on to **Vence** (p. 267) for a visit to the great Henri Matisse's artistic masterpiece, **Chapelle du Rosaire** (p. 269). From there, it's just 24km (15 miles) southeast to Nice, where you can enjoy dinner at a typical Niçois bistro.

Day 14: Nice to Menton ★★

While still overnighting in Nice, head east for the most thrilling drive in all of France, a trip along the **Grande Corniche** highway, which stretches 31km (19 miles) east from Nice to the little resort of **Menton** near the Italian border. Allow 3 hours for this trip. Highlights along this road include **Roquebrune-Cap Martin** and **La Turbie.** The greatest view along the Riviera is at the **Eze Belvedere,** at 1,200m (3,936 ft.). Return to Nice to wind down your travels and prepare for your trip home.

FRANCE FOR FAMILIES

France offers many attractions for kids. Our suggestion is to limit the bustle of **Paris** to 2 days, and then spend a day wandering the spectacular grounds and glittering interiors of **Versailles,** 2 days in **Disneyland Paris,** and 2 days on the **Riviera.**

Days 1 & 2: Paris ★★★

Take the kids for a morning visit to **Notre-Dame** (p. 75). The highlight is climbing the 387 narrow and winding steps to the top of one of the towers for a fabulously Quasimodo view of the gargoyles and Paris. After a visit, head over to the street market along rue Cler to pick up picnic goodies, best enjoyed in the nearby **Champ de Mars,** which also stages great puppet shows. After lunch, scale the iconic **Eiffel Tower** (p. 104). Then take the children for a stroll through the **Jardin des Tuileries** (p. 79), which offers seasonal fun fairs, ice-cream stands, and a giant Ferris wheel. At the circular pond, you can rent a toy boat.

Aerial view of Champ de Mars, from the Eiffel Tower, Paris.

On Day 2, visit the **Musée du Louvre** (p. 81). Even if your child is not a museum lover or bores easily, he or she is bound to find something interesting among the thousands of objects and paintings. Kids seem to be particularly fascinated by the Egyptian art and antiquities in the Sully and Denon wings as well as the gems and jewels in the Galerie d'Apollon.

After the Louvre, take the Métro to Porte de la Villette, where you can spend 2 or 3 hours at **Cité des Sciences et de l'Industrie.** The mammoth structure is home to a planetarium, a 3-D cinema, and interactive exhibits, as well as the kid-friendly Cité des Enfants.

As the afternoon fades, head for **Butte Montmartre,** with its fiesta atmosphere. Take the Métro to Anvers and walk to the funicular, the cable car that carries you to the **Basilique du Sacré-Coeur** (p. 96). From here you can take your brood for a merry-go-round ride at **place des Abbesses** (p. 96).

Day 3: Versailles ★★★

Tear yourself away from the glories of Paris for a day spent at the **Château de Versailles** (p. 123). Take the RER line C to the Versailles/ Rive Gauche station. If the kids get bored in the château, you can offer them a rowboat outing on the Grand Canal. Let them get their ya-yas out running around in the vast grounds, where you can also picnic (buy picnic fixings ahead of time in Paris or purchase a sandwich at one of the stalls placed in discreet corners of the garden).

Days 4 & 5: Disneyland Paris ★★

Disneyland Paris is the top family vacation destination in France. Allow a full day to see the highlights of the park, plus another day to absorb some or all of its secondary adventures. Our recommendation is to visit **Main Street, U.S.A., Frontierland,** and **Adventureland** on the first day, saving **Fantasyland, Discoveryland, Walt Disney Studios,** the entertainment center at **Village Disney,** and **Sleeping Beauty Castle** for the second day. The RER commuter express train A takes you from Etoile in Paris to Marne-la-Vallée/Chessy in 45 minutes.

Day 6: Nice ★★★

Return to Paris and fly to Nice, capital of the French Riviera. If you flew Air France transatlantic, Nice can often be attached as a low-cost extension of your round-trip fare.

In Nice, you can check into your hotel for 2 nights, as the city has the most affordable accommodation on the coast. Set out to explore this old city. There's always a lot of free entertainment in summer along Nice's seafront boardwalk, the **promenade des Anglais** (p. 277), and the people-watching on the Riviera—particularly on the beach—is likely to leave your kids wide-eyed. Be sure to spend an hour or two at the city's new **Promenade du Paillon** (p. 278) public park, where younger kids can go wild on the animal-themed playgrounds or splash around in the open expanse of dancing fountains.

In the afternoon, journey to the evocative hill town of **St-Paul-de-Vence** (p. 264). Children can race along the ramparts, meander the pedestrian-only rue Grande, or explore the sculpture garden at the **Fondation Maeght** (p. 266), one of France's greatest modern-art museums.

Return to Nice for the evening and take your kids for a stroll through the Old Town, dining as the sun dips over the Mediterranean.

Fountains at Promenade du Paillon.

Day 7: Monaco ★★★

While still based in Nice, head for the tiny principality of Monaco, which lies only 18km (11 miles) east of Nice. Frequent buses and trains ply the coastal route between the two cities.

Children will enjoy the changing-of-the-guard ceremony at **Les Grands Appartements du Palais** (p. 296), where Prince Albert married South African swimmer Charlene Wittstock in July 2011. But the best part of Monaco for kids is the **Musée Océanographique de Monaco** (p. 296), home to sharks and other exotic sea creatures. Hundreds of cool vintage cars are also on display at the **Collection des Voitures Anciennes de S.A.S. le Prince de Monaco** (p. 296).

Return to Nice that night and prepare for your flight home in the morning.

ART LOVERS' TOUR OF FRANCE

From contemporary art to modern masters, France is infused with art. Art aficionados can experience an unforgettable trip taking in Paris (2 days), Aix-en-Provence (1 day), and then the Riviera between St-Tropez and Nice (4 days).

Days 1 & 2: Paris ★★★

Start your art tour of Paris with a quick check of what's currently on the city: The **Grand Palais** (p. 90), **Musée de Luxembourg,** and the **Pinacothèque de Paris** all host excellent temporary exhibitions.

You can attend a show at any of these venues, or begin your day at the newly renovated **Musée de Montmartre** (p. 96), formerly home to both Renoir and Utrillo. Then hop onto the Métro and head south to the Jardin du Luxembourg. The small house that is **Musée Zadkine,** dedicated to Russian sculptor Ossip Zadkine, is located nearby. Enjoy a leisurely lunch at one of the neighborhood's many bistros. Round out the afternoon by taking in a cutting-edge contemporary exhibition at the iconic **Palais de Tokyo** (p. 94).

On Day 2, spend the morning enjoying the **Musée Picasso** and then stroll around the **Marais** (p. 86), the city neighborhood currently boasting the highest concentration of art galleries.

Midafternoon, jump aboard one of the many TGV trains heading south to Aix-en-Provence. The journey takes around 3 hours, leaving you plenty of time to enjoy a typical Provençal dinner upon arrival.

Day 3: Aix-en-Provence ★★

Paul Cézanne is Aix's most celebrated son. Begin your day at his **Atelier** (p. 219), almost perfectly preserved, as it was when the great artist worked here more than a century ago. There are regularly scheduled English-language tours of the site. Afterward, a visit to the city's famed **Musée Granet** (p. 220)—one of the region's most superb modern-art museums—is a must.

Aix's plane-tree-shaded **cours Mirabeau** is almost a work of art in itself. Be sure to stop into **Brasserie Les Deux Garçons** (p. 219), where Cézanne used to drink and debate with the famous French writer Émile Zola.

After lunch, rent a car and drive to **St-Tropez** (p. 236). Warm evenings are best enjoyed strolling the port's pretty quays or taking in the million-dollar panoramas from the hilltop **Citadelle** (p. 239).

Day 4: St-Tropez ★★★

Since the 1890s, when Signac and Bonnard stumbled upon St-Tropez, artists and their patrons have been drawn to the French Riviera. Spend the morning appreciating the **Musée de l'Annonciade**'s (p. 239) Impressionist paintings, many of them depicting St-Tropez and the surrounding coast.

After lunch in one of the town's sidewalk cafes, drive around 100km (62 miles) east along the coast until you reach Nice, where you'll base yourself for the next 3 nights. Return your rental car here—traffic-heavy roads, combined with excellent public transportation, make your own vehicle unnecessary.

Day 5: Antibes & Vallauris ★★

Today you'll spend the day following in the footsteps of one of the 20th century's modern masters: Pablo Picasso. Take one of the frequent trains from Nice to Antibes (20 min.). On the edge of the picturesque, strollable Old Town sits the 14th-century Grimaldi Château, now home to the **Musée Picasso** (p. 262). The Spanish artist lived and worked in this castle in 1946.

Stroll through Antibes' covered market, then—appetite piqued—stop into a small bistro, such as **Entre 2 Vins** (p. 261), for a light lunch. Next,

Musée Picasso, Antibes.

make your way to Antibes' bus station, where frequent buses depart for Vallauris (35 min.). Picasso moved to this hilltop village during the 1950s, reviving the local ceramic-making industry and personally producing thousands of pieces of pottery. Visit Picasso's mammoth paintings in the **Musée National Picasso La Guerre et La Paix** (p. 254), the artist's tribute to pacifism.

Make your way back to Nice (it's quickest to simply reverse your route). Spend the evening strolling the promenade des Anglais or wandering the city's atmospheric Old Town.

Days 6 & 7: Nice ★★★

Begin your Day 6 citywide explorations in the neighborhood of Cimiez, where both the famed **Musée Matisse** (p. 279) and the **Musée National Message Biblique Marc Chagall** (p. 279) are located. It's possible to walk between the two (around 15 min.), but be sure to hit the Matisse Museum first—then it's downhill all the way to see Chagall's ethereal artworks. Midafternoon, make your way over the **Musée Masséna** (p. 278), where a combination of local art and history gives visitors a peek at the ritzy French Riviera of the past.

Use your final day to make a day trip to the hilltop village of **St-Paul-de-Vence** (p. 264), 20km (12 miles) to the north. Wander the St-Paul-de-Vence's ramparts for half an hour, before descending to the world-class modern art on display at the **Fondation Maeght** (p. 266). En route back to Nice, stop into the **Musée Renoir** in Cagnes-sur-Mer. The recently renovated museum spills over the artist's former family home, studio, and gardens.

PARIS

by Margie Rynn

T he word "Paris" conjures up such a potent brew of images and ideas that it's sometimes hard to find the meeting point between myth and reality. But the city's graceful streets, soaked in history, really are as elegant as they say, its monuments and museums as extraordinary; and a slightly world-weary, *fin-de-siècle* grandeur really is part of day-to-day existence.

4

Where to begin? With so many wonderful things to see, it's easy to get overwhelmed in the City of Light. If you are here for only a few days, you'll probably be spending most of your time in the city center, the nucleus of which is the Île de la Cité. The **top neighborhoods** on most short-term visitors' hit parade are the 1st through 8th arrondissements (see "City Layout," below), which includes the Île de la Cité, the Louvre area, the Champs Elysées, the Eiffel Tower, the Latin Quarter, the Marais, and St-Germain. **If you have a bit more time,** you should explore some of the outlying neighborhoods, like the funky and dynamic eastern areas of Mesnilmontant, Belleville, Canal St-Martin, and Bastille, or the elegant, museum-rich depths of the 16th arrondissement. Whether you're here for a few days or longer, this chapter is designed to give you the essential information you need to create a Paris itinerary that's just right for you.

ESSENTIALS & ORIENTATION

Arriving

BY PLANE

Paris has two international airports: **Aéroport d'Orly,** 18km (11 miles) south of the city (www.aeroportsdeparis.fr; for both airports: ☎ **00-33-1-70-36-39-50** from abroad, or **39-50** from France), and **Aéroport Roissy-Charles-de-Gaulle** (also known as CDG), 30km (19 miles) northeast. If you are taking Ryanair or another discount airline that arrives at **Beauvais** (www.aeroportbeauvais. com; ☎ **08-92-68-20-66,** .34€ per min), be advised that that airport is located about 80km (50 miles) from Paris.

Getting to the City Center from the Airport

CHARLES DE GAULLE AIRPORT (ROISSY) **By commuter train:** The quickest way into central Paris is the RER B (www.ratp. fr), suburban trains that leave every 10 to 15 minutes between 5am and 10pm (midnight on weekends). It takes about 40 minutes to get to Paris, and RER B stops at several Métro stations including Châtelet-Les-Halles, Saint-Michel-Notre-Dame, and Luxembourg. A single ticket costs 9.75€ and you can buy it from the machines at the stations in both terminals.

By bus: Air France operates two bus routes (**Les Cars Air France;** www.lescarsairfrance.com; ✆ **08-92-35-08-20**) from the airport to Port Maillot/Charles de Gaulle–Etoile and Gare de Lyon/Gare Montparnasse. Depending on the route, a one-way trip costs 17€ to 18€ adults and 8.50€ to 9€ children 2 to 11; both trips take about an hour, depending on traffic. Buses leave every 30 minutes between 6am and 11pm. The **Roissybus** (www.ratp.fr; ✆ **32-46** from France only) departs from the airport daily from 6am to 12:30am and costs 11€ for the 60-minute ride. The bus leaves you in the center of Paris, at the corner of rue Scribe and rue Auber, near the Opera House.

By taxi: A taxi from Roissy into the city will cost at least 50€, not including 1€ per item of luggage, and the fare is 20% higher from 5pm to 10am, as well as on Sundays and bank holidays.

ORLY AIRPORT **By commuter train:** Take the 8-minute monorail **Orly-Val** to the station in the town of Antony, and take the **RER B** into the center. Combined travel time is about 40 minutes. Trains run between 6am and 11pm, and the one-way fare for the OrlyVal plus the RER B is 12€ adults and 6€ children under 10.

By bus: Les Cars Air France (www.cars-airfrance.com; ✆ **08-92-35-08-20**) leaves every 20 minutes between 6am and 11:40pm, stopping at Gare Montparnasse, Invalides, and Charles de Gaulle-Etoile. The fare is 13€ one-way, and 6.50€ children ages 2 to 11. In normal traffic, the trip takes about an hour. The **Orlybus** (www.ratp.fr), which leaves every 15 minutes between 5am and midnight, links the airport with Place Denfert-Rochereau, a 30-minute trip that costs 7.70€ for adults.

By taxi: A taxi from Orly to central Paris will cost at least 50€, not including 1€ per item of luggage, and the fare is 20% higher from 5pm to 10am, as well as on Sundays and Bank Holidays.

BEAUVAIS AIRPORT Buses leave about 20 minutes after each flight has landed, and, depending on the traffic, take about 1 hour and 15 minutes to get to Paris. The bus drops you at Porte Maillot (Métro: Porte Maillot) on the western edge of the city. To return to Beauvais, you need to be at the bus station at least 3 hours before the departure of your flight. A one-way ticket costs 17€.

BY TRAIN

Paris has six major train stations: **Gare d'Austerlitz** (13th arrond.), **Gare de Lyon** (12th arrond.), **Gare Montparnasse** (14th arrond.), **Gare St-Lazare** (8th arrond.), **Gare de l'Est** (10th arrond.), and **Gare du Nord** (10th arrond.). Each station can be reached by bus or Métro; details can be found on the **SNCF** station site (www.gares-connexions.com/en). *Warning:* As in most major cities, the stations and surrounding areas are rather seedy and frequented by pickpockets. Be alert, especially at night.

Paris Neighborhoods

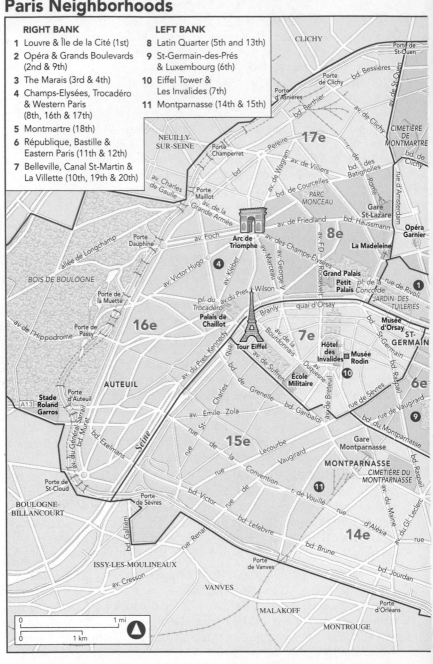

RIGHT BANK

1 Louvre & Île de la Cité (1st)
2 Opéra & Grands Boulevards (2nd & 9th)
3 The Marais (3rd & 4th)
4 Champs-Elysées, Trocadéro & Western Paris (8th, 16th & 17th)
5 Montmartre (18th)
6 République, Bastille & Eastern Paris (11th & 12th)
7 Belleville, Canal St-Martin & La Villette (10th, 19th & 20th)

LEFT BANK

8 Latin Quarter (5th and 13th)
9 St-Germain-des-Prés & Luxembourg (6th)
10 Eiffel Tower & Les Invalides (7th)
11 Montparnasse (14th & 15th)

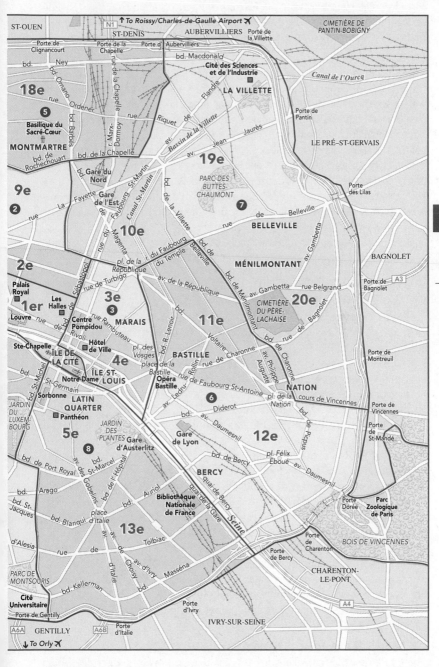

BY BUS

Most long-haul buses arrive at the **Eurolines France** station on the eastern edge of the city, 23 av. du Général-de-Gaulle, Bagnolet (www.eurolines.fr; ℂ in France **08-92-89-90-91,** other countries **01-41-86-24-21;** Métro: Gallieni).

BY CAR

While I wouldn't recommend driving in Paris to my worst enemy, renting a car and driving around France before or after your Paris trip can be a lovely way to see the country. All of the major car-rental companies have offices here (see below), but you'll often get better deals if you reserve before you leave home. **AutoEurope** (www.autoeurope.com) is an excellent source for discounted rentals. Check its prices against **Avis** (www.avis.com; ℂ **08-21-23-07-60,** .12€ per min); **Budget** (www.budget.com; ℂ **08-25-00-35-64,** .15€ per min); **Europcar** (www.europcar.com; ℂ **08-25-358-358,** .15€ per min); **Hertz** (www.hertz.com; ℂ **08-25-861-861,** .15€ per min); **Rent-a-Car** (www.rentacar.fr; ℂ **08-91-700-200,** .25€ per min); and **Thrifty** (www.thrifty.com; ℂ **01-82-88-16-77**).

Before you step on the gas, at the very least, try to get hold of a list of international road signs; your rental agency should have one.

Getting Around Town

For everything you ever wanted to know about the city's public transport, visit the **RATP** (www.ratp.fr; ℂ **32-46** in France). Paris and its suburbs are divided into six travel zones, but you'll probably only be concerned with the city center, zones 1 and 2.

RATP tickets are valid on the Métro, bus, and RER. You can buy tickets over the counter (if you are lucky—ticket booths are an endangered species) or from machines at most Métro entrances. The machines take coins and chip-enabled credit cards. A **single ticket** costs 1.80€ and a *carnet* of 10 tickets costs 14€. Children 4 to 9 years old pay half price; kids under 4 ride free. The tourist-oriented **Paris Visite** pass offers unlimited travel in zones on bus, Métro, and RER, and discounts on some attractions, but its usefulness is limited. Paris is a relatively small city and you'll probably end up walking a lot; in the end a cheaper *carnet* of 10 tickets may do the trick (and you can share it with your fellow travelers). A 1-day Paris Visite adult pass for zones 1 to 3 costs 11€, a 2-day pass 18€, a 3-day pass 25€, and a 5-day pass 36€. Each day begins at midnight and finishes at midnight the following day. It is also possible to buy more expensive passes for zones 1 to 5, which will also get you to the airport. For a slightly cheaper 1-day pass, try a **Mobilis** ticket, which offers unlimited travel in zones 1 up to 5; a pass for zones 1 and 2 costs 7€. For travelers under 26, look for the **Ticket Jeunes,** a 1-day ticket that can be used on a Saturday, Sunday, or bank holiday and provides unlimited travel in zones 1 to 3 for 3.85€, or zones 1 to 5 for 8.35€.

BY MÉTRO OR RER (SUBWAY)

The city's first Métro, or subway, was inaugurated on July 19, 1900. Today, more than a century later, it still functions very well. Aside from the

Essentials & Orientation

occasional strike or work slowdown, the Métro is usually efficient and civilized, especially if you avoid rush hour (7:30–9:30am and 6–8pm). It's generally safe at night (although you might want to think twice about using it to get to more isolated parts of the city); the service shuts down between midnight and 1am weekdays, and at 2am on Friday, Saturday, and pre-holiday evenings. The suburban trains (the RER; see below) close down around the same time (without the weekend bonus hour). The **RER** (pronounced "ehr-euh-ehr") is the suburban train network that dashes through the city making limited stops. The downsides are (a) they don't run as often as the Métro, and (b) they're hard to figure out since they run on a different track system and the same lines can have multiple final destinations. *Important:* Make sure to hold on to your ticket; you'll need it to get *out* of the turnstile on the way out.

BY BUS

Thanks to an increase in dedicated bus lanes, the buses can be an efficient way to get around town, and you'll get a scenic tour to boot. The majority start running around 6:30am and stop anywhere from 9:30pm to midnight; service is reduced on Sundays and holidays. You can use Métro tickets on the buses or you can buy tickets directly from the driver (2€). Tickets need to be validated in the machine next to the driver's cabin. Your regular Métro ticket gives you a free transfer, to be used within 1½ hours; if you buy your ticket on the bus there is no transfer included.

BY TRAM

Over the past few years, Paris has developed its tramway network, with several extensions and new lines in progress. They connect Paris with its suburbs; within Paris they run along the outer boulevards that trace the city limits. You can use Métro tickets on the tram.

BY BICYCLE

Cycling in Paris has been revolutionized by the hugely successful **Velib'** bike rental scheme (the name comes from *vélo* meaning bicycle and *liberté* meaning freedom) launched in 2007. It takes a little effort for a tourist to sign up, but it's worth it to see Paris from two wheels (see box, below).

Alternatively, you can rent a bike from **Paris à vélo, c'est sympa!**, 22 rue Alphonse Baudin (www.parisvelosympa.com; ✆ **01-48-87-60-01**; Métro: St-Sébastien-Froissart or Richard Lenoir). Rentals cost 12€ for half a day and 15€ for a full day, but they do require a safety deposit of at least 250€, depending on what kind of bike you rent.

BY CAR

Driving is *not* recommended in Paris, but the auto-adventurous may want to try tooling around in a small electric car through **Autolib'** (www.autolib.eu; ✆ **08-00-94-20-00**), the recent outgrowth of the popular Velib' bicycle rental program (see above). A similar concept to its cycling cousin, the scheme involves short-term electric car rental. To register you can go to one of the Autolib' subscription kiosks (with a chip-enabled credit card) or to the Autolib' information center (5 rue Edouard VII, 9th arrond.) with your driving

Velib': A Great Way to Cycle Around Paris

Since July 2007, when the city of Paris inaugurated the **Velib'** (vel-LEEB) system of low-cost bike rentals, Parisians have been pedaling up a storm. Traffic be dammed: It's fun to ride around town, drop off your bike near your destination, and not have to worry about locking it up. The way it works is this: You buy a 1- or 7-day subscription (1.70€ or 8€, respectively) from the machine at one of hundreds of bike stands, which gives you the right to as many half-hour rides as you'd like for 1 or 7 days. If you want to go over a half-hour, you pay 1€ for your extra half-hour, 2€ for the half-hour after that one and 4€ for the third half-hour on. Everything is meticulously explained, in English, on the website, www.velib.fr, and there's even a number you can call for English-speaking assistance (✆ **01-30-79-79-30**). There's one big catch, however—to use the machines you must have a credit or debit card with a chip in it. This can be a problem for North American tourists, so I advise either getting a TravelEx "cash passport" with money on it (www.travelex.com), or, even easier, just **buy your subscription ahead of time online** (make sure you have your secret code to punch in on the stand). Helmets are not provided, so if you're feeling queasy about launching into traffic, bring one along. There are few bike lanes so far, but success has been such that new ones are being added, and cyclists have the right to ride in the bus lanes. *One more tip:* Before you ride, get a map of the city that shows where the bike stands are so you don't waste precious time looking for a place to check in or check out. Or better yet, download the Velib' application from the website.

license, a valid form of I.D., and a credit card, or you can simply **register online.** A 1-day subscription is free, but you pay 9€ per half-hour. A 7-day subscription is 10€ plus 7€ per half-hour, a month is 25€ plus 6.50€ per half-hour, and a year is 120€ plus 5.5€ per half-hour. You are given a badge that you then pass over a sensor at a rental station to unlock the car. Unplug it from the charger and drive away. To return it, just use the GPS to find a spot at an Autolib' station and plug in your car.

Visitor Information

A good place to start any information quest is at the Paris Tourist Office (25 rue des Pyramides, 1st arrond.; www.parisinfo.com; ✆ **01-49-52-42-63;** Métro: Pyramides). There's always a multilingual person on the other end of the line when you call (if you'd prefer not to spring for an international call, surf to their comprehensive website). The Tourist Office has several branches sprinkled around the city; check the website for addresses and hours.

City Layout

Paris is relatively small. It's not a sprawling megalopolis like Tokyo or London; in fact, Paris *intramuros,* or inside the long-gone city walls, numbers a mere 2.27 million habitants, and, excluding the large exterior parks of Bois de Vincennes and the Bois de Boulogne, measures about 87 sq. km (34 sq. miles). (The suburbs, on the other hand, are sprawling, but chances are you won't be spending much, if any, time there.) So getting around is not difficult, provided you have a general sense of where things are.

The city is vaguely egg shaped, with the Seine cutting a wide upside-down "U"-shaped arc through the middle. The northern half is known as the **Right Bank,** and the southern, the **Left Bank.** To the uninitiated, the only way to remember is to face west, or downstream, so that the Right Bank will be to your right, and the Left to your left.

If you can't get your banks straight, don't worry, because most Parisians don't talk in terms of Right or Left Bank, but in terms of *arrondissements,* or districts. The city is neatly split up into 20 official arrondissements, which spiral out from the center of the city. So the lower the number, the closer you'll be to the center, and as the numbers go up, you'll head toward the outer limits. Though their borders don't always correspond to historical neighborhoods, they do chop up the city into easily digestible chunks, so if you know what arrondissement your destination is in, your chances of finding it easily go way up. Your chances will be even better if you have a good map. Even if you're only in the city for a week, it's worthwhile to invest in a purse-size map book (ask for a "Paris par Arrondissement" at bookstores or larger newsstands), which costs around 8€. The book should include a street index and a detailed set of maps by arrondissement—one of the best is called "Le Petit Parisien," which includes separate Métro, bus, and street maps for each district. To get a general sense of where the arrondissements are, see the map on p. 40.

[Fast FACTS] PARIS

ATMs/Banks ATMs can be found all over the city. For currency exchange, look for **Travelex** (www.travelex. fr) counters at Paris airports and train stations.

Dentists & Doctors Download a list of English-speaking dentists and doctors in Paris from the US embassy website (http://france.usembassy. gov, click on "Resources for US Citizens"). Or call U.S. Citizens Services at ☏ **01-43-12-22-22.**

Hospitals Paris has good public hospitals; visit www. aphp.fr for locations and details on specialties. Private hospitals with English-speaking staff: **American Hospital of Paris** (63 bd.

Victor Hugo, 92200 Neuilly-sur-Seine; www.american-hospital.org; ☏ **01-46-41-25-25**) and **Institut Hospitalier Franco-Britannique** (3 rue Barbès or 4 rue Kleber, Levallois; www.ihfb.org/en; ☏ **01-47-59-59-59**).

Embassies See planning chapter, p. 306.

Emergencies Emergency services: ☏ **112.** The fire brigade (*Sapeurs-Pompiers;* ☏ **18**) deals with all kinds of medical emergencies, not just fires. For an ambulance, call ☏ **15.** For the police, call ☏ **17.**

Lost & Found Bureau des Objets Trouvés (36 rue des Morillons, 15e; ☏ **08-21-00-25-25,** .12€ per min).

Mail & Postage There are post offices (**La Poste,** www.laposte.fr, ☏ **36-31**) in every arrondissement. Most are open Mon–Fri 8:30am–8pm, Sat 8am–1pm; the main post office (52 rue du Louvre; Métro: Louvre-Rivoli) is open Mon–Sat 7:30am–6am and Sunday 10am–6am. Stamps are also sold in *tabacs* (tobacconists).

Pharmacies There are pharmacies all over the city; both the **Pharmacie les Champs** (84 av. des Champs-Élysées; ☏ **01-45-62-02-41**) and the **Pharmacie Européene** (6 place de Clichy; ☏ **01-48-74-65-18**) are open 24 hours daily.

Safety In general, Paris is a safe city and it is safe to use the Métro at any time, though it's best to avoid the RER late at night. **Beware of pickpockets,** especially in tourist areas and the Louvre; organized gangs will even use children as decoys.

Toilets Paris is full of gray-colored, street toilet kiosks, which are a little daunting to the uninitiated, but free, and are automatically washed and disinfected after each use.

WHERE TO STAY

Paris has more than 1,500 hotels, from palaces fit for a pasha to tiny family-run operations. In theory, you should be able to find something in line with your budget, timeframe, and personal tastes. But even if you can't find the hotel of your dreams in the list below, don't despair—at the end of this section I list a few alternative lodging options, including bed-and-breakfasts and short-term apartment rentals.

The Right Bank

LOUVRE & ÎLE DE LA CITÉ (1ST ARRONDISSEMENT)

The area surrounding the Louvre is littered with hotels, most of which are dreadfully overpriced. Yes, if you only are in town for 1 or 2 days, a central locale is key, since time is of the essence. But if you have a little more time, you'll find much more comfortable lodgings, at the same or lower prices, a 10-minute walk away.

Expensive

Hotel Brighton ★★   Did someone say "view"? How about a panorama of the Louvre and the Tuileries gardens from your bed? While not every room in this gracious hotel has the jackpot view, those in the "deluxe" and "executive" categories do, and all have a subdued, classic look with elegant fabrics draping windows and tasteful decorative touches. This classy establishment under the arcades of the rue de Rivoli may not be not quite as grand as the Meurice, just down the block, but it is also about one-third the price. Rooms with views book up early, so plan ahead.

218 rue de Rivoli, 1st arrond. www.paris-hotel-brighton.com. ℭ **01-47-03-61-61.** 61 units. 199€–391€ double; 310€–422€ suite. Métro: Tuileries. **Amenities:** Bar, concierge, laundry service, room service, tea room, Wi-Fi (free).

Moderate

Hôtel Thérèse ★★   Just a few steps from the Palais Royal and the Louvre, these recently overhauled lodgings combine old-fashioned Parisian charm with modern Parisian chic. Soft grey/teal blues highlight a creative decor that complements the building's age instead of fighting it. Comfy sofas invite you to relax in the lobby, whose stylish look includes mirrors, bookcases, and unique lighting fixtures. The comfort factor extends to the rooms, many of which have very high ceilings, interesting drapery fabrics, and upholstered headboards.

5–7 rue Thérèse, 1st arrond. www.hoteltherese.com. ℭ **01-42-96-10-01.** 40 units. 180€–390€ double. Métro: Palais-Royal or Pyramides. **Amenities:** Concierge, library/bar, Wi-Fi (free).

Inexpensive

Hôtel du Cygne ★   Chock-full of exposed beams and stone walls, this 17th-century building has been carefully restored, and the simple lodgings receive ongoing tender loving care. Most rooms are predictably small but cheerfully decorated, with fresh white walls, floral bedspreads, and the owner's personal touch. If you can handle the climb to the top floor, you'll be rewarded with a roomy suite that sleeps three. The hotel is located near Les Halles (a little seedy at night) and the Montorgueil neighborhood (very hip at night). There is no elevator.

3–5 rue du Cygne, 1st arrond. www.cygne-hotel-paris.com. ✆ **01-42-60-14-16.** 18 units. 90€–165€ double; 155–185€ suite. Métro: Etienne Marcel. RER: Les Halles. **Amenities:** Wi-Fi (free).

LE MARAIS (3RD & 4TH ARRONDISSEMENTS)

Centuries ago, this neighborhood was a swamp *(marais)*, but now it's merely swamped with stylish boutiques, restaurants, and people who seem to have just stepped out of a hair salon. Stunning 16th- and 17th-century mansions house terrific museums; the narrow streets harbor clothing stores, cool bars, clubs, and the remnants of the city's historic Jewish quarter.

Expensive

Pavillon de la Reine ★★★   Just off the place des Vosges, the "Queen's Pavilion" harkens back to the days when the magnificent square was home to royalty. Set back from the hustle and bustle of the Marais, this heavenly hideaway feels intimate, like a lord's private hunting lodge in the country. The decor is a suave combination of subtle modern and antique: The dark period furniture blends with rich colors on the walls and beds; choice objects and historic details abound. Several deluxe duplexes have staircases leading to cozy sleeping lofts.

28 place des Vosges, 3rd arrond. www.pavillon-de-la-reine.com. ✆ **01-40-29-19-19.** 54 units. 385€–550€ double; 600€–1,200€ suite. Métro: Bastille. **Amenities:** Bar; concierge; fitness room, laundry service, room service, sauna, spa, Wi-Fi (free).

Moderate

Hôtel Caron de Beaumarchais ★★★   In the 18th century, Pierre Auguste Caron de Beaumarchais—author of "The Barber of Seville"—lived near here, and this small hotel celebrates both the playwright and the magnificent century he lived in. Delightful details give you a taste of what life was like back in the day: Walls are covered in high-quality reproductions of period fabrics; rooms are furnished with authentic antique writing tables; and period paintings and first-edition pages of "The Barber of Seville" hang on the walls. A pianoforte that dates from 1792 stands in the lobby, next to an antique card table set up for a game. You half expect Pierre Auguste himself to come prancing through the door.

12 rue Vieille-du-Temple, 4th arrond. www.carondebeaumarchais.com. ✆ **01-42-72-34-12.** 19 units. 120€–200€ double. Métro: St-Paul or Hôtel de Ville. **Amenities:** Wi-Fi (free).

Right Bank Hotels & Restaurants

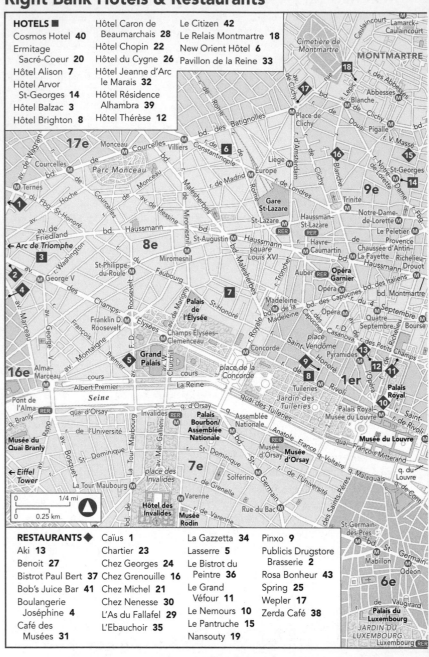

HOTELS ■
Cosmos Hotel **40**
Ermitage
  Sacré-Coeur **20**
Hôtel Alison **7**
Hôtel Arvor
  St-Georges **14**
Hôtel Balzac **3**
Hôtel Brighton **8**

Hôtel Caron de
  Beaumarchais **28**
Hôtel Chopin **22**
Hôtel du Cygne **26**
Hôtel Jeanne d'Arc
  le Marais **32**
Hôtel Résidence
  Alhambra **39**
Hôtel Thérèse **12**

Le Citizen **42**
Le Relais Montmartre **18**
New Orient Hôtel **6**
Pavillon de la Reine **33**

RESTAURANTS ◆
Aki **13**
Benoit **27**
Bistrot Paul Bert **37**
Bob's Juice Bar **41**
Boulangerie
  Joséphine **4**
Café des
  Musées **31**

Caïus **1**
Chartier **23**
Chez Georges **24**
Chez Grenouille **16**
Chez Michel **21**
Chez Nenesse **30**
L'As du Fallafel **29**
L'Ebauchoir **35**

La Gazzetta **34**
Lasserre **5**
Le Bistrot du
  Peintre **36**
Le Grand
  Véfour **11**
Le Nemours **10**
Le Pantruche **15**
Nansouty **19**

Pinxo **9**
Publicis Drugstore
  Brasserie **2**
Rosa Bonheur **43**
Spring **25**
Wepler **17**
Zerda Café **38**

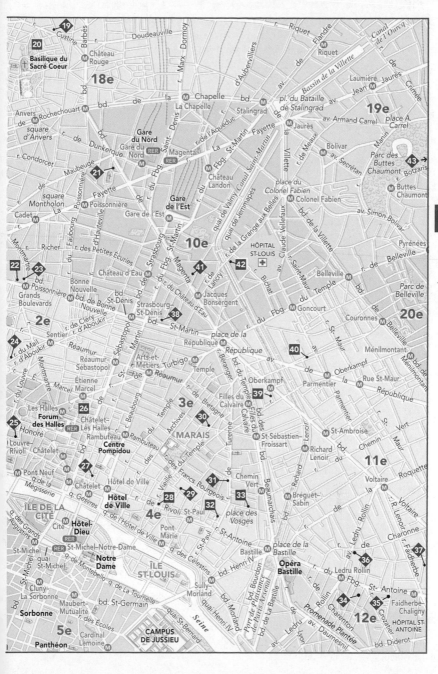

Inexpensive

Hôtel Jeanne d'Arc le Marais ★★ With a prime location, comfortable rooms, and great prices, it's no wonder this hotel books up months in advance. It's located in the lower Marais, right next to the leafy place du Marché St-Catherine. While definitely not luxurious, the rooms are in excellent shape, decked out in warm colors and old-fashioned prints; several have been given a more modern makeover and new bathrooms. Families will be interested in the reasonably priced quads as well as the two communicating rooms on the sixth floor. *Note:* There is another hotel with the same name in the 13th arrondissement—make sure you contact the right one when you reserve, or you'll be in for an unpleasant surprise.

3 rue de Jarente, 4th arrond. www.hoteljeannedarc.com. ℂ **01-48-87-62-11.** 35 units. 120€–150€ double; 250€ triple or quad. Métro: St-Paul. **Amenities:** Computer in lobby, Wi-Fi (free).

CHAMPS-ÉLYSÉES, TROCADÉRO & WESTERN PARIS (8TH, 16TH & 17TH ARRONDISSEMENTS)

Affordable lodgings are scarce in this opulent environment, especially near the Champs and the Arc de Triomphe, where high prices often have more to do with location than the quality of the lodging. Ironically, the location is not particularly central; it's a good hike from here to Notre-Dame.

Expensive

Hôtel Balzac ★★★ Chandeliers and swags of rich fabric await you in the lobby of this classy townhouse, which was built for the director of the Paris Opéra in 1853. Just a few steps away from the Champs-Élysées, the spacious rooms here feature huge beds, high thread-counts, and chiffon and velour around the bed and windows. The ambiance is classic and very French, with reproduction antiques, high ceilings, and subtle colors. There's a covered interior courtyard where you can enjoy a drink on a plush sofa; if you're itching to get out, Louis Vuitton and Fouquet's are just around the corner. This is luxury on a small, personal scale; the service is impeccable and polite without being haughty, and the hotel is small enough to still feel intimate. Pierre Gagnaire, a Michelin three-star gourmet pleasure palace, is in the same building.

6 rue Balzac, 8th arrond. www.hotelbalzac.com. ℂ **01-44-35-18-00.** 69 units. 300€–660€ double; 480€–1,320€ suite and junior suites; 1,440€–2,200€ Royal and Presidential suites. Métro: George V. **Amenities:** Restaurant, bar, business center, dry cleaning, room service, concierge, private parking (23€), Wi-Fi (free).

Moderate

Hôtel Alison ★★ While the lobby decor at this comfortable, family-run hotel hasn't changed since at least 1982 (think Almodóvar movies), it's impeccably clean and shiny, as are the relatively spacious rooms. However you feel about beige walls and chocolate carpets, you should be pleased with the generally high level of comfort here, and the location is excellent: around the corner from the Madeleine and a short stroll to the Champs Elysées and the place de la Concorde.

21 rue de Surène, 8th arrond. www.hotel-alison.com. © **01-42-65-54-00.** 34 units. 132€–189€ double; triple 189€–209€; family suite 240€–388€. Métro: Madeleine or Concorde. **Amenities:** Bar, Wi-Fi (free).

Inexpensive

New Orient Hôtel ★★★ This lovely hotel, which offers comfortable rooms with high ceilings, 19th-century moldings, and antique headboards and armoires, may not be on top of the Champs Elysées, but it's not far, and it is close to stately Parc Monceau and a quick trot to the Saint Lazare train station. The friendly owners, inveterate flea market browsers, have refinished and restored the antique furniture themselves. Rooms (many of which have small balconies) are in tip-top shape, and bathrooms sparkle. There's an elevator, but you'll have to negotiate stairs to get to it.

16 rue de Constantinople, 8th arrond. www.hotelneworient.com. © **01-45-22-21-64.** 30 units. 110€–190€ double, 185€–240€ family room for 4. Métro: Villiers, Europe, or St-Lazare. **Amenities:** Computer in lobby, Wi-Fi (free).

OPÉRA & GRANDS BOULEVARDS (2ND & 9TH ARRONDISSEMENTS)

This area offers a lovely mix of hip bars and restaurants and old-time Paris, with a sprinkling of small museums for a dose of culture. While the area has few big monuments, its up sides include lower room rates and a more neighborhood-y feel.

Moderate

Hôtel Arvor Saint Georges ★★ Located in the charming "New Athens" neighborhood, where 19th-century Romantics like George Sand and Frédéric Chopin lived and worked, these spiffy lodgings offer an arty yet relaxed atmosphere, where fresh white walls show off modern photography and contemporary prints. Rooms are a little small, but simple and chic, with white walls, a splash of color, and a distinctive table or armchair. The airy lobby area, with large windows and bookshelves is an invitation to kick back and read or sip a cup of tea. The tasty breakfast is served here or outside in the flower-filled patio when the weather is nice.

8 rue Laferrière, 9th arrond. www.hotelarvor.com. © **01-48-78-60-92.** 30 units. 120€–200€ double; 200€–280€ suite. Métro: St-Georges. **Amenities:** Bar; Wi-Fi (free).

Inexpensive

Hôtel Chopin ★ Nestled at the back of the delightful Passage Jouffroy, this budget hotel has remarkably quiet rooms considering its location in the middle of the rush and bustle of the Grands Boulevards. The staircase is a little creaky (you have to climb a flight to get to the elevator), and the decor is nothing to write home about, but the rooms are clean and colorful and the bathrooms are spotless. Rooms on the upper floors get more light; many have nice views of Parisian rooftops.

10 bd. Montmartre or 46 passage Jouffroy, 9th arrond. www.hotel-chopin.com. © **01-47-70-58-10.** 36 units. 106€–124€ double; 147€ triple. Métro: Grands Boulevards or Richelieu-Drouot. **Amenities:** Wi-Fi (free).

MONTMARTRE (18TH ARRONDISSEMENT)

Once you leave behind the tourist hordes that invade the Sacré-Coeur and place du Tertre, you'll find a neighborhood of lovely little lanes and small houses, harkening back to the days when Picasso and the boys were at the Bateau Lavoir. Unfortunately, the pickings are slim if you want to actually sleep here. Another consideration: Although Montmartre is charming, it's on the northern edge of the city, so you'll need to budget extra time to get back down the hill to the center of town.

Moderate

Le Relais Montmartre ★★   These comfortable lodgings include small but impeccable rooms decked out in light, warm colors and a classic decor. Nothing particularly hip or stylish here, just quality accommodations in tasteful floral prints, plus reliable service. The one decorative quirk: exposed beams on the ceilings in shades of lavender and blue. The hotel is located on a peaceful little side street, right around the corner from a delicious stretch of food shops on rue Lepic. There are connecting rooms for families, and a small patio for breakfasting in good weather.

6 rue Constance, 18th arrond. www.hotel-relais-montmartre.com. ☏ **01-70-64-25-25.** 26 units. 139€–259€ double, 218€–289€ triple. Métro: Blanche. **Amenities:** Concierge service, laundry service, iPad for guests, Wi-Fi (free).

Inexpensive

Ermitage Sacré-Coeur ★★★   Built in 1890 by a rich gentleman for his mistress, this beautifully preserved townhouse has been lovingly converted into an intimate hotel. It may not offer room service (although a complimentary breakfast is served in your room) or much by way of amenities, but the ambience is unique. Tucked behind the Sacré-Coeur, this small mansion still feels like a private home. In fact, it virtually is: The Canipel family has run these unconventional lodgings for more than 40 years. Each of the five rooms is decorated in period prints and draperies, with beautiful antique bedsteads and armoires. The hallways are done up in deep blues and gold leaf; the wall murals and paintings are the works of a local artist. The hotel has no elevator. The Canipels also rent nearby studios and apartments that sleep up to four.

24 rue Lamarck, 18th arrond. www.ermitagesacrecoeur.fr. ☏ **01-42-64-79-22.** 5 units. 125€–140€ double; 160€ triple; 180€ quad. Rates include breakfast. No credit cards. Métro: Lamarck-Caulaincourt. Parking 20€. **Amenities:** Wi-Fi (free).

RÉPUBLIQUE, BASTILLE & EASTERN PARIS (11TH & 12TH ARRONDISSEMENTS)

Encompassing the recently overhauled place de la République, as well as the historic place de la Bastille, this area is a good choice for both budget travelers and creatures of the night—it includes the bars and clubs of the Oberkampf and Charonne neighborhoods, and is close to the Marais.

Inexpensive

Cosmos Hotel ★★   Just around the corner from the animated Oberkampf neighborhood, this budget option is one of the best deals in town. The modern rooms are generally spotless; aside from a few nicks on the walls, everything from the bed linens to the floor covering looks spanking new. And such good value—only 70€ to 80€ a double. Furthermore, the staff is friendly and helpful. The only downside: Weekend nights can be noisy as people spill out of the busy bars and cafes nearby.

35 rue Jean-Pierre Timbaud, 11th arrond. www.cosmos-hotel-paris.com. *C* **01-43-57-25-88.** 36 units. 70€–80€ double; 90€ triple; 98€ quad. Métro: Parmentier. **Amenities:** Wi-Fi (free).

Hôtel Résidence Alhambra ★   This budget classic now sports a lobby in chic shades of gray and lots of polished concrete. Rooms are polished as well, with splashes of bright color. Tucked in the crook of this L-shaped hotel is a large, leafy garden with tables for alfresco breakfasts. You can even bring your own eats and picnic here after 10am. Eight of the guest rooms on the bottom floor open directly onto a balcony over the garden; about half of the others face onto it. Requests for garden views are taken, but there's no guarantee you'll get it.

13 rue de Malte, 11th arrond. www.hotelalhambra.fr. *C* **01-47-00-35-52.** 53 units. 129€–200€ double; 169€–299€ triple; 209€–349€ quad; 209€–349€ family suite. Métro: Oberkampf. **Amenities:** Computer and printer in lobby, Wi-Fi (free).

BELLEVILLE, CANAL ST-MARTIN & LA VILLETTE (10TH, 19TH & 20TH ARRONDISSEMENTS)

When historic arty neighborhoods like St-Germain and Montmartre became too expensive for up-and-coming artists, many immigrated to these more proletarian neighborhoods, giving the area a funky, bohemian feel. Even though it's gentrifying, Belleville is still known for artists' studios, while dozens of hip cafes and restaurants have popped up along the Canal St-Martin and the Bassin de la Villette. The young and adventurous will appreciate this part of town, but others may find it too much of a commute to the city center.

Moderate

Le Citizen ★★   Maybe it's the smiling young staff in jeans, or the ecological ethos, but there's something alternative in the air at this adorable boutique hotel on the Canal St-Martin. While the rooms are on the small side, they are light and airy, with lots of blonde wood and clean lines; all look out on the tree-lined canal. When you check in, you'll be handed an iPad loaded with information and apps on Paris. Minibar and a delicious buffet breakfast are included in your room rate.

96 quai de Jemmapes, 10th arrond. www.lecitizenhotel.com. *C* **01-83-62-55-50.** 12 units. 199€–296€ double, 304€–334€ suite, 480€ apartment. Rates include breakfast. Métro: Jacques Bonsergent. **Amenities:** Room service, minibar (free), iPad, Wi-Fi (free).

The Left Bank

LATIN QUARTER (5TH & 13TH ARRONDISSEMENTS)

Central and reasonably priced, the Latin Quarter is a long-time favorite for travelers in search of affordable accommodations. As a consequence, a few corners of this famously academic neighborhood are overrun with tourists and

Left Bank Hotels & Restaurants

RESTAURANTS ◆

Bonjour Vietnam **28**
Café Constant **2**
Café de Flore **15**
Café de la Mairie **19**
Cobéa **13**
Crêperie de
  Saint Malo **11**
Dans les Landes **31**
Itinéraires **25**
L'Arpège **8**
La Régalade **14**
Le Casse Noix **1**
Le Comptoir
  du Relais **21**
Le P'tit Fernand **20**
Le Pré Verre **24**
Le Relais Louis XIII **18**
Les Deux Magots **16**
Mangetout **17**
Restaurant Auguste **7**
Restaurant Polidor **23**

HOTELS ■

Hôtel des Bains **12**
Hôtel des Grandes
  Ecoles **29**
Hôtel du Champ
  de Mars **4**
Hôtel Eber Mars **5**
Hôtel Les Jardins
  du Luxembourg **27**
Hôtel Londres Eiffel **3**
Hôtel Mayet **10**
Hôtel Muget **6**
Hôtel Saint-Jacques **26**
Hôtel Signature St-
  Germain-des-Prés **9**
L'Apostrophe **30**
Relais St-Germain **22**

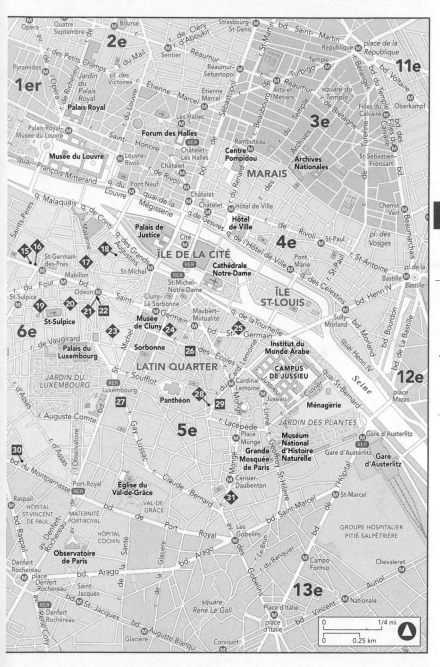

trinket shops. The streets immediately surrounding the place St-Michel (especially around rue de la Huchette) are where you'll find the worst tourist traps, both hotel and restaurant-wise; better prices and quality are to be had in the quieter and more authentic areas around the universities, a little farther from Notre-Dame but still within easy walking distance.

Moderate

Hôtel des Jardins du Luxembourg ★★ Just around the corner from its glorious namesake, these intimate lodgings are tucked away on a quiet cul-de-sac, an excellent hideaway for a romantic honeymoon or cozy retreat. The building's claim to fame is that Sigmund Freud stayed here on his first visit to Paris; perhaps this has something to do with the 1930s and 1940s touches to the decor. The Art Deco ambience of the lobby and lounge invites deep reflection or at least a nice rest in one of the plush armchairs; for full relaxation, indulge in a visit to the sauna. While the standard rooms are quite pretty, with curly wrought-iron headboards and puffy comforters (cotton or feather), the superior rooms, which cost only a few euros more, have nicer views, small balconies, snazzy bathrooms, and designer-fabric-covered walls.

5 impasse Royer-Collard, 5th arrond. www.les-jardins-du-luxembourg.com. ℂ **01-40-46-08-88.** 26 units. 110€–212€ double. Métro: Cluny–La Sorbonne. RER: Luxembourg. **Amenities:** Bar; sauna; Wi-Fi (free).

Hôtel Saint-Jacques ★★ The spacious rooms in this delightful hotel retain lots of architectural details from its Belle Epoque past. Most of the ceilings are adorned with masses of curlicues, and some have restored 18th-century murals to gaze at while you laze in bed. Modern reproductions of famous French paintings hang on the walls; Second Empire–themed murals decorate the lobby and breakfast room. The romantic decor has a light, feminine feel, all shades of light blue, cream, and gray—considerably more inviting than when the hotel served as a set for the Audrey Hepburn/Cary Grant classic "Charade."

35 rue des Ecoles, 5th arrond. www.paris-hotel-stjacques.com. ℂ **01-44-07-45-45.** 26 units. 114€–342€ double; 112€–328€ triple. Métro: Maubert-Mutualité, RER: St-Michel–Notre-Dame. **Amenities:** Babysitting, bar, Wi-Fi (free).

Inexpensive

Hôtel des Grandes Ecoles ★★★ Tucked into a private garden on the slope of the Montagne St-Geneviève, this hotel makes you feel as if you have just walked out of Paris and into the countryside. A path leads to a flower-bedecked interior courtyard, where birds chirp in the trees; the reception area adjoins an inviting breakfast room with potted plants and an upright piano. The spotless rooms are filled with country-style furniture and papered in old-fashioned prints; crocheted bedspreads and framed etchings of flowers complete the look. The calm is such that the hotel has nixed TVs. What's more, this unique ambience comes at a reasonable price. Families will appreciate the six large suites that can sleep four.

75 rue de Cardinal-Lemoine, 5th arrond. www.hotel-grandes-ecoles.com. ℂ**01-43-26-79-23.** 51 units. 135€–165€ double, 185€ family room. Parking 30€. Métro: Cardinal Lemoine or Place Monge. **Amenities:** Wi-Fi (free).

ST-GERMAIN-DES-PRÉS & LUXEMBOURG (6TH ARRONDISSEMENT)

Sleek boutiques and restaurants abound in this legendary neighborhood; historic cafes and monuments lend plenty of atmosphere. Unlike some other Parisian neighborhoods, this one is lively even late at night; it is also centrally located and within walking distance of many top sights.

Expensive

Relais St-Germain ★★★ Fashioned from three adjoining 17th-century townhouses, this intimate hotel mixes old-world charm and jazzy modernity. Exposed beams abound in the spacious rooms, even the smallest of which are equipped with a comfortable sitting area. The decor artfully blends period furniture with modern prints, like the Louis XV armchair covered in zigzagged leather, or the 18th-century painting hung in the middle of a wall of mirrors. The effect is both stylish and deeply comforting. There are some extra stairs between floors, so if you have mobility issues, be sure to make that clear when you reserve. Guests have priority at the hotel restaurant, **Le Comptoir** (p. 69), where you might otherwise have a 6-month wait for a reservation. Book your room at least a month in advance.

9 carrefour de l'Odéon, 6th arrond. www.hotelrsg.com. ℂ **01-44-27-07-97.** 22 units. 295€ double; 460€ suite. Rates include breakfast. **Amenities:** Restaurant; free Wi-Fi. Métro: Odéon.

Inexpensive

Hotel Mayet ★★ The lobby of this young-at-heart hotel sports two murals, one by American graffiti artist JohnOne and the other by his French counterpart André. Rooms are snug but colorful, with white walls and touches of bright orange. The hotel has a lighthearted North African theme, with paintings of camels in the desert and vintage photos of beautiful Moroccan movie stars. This family-run enterprise also has an apartment for rent next door that sleeps four with a kitchen and washer-dryer.

3 rue Mayet, 6th arrond. www.mayet.com. ℂ **01-47-83-21-35.** 23 units. 110€–200€ double; 180€–300€ triple. Métro: Duroc. **Amenities:** Bar, free Wi-Fi.

EIFFEL TOWER & NEARBY (7TH ARRONDISSEMENT)

Many visitors to Paris clamor for hotels that are right near the Eiffel Tower, perhaps under the mistaken impression that this is a central location. It isn't. Still, there's no denying that this extremely posh area is beautiful.

Expensive

Hôtel Signature St-Germain-des-Près ★★★ Recently overhauled, this hotel is now run by the friendly Prigent family (who are also at the helm of the Hôtel Londres Eiffel; see below). Bright colors on the walls blend harmoniously with subdued bedsteads and linens; smart mid-century reproduction furniture and faux antique phones take the edge off sleek modern lines. The "Prestige" rooms cost more, but are especially roomy (30 sq. m/323 sq. ft.), a rarity even in upscale Parisian hotels. In addition to particularly attentive service, this hotel is also blessed with an excellent location for shopping addicts: It's just down the street from Bon Marché.

5 rue Chomel, 7th arrond. www.signature-saintgermain.com. (℃) **01-45-48-35-53.** 26 units. 190€–380€ double; 370–420€ triple; two-room connecting family suite 440€–540€. Métro: Sèvres-Bablylone or St-Sulpice. **Amenities:** Concierge service, Wi-Fi (free).

Moderate

Hôtel Eber Mars ★★   When you walk in the door, chances are you will be greeted by none other than Monsieur Eber himself, who has spent the last decade lovingly renovating his hotel. The 1930s-era decor is low-key and specifically Parisian. Walls in the spacious rooms are papered in period patterns in neutral colors, lit by authentic Art Deco hanging fixtures found at antiques fairs. Old-fashioned radiators have been scraped and lacquered; prints dating from the Universal Exposition of 1889 (which unveiled the Eiffel Tower—another decor theme) are hung on the walls. Rooms in this hotel are unusually large for Paris; the triples and connecting suites are ideal for families.

117 av. de la Bourdonnais, 7th arrond. www.hotelebermars.com. (℃) **01-47-05-42-30.** 25 units. 120€–280€ doubles, 180€–300€ triples. Métro: Ecole Militaire. **Amenities:** Bar, Wi-Fi (free).

Hôtel Londres Eiffel ★★   From the moment you enter, you feel like you are in a private home. In fact, you may very well be welcomed by Samba, the lovely golden retriever, before you meet the Prigents, the hospitable owners. Knickknacks line the wood bookshelves in the neo-retro lobby, an old-fashioned, yet cheerfully modern look that extends to the guestrooms. Polished wood banisters lead up spiral staircases to narrow hallways and cozy rooms decorated with a personal touch. Walls are covered with tasteful printed fabrics featuring slightly kitsch 19th-century motifs, while the furniture harkens back to the 1940s, with lots of wood in soft shades of beige and brown. Connecting rooms are available for families.

1 rue Augereau, 7th arrond. www.hotel-paris-londres-eiffel.com. (℃) **01-45-51-63-02.** 30 units. 160€–275€ double; 330€ triple. Métro: Ecole Militaire. **Amenities:** Wi-Fi (free).

Hôtel Muget ★★★   Known for its impeccable service and comfort level, the lovely rooms at this personable hotel are fitted with faux-antique furniture, big wood headboards hand-painted with a lily-of-the-valley (muguet) motif, and pretty bathrooms with old-fashioned wood washstands and mirror frames. Rooms are relatively large for Paris, and the triples are downright spacious. Five doubles have a great view of the Eiffel Tower, three others of Les Invalides; needless to say they book up months in advance. The others, which are equally comfy and less expensive, look out on either the quiet street or the airy courtyard. Three rooms on the ground floor face directly into a small but lush garden.

11 rue Chevert, 7th arrond. www.hotelmuguet.com. (℃) **01-47-05-05-93.** 43 units. 165€–280€ double; 250€–350€ triple. Métro: Varenne or La Tour Maubourg. **Amenities:** Computer and printer in lobby; Wi-Fi (free).

Inexpensive

Hôtel du Champ de Mars ★★ An adorable and affordable little inn right around the corner from the food shops of rue Cler—what more could you ask for? The impeccably maintained rooms are decorated with the kind of care people generally reserve for their own homes: thick cotton bedspreads, framed etchings, and printed fabrics in warm colors on the walls and windows. Two rooms have a tiny courtyard, while those on the upper floors get lots of light. The friendly staff includes a delightful cocker spaniel named Cannelle.

7 rue du Champ de Mars, 7th arrond. www.hotelduchampdemars.com. ⓒ **01-45-51-52-30.** 25 units. 130€–170€ double. Métro: Ecole Militaire. **Amenities:** Laptop loan for guests; Wi-Fi (free).

MONTPARNASSE & NEARBY (14TH & 15TH ARRONDISSEMENTS)

Montparnasse is more centrally located than it might seem—it's right on the border of St-Germain and close to the Luxembourg gardens. Also, the train station is a major transit hub for a bundle of Métro lines and bus routes. Though the utterly unaesthetic Tour Montparnasse now casts a shadow over this ancient artists' haunt (Henry Miller, Man Ray, Chagall, Picasso . . .), the little streets in the area are still full of personality.

Moderate

L'Apostrophe ★★ Honoring the neighborhood's literary history (nearby writers' haunts include La Coupole and the Closerie des Lilas), this "poem hotel" is dedicated to the beauty and mystery of writing. The decor is a little off the wall, but very tastefully so, starting with an impressive silhouette of a tree on the hotel's facade. Inside, rooms are themed: "Caligraphy" has Chinese characters splashed on royal blue walls, "Musique" features stenciled sheet music, instruments, and giant piano keys. The larger rooms include a Jacuzzi bathtub right in the room.

3 rue de Chevreuse, 6th arrond. www.apostrophe-hotel.com. ⓒ **01-56-54-31-31.** 16 units. 169€–310€ standard double; 220€–353€ double with a Jacuzzi. Métro: Vavin. **Amenities:** Bar; free Wi-Fi.

Inexpensive

Hôtel des Bains ★★★ With cute, comfortable rooms and excellent rates, this friendly hotel is one of the best deals on the Left Bank, especially for families. In a city where large rooms are rare, it offers several good-size, two-room suites for up to four people. Doubles are amply sized as well, with high ceilings; the largest ones face the pretty courtyard. The decor is simple but nicely accessorized with objects and artwork from the art market that takes place on the nearby square every Sunday. Most rooms have wood floors and a few have tiny balconies. The elevator stops at a landing between floors, which have a few stairs.

33 rue Delambre, 14th arrond. www.hotel-des-bains-montparnasse.com. ⓒ **01-43-20-85-27.** 42 units. 105€ double; 140€–175€ suites for 2–4 people. Métro: Vavin, Edgar Quinet, or Montparnasse. **Amenities:** Wi-Fi (free).

WHERE TO EAT

Boulangeries (bakeries) with buttery croissants and decadent pastries lurk on every street corner; open-air markets tempt the senses; and restaurants with intriguing menus sprout up on every block.

Recently, a whole new crop of "neo-bistros" has emerged, offering high-quality eats for a fraction of what you would pay in a gourmet palace. One outgrowth of this movement is the obsession with "noble" ingredients—that is, high-quality, regional produce or products, often from a specific small-scale farm or artisan, sometimes organic, but always in keeping with the oldest and best traditions.

Note: Restaurants tend to be small in Paris, and when it comes to reservations, size matters. To be sure to get a table, reserve ahead for most of the restaurants listed below under the "Expensive" or "Moderate" categories.

The Right Bank

LOUVRE & ÎLE DE LA CITÉ (1ST ARRONDISSEMENT)

Dining near the Louvre can be an expensive and frustrating affair; it's rife with overpriced, mediocre tourist restaurants boasting menus in at least five languages. If you poke around some of the smaller streets however, you'll discover plenty of little restaurants where you can eat well and affordably. That said, if you are ready to spend, gourmet opportunities abound.

Expensive

Le Grand Véfour ★★★ CLASSIC FRENCH   Channel centuries of history at this illustrious restaurant, where Napoléon, Danton, Hugo, Colette, and Cocteau all once dined. Thanks to Guy Martin, chef and owner, the food is as memorable as the magnificently preserved 18th-century salon: Signature dishes like Prince Rainier III pigeon and truffled oxtail parmentier share the menu with new creations with contemporary flavors like sumac and star anise. Reserve at least 2 weeks in advance.

17 rue de Beaujolais, 1st arrond. www.grand-vefour.com. ✆ **01-42-96-56-27.** Main courses 88€–108€; fixed-price lunch 98€, fixed-price dinner 298€. Mon–Fri 12:30–1:45pm and 8–9:45pm. Closed Aug. Métro: Louvre–Palais-Royal or Pyramides.

Spring ★★★ MODERN FRENCH   One of the city's most talked-about restaurants has a chef who is—gasp—American! Try not to think about that and just enjoy the amazing dishes that come out of the kitchen. Chef Daniel Rose, native of Chicago, pays utmost respect to all things French while adding a dash of Yankee bravado to his superb creations. The seasonal menu might start with zucchini with mint and curry oil, followed by quail with cherries and purée of almonds. Desserts might include a tea sorbet with grapefruit or chocolate with blackberries. It's a four-course fixed-price menu only, which doesn't seem to be a problem for diners, who fight for a seat here. Reserve at least 1 month in advance.

6 rue Bailleul, 1st arrond. www.springparis.fr. ✆ **01-45-96-05-72.** Fixed-price dinner 84€. Tues–Sat 6:30–10:30pm. Métro: Louvre-Rivoli.

It's 3pm. All of the restaurants are closed and you are dreaming of something light and healthy to eat. Fear not: Look for one of the following healthy gourmet chains that are multiplying around offices and shopping areas. Locations are listed on the restaurants' websites.

Cojean (24 locations; www.cojean.fr): A creation of an ex-McDonald's executive with an almost religious fervor for fresh, healthy food, these airy, modern boutiques serve innovative salads, as well as quiches, sandwiches, and fresh-squeezed juices. Many veggie options. Open until 4 or 5pm in most locations.

Exki (11 locations; www.exki.com): This Belgian chain (pronounced "ex-KEY," like the French word for "exquisite") offers a terrific array of tasty, healthy sandwiches, soups, and desserts (vegetarian choices too), until 9 or 10pm. It uses lots of organic, free-trade, seasonal ingredients and has a low ecological footprint.

Boco (three locations; www.boco.fr): This place is almost too good to be true. Organic takeout from Michelin-starred chefs for under 15€? Be still, my beating heart. Hot food, cold food, light meals, and desserts are served daily from 11am until 8 or 10pm (St-Lazare location lunch only). Main dishes run 7€ to 10€, and, gasp, a fixed menu (changes daily) three-course meal costs 15€.

Moderate

Pinxo ★★★ MODERN FRENCH/TAPAS   Sample renowned chef Alain Dutournier's exquisite cooking in a relaxed atmosphere at this modern tapas restaurant where food is made to be shared. Everyone grazes on small plates with magnificent mouthfuls (each dish is priced per person on the menu), such as baby squid with fried ginger; terrine of goat cheese with eggplant; or sliced Chalosse beef à la plancha. The best way to wash it all down is with a glass of wine—choose from 120 bottles, many of which are available by the glass.

9 rue d'Alger, 1st arrond. www.alaindutournier.com. ℭ **01-40-20-72-00.** Portions per person 6€–9€, meal per person 35€–40€. Mon–Fri 12:15–2:15pm and 7–10:30pm, Sat 7–10:30pm. Closed Aug. Métro: Tuileries.

Inexpensive

Aki ★★ JAPANESE   Of the dozens of Japanese restaurants on rue Ste-Anne, this one, which specializes in *okonomiyaki*, stands out. This delicious dish is a sort of grilled omelet topped with meat or seafood and a yummy sauce. Watch the cooks create yours on a griddle in the open kitchen. It also serves udon and soba noodles. Arrive early or be prepared to wait in line.

11bis rue Sainte Anne, 1st arrond. www.akirestaurant.fr. ℭ **01-42-97-54-27.** 12€–15€, fixed-price lunch or dinner 13€–15€. Mon–Sat 11:30am–10:45pm. Métro: Pyramides.

OPÉRA & GRANDS BOULEVARDS (2ND & 9TH ARRONDISSEMENTS)

Buzzing with cafes and theaters back in the 19th century, the long-overlooked Grand Boulevards have come back to life, especially near the Opéra and the hip part of the 9th arrondissement that borders Montmartre. Less trendy, but also less expensive, the little streets around the Bourse (the French stock exchange) have a wide range of restaurant options, especially at lunchtime.

Expensive

Chez Georges ★★ TRADITIONAL FRENCH   A step back in time, this is how Parisian restaurants were before cuisine became nouvelle, or vanilla infusions were allowed to touch a fish dish. The room is crowded and lively; the cooking is old-fashioned and delicious. Many of the customers are regulars who work at the nearby stock exchange. The handwritten menu features beautifully executed classics like fillet of sole, *pot-au-feu* (beef simmered with vegetables), and sweetbreads with morels. Save room for the profiteroles at dessert.

1 rue du Mail, 2nd arrond. ⓒ **01-42-60-07-11.** Main courses 20€–43€. Mon–Fri noon–2:30pm and 7–11pm. Closed Aug. and the last week of Dec. Métro: Bourse.

Moderate

Chez Grenouille ★ TRADITIONAL FRENCH   Chef Alexis Blanchard has won prizes for his pâtés and *boudins* (blood sausage), so you'll find all manner of charcuterie on the menu here, plus classics such as roast suckling pig, sweetbreads with morels and *vin jaune,* and the chef's famous *andouillette* (tripe sausage), plus a fish dish or two for lighter eaters. There's nothing fussy or huffy about the decor or the service; this is a friendly and relaxed place where the food comes first, and it is hearty and delicious. Finish with the crème caramel made with salted butter.

52 rue Blanche, 9th arrond. www.chezgrenouille.com. ⓒ **01-42-81-34-07.** Main courses 22€–28€; fixed-price lunch 18€–23€. Mon–Fri noon–2:30pm and 7–11pm; Sat 7–11pm Métro: Trinité.

Le Pantruche ★★ TRADITIONAL FRENCH/BISTRO   The name is old-fashioned slang for Paris, but this little bistro has a decidedly modern feel to it. Another case of a runaway chef from Michelin-starred restaurants, Le Pantruche offers flavorful updated bistro fare like braised sweetbreads with carrots in a licorice glaze, or suckling pig with pears, celery root, and chestnuts. The atmosphere is relaxed, and the fixed-price menus at lunch and dinner are a terrific value.

3 rue Victor Massé, 9th arrond. www.lepantruche.com. ⓒ **01-48-78-55-60.** Main courses: 19€–26€; fixed-price lunch 19€, fixed-price dinner 35€ Mon–Fri 12:30–2:30pm and 7:30–9:30pm. Closed first 3 weeks of Aug. Métro: Pigalle.

Inexpensive

Chartier ★ TRADITIONAL FRENCH   With a dining room that can seat over 300, this gargantuan establishment is one of the last of the *bouillons,* or workers' restaurants, found all over Paris back in the 19th century. The idea was to offer good food at modest prices, a concept that still speaks to working Parisians some 100 years later, if the line out the door is any indication. You come here for the experience more than for the food, which is tasty but certainly won't win any prizes. The menu includes traditional dishes like roast chicken with fries, or rump steak with pepper sauce. Service is fast and furious (how could it not be with this many tables?), but it's all part of the atmosphere, which is something that belongs to another time and place. It takes no reservations, so be prepared to wait.

7 rue du Faubourg Montmartre, 9th arrond. www.restaurant-chartier.com. ℂ **01-47-70-86-29.** Main courses 8.70€–13€. Daily 11:30am–10pm. Métro: Grands-Boulevards.

LE MARAIS (3RD & 4TH ARRONDISSEMENTS)

Between its working-class roots and its more recent makeover, it offers a wide range of choices, from humble falafel joints to trendy brasseries.

Expensive

Benoit ★★ TRADITIONAL FRENCH   This historic bistro had already hosted a century's worth of Parisian notables when Alain Ducasse took the helm in 2005. The dining room is still lined with mirrors, zinc, and tiles, while the classic menu has been given an extra dash of pizzazz. Dishes like escargots in garlic butter and brill braised with Jura wine share the stage with homemade cassoulet and beef filet bordelaise. The sommelier will help you navigate the huge wine list.

20 rue St-Martin, 4th arrond. www.benoit-paris.com. ℂ **01-42-72-25-76.** Main courses 26€–54€; fixed-price lunch 39€. Daily noon–2pm and 7:30–10pm. Closed first 3 weeks of Aug. Métro: Hôtel-de-Ville.

Moderate

Café des Musées ★ TRADITIONAL FRENCH/BISTRO   Weary culture vultures who've tried to do both the Picasso museum and the Musée Carnavalet on the same day will appreciate this bustling corner cafe with its appealing sidewalk tables. This is not just any old corner cafe, mind you, but one where the inventive chef works wonders with bistro classics like steak frîtes and *andouillette* (tripe sausage) as well as lighter fare like a seasonal vegetable casserole with basil oil, or a *grand aioli,* poached cod with aioli mayonnaise and vegetables. The lunch fixed-price menu is particularly good value.

49 rue de Turenne, 3rd arrond. www.lecafedesmusees.fr. ℂ **01-42-72-96-17.** Main courses 16€–27€; fixed-price lunch 17€, Daily noon–3pm and 7–11pm. Closed last 2 weeks of Aug. Métro: St. Paul or Chemin Vert.

Inexpensive

Chez Nenesse ★★★ TRADITIONAL BISTRO   This neighborhood haunt has stayed true to its proletarian roots in a frighteningly hip part of the northern Marais. At lunchtime, the chef sends out traditional bistro fare (such as blanquette de veau, or rump steak) into the busy dining room, while dinner comes with a change in menus and ambience—the checked plastic tablecloths are traded for white linen, and *magret de canard au cassis* (duck breast with cassis liqueur) and *filet d'agneau a l'estragon* (lamb steak with tarragon) take center stage. Thursday is steak-frites day, when regulars crowd in at lunch for their weekly dose of the yummy house fries.

17 rue Saintonge, 3rd arrond. ℂ **01-42-78-46-49.** Main courses lunch 11€–12€, dinner 16€–22€. Mon–Fri noon–2:15pm and 8–10:15pm. Closed Aug and from Christmas to New Years. Métro: Filles de Calvaire or Oberkampf.

L'As du Fallafel ★★ FALAFEL/ISRAELI   This Marais institution offers, without a doubt, the best falafel in Paris. True, falafel joints are scarce in this city, but that doesn't take away from the excellence of these overstuffed beauties, brimming with cucumbers, pickled turnips, shredded cabbage, tahini, fried eggplant, and those crispy balls of fried chickpeas and spices. Wash it down with an Israeli beer. Service is fast and furious, but basically friendly—be prepared to deal with hordes of tourists and locals at lunch. Closed Friday afternoon and all day Saturday.

34 rue des Rosiers, 4th arrond. ℂ **01-48-87-63-60.** Main courses 8€–20€. Sun–Thurs 11am–midnight; Fri 11am–3pm. Métro: St. Paul.

CHAMPS-ÉLYSÉES & WESTERN PARIS (8TH, 16TH & 17TH ARRONDISSEMENTS)

Champs-Elysées is a difficult place to find a good meal, unless you are willing to spend a lot of money. Mediocre chain restaurants abound on the grand avenue itself, and kebob joints mingle with frighteningly expensive gourmet palaces on the surrounding side streets.

Expensive

Caïus ★★★ MODERN FRENCH   While the chef at this elegant dining room is a fan of spices and herbs from faraway lands, Jean-Marc Notelet's subtle cuisine also makes use of top-quality French ingredients, like mussels from Brittany, veal from Corrèze, and free-range pork raised on apples and acorns. Menu must-haves include cod with lemongrass and combava, grilled duck with sumac, and beef confit with tonka beans and niora. Be sure to reserve: Tables fill quickly with a devoted local clientele.

6 rue d'Armaillé, 17th arrond. www.caius-restaurant.fr. ℂ **01-42-27-19-20.** Main courses 20€–25€; fixed-price dinner 42€. Mon–Fri noon–2pm and 7:30–10:30pm. Closed 3 weeks in Aug and last week in Dec. Métro: Argentine.

Lasserre ★★★ GOURMET FRENCH   André Malraux, Salvador Dali, Audrey Hepburn, Marlene Dietrich—the list of celebrities who have dined at this legendary restaurant is understandably long. What famous person wouldn't want to eat in this superb dining room, where the ceiling opens when the weather is willing? A silk-draped, arch-windowed affair, the room glistens with fine porcelain, silver knickknacks, and crystal candelabras. The young chefs have recently brought new life to the classic menu, adding their own subtle creations, such as sea bass with vegetables in chardonnay, or roasted lamb confit with artichokes and apples. Reserve at least 2 weeks ahead. Dinner jackets required for men.

17 av. Franklin D. Roosevelt, 8th arrond. www.restaurant-lasserre.com. ℂ **01-43-59-02-13.** Main courses 85€–220€; fixed-price lunch 90€ and 120€, fixed-price dinner 220€. Tues–Wed and Sat 7–10pm; Thurs–Fri noon–2pm and 7–10pm. Closed Aug. Métro: Franklin Roosevelt.

Moderate

Publicis Drugstore Brasserie ★★ MODERN BRASSERIE   You won't find toothpaste at this "drugstore," whose name comes from a former

1950s incarnation that consisted of a warren of shops, restaurants, and services "à l'americaine." This ultra-modern, oh-so-chic complex has kept the multi-functional concept with shops, restaurants, and a cinema. The Brasserie is the most accessible eating option—a light-filled expanse with a great street-side view of the Champs and the Arc de Triomphe. The food is high-end casual: gourmet hamburgers, grilled fish, and steak tartare, delivered by a young and beautiful waitstaff. Meals are served non-stop until 2am, and there is an "early lunch" deal for 15€–20€ during the week from 11:30am–12:30pm.

133 av. des Champs Elysées, 8th arrond. www.publicisdrugstore.com. ℂ **01-44-43-77-64.** Main courses 22€–42€; fixed-price "early lunch" 15€–20€; Sunday brunch 38€. Mon–Fri 8am–2am. Sat–Sun 10am–2am. Métro: Charles de Gaulle–Etoile.

Inexpensive
Boulangerie Joséphine ★ BAKERY/SANDWICHES/FRENCH   This terrific bakery near the Arc de Triomphe has a nice outdoor terrace and a pretty upstairs dining room that fills quickly with local office workers and business-people at lunchtime. You can buy sandwiches and salads (and desserts, of course) to go, or sit down for table service (noon–3pm) and sample one of the excellent daily specials, like stuffed vegetables, roast chicken, or osso buco (Milanese veal stew). Also open for continental breakfast from 8am.

69 av. Marceau, 8th arrond. www.josephine-boulangerie.com. ℂ**01-47-20-49-62.** Main courses 5€–15€. Mon–Fri 8am–8pm. Closed for 2 weeks in mid-Aug. Métro: Charles de Gaulle–Etoile.

MONTMARTRE (18TH ARRONDISSEMENT)
When you get away from the tourist traps of Place du Tertre, you start to understand why this neighborhood is a favorite with the arty-hipster set. And where there's art, you are bound to find an artist in the kitchen.

Moderate
Nansouty ★★★ MODERN FRENCH   Just north of the Butte de Mont-martre, this popular wine bar will appeal to both gourmets and wine enthu-siasts. Choose from more than 100 bottles on the massive blackboard, and supplement with top-quality nibbles. Can't make up your mind? Just ask the waitstaff, who are wise in the ways of Bacchus. Success has been such that Nansouty is now open at both lunch and dinner, offering affordable fixed-price menus and seasonal specialties.

35 rue Ramey, 18th arrond. ℂ **01-42-52-58-87.** Main courses 18€; fixed-price lunch 17€, fixed-price dinner 30€ Tues–Fri noon–2:30pm and 8–11pm; Sat and Mon 8–11pm. Métro: Lamarck-Caulincourt or Château Rouge.

Wepler ★★ FRENCH BRASSERIE   Picasso and Modigliani used to hang out at this venerable brasserie on Place de Clichy, as did writer Henry Miller, who made it his headquarters. Today the atmosphere is quite sedate, but it's still a wonderful place to sit and watch the world go by, and the prices are accessible enough that it is still frequented by artists and writers. The menu is classic brasserie (steak tartare, shellfish platters, poached haddock in *beurre blanc*) but with a light, gourmet touch. If you don't want a big meal, ask for the less expensive cafe menu on the covered terrace, which features delicate omelets, a *plat du jour*, and meal-sized salads.

14 place de Clichy, 18th arrond. www.wepler.com. © **01-45-22-53-24.** Main courses 18€–39€; fixed-price lunch or dinner 25€–35€. Daily 8am–midnight. Métro: Place de Clichy.

RÉPUBLIQUE, BASTILLE & EASTERN PARIS (11TH & 12TH ARRONDISSEMENTS)

Home to a mix of working-class families, hipsters, and *bobos* (bourgeois bohemians), the area between République and Nation is diverse, young, and fun. This might be why there are so many good restaurants around here. It's also a good place to discover the flavors of Africa in restaurants featuring dishes from France's former colonies.

Moderate

Bistrot Paul Bert ★★★ BISTRO/TRADITIONAL FRENCH   Ask any local food writer to name his or her favorite classic bistro, and there's a good chance you'll be directed here. The chalkboard menu changes with the seasons, but you can usually count on one of the city's best steak frîtes (here crowned with a glistening morsel of marrow), followed by a generous slice of *tarte tatin* (apple tart) served with thick crème fraîche. The decor is a jumble of wooden tables, tile floors, flea market finds, and a polished zinc bar—exactly how you imagine a neighborhood bistro should be.

18 rue Paul Bert, 11th arrond. © **01-43-72-24-01.** Main courses 27€; fixed-price lunch 19€ and 38€, fixed-price dinner 38€. Tues–Sat noon–2pm and 7:30–11pm. Closed Aug. Métro: Faidherbe-Chaligny.

La Gazzetta ★★★ MODERN FRENCH   Just down the street from the bustling outdoor food market at Aligre, this atmospheric, old-fashioned-looking bistro is helmed by a chef whose cooking is anything but traditional. How about spelt risotto with nettles, or mackerel with burnt spring onions—topped off with goat-cheese ice cream with roasted apricots for dessert? It may sound strange, but it tastes fantastic. If everyone at your table is of like mind, you can savor the five-course tasting menu for 59€; at lunch the less adventurous can order a fixed-price menu with three tiny appetizers and a main dish for 19€, an excellent price for this level of quality.

29 rue de Cotte, 12th arrond. www.lagazzetta.fr. © **01-43-47-47-05.** Main courses 16€–28€. Fixed-price lunch 19€–24€; fixed-price dinner 39€–59€. Tues–Sat noon–3pm and 7–10:30pm, Sun noon–3pm. Closed mid-July to mid-Aug. Métro: Ledru-Rollin.

Inexpensive

L'Ebauchoir ★★   Located in an unlikely corner of the 12th arrondissement, this neighborhood hangout offers a great selection of modern bistro cooking at reasonable prices. The high ceilings, sunny yellow walls, and wooden fixtures create a friendly atmosphere for Mediterranean-inspired dishes like roast lamb with sweet spices and Thai basil, or magret (breast) of duck with vanilla and pineapple. There's usually a nice vegetarian option here, like a vegetable "cake" with sautéed shiitake mushrooms, asparagus, and hummus. With a three-course lunch deal at 16€, this place gets jammed at noon, so try to reserve.

43 rue des Citeaux, 12th arrond. www.lebauchoir.com. ✆ **01-43-42-49-31.** Main courses dinner 18€–23€; fixed-price lunch 14€–28€. Mon 8–11pm, Tues–Fri noon–2:30pm and 8–11pm, Fri–Sat noon–2:30pm and 7:30–11pm. Closed 1 week mid-Aug. Métro: Faidherbe Chaligny or Reuilly Diderot.

BELLEVILLE, CANAL ST-MARTIN & NORTHEAST PARIS (10TH, 19TH & 20TH ARRONDISSEMENTS)

One of the last strongholds of Paris's bohemian set, here you can find both gourmet bistros and funky cheap eats, as well as a good number of wine bars that serve both nibbles and the fruit of the vine.

Moderate

Chez Michel ★★★ BRETON/SEAFOOD   Prices have barely budged in a decade at this popular restaurant, where the atmosphere is homey and relaxed, and the food is simply excellent. A few short blocks from the Gare du Nord, you can stumble off the Eurostar and within minutes be settling in at your table—provided you've reserved. Fans come from far and wide to enjoy Chef Thierry Breton's creations, much of which is inspired by the cuisine of Brittany, where he hails from. The chalkboard menu includes specialties like *Kotriade,* a Breton fish stew, and lots of beautifully prepared seafood, as well as plenty of elegant renditions of down-home French cooking, like veal fricassee with vegetables, beef cheeks with artichokes, or roast chicken "chasseur." For dessert, try the copious rice pudding or the awe-inspiring Paris-Brest (a choux pastry filled with praline cream).

10 rue de Belzunce, 10th arrond. www.restaurant-chez-michel.com. ✆ **01-44-53-06-20.** Fixed-price lunch 29€, fixed-price dinner 35€. Tues–Fri noon–2pm and Mon–Fri 7pm–midnight. Closed Aug. Métro: Gare du Nord.

Rosa Bonheur ★ TAPAS   This unconventional space is named after an unconventional 19th-century painter/sculptress. Yes, it's a tapas bar, but it's also a sort of off-the-wall community center, hosting various expositions and events—it even has its own chorus and soccer team. Located in an old *buvette* (refreshment pavilion) inside the Parc des Buttes Chaumont, dating from the Universal Exposition of 1900, the restaurant boasts a sprawling terrace and one of the best panoramic views in town. A huge crowd gathers to drink and nibble tapas both indoors and out. An indoor play area and kids' menu make this a good family option. There is a second location on a docked barge on the Seine, **Rosa Bonheur Sur Seine** (right near the Pont des Invalides on the Left Bank). The barge is open year round; from April to October there is outdoor seating and a pizza stand on the quay.

2 allée de la Cascade, 19th arrond. www.rosabonheur.fr. ✆ **01-42-00-00-45.** Tapas 3€–9€. Wed–Fri noon–midnight, Sat–Sun 10am–midnight. Closed first 2 weeks in Jan. Métro Botzaris.

Inexpensive

Bob's Juice Bar ★ VEGETARIAN   Hip Parisians are tripping all over themselves to try "smoossies" (that is, smoothies) these days, and some of the best can be found at this terrific vegetarian restaurant, which has muffins, bagels, soups, and other delicious goodies. The brainchild of Marc Grossman (alias "Bob"), an erstwhile New Yorker, this may not be the most authentically French experience, but it certainly is a tasty one. Sit down or take out here, or try the **Bob's Kitchen** in the Marais (74 rue des Gravilliers), or **Bob's Bake Shop** in the 18th (Halle Pajol, 12 Esplanade Nathalie Sarraute), both of which are open on Sundays.

15 rue Lucien Sampaix, 10th arrond. *©* **09-50-06-36-18.** Smoothies and juices 5€–7.50€; main courses 6€–8€. Mon–Fri 7:30am–3pm, Sat 8:30am–4pm. Métro: Jacques Bonsergent.

Zerda Café ★★ NORTH AFRICAN/COUSCOUS Intricately carved Moorish designs cover the walls of this friendly restaurant, which serves some of the best couscous in Paris. A steaming heap of fine couscous, a savory bouillon with vegetables, and delicately grilled or roasted meat are the three main components of this dish, originally imported from North Africa and now wildly popular in France. Zerda offers a choice of lamb, chicken and *merguez* (spicy lamb sausage) versions; recommended is the meltingly tender "lamb cooked in sauce," but they are all good. If you prefer one of their scrumptious tagines (stews including ingredients such as dried fruits, olives, or preserved lemons), be patient: They take 20 minutes to prepare. There is a second location at 125 rue de Tocqueville, in the 17th arrondissement.

15 rue René Boulanger, 10th arrond. www.zerdacafe.fr. *©* **01-42-00-25-15.** Main courses 15€–22€. Mon and Sat 7pm–midnight, Tues–Fri and Sun noon–4pm and 7–midnight. Closed 2 weeks in Aug. Métro: Strasbourg–St-Denis.

The Left Bank
LATIN QUARTER (5TH & 13TH ARRONDISSEMENTS)
Steer clear of the unbearably touristy area around rue de la Huchette and the often mediocre restaurants on rue Moufftard. Venture farther afield, where innovative restaurateurs have been cultivating a knowledgeable clientele of professors, professionals, and savvy tourists like yourself.

Expensive
Itinéraires ★★ FRENCH FUSION After earning acclaim at 24 years old with his tiny tapas bistro in the 11th arrondissement, gifted chef Sylvain Sendra has opened this elegant enterprise devoted to finding the meeting point between French and more far-flung cuisines. The seasonal menu features lots of organic ingredients and might include griddled sea bass with kabocha, capers, and olives; roasted lamb from the Lozère with puréed carrots; or a chocolate crumble with banana-passion fruit ice cream for dessert. If everyone in your party is of a like mind, you can order a tasting menu either at lunch (49€) or at dinner (89€).

5 rue de Pontoise, 5th arrond. www.restaurant-itineraires.com. *©* **01-46-33-60-11.** Main dishes 34€–38€, fixed-price lunch 49€, fixed-price dinner 65€–69€. Tues–Fri noon–2pm and 7–10:30pm, Sat 7–10:30pm. Closed Aug. Métro: Maubert-Mutualité.

Moderate
Dans les Landes ★ SOUTHWESTERN FRENCH/TAPAS Chef Julien Duboué takes inspiration from his native homeland and neighboring Basque

country to create luscious tapas: fried *chipirions* (small squid that are crisp, golden, and dusted with smoky pepper), polenta with smoked duck breast, Basque-style mussels—the list is long and tempting—and best sampled with (many) glasses of great regional wines. It's packed at night, so get there early or reserve a table.

119 bis rue Monge, 5th arrond. www.dansleslandesmaisaparis.com. ℂ **01-45-87-06-00.** Tapas 8€–25€. Daily noon–11pm. Closed last week of Dec, first week of Jan. Métro: Censier-Daubenton.

Le Pré Verre ★★ MODERN FRENCH/ASIAN FUSION This crowded and convivial gourmet wine bar offers dishes that are a scrumptious blend of traditional French and exotic ingredients—not particularly flashy or trendy or even spicy, just deliciously unexpected. One of the signature dishes is a meltingly tender *cochon de lait* (milk-fed pork) served with a smooth cinnamon-infused sauce and a delectably crunchy mass that turns out to be cabbage. The weekday lunch menu is a particularly great deal: You get an appetizer, a main dish, a glass of wine, and coffee for 15€.

8 rue Thenard, 5th arrond. www.lepreverre.com. ℂ **01-43-54-59-47.** Main courses 20€; fixed-price lunch 15€ and 32€, fixed-price dinner 32€. Tues–Sat noon–2pm and 7:30–10:30pm. Closed last week of Dec. Métro: Maubert-Mutualité or Cluny-La Sorbonne.

Inexpensive

Bonjour Vietnam ★★ VIETNAMESE This postage-stamp of a restaurant serves deliciously authentic Vietnamese dishes like *bò bún* (a heap of rice vermicelli, sliced beef, and crispy spring rolls in a tangy sauce) or a steaming bowl of *pho* (beef broth with vegetables and noodles, topped with fresh basil, mint, and bean sprouts). The less adventurous might prefer caramel pork or ginger chicken, both featured on the 12€ lunch set menu. The steamed raviolis are particularly popular as a starter. All dishes are made to order, so don't expect instant service.

6 rue Thouin, 5th arrond. ℂ **01-43-54-78-04.** Main courses 12€–14€. Fixed-price lunch 12€. Wed–Mon noon–2:30pm and 7–11pm. Métro: Cardinal Lemoine.

ST-GERMAIN-DES-PRÉS (6TH ARRONDISSEMENT)

Saint Germain is a mix of expensive eateries that only the lucky few can afford and stalwart holdouts from the days when poverty-stricken intellectuals and artists frequented the Café de Flore. The restaurants hugging the perimeter of Marché St-Germain offer a wide range of possibilities.

Expensive

Le Comptoir du Relais ★★★ TRADITIONAL FRENCH/BISTRO The brainchild of super-chef Yves de Camdeborde, this scrumptious bistro is still bringing in the crowds almost a decade after it opened. During the day, it's a bistro serving relatively traditional fare, say, a slice of lamb with thyme sauce or maybe the *panier de cochonaille,* a basket of the Camdeborde family's own brand of smoked meats. On weeknights, it's a temple to haute cuisine, with a five-course tasting menu. You must reserve several weeks (at least) in advance for this set meal, which changes every night. There are no reservations at

4

PARIS | Where to Eat

lunch or on the weekends, when the bistro menu is served from noon to 11pm, so arrive early or be prepared to wait.

9 carrefour de l'Odéon, 6th arrond. www.hotel-paris-relais-saint-germain.com. ℭ **01-44-27-07-50.** Main courses weekends and weekdays 15€–29€; fixed-price dinner weeknights 60€. Daily noon–11pm. Métro: Odéon.

Le Relais Louis XIII ★★★ CLASSIC FRENCH   This esteemed restaurant pays homage to traditional French cuisine. No tonka beans or reduced licorice sauce here—Chef Manuel Martinez lends his formidable skills to classic sauces and time-honored dishes like sea-bass *quenelles* and roast duck, though he's not opposed to topping off the meal with a little lemon-basil sherbet. Signature dishes include lobster and foie gras ravioli, or braised sweetbreads with wild mushrooms. The atmospheric dining room, crisscrossed with exposed beams and ancient stonework, makes you wonder if the Three Musketeers might tumble through the doorway bearing your mille-feuille with bourbon vanilla cream.

8 rue des Grands-Augustins, 6th arrond. www.relaislouis13.fr. ℭ **01-43-26-75-96.** Main courses 60€; fixed-price lunch 55€; fixed-price dinner 85€–140€. Tues–Sat 12:15–2:30pm, 7:30–10:30pm. Closed Aug. Métro: Odéon or St-Michel.

Moderate
Le P'tit Fernand ★★ TRADITIONAL FRENCH/BISTRO   This tiny slice of a restaurant packs a flavorful punch. Red-checked tablecloths provide a homey background for excellent bistro dishes like thick steak with a confit of shallots and creamy mashed potatoes, or duck *magret* (breast) served with morello-cherry sauce. You could start with a nice light beet and rhubarb gazpacho or go nuts and order the homemade terrine of foie gras. Whatever it is, it will be executed with loving care and quality ingredients, which is why this restaurant has a devoted clientele.

7 rue Lobineau, 6th arrond. ℭ **01-40-46-06-88.** Main courses 18€–26€. Daily noon–2pm and 7–10:30pm. Métro: Mabillon.

Mangetout ★★★ MODERN FRENCH   This intimate restaurant comes courtesy of Michelin-starred chef Alain Dutournier, the force behind Pinxo (p. 61), and considering the high standard of cuisine offered, the affordable price tag is most definitely a deal. You could start with mushroom-infused scallops in herbs, proceed to milk-fed lamb with spring vegetables, and finish with a decadent chestnut cream *Mont Blanc* and still get out for under 50€. As the dining room is tiny, dinner reservations are essential.

82 rue Mazarine, 6th arrond. www.alaindutournier.com/wp/mangetout. ℭ **01-43-54-02-11.** Main courses 13€–29€. Tues–Sat noon–2pm and 7–10:30pm. Closed in Aug. Métro: Mabillon or Odéon.

Inexpensive
Restaurant Polidor ★ TRADITIONAL FRENCH/BISTRO   An unofficial historic monument, Polidor is not so much a restaurant as a snapshot of a bygone era. The decor has not changed substantially for at least 100 years, when Verlaine and Rimbaud, the bad boys of poetry, would come here for a cheap

meal. The bistro would continue to be a literary lunch room for decades: In the 1950s it was dubbed "the College of Pataphysics" by a rowdy group of young upstarts that included Max Ernst, Boris Vian, and Eugene Ionesco; André Gide and Ernest Hemingway were reputed regulars. The menu features hefty bistro standbys like boeuf bourguignon and *blanquette de veau* (veal stew with white sauce), but you'll also find lighter fare like salmon with basil and chicken breast with morel sauce. These days, the arty set has moved elsewhere; you'll probably be sharing the long wooden tables with other tourists, along with a dose of locals.

41 rue Monsieur-le-Prince, 6th arrond. www.polidor.com. © **01-43-26-95-34.** Main courses 11€–25€; fixed-price menu 22€–35€. Mon–Sat noon–2:30pm and 7pm–12:30am, Sun noon–2:30pm and 7–11pm. Métro: Odéon.

EIFFEL TOWER & NEARBY (7TH ARRONDISSEMENT)

Crowded with ministries and important people, this neighborhood is so grand. Though it's a rather staid neighborhood, a few streets are fairly lively, namely rue Cler, a pretty market street, and rue St-Dominique, home to some of the best restaurants on this side of the Seine.

Expensive

Arpège ★★★ MODERN FRENCH   This is probably the only Michelin-three-star restaurant where vegetables are the stars of the show. You can still find meat on the menu, but it takes a back seat to carrots, turnips, sweet peas, or whatever other lovely plant life is in season. This pristine produce, which comes from Chef Alain Passard's farm, is often picked in the morning and ends up on diners' plates the same evening. The menu comes in two sections: the "grand crus" of the vegetable garden, and the "memory" dishes: medallions of lobster in honey with a "transparence" of Atlantic turnip, or a creamy risotto with "garden treasures." Don't miss the *tarte aux pommes bouquet de roses* (tart composed of apple ribbons rolled into tiny rosettes). Reservations are required at least 2 weeks in advance.

84 rue de Varenne, 7th arrond. www.alain-passard.com. © **01-47-05-09-06.** Main courses 86€–140€; fixed-price lunch 140€, fixed-price tasting menu (lunch and dinner) 240€ and 320€. Mon–Fri noon–2pm and 7–10:30pm. Métro: Varenne.

Restaurant Auguste ★★ MODERN FRENCH/SEAFOOD   It's not every famous chef that can call himself "Mr. Goodfish." Gael Orieux's love of the sea and everything in it has led him to become spokesperson for an association dedicated to protecting the oceans. Naturally, that means what you see on your plate is not only delicious, but also sustainable. Let's hope he makes an impact on his clientele, many of whom are politicians from the nearby Assemblée Nationale. Your dish will look like artwork, whether it's scallops with foie gras and enoki mushrooms, or lacquered monkfish with lobster oil and nutmeg. Meat-eaters might appreciate the blackened lamb with Cajun spices, white cherry juice, and yellow zucchini.

54 rue de Bourgogne, 7th arrond. www.restaurantauguste.fr. © **01-45-51-61-09.** Main courses 36€–55€; fixed-price lunch 37€, fixed-price dinner 88€. Mon–Fri noon–2:30pm and 7–10:30pm. Closed 3 weeks in Aug. Métro: Varenne.

Moderate

Le Casse Noix ★★ TRADITIONAL FRENCH/BISTRO   The result of yet another great chef realizing his bistro dreams, this relaxed restaurant offers high-caliber food in a casual, affordable setting. The decor is nostalgic (note the nutcracker collection and vintage advertisements), and the traditional French cooking is sincere and generous, featuring dishes like roast pork shoulder Ibaïona with olive puree, or a classic *petit salé* (lentils with smoky ham). About a 10-minute walk from the Eiffel Tower, this is a good bet for those looking for a bit of authenticity in an otherwise very touristy neighborhood. At dinnertime, the fixed-price menu is *obligatoire,* so no à la carte ordering. Lunch is more flexible.

56 rue de la Fédération, 15th arrond. www.le-cassenoix.fr. ℰ **01-45-66-09-01.** Main courses at lunch 19€–23€; fixed-price lunch 21€ and 26€, fixed-price dinner 33€. Mon–Fri noon–2:30pm and 7–10:30pm. Closed Aug and between Christmas and New Year. Métro: Dupleix.

Inexpensive

Café Constant ★★ TRADITIONAL FRENCH/BISTRO   Of the three Christian Constant restaurants on this street, this one is the most relaxed; you may find the master himself at the bar smoking a cigar here during his off hours. The menu features modern versions of French comfort food like tangy poached cod with aioli, melt-in-your-mouth beef *daube* (stew) with carrots, or steak with shallots and creamy potato puree. The weekday lunch *formule* is a two-course meal (chef's choice) for 16€, a terrific deal for this level of quality. No reservations.

139 rue Saint-Dominique, 7th arrond. www.maisonconstant.com. ℰ **01-47-53-73-34.** Main courses 16€–29€; lunch fixed-price menu 16€–23€. Daily 7–11am and noon–11pm. Métro: Ecole Militaire.

MONTPARNASSE & NEARBY (14TH & 15TH ARRONDISSEMENTS)

The famous cafes where struggling writers and artists like Picasso, Hemingway, and Chagall once hung out are now much too expensive for most ordinary mortals, so having a drink is probably the best way to enjoy them. But

CAFE SOCIETY: PARIS'S top cafes

Cafe life is an integral part of the Parisian scene, and it simply won't do to visit the capital without joining in. Here are a few sure fire options. *Tip:* Coffee or other drinks at the bar often cost half of what they do at a table.

Café de Flore
Every great French intellectual and artist seems to have had their moment here: Apollinaire, André Breton, Picasso, Giacometti and of course, Simone de Beauvoir and Jean-Paul Sartre, who virtually lived here during WWII. The atmosphere today is less thoughtful and more showbiz, but it's still worth an overpriced cup of coffee just to come in and soak it up.

172 bd. St-Germain, 6th arrond. www.cafe deflore.fr. ℭ **01-45-48-55-26.** Daily 7am–2am. Métro: St-Germain-des-Prés.

Les Deux Magots
The literary pedigree here is impressive: Poets Verlaine and Rimbaud camped out here, as did André Gide and Albert Camus. Sartre and de Beauvoir moved in postwar and stayed for decades. The outdoor terrace is pleasant early in the morning before the crowds awake.

6 place St-Germain-des-Prés, 6th arrond. www. lesdeuxmagots.fr. ℭ **01-45-48-55-25.** Daily 7:30am–1am. Métro: St-Germain-des-Prés.

Le Bistrot du Peintre
Artists, hipsters, and other fauna from the bustling rue de Charonne area flock to this popular spot, which sports an authentic Art Nouveau interior with the original peeling paint.

116 av. Ledru-Rollin, 11th arrond. www.bistrot dupeintre.com. ℭ **01-47-00-34-39.** Daily 7am–2am; Métro: Ledru-Rollin.

Café de la Mairie
What could be nicer than sitting outdoors at a sidewalk cafe on the place St-Sulpice? Indoors, it's a 1970s archetype: Formica bar, boxy chairs, and an odd assortment of pensioners, fashion victims, students, and would-be novelists.

8 place St-Sulpice, 6th arrond. ℭ **01-43-26-67-82.** Mon–Fri 7am–2am. Sat 8am–2am, Sun 9am–2am. Métro: Mabillon or St-Sulpice.

Le Nemours
Cuddled up in a corner next to the Comédie-Française, this beautiful cafe has a great terrace stretching out onto the Place Colette. The ideal spot for taking a load off after a day at the nearby Louvre.

2 place Colette. ℭ **01-42-61-34-14.** Mon–Fri 7am–1am, Sat 8am–1am. Métro: Palais-Royal Musée du Louvre or Pyramides.

there are plenty of other good options, from Breton crêperies near the train station to a bundle of new gourmet bistros farther south.

Expensive

Cobéa ★★★ MODERN FRENCH   Chef Philippe Bélissent invents concoctions that are as delicate and refined as the dining room in this pretty little house: perfectly cooked veal with fava beans and polenta; freshly caught John Dory; or pigeon with artichokes and olives might show up on the mix-and-match menu. The concept at dinner is as follows: There is one menu, from which you decide whether you'd like to try four (79€), six (99€), or eight (119€) courses. Each serving is small but exquisite; by the time you finish your dessert, both your stomach and your soul are thoroughly satiated. Service is impeccable.

11 rue Raymond Losserand, 14th arrond. www.cobea.fr. ℭ **01-43-20-21-39.** Fixed-price lunch 49€–69€, fixed-price dinner 79€–119€. Tues–Sat 12:15–1:15pm, 7:15–9:15pm. Closed in Aug. Métro: Gaïté or Pernety.

Moderate

La Régalade ★★★ TRADITIONAL FRENCH/BISTRO With its cracked tile floors, polished wood, and burgundy banquettes, chef Bruno Doucet's neo-bistro is an homage to the good things in life, like foie gras in asparagus bouillon or marinated sea scallops with basil and Parmesan. Main dishes are generally variations on French comfort food, such as a succulent pork breast with sweet peas, or lively innovations like a creamy squid risotto with sautéed prawns. Dessert could be a stinky Reblochon cheese, a molten Guanaja chocolate cake, or the house specialty, rice pudding. Reserve a week in advance.

14 av. Jean-Moulin, 14th arrond. ✆ **01-45-45-68-58.** Fixed-price menu 37€. Tues–Fri noon–2:30pm; Mon–Fri 7–11pm. Closed first 3 weeks of Aug. Métro: Alésia.

Inexpensive

Crêperie de Saint Malo ★★ CREPERIE Of the dozens of crêperies concentrated near the Montparnasse train station, this is one of the best. The *galettes* and crêpes are perfectly cooked with lacy, crispy edges, and what's more, they use organic flour. It may be difficult but it's worth trying to save room for a sweet variety for dessert. Tradition demands that this meal be accompanied by a bowl of hard cider (low alcohol content, for adults only). The friendly service and easy-going atmosphere makes this a good choice for families with kids.

53 rue du Montparnasse, 14th arrond. ✆ **01-43-20-87-19.** Main courses 6.90€–12€; fixed-price menu 14€. Daily 11:30am–2:30pm and 6:30–11:30pm. Métro: Edgar Quinet.

EXPLORING PARIS

With more than 130 world-class museums to visit, scores of attractions to discover, extraordinary architecture to gape at, and wonderful neighborhoods to wander, Paris is an endless series of delights. Fortunately, you can have a terrific time in Paris even if you don't see everything. Some of your best moments may be simply roaming around the city without a plan.

The following pages highlight the best that Paris has to offer, from iconic sights to quirky museums and hidden gardens, from medieval castles to galleries celebrating the most challenging contemporary art.

The Right Bank

LOUVRE & ÎLE DE LA CITÉ (1ST ARRONDISSEMENT)

Back in the city's misty and uncertain beginnings, the Parisii tribe set up camp on the right bank of the Seine and started hunting on the Île de la Cité. Many centuries later, the **Louvre** popped up, first as a fortress and now one of the world's mightiest museums. The city's epicenter packs in a high density of must-see monuments and museums, but don't miss the opportunity for aimless strolling, in the magnificent **Tuileries Gardens,** say, or over the **Pont Neuf.** *Note:* For simplicity's sake, the entire Île de la Cité has been included in this section, though technically half of it lies in the 4th arrondissement.

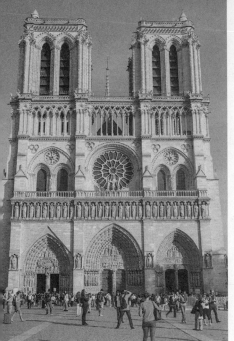

Cathédrale de Notre-Dame, one of Paris's most-visited tourist attractions.

Cathédrale de Notre-Dame

★★★ CATHEDRAL   This remarkably harmonious ensemble of carved portals, huge towers, and flying buttresses has survived close to a millennium's worth of French history and served as a setting for some of the country's most solemn moments. Napoléon crowned himself Emperor here, Napoléon III was married here, and the funerals of some of France's greatest generals (Foch, Joffre, Leclerc) were held here. In August 1944, the liberation of Paris from the Nazis was commemorated in the cathedral, as was the death of General de Gaulle in 1970.

Construction on the cathedral began in 1163 and lasted more than 200 years. The building was relatively untouched up until the end of the 17th century, when monarchs started meddling with its windows and architecture. By the time the Revolutionaries decided to convert it into a "Temple of Reason," the cathedral was already in sorry condition—and the pillaging that ensued didn't help. The interior was ravaged, statues were smashed, and cathedral became a shadow of its former glorious self.

We can thank the famous "Hunchback" himself for saving Notre Dame. Victor Hugo's novel "The Hunchback of Notre Dame" drew attention to the state of disrepair, and other artists and writers began to call for the restoration of the edifice. In 1844 Louis-Phillipe hired Jean-Baptiste Lassus and Viollet-le-Duc to restore the cathedral, which they finished in 1864.

Begin your visit at **Point Zéro,** just in front of the building on the parvis (the esplanade). This is the official center of Paris and the point from which all distances relative to other French cities are calculated. Before you are three enormous **carved portals** depicting (from left to right) the Coronation of the Virgin, the Last Judgment, and scenes from the lives of the Virgin and St-Anne. Above is the **Gallery of the Kings of Judah and Israel**—thought to be portraits of the kings of France, the original statues were chopped out of the facade during the Revolution; some of the heads were eventually found in the 1970s and now are in the Musée National du Moyen Age/Thermes de Cluny.

Upon entering the cathedral, you'll be immediately struck by two things: the throngs of tourists clogging the aisles, and, when you look up, the heavenly dimensions of the pillars holding up the ceiling. Soaring upward, these delicate archways give the impression that the entire edifice is about to take

Paris Attractions

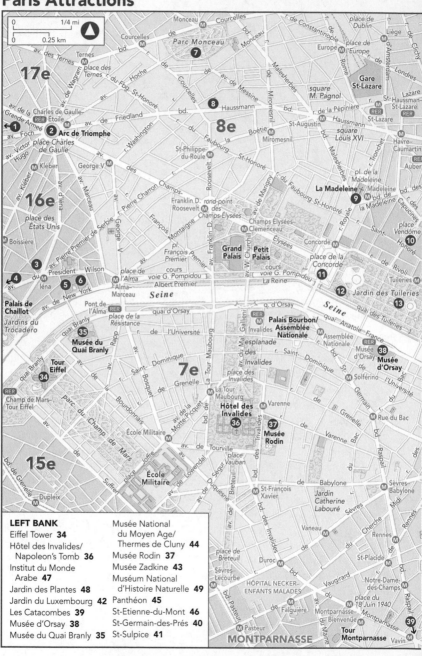

LEFT BANK

Eiffel Tower **34**
Hôtel des Invalides/
 Napoleon's Tomb **36**
Institut du Monde
 Arabe **47**
Jardin des Plantes **48**
Jardin du Luxembourg **42**
Les Catacombes **39**
Musée d'Orsay **38**
Musée du Quai Branly **35**

Musée National
 du Moyen Age/
 Thermes de Cluny **44**
Musée Rodin **37**
Musée Zadkine **43**
Muséum National
 d'Histoire Naturelle **49**
Panthéon **45**
St-Etienne-du-Mont **46**
St-Germain-des-Prés **40**
St-Sulpice **41**

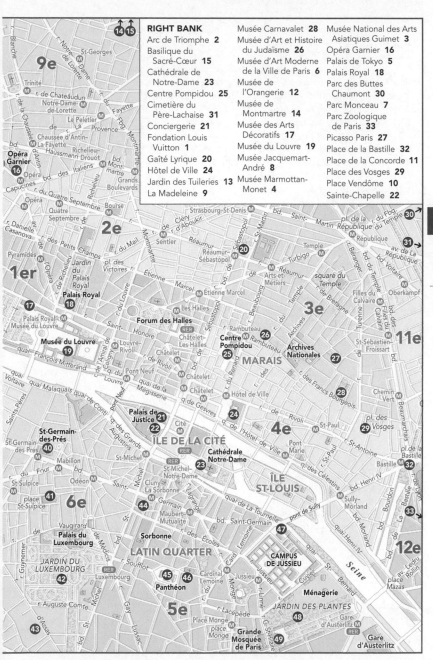

RIGHT BANK

Arc de Triomphe **2**
Basilique du
Sacré-Cœur **15**
Cathédrale de
Notre-Dame **23**
Centre Pompidou **25**
Cimetière du
Père-Lachaise **31**
Conciergerie **21**
Fondation Louis
Vuitton **1**
Gaîté Lyrique **20**
Hôtel de Ville **24**
Jardin des Tuileries **13**
La Madeleine **9**

Musée Carnavalet **28**
Musée d'Art et Histoire
du Judaïsme **26**
Musée d'Art Moderne
de la Ville de Paris **6**
Musée de
l'Orangerie **12**
Musée de
Montmartre **14**
Musée des Arts
Décoratifs **17**
Musée du Louvre **19**
Musée Jacquemart-
André **8**
Musée Marmottan-
Monet **4**

Musée National des Arts
Asiatiques Guimet **3**
Opéra Garnier **16**
Palais de Tokyo **5**
Palais Royal **18**
Parc des Buttes
Chaumont **30**
Parc Monceau **7**
Parc Zoologique
de Paris **33**
Picasso Paris **27**
Place de la Bastille **32**
Place de la Concorde **11**
Place des Vosges **29**
Place Vendôme **10**
Sainte-Chapelle **22**

Views from the Two Towers

The lines are long and the climb is longer, but the view from the **rooftop balcony** at the base of the cathedral's towers is possibly the most Parisian of all views. After trudging up some 255 steps (in a narrow winding staircase—not for small children or anyone with mobility concerns), you'll be rewarded with a panorama that not only encompasses the Île de la Cité, the Eiffel Tower, and Sacré-Coeur, but is also framed by a collection of photogenic **gargoyles.** One of the most famous is the **Stryga,** a horned and winged beasty holding his head in his hands, pensively sticking his tongue out at the city below. Another 147 steps up a narrow stairway lead to the summit of the **south tower,** from which you get an endless view of Paris. Come in the morning before the crowds get thick, and avoid weekends (www.monuments -nationaux.fr; ℂ **01-53-40-60-80;** 8.50€ adults, 5.50€ under 26, free under 18; Apr–June and Sept 10am–6pm; July–Aug Mon–Fri 10am–6pm, Sat–Sun 10am–11pm; Oct–Mar 10am–5:30pm).

4

Exploring Paris

PARIS

off into the sky. Up there in the upper atmosphere are three remarkable stained-glass **rose windows.** The north window retains almost all of its 13th-century stained glass; the other two have been heavily restored. An impressive **treasury** is filled with relics of various saints including the elaborate cases for the **Crown of Thorns,** brought back from Constantinople by Saint Louis in the 13th century. The crown itself is not on display; however, it can be viewed, along with a nail and some pieces of the Holy Cross, on the first Friday of the month (3pm), every Friday during Lent (3pm) and Good Friday (10am–5pm). For a detailed look at the cathedral, take advantage of the **free guided tours in English** (Wed–Thurs 2pm, Sat 2:30pm) or rent an **audioguide** for 5€.

When you leave, be sure to take a stroll around the outside of the cathedral to admire the other portals and the famous flying buttresses.

Place du Parvis Notre-Dame, 4th arrond. www.notredamedeparis.fr. ℂ **01-53-10-07-02.** Free admission to cathedral. Treasury 4€ adults, 2€ students and seniors, 1€ ages 6–12, free children 5 and younger. Cathedral Mon–Fri 8am–6:45pm, Sat–Sun 8am–7:15pm. Treasury Mon–Fri 9:30am–6pm; Sat 9:30am–6:30pm; Sun 1:30–6:30pm. Métro: Cité or St-Michel. RER: St-Michel.

Conciergerie ★ HISTORIC SITE   A relic of the darker side of the Revolution, this famous prison commemorates The Terror, when murderous infighting between the various revolutionary factions engendered panic and paranoia that led to tens of thousands of people throughout the country being arrested and executed. Many of the Revolution's most pivotal characters spent their final days here before making their way to the guillotine, including the queen, Marie Antoinette.

Though it's been a prison since the 15th century, the building itself is actually what remains of a 14th-century royal palace built by Philippe le Bel. The enormous **Salle des Gens d'Arms,** with its 8.4m-high (28-ft.) vaulted ceiling, is an impressive reminder of the building's palatial past. As for the prison,

Famously called "the belly of Paris," **Les Halles** was the city's primary wholesale fruit, meat, and vegetable market for 8 centuries. The smock-clad vendors, beef carcasses, and baskets of vegetables all belong to the past, as the market was relocated to the suburb of Rungis in the early '70s. In a fit of modernity, all the pretty 19th-century pavilions were torn down and in their place a weird, partly underground shopping mall was constructed around a giant hole in the ground: the **Forum des Halles** (1–7 rue Pierre-Lescot, 1st arrond.). Fortunately, the city has embarked on a massive renovation program to overhaul the shopping center and the surrounding gardens, which is why the entire area has been temporarily transformed into a construction zone. "The canopy," an immense, undulating sheet of glass and metal that gently floats over the Forum was completed in 2015, but other areas are still under construction. For information, visit www.parisleshalles.fr.

though the cells have been outfitted with displays and re-creations of daily life (including wax figures), it's a little difficult to imagine what it was like in the bad old days. However, the **Cours des Femmes** (the women's courtyard) virtually hasn't changed since the days when female prisoners did their washing in the fountain. In a curious attempt to spice up its offerings, the site has recently been hosting contemporary art exhibits, so don't be surprised to see conceptual art as you wander around the prison cells.

2 bd. du Palais, 1st arrond. www. monuments-nationaux.fr. Admission ✆ **01-53-40-60-80.** 8.50€ adults, 5.50€ ages 18–25, free for 17 and younger. Daily 9:30–6pm. Métro: Cité, Châtelet, or St-Michel. RER: St-Michel.

Bronze sculpture "The Three Nymphs," by Aristide Maillol in Jardin de Tuileries.

Jardin des Tuileries ★★★

GARDENS This exquisite park spreads from the Louvre to the place de la Concorde. What you see today is based on the design by 17th-century master landscape artist André Le Nôtre—the man behind the gardens of Versailles. Le Nôtre's elegant geometry of flowerbeds, parterres, and groves of trees made the Tuileries Gardens the ultimate stroll for the era's well-to-do Parisians. It continues to delight both tourists and locals in the 21st century.

During World War II, furious fighting went on here, and many statues were damaged. Little by little in the postwar years the garden put itself back together. Seventeenth- and 18th-century representations of various gods and goddesses were repaired, and the city added new works by modern masters such as Alberto Giocometti, Jean Dubuffet, and Henry Moore. Rodin's "The Kiss" and "Eve" are here, as well as a series of 18 of Maillol's curvaceous women, peeking out of the green **labyrinth** of hedges in the Carousel Gardens near the museum.

Pulling up a metal chair and sunning yourself on the edge of the large **fountain** in the center of the gardens (the **Grande Carrée**) is a delightful respite for tired tourists after a day in the Louvre; tots will enjoy playing with one of the wooden **toy sailboats** that you can rent from a stand (2.50€/half-hour).

Near place de la Concorde, 1st arrond. ✆ **01-40-20-90-43.** Free admission. Daily 7:30am–dusk. Métro: Tuileries or Concorde.

4

Musée de l'Orangerie ★★ MUSEUM   Since 1927, this former royal greenhouse has been the home of Monet's stunning "Nymphéas," or **water lilies,** which he conceived as a "haven of peaceful meditation." Two large oval rooms are dedicated to these masterpieces, in which Monet tried to replicate the feeling and atmosphere of his garden at Giverny. He worked on these enormous canvases for 12 years, with the idea of creating an environment that would soothe the "overworked nerves" of modern men and women—in what could be called one of the world's first art installations.

The other highlight here is the Guillaume collection, an impressive assortment of late-19th- and early-20th-century paintings. The first, light-filled gallery displays works by Renoir and Cezanne. Mostly portraits and still lifes, they include Renoir's glowing, idyllic "Femme Nu dans un Paysage" and Cézanne's rather dour-looking "Madame Cézanne." The rest of the collection includes slightly sinister landscapes by Rousseau, enigmatic portraits by Modigliani, distorted figures by Soutine, as well as some kinder, gentler Picassos ("Les Adolescents" bathed in pink and rust tones).

Jardin des Tuileries, 1st arrond. www.musee-orangerie.fr. ✆ **01-44-77-80-07.** Admission 9€ adults, 6.50€ ages 18–25, free ages 17 and younger. Wed–Mon 9am–6pm. Métro: Concorde.

Musée des Arts Décoratifs ★★ MUSEUM   Possessing some 150,000 items in its rich collection, this fascinating museum offers a glimpse of history through the prism of decorative objects, with a spectrum that ranges from medieval traveling trunks to Philippe Starck stools. The collection is organized in more or less chronological order, so on your journey you will pass by paintings from the First Italian Renaissance, through a room filled with exquisite 15th-century intarsia ("paintings" made out of intricately inlaid wood), before gaping at huge, intricately carved 17th-century German armoires. Other highlights include a tiny room covered in gilded woodwork from an 18th-century mansion in Avignon, a 19th-century courtesan's bedroom, and a stunning Art Nouveau dining room.

The collection weakens after 1930; it's hard to tell if this is due to a lack of imagination on the part of the museum or on the part of 20th-century designers. The chronological sequence can be hard to follow; note that the visit starts on the third floor. There are two other museums in the building (which is actually one of the extremities of the Louvre): the **Musée de la Publicité,** which takes on the history of advertising, and the **Musée de la Mode et du Textile,** which hosts exhibits on the many facets of clothing, including the works of famous couture houses like Jean-Paul Gaultier and Dior (both have the same hours as the main museum and are included in the ticket price to Arts Décoratifs).

Palais du Louvre, 107 rue de Rivoli, 1st arrond. www.lesartsdecoratifs.fr. *(C)* **01-44-55-57-50.** Admission 11€ adults, 8.50€ ages 18–25, free for children 17 and younger. Tues–Sun 11am–6pm. Métro: Louvre-Palais-Royal or Tuileries.

Musée du Louvre ★★★ MUSEUM   The best way to thoroughly visit the Louvre would be to move in for a month. Not only is it one of the largest museums in the world, with more than 35,000 works of art displayed over 60,000 sq. m (645,835 sq. ft.), but it's packed with enough artistic master-pieces to make the Mona Lisa weep. Rembrandt, Rubens, Botticelli, Ingres, and Michelangelo are all represented here; subjects range from the grandiose (Antoine-Jean Gros's gigantic "Napoleon Bonaparte Visiting the Plague-Stricken in Jaffa") to the mundane (Vermeer's tiny, exquisite "Lacemaker"). You can gape at a diamond the size of a golf ball in the royal treasury, or marvel over exquisite bronze figurines in the vast Egyptian section.

With 8.8 million annual visitors, the Louvre is consistently the most visited museum worldwide.

Today, the building is divided into three wings, Sully, Denon, and Richelieu, each one with its own clearly marked entrance, found under I.M. Pei's glass pyramid. Get your hands on a museum map (there's an excellent interactive map on the museum's website), choose your personal "must-sees," and plan ahead. There's no way to see it all, and you'll be an instant candidate for early retirement if you try. Merci-fully, the museum is well organized and has been very reasonably arranged into color-coded sections. If you're really in a rush or you just want to get an overall sense of the place, you can take the introductory guided tour in English (1½ hr.; 11:15am, 2pm; Wed–Sun except the first Sun of the month; 12€).

The museum's three biggest stars are all located in the Denon wing. La Joconde, otherwise known as the **"Mona Lisa,"** now has an entire wall to herself, making it easier to contemplate her enigmatic smile. Another inscrutable female in this wing is the **"Venus de Milo,"** who was found on a Greek island in 1820. Possibly the most photographed woman in the world, this armless marble goddess gives no hint of the original position of her limbs or her exact identity. Recently restored and lovelier than ever, the **"Winged Victory of Samothrace,"** is the easiest to locate. Standing at the top of a majestic flight of stairs, her powerful body pushing forward as if about to take flight, this headless, yet magnificent, Greek sculpture once guarded the Sanctuary of the Great Gods on the island of Samothrace.

Because a complete listing of the Louvre's highlights would fill a book, below is a decidedly biased selection of my favorite areas:

13TH- TO 18TH-CENTURY ITALIAN PAINTING   A few standouts in the immense Italian collection include the delicate fresco by Botticelli called "Venus and the Three Graces Presenting Gifts to a Young Woman," Veronese's enormous "Wedding Feast at Cana," and of course, the "Mona Lisa." The Divine Miss M is in a room packed with wonders, including several Titians and Tintorettos. Once you've digested this rich meal, stroll down the endless Grande Galerie, past more da Vincis ("Saint John the Baptist," "The Virgin of the Rock"), as well as works by Raphael, Caravaggio, and Gentileschi.

GREEK & ROMAN SCULPTURE   While the "Venus de Milo" and the "Winged Victory of Samothrace" are not to be missed, the Salle des Caryatides (the room itself is a work of art) boasts marble masterworks like "Artemis" hunting with her stag and the troubling "Sleeping Hermaphrodite," an alluring female figure from behind—and something entirely different from the front.

THE GALERIE D'APOLLON   The gold-encrusted room is an excellent example of the excesses of 17th-century French royalty. Commissioned by Louis XIV, aka "The Sun King," every inch of this gallery is covered with gilt stucco sculptures and flamboyant murals invoking the journey of the Roman sun god Apollo (ceiling paintings are by Charles Le Brun). The main draw here is the collection of crown jewels. Among necklaces bedecked with quarter-sized sapphires and tiaras dripping with diamonds and rubies is the jewel-studded crown of Louis XV and the pearl-and-diamond diadem of Empress Eugenie.

THE EGYPTIANS   The largest collection outside of Cairo, thanks in large part to Jean-François Champollion, the 19th-century French scientist and scholar who first decoded Egyptian hieroglyphs. Sculptures, figurines, papyrus documents, steles, musical instruments, and of course, mummies, fill numerous rooms in the Sully Wing, including the colossal statue of Ramses II and the strangely moving Seated Scribe. He gazes intently out of intricately crafted inlaid eyes: A combination of copper, magnesite, and polished rock crystal create a startlingly lifelike stare.

Don't want to wait in line for tickets to the Louvre? Order tickets in advance online (in English) at **www.fnactickets. com** or by calling 📞 **08-92-68-36-22,** .34€/min; you can print out your tickets, get them mailed to you, or you can pick them up at any French branch of the FNAC bookstore chain. Note that the Louvre is open until 9:30pm on Wednesday and Friday—usually quiet times to visit. If you are of an improvisational bent, however, and prefer to pick up tickets at the entrance, here are a few ways to avoid the lines that often snake around the pyramid entryway: 1) Enter directly from the Palais Royal–Musée du Louvre Métro stop; 2) Take one of the two staircases on either side of the Arc du Carrousel in the Tuileries Gardens that lead directly down to the ticketing area; or 3) Enter at the Porte des Lions (in the Denon Wing).

LARGE-FORMAT FRENCH PAINTINGS Enormous floor-to-ceiling (and these are high ceilings!) paintings of monumental moments in history cover the walls in these three rooms. The "Coronation of Napoléon" by Jacques-Louis David depicts the newly minted Emperor crowning Josephine, while the disconcerted pope and a host of notables look on. On the facing wall, "Madame Récamier" (also by David), one of Napoléon's loudest critics, reclines fetchingly on a divan. Farther on are several tumultuous canvases by Eugène Delacroix, including "Liberty Guiding the People," which might just be the ultimate expression of French patriotism. In the painting, which evokes the events of the revolution of 1830, Liberty—breast exposed, a rifle in one hand, the French flag in the other—leads the crowd over a sea of dead bodies. High ideals and gore—sort of sums up the French revolutionary spirit.

Note: When visiting the museum, **watch your wallets and purses**—there has been an unfortunate increase in pickpockets; organized groups even use children to prey on unsuspecting art lovers.

Quai du Louvre, 1st arrond. Main entrance in the glass pyramid, cour Napoléon. www. louvre.fr. 📞 **01-40-20-50-50.** Admission 12€ adults, children 17 and younger free. Sat–Mon and Thurs 9am–6pm; Wed and Fri 9am–9:30pm. Métro: Palais-Royal–Musée du Louvre.

Palais Royal ★★ HISTORIC SITE/GARDEN The gardens and long arcades of the Palais Royal are not only a delight to stroll through, they were also witness to one of the most important moments in French history. Built by Cardinal Richelieu, the lavish palace eventually came into the hands of a certain Duke Louis Phillippe d'Orleans at the end of the 18th century. An inveterate spendthrift, the young lord soon found himself up to his ears in debt. To earn enough money to pay off his creditors, he came up with the shockingly modern idea of opening the palace gardens to development, building apartments on the grounds. The bottom floor of the galleries, which make up three sides of the enclosure you see today, were let out as shops, cafes, and boutiques. Gambling houses and bordellos sprang up between the shops and cafes, and the gardens became the central meeting place for revolutionaries.

Things came to a head on July 12, 1789, when Camille Desmoulins stood up on a table in front of the Café de Foy and called the people to arms—2 days later, the mob would storm the Bastille, igniting the French Revolution. In more recent times, the palace was taken over by various government ministries, and the apartments were rented to artists and writers, including Colette and Jean Cocteau.

Today the shops in the arcades are very subdued, and very expensive—mostly antique toy and stamp dealers, a smattering of high-end designer clothes, and a couple of pricey restaurants, including the legendary Grand Véfour (p. 60). The *cour d'honneur* on the south end is filled with black-and-white-striped columns by Daniel Buren; though most Parisians have now gotten used to this unusual installation, when it was unveiled in 1987 it caused almost as much of a stir as Camille Desmoulins did on that fateful day.

Rue St-Honoré, 1st arrond. Free admission to gardens and arcades, buildings closed to public. Gardens daily 7:30am–dusk. Métro: Palais Royal–Musée du Louvre.

Place Vendôme ★★ SQUARE   In 1686, Louis XIV decided the time had come to design a magnificent square, at the center of which would stand a statue of His Royal Highness. Though the statue is long gone, this is still one of the classiest squares in the city. The work of Jules Hardouin-Mansart, this über-elegant octagonal ensemble of 17th-century buildings today is the home of the original Ritz Hôtel, as well as the world's most glitzy jewelry makers, including Cartier, Van Cleef & Arpels, and Boucheron. The statue reigned over the square up until the Revolution, when it was melted down for scrap. When Napoléon took over, he erected a huge Roman-style column honoring his glorious army (yes, once again), this time documenting its victory at Austerlitz. A long spiral of bas-reliefs recounting the campaign of 1805 march up the Colonne de la Grande Armée, which is crowned by a statue of the Emperor himself.

Enter by rue de Castiglione, 1st arrond. Métro: Tuileries or Concorde.

Sainte-Chapelle ★★★ CHURCH   A wall of color greets visitors who enter this magnificent chapel. Stained-glass windows make up a large part of the upper level of the church, giving worshippers the impression of standing inside a jewel-encrusted crystal goblet. What isn't glass is elaborately carved and painted in gold leaf and rich colors: vaulting arches, delicate window casings, and an almost Oriental wainscoting of arches and medallions. The 15 windows recount the story of the Bible, from Genesis to the Apocalypse, as well as the story of St-Louis, who was responsible for the chapel's construction. During the Crusades, Louis IX (who was later canonized) brought home some of the holiest relics in Christendom from Constantinople: the Crown of Thorns and a piece of the Holy Cross. Such a treasure required an appropriately splendid chapel in the royal palace, and thus the chapel was built (the relics are now in the treasury of Notre-Dame). The record is not clear, but the architect may have been the illustrious Pierre de Montreuil, who worked on the cathedrals of St-Denis and Notre-Dame. What is sure is that the mysterious architect was brilliant: He managed to support the structure with arches and buttresses in such a way that the walls of the upper chapel are almost entirely glass.

The **lower chapel,** which was meant for the servants, has a low, vaulted ceiling painted in blue and red and gold and covered with fleur-de-lis motifs. Up a small staircase is the **upper chapel,** clearly meant for the royals. This masterpiece suffered both fire and floods in the 17th century and was pillaged by zealous Revolutionaries in the 18th. By the mid–19th century, the chapel was being used to store archives—2m (6½ ft.) of the bottom of each window was removed to install shelves. Fortunately, renewed interest in medieval art eventually led to a conscientious restoration by a team that was advised by master restorer Viollet-le-Duc. The quality of the work on the windows is such that it is almost impossible to detect the difference between the original and the reconstructed stained glass (which makes up about one-third of what you see).

Palais de Justice, 4 bd. du Palais, 1st arrond. www.monuments-nationaux.fr. ✆ **01-53-40-60-80.** 8.50€ adults, 5.50€ ages 18–25, free 17 and younger. Mar–Oct daily 9:30am–6pm; Nov–Feb daily 9am–5pm. Métro: Cité, St-Michel, or Châtelet–Les Halles. RER: St-Michel.

OPÉRA & GRANDS BOULEVARDS (2ND & 9TH ARRONDISSEMENTS)

The grandiose **Opéra Garnier** reigns over this bustling neighborhood, which teems with office workers, tourists, and shoppers scuttling in and around the Grands Magasins (the big department stores) on Boulevard Haussmann. Which may account for why there are perhaps more opportunities for outstanding retail experiences here than for cultural ones.

Opéra Garnier ★★ OPERA HOUSE Flamboyant, extravagant, and baroque, this opulent opera house is a splendid example of Second Empire architectural excess. Corinthian columns, loggias, busts, and friezes cover the **facade** of the building, which is topped by a gold dome. The interior of the building is no less dramatic. The vast **lobby,** built in a spectrum of different colored marble, holds a spectacular double staircase that sweeps up to the different levels of the auditorium, as well as an array of glamorous antechambers, galleries, and ballrooms that make you wonder how the opera scenery could possibly compete. Mosaics, mirrors, gilt, and marble line these grand spaces, whose painted ceilings dance with fauns, gods, and nymphs. The main event, of course, is the **auditorium,** which might seem a bit small, considering the size of the building. In fact, it holds not even 2,000 seats. The beautiful **ceiling** was painted with colorful images from various operas and ballets by Marc Chagall in 1964.

All of this (with the exception of the Chagall ceiling) sprang from the mind of a young, unknown architect named Charles Garnier, who won a competition launched by Napoléon III. Though the first stone was laid in 1862, work was held up by war, civil unrest, and a change in regime; the Palais Garnier was not inaugurated until 1875. Some contemporary critics found it a bit much (one called it "an overloaded sideboard"), but today it is generally acknowledged as a masterpiece of the architecture of the epoch.

And what about that phantom? Gaston Leroux's 1911 novel, "The Phantom of the Opera," clearly was inspired by the building's **underground lake,** which was constructed to help stabilize the building.

You can visit the building on your own (for a fee; see ticket prices below), but you might want to take advantage of the **guided visits in English** (14€ adults, 13€ children under 10; Wed, Sat and Sun at 11:30am and 2:30pm; July–Aug and French school vacations daily 11:30am and 2:30pm). Either way, your visit will be limited to the lobby, the surrounding foyers, the museum, and if there's not a rehearsal in progress, the auditorium—sorry, you won't get to see the lake. Or simply **buy tickets to a show;** consult the Opéra website to see what's on at the Palais Garnier.

Corner of rue Scribe and rue Auber, 9th arrond. www.operadeparis.fr. ℭ **08-92-89-90-90** (.34€ per min). Admission 10€ adults, 6€ students and ages 10–25, free children under 10. Oct to mid-July daily 10am–4:30pm, mid-July to Sept 10am–5:30pm. Métro: Opéra.

LE MARAIS (3RD & 4TH ARRONDISSEMENTS)

Home to royalty and aristocracy between the 14th and 17th centuries, the Marais still boasts remarkable architecture, some of it dating back to the Middle Ages. One of the few neighborhoods that was not knocked down during Baron Haussmann's urban overhaul, Marais has narrow streets still lined with magnificent *hôtels particuliers* (that is, mansions) as well as humbler homes from centuries past. In addition to the **Pompidou Center,** the Marais harbors a wealth of terrific smaller museums, as well as the delightful **Place des Vosges.** The remnants of the city's **historic Jewish quarter** are found on rue des Rosiers, which has been invaded by clothing shops in recent years. These days, the real Jewish neighborhood is in the 19th arrondissement.

Centre Pompidou ★★ MUSEUM   The bizarre architecture of this odd building provokes such strong emotions, it's easy to forget that there is something inside. It was designed in 1971 by Italo-British architects Renzo Piano and Richard Rogers, whose concept was to put the support structure on the outside of the building, thereby liberating space on the inside for a museum and cultural center. The result was a gridlike exoskeleton with a tubular escalator inching up one side and huge multicolored pipes and shafts covering the other. To some, it's a milestone in contemporary architecture; to others, it's simply a horror. Either way, it's one of the most visited structures in France, for the Pompidou is much more than an art museum. Its some 100,000 sq. m (1,076,390 sq. ft.) of floor space includes a vast **reference library,** a **cinema archive,** bookshops, and a **music institute,** as well as a performance hall, a **children's gallery,** and areas for educational activities. The actual museum, the **Musée National d'Art Moderne,** is on the fourth and fifth floors.

The Pont Neuf

Since it's recently had a makeover, it does indeed look brand-spanking *neuf* (new), even though it is, in fact, the oldest bridge in Paris. The bridge was an instant hit when it was inaugurated by Henri IV in 1607: Ample sidewalks, and the fact that it was the first bridge sans houses, made it a delight for pedestrians. It still is, especially if you ignore the cars and just take in the lovely views.

Because the museum collection is in constant rotation, it's impossible to say what you're likely to see on your visit, but the emphasis is generally on works from the second half of the 20th century, with a good dose of surrealism, Dada, and other modern movements from the first half. It includes relatively tame abstracts by **Picasso** and **Kandinsky** to **Andy Warhol**'s multi-headed portrait of Elizabeth Taylor to a felt-wrapped piano by **Joseph Beuys.** Just outside of the front of the center is the **Atelier Brancusi,** where the sculptor's workshop has been reconstituted in its entirety.

Take note of the monumental sculpture/mobile by Alexander Calder on the vast esplanade that slopes down towards the building, and don't miss the delightful **Stravinsky Fountain** around the side; kids are mesmerized by its colorful mobile sculptures by Niki de Saint Phalle and Jean Tinguely.

Place Georges-Pompidou, 4th arrond. www.centrepompidou.fr. (℘ **01-44-78-12-33.** Admission 11€–13€ adults, 9€–10€ students, free children 17 and younger; admission varies depending on exhibits. Wed–Mon 11am–10pm. Métro: Rambuteau, Hôtel de Ville, or Châtelet–Les Halles.

Gaîté Lyrique ★ CULTURAL CENTER   One of the newer additions to the city's cultural scene, this gallery space/concert hall/educational center is devoted to exploring mixed-media and digital art forms. Set in an abandoned 19th-century theater (hence the name), the building has been transformed to host rotating exhibits that range from music and multimedia performances to design, fashion, and architecture to new media—there's even an interactive room dedicated to video games.

3 bis rue Papin, 3rd arrond. www.gaite-lyrique.net. (℘ **01-53-01-52-00.** Tues–Sat 2–8pm, Sun noon–6pm. 7.50€ adults, 5.50€ under 26 and over 60. Métro: Réaumur-Sébastopol or Arts et Metiers.

Hôtel de Ville ★ HISTORIC SITE   This enormous Neo-Renaissance wedding cake is Paris's city hall, and you can't go inside. But you can feast on the lavish exterior, which includes 136 statues representing historic VIPs of Parisian history. Since the 14th century, this spot has been an administrative seat for the municipality; the building you see before you dates from 1873, but it is a copy of an earlier Renaissance version that stood in its place up until 1870, when it was burned down during the Paris Commune. The vast square in front of the building was the stage for several important moments in the city's history, particularly during the Revolution: Louis XVI was forced to kiss the new French flag here, and Robespierre was shot in the jaw and arrested here during an attempted coup. Today the square is host to more peaceful activities: There's usually a merry-go-round or two to captivate the little ones, and in winter an **ice-skating rink** is set up.

29 rue de Rivoli, 4th arrond. www.paris.fr. ℭ **01-42-76-43-43.** Free admission. Métro: Hôtel-de-Ville.

Musée Carnavalet ★★★ MUSEUM   Starting with a prehistoric canoe from 4600 BC and continuing into the 20th century, the history of Paris is recounted at this fascinating museum, through items as diverse as Gallo-Roman figurines, Napoléon's toiletry kit, and an 18th-century portrait of Benjamin Franklin when he was the U.S. ambassador to France.

The museum is housed in two magnificent 17th-century mansions, one of which was the home of prodigious letter-writer and woman of the world Madame de Sévigné from 1677 until her death in 1696. Little of the original interior decoration remains in either building, but this is made up for by the importation of entire rooms, including wall paneling and furniture, from various private mansions of different epochs. Highlights include the Louis XV–style **Salon des Philosophes,** with its beautiful *boiseries* (carved wood paneling) and historical objects like the inkwell of Jean-Jacques Rousseau; and the 18th-century **Café Militaire,** a room from an officer's cafe with gilded and sculpted wood paneling representing military motifs like shields, standards, and crowns of laurels.

The section on the French Revolution includes several fascinating mementos, such as the keys to the Bastille prison and a copy of the Declaration of the Rights of Man that once hung behind the president of the Convention. Particularly moving are the personal objects of the royal family from their last days in prison—a lock of Marie Antoinette's hair, Louis XVI's razor and water glass, the young Dauphin's writing exercises—reminders that these iconic figures were in fact made of flesh and blood.

All the labels and descriptions are in French, so you may want to invest in an English-language audioguide (5€); even without translations, most of the art and objects speak for themselves. *Note:* In December 2016 the museum will close for extensive renovations for a period of 3 years.

16 rue des Francs-Bourgeois, 3rd arrond. www.carnavalet.paris.fr. ℭ**01-44-59-58-58.** Free admission for permanent collection. Tues–Sun 10am–6pm. Métro: St-Paul or Chemin Vert.

Musée d'Art et Histoire du Judaïsme ★★ MUSEUM   Housed in the magnificent Hôtel de Saint Aignan, this museum chronicles the art and history of the Jewish people in France and in Europe. It features a superb collection of objects of both artistic and cultural significance (a splendid Italian Renaissance Torah ark, a German gold and silver Hanukkah menorah, a 17th-c. Dutch illustrated Torah scroll, documents from the Dreyfus trial), interspersed with texts, drawings, and photos telling the story of the Jews and explaining the basics of both Ashkenazi and Sephardic traditions. The final rooms include a collection of works by Jewish artists, including Modigliani, Soutine, Lipchitz, and Chagall. In recent years, this museum has hosted some terrific temporary exhibits on offbeat subjects like the (Jewish) origins of Superman, Radical Jewish Culture, and the Walter Benjamin archives. Be prepared for airportlike security at the entrance.

71 rue du Temple, 3rd arrond. www.mahj.org. ℗ **01-53-01-86-53.** Admission 8€ adults, 6€ ages 18–25, free 17 and younger. Mon–Fri 11am–6pm; Sun 10am–6pm. Métro: Rambuteau or Hôtel de Ville.

Picasso Paris ★★★ MUSEUM   After 5 years of renovations, this shrine to all things Picasso has at last reopened with double the exposition space and a more comfortable visit for the millions of visitors that tramp through its doors. Housed in the stunning Hôtel Salé, a 17th-century mansion, this unique institution valiantly strives to make sense of the incredibly diverse output of this prolific genius. Some 400 carefully selected paintings, sculptures, collages, and drawings are presented in a more or less chronological and thematic order, which is no small task when dealing with an artist who experimented with every style, from neoclassicism to surrealism, to his own flamboyantly abstract inventions. Impressionist portraits ("Portrait of Gustave Coquiot," 1901), cubist explorations ("Man with Guitar," 1911), mannerist allegories ("The Race," 1922), deconstructionist forms ("Reclining Nude," 1932), make up only part of his oeuvre, which has been estimated to include some 50,000 works. Not only that, Picasso often worked in wildly different styles during the same period, sometimes treating the same subjects. For example, the rounded yet realistic lovers dancing in "La Danse des Villageois" painted in 1922, hangs next to two forms in a blaze of color representing "The Kiss" painted in 1925. There is also a sampling of the highly abstract and somewhat disturbing portraits of the many women in his life, including portraits of Dora Maar and Marie-Thérèse, both painted in 1937. On the top floor is Picasso's private collection, which includes works by artists he admired like Courbet and Cézanne, as well as paintings by his friends, who included masters like Braque and Matisse.

All in all, what you see on the walls is less than 10% of the 5,000 works in the museum's collection; the presentation will rotate every couple of years. Unless you enjoy waiting in long lines exposed to the elements, **buy your ticket in advance online;** you'll usually walk right in with your e-ticket.

5 rue de Thorigny, 3rd arrond. www.museepicassoparis.fr. ℗ **01-85-56-00-36.** Admission 11€ adults, free 17 and younger. Tues–Fri 11:30am–6pm, Sat–Sun 9:30am–6pm. Métro: St-Paul or Chemin Vert.

Place des Vosges ★★★ PLAZA   Possibly the prettiest square in the city, this beautiful spot combines elegance, greenery, and quiet. Nowhere in Paris will you find such a unity of Renaissance-style architecture; the entire square is bordered by 17th-century brick townhouses, each conforming to rules set down by Henri IV himself, under which run arched arcades. The square's history dates back to a royal mishap in 1559, when the site was occupied by a royal palace. During a tournament, feisty king Henri II decided to fight Montgomery, the captain of his guard. A badly aimed lance resulted in Henri's untimely death; his wife, Catherine de Médicis, was so distraught she decided to have the palace demolished. His descendant, Henri IV, took advantage of the free space to construct a royal square. Over the centuries, a number of celebrities lived in the 36 houses, including Mme. de Sévigny and Victor Hugo. Today the homes are for the rich, as are many of the chic boutiques under the arcades, but the lush lawns, trees, fountains, and the children's playground are for everyone.

4th arrond. Métro: St-Paul.

Arc de Triomphe.

CHAMPS-ÉLYSÉES, TROCADÉRO & WESTERN PARIS (8TH, 16TH & 17TH ARRONDISSEMENTS)

Decidedly posh, this is one of the wealthiest parts of the city in both per-capita earnings and cultural institutions. While the **Champs-Elysées** is more glitz than glory, the surrounding neighborhoods offer high-end shops and restaurants as well as some terrific museums and concert halls. This is also where you will find grandiose architectural gestures, like the **Arc de Triomphe** and the **Place de la Concorde,** which book-end the Champs, and the **Grand Palais** and **Petit Palais,** leftovers from the legendary 1900 Universal Exposition.

Arc de Triomphe ★★★ MONUMENT   If there is one monument that symbolizes "La Gloire," or the glory of France, it is this giant triumphal arch. Crowning the Champs-Elysées, this mighty archway both celebrates the military victories of the French army and memorializes the sacrifices of its soldiers. Over time, it has become an icon of the Republic and a setting for some of its most emotional moments: the lying in state of the coffin of Victor Hugo in 1885, the burial in 1921 of the ashes of an unknown soldier who fought in World War I, and General de Gaulle's pregnant pause under the arch before striding down the Champs-Elysées before the cheering crowds after the Liberation in 1944.

It took a certain amount of chutzpah to build such a shrine, and sure enough, it was Napoléon who instigated it. In 1806, still glowing after his victory at Austerlitz, the Emperor decided to erect a monument to the Imperial Army along the lines of a Roman triumphal arch. Unfortunately, the

Empire came to an end before the arch was finished, and it didn't get completed until 1836.

The arch is covered with bas-reliefs and sculptures, the most famous of which is the enormous "Depart of the Volunteers" of 1792, by François Rude. Just above is one of the many smaller panels detailing Napoleonic battles—in this case, Aboukir—wherein the Emperor treads victoriously over the Ottomans. At the base of the arch is the Tomb of the Unknown Soldier, over which a flame is relit every evening. The inscription reads ICI REPOSE UN SOLDAT FRANÇAIS MORT POUR LA PATRIE, 1914–1918 ("Here lies a French soldier who died for his country").

Don't even think about crossing the vast traffic circle to get to the arch; instead take the underpass near the Métro entrances. You can visit the area under the arch free of charge, but if you want to enjoy the view from the rooftop terrace, you have to pay. You also have to climb 284 stairs to get there (only the very young, the very old, and the disabled get to use the elevator). Though you are not as high up as the viewing platforms on the Eiffel Tower, the panorama is quite impressive. Directly below you will see the 12 boulevards that radiate from the star-shaped intersection (hence the moniker "Etoile"), most of which are named after Napoleonic battles.

Place Charles de Gaulle–Etoile, 8th arrond. www.monuments-nationaux.fr ✆ **01-55-37-73-77.** Admission 9.50€ adults, 6€ ages 18–24, free 17 and under. Apr–Sept daily 10am–11pm; Oct–Mar daily 10am–10:30pm. Métro: Charles-de-Gaulle–Etoile.

Fondation Louis Vuitton ★ Designed by mega-architect Frank Gehry, this stunning contemporary art museum is swathed in a mass of billowing "sails" of glass, giving the impression it is about to sail off into the lush greenery of the Bois de Boulogne, a large park on the western edge of the city (p. 44). Once you've taken in the arty outside, you have two choices: 1) stand in line to see the sophisticated collection of ultra-contemporary art, or 2) go eat an ice cream cone at the Jardin d'Acclimatation, a small amusement park just behind the museum. The best strategy for avoiding lines to the museum is to buy a ticket ahead of time on the Internet and then enter through the Jardin d'Acclimatation, where there is a shorter line than at the main entrance. If you are not big on heady modern and conceptual art, you should probably stick to option number 2.

8 ave. du Mahatma Gandhi, Bois de Boulogne, 16th arrond. www.fondationlouis vuitton.fr. ✆ **01-40-69-96-00.** 14€ adults, 10€ ages 18–26, 5€ artists and children 3–17, free 2 and under; ticket includes entry to the Jardin d'Acclimatation. Mon, Wed–Thurs noon–7pm, Fri noon–11pm, Sat–Sun 11am–8pm. Métro: Les Sablons or Porte Maillot. Shuttle bus 1€ from Place Charles de Gaulle–Etoile, corner of ave. Friedland.

La Madeleine ★ CHURCH As you peer up the rue Royale from the place de la Concorde, you'll see something that very closely resembles a Roman temple. When the first stone was laid in 1763, it was destined to be a church with a neoclassical facade. But then the Revolution broke out, and construction ground to a halt. Napoléon finally strode onto the scene and declared that it would become the Temple de La Gloire, to honor the glorious victories of his army. He wanted something "solid" because he was sure that the monument would last "thousands of years." When military defeats and mounting debt again delayed construction, Napoléon decided that maybe it wouldn't be such a bad idea to make it a church after all—that way Rome would foot the bill. However, it wasn't until 1842, under the Restoration, that La Madeleine was finally consecrated.

The inside of the church is pretty dark, due to a lack of windows, but there are some interesting works of art here, if you can make them out in the gloom. On the left as you enter is François Rude's "Baptism of Christ"; farther on is James Pradier's sculpture "La Marriage de la Vierge."

Place de la Madeleine, 8th arrond. www.eglise-lamadeleine.com. ℂ **01-44-51-69-00.** Free admission. Daily 9:30am–7pm. Métro: Madeleine.

Musée d'Art Moderne de la Ville de Paris ★ MUSEUM   Housed in a wing of the massive Palais de Tokyo, this municipal modern-art museum covers ground similar to that of the Pompidou Center but on a smaller scale. Though several big names are represented (Picasso, Rouault, and Picaba, to name a few), in general these are not their best-known works; highlights include a room dedicated to surrealism (the personal collection of André Breton) and a series of paintings by Delaunay and Léger. The contemporary section, from 1960 on, covers seriously abstract movements like Fluxus and Figuration. In recent years, the collection has acquired several new works from the 1980s on, but for the most cutting edge ideas, you are probably better off at the Palais de Tokyo museum (see below) in the wing next door. There's also a huge room entirely covered with brilliant wall murals by Raoul Dufy ("La Fée Electricité"), as well as another with two enormous versions of "La Danse" by Matisse.

11 av. du Président-Wilson, 16th arrond. www.mam.paris.fr. ℂ **01-53-67-40-00.** Free admission to permanent collections. Tues–Sun 10am–6pm. Métro: Iéna or Alma-Marceau.

Musée Jacquemart-André ★★★ MUSEUM   The love child of a couple of passionate art collectors, this terrific museum takes the form of a 19th-century mansion filled with fine art and decorative objects. Not only is the collection superb, it is also of a blissfully reasonable size—you can see a wide range of beautiful things here without wearing yourself to a frazzle.

The house itself is a work of art: At its inauguration in 1875, the marble Winter Garden with its spectacular double staircase was the talk of the town. Nélie Jacquemart and Edouard André devoted their lives to filling this splendid dwelling with primarily 18th-century French art and furniture. The paintings of Fragonard, Boucher, and Chardin are in evidence, as is an impressive assortment of Louis XV– and Louis XVI–era decorative objects. There are many superb portraits, including that of an officious-looking "Comte Français de Nantes" by David. To honor the artists that influenced these French painters, the couple also amassed a number of 17th-century Dutch paintings, including a jaunty "Portrait of a Man" by Frans Hals, and Rembrandt's evocative "Pilgrims at Emmaus."

The peripatetic couple, who traveled frequently in search of new items for their collection, also took an interest in Renaissance Italian art; though at the time considered "primitive" by most art fans, that didn't stop Jacquemart and André from snapping up Quattrocento masterpieces like Botticelli's "Virgin and Child." The Italian collection (on the second floor) is the most awe-inspiring part of the museum—not only are there works by masters like Bellini, Uccello, and Mantegna, but they are presented in an intimate space with excellent lighting. You feel like you are walking into a felt-lined jewel box. Leave time to eat a light lunch or have tea in the Jacquemart-André's lovely dining room.

158 bd. Haussmann, 8th arrond. www.musee-jacquemart-andre.com. ℂ 01-45-62-11-59. Admission 12€ adults, 10€ students and children 7–17, free for children 6 and younger. Daily 10am–6pm. Métro: Miromesnil or St-Philippe-du-Roule.

Musée Marmottan Monet ★★ MUSEUM

Boasting the world's largest collection of Monets, this museum offers an in-depth look at this genius and some of his talented contemporaries. Among the dozens of Monet canvases is the one that provided the name of an entire artistic movement. Pressed to give a name to this misty play of light on the water for the catalog for an 1874 exposition that included Cézanne, Pissarro, Renoir, and Degas, Monet apparently said, "put 'impression.'" The painting, "Impression, Sunrise," certainly made one, as did the show—thereafter the group was referred to as the Impressionists. Monet never stopped being fascinated with the interaction of light and water, be it in a relatively traditional portrait of his wife and daughter against the stormy sea in "On the Beach at Trouville," or in an almost abstract blend of blues and grays in "Charing Cross Bridge." Monet often painted the same subject at different times of the day, as in his famous series on the Cathedral of Rouen, one of which is here: "Effect of the Sun at the End of the Day." Fans of the artist's water lily series will not be disappointed; the collection includes dozens of paintings of his beloved garden in Giverny.

Paintings by Renoir, Sisley, Degas, Gauguin, and other contemporaries can be seen in the light-filled rooms on the upper floor, as are works by one of the only female members of the group, Berthe Morisot, who gets an entire room devoted to her intimate portraits and interiors.

2 rue Louis-Boilly, 16th arrond. www.marmottan.fr. ℂ 01-44-96-50-33. Admission 11€ adults, 6.50€ students under 25 and ages 8–24, free for children 7 and younger. Tues–Wed and Fri–Sun 10am–6pm; Thurs 10am–9pm. RER: Bouilainvilliers.

Musée National des Arts Asiatiques Guimet ★★ MUSEUM

Founded in 1889 by collector and industrialist Emile Guimet, today this vast collection of Asian art is one of the largest and most complete in Europe. Here you'll find of exquisite works from Afghanistan, India, Tibet, Nepal, China, Vietnam, Korea, Japan, and other Asian nations. You could spend an entire day here, or you could pick and choose regions of interest (displays are arranged geographically); the free audio guide is a good bet for finding stand-outs and providing cultural context. Highlights include a Tibetan bronze sculpture ("Hevajra and Naîrâtmya") of a multi-headed god embracing a fero-cious goddess with eight faces and 16 arms; a blissfully serene stone figure of a 12th-century Cambodian king ("Jayavarman VII") who presided over a short-lived Khmer renaissance; and superb Chinese scroll paintings, including a magnificent 17th-century view of the Jingting mountains in autumn.

6 place d'Iéna, 16th arrond. www.guimet.fr. © **01-56-52-53-00.** Admission to perma-nent collection 7.50€ adults, 5.50€ ages 18–25, free for ages 17 and younger. Wed–Mon 10am–6pm. Métro: Iéna.

Palais de Tokyo ★★ MUSEUM/PERFORMANCE SPACE If you're traveling with cranky teenagers who've had enough of La Vieille France, or if you're also sick of endless rendezvous with history, this is the place to come for a blast of contemporary madness. This vast art space not only offers a rotating bundle of expositions, events, and other happenings, but it's also one of the only museums in Paris that stays open until midnight. While some might quibble over whether or not the works on display are really art, there's no denying that this place is a lot more fun than its stodgy neighbor across the terrace (see above). There's no permanent collection, just continuous tempo-rary exhibits, installations, and events, which include live performances and film screenings. The center underwent a major expansion in 2012 that almost tripled its size—it is now one of the largest sites devoted to contemporary creativity in Europe. In warm weather, you can eat on the splendid terrace or repair to its arty-cool restaurant, **Tokyo Eat.**

13 av. du Président-Wilson, 16th arrond. www.palaisdetokyo.com. © **01-81-97-35-88.** Admission 10€ adults, 8€ ages 18–25, free for ages 17 and younger. Wed–Mon noon–midnight. Métro: Iéna.

Parc Monceau ★★ PARK/GARDENS Marcel Proust used to laze under the trees in this beautiful park, and who could blame him? The lush lawns and leafy trees of this verdant haven would brighten the spirits of even the most melancholy writer. Located in a posh residential neighborhood and ringed by stately mansions, this small park, commissioned by the duke of Chartres in 1769, is filled with *folies,* faux romantic ruins, temples, and antiquities inspired by exotic faraway places. Don't be surprised to stumble upon a mina-ret, a windmill, or a mini-Egyptian pyramid here. The most famous *folie* is the **Naumachie,** a large oval pond surrounded in part by Corinthian columns. You'll find a sizeable **playground** in the southwest corner, as well as a **merry-go-round** near the north entrance.

35 bd. de Courcelles, 8th arrond. www.paris.fr. Free admission. 8am–sundown. Métro: Monceau or Villiers.

Place de la Concorde ★★★ PLAZA Like an exclamation point at the end of the Champs-Elysées, the place de la Concorde is a magnificent arrangement of fountains and statues, held together in the center by a

Place de la Concorde, Paris.

3,000-year-old Egyptian obelisk (a gift to France from Egypt in 1829). Today it is hard to believe that this magnificent square was once bathed in blood, but during the Revolution it was a grisly stage for public executions. King Louis XVI and his wife, Marie Antoinette, both bowed down to the guillotine here, as did many prominent figures of the Revolution, including Danton, Camille Desmoulins, and Robespierre. Once the monarchy was back in place, the plaza hosted less lethal public events like festivals and trade expositions.

In 1835 the *place* was given its current look: Two immense fountains, copies of those in St. Peter's Square in Rome, play on either side of the obelisk; 18 sumptuous columns decorated with shells, mermaids, and sea creatures each hold two lamps; and eight statues representing the country's largest cities survey the scene from the edges of the action. On the west side are the famous **Marly Horses,** actually copies of the originals, which were suffering from erosion and have since been restored and housed in the Louvre. On the north side of the square are two palatial buildings that date from the square's 18th-century origins: On the east side is the **Hôtel de la Marine,** and on the west side is the **Hôtel Crillon,** where on February 6, 1778, a treaty was signed by Louis XVI and Benjamin Franklin, among others, wherein France officially recognized the United States as an independent country and became its ally.

8th arrond. Métro: Concorde.

MONTMARTRE (18TH ARRONDISSEMENT)

Few places in this city fill you with the urge to belt out sappy show tunes like the *butte* (hill) of Montmartre. Admiring the view from the esplanade in front of the oddly Byzantine **Basilique du Sacré-Coeur,** you'll feel as if you've finally arrived in Paris, and that you now understand what all the fuss is about. Ignore the tour buses and crowds mobbing the church and the hideously touristy **place du Tertre** behind you and wander off into the warren of streets towards the **place des Abbesses** or up **rue Lepic,** where you'll eventually stumble across the **Moulin de la Galette** and **Moulin du Radet,** the two surviving windmills (there were once 30 on this hill).

Basilique du Sacré-Coeur ★ CHURCH   Poised at the apex of the hill like a *grande dame* in crinolines, this odd-looking 19th-century basilica has become one of the city's most famous landmarks. After France's defeat in the Franco-Prussian War, prominent Catholics vowed to build a church consecrated to the Sacred Heart of Christ as a way of making up for whatever sins the French may have committed that had made God so angry at them. Since 1885, prayers for humanity have been continually chanted here (the church is a pilgrimage site, so dress and behave accordingly). Inspired by the Byzantine churches of Turkey and Italy, this multi-domed confection was begun in 1875 and completed in 1914, though it wasn't consecrated until 1919 because of World War I. The white stone was chosen for its self-cleaning capabilities: When it rains, it secretes a chalky substance that acts as a fresh coat of paint. Most visitors climb the 237 stairs to the **dome,** where the splendid city views extend over 48km (30 miles).

Parvis de la Basilique, 18th arrond. www.sacre-coeur-montmartre.com. (℃) **01-53-41-89-00.** Free admission to basilica, joint ticket to dome and crypt 8€ adults, 5€ ages 4–16, free under 4. Basilica daily 6am–10:30pm; dome and crypt daily 8:30am–8pm May–Sept, 9am–5pm Oct–Apr. Métro: Abbesses; take elevator to surface and follow signs to funicular.

Musée de Montmartre ★★ MUSEUM   The main reason to visit this small museum is to get an inkling of what Montmartre really was like back in the days when Picasso, Toulouse-Lautrec, Van Gogh, et al. were painting and cavorting up here on the *Butte* (as opposed to the hideously commercial version up the hill on Place du Tertre). While there are few examples of the artists' works here, there are plenty of photos, posters, and even films documenting the neighborhood's famous history, from the days when its importance was mainly religious, to the gory days of the Paris Commune, and finally to the artistic boom in the 19th and 20th centuries. Next to an original poster of Jane Avril by Toulouse-Lautrec, for example, you'll see a photo of the real Jane Avril, as well as other Montmartre cabaret legends like Aristide Bruant and La Goulue. The 17th-century house that shelters the museum was at various times the studio and home of Auguste Renoir and Raoul Dufy, as well as Susan Valadon and her son, Maurice Utrillo, whose studio can now be visited. English-language audio-guides are a big help here.

12 rue Cortot, 18th arrond. www.museedemontmartre.fr. (℃) **01-49-25-89-37.** Admission 9€ adults, 7€ ages 18–25, 5€ ages 10–17, free under 10. Daily 10am–6pm. Métro: Lamarck-Caulaincourt.

RÉPUBLIQUE, BASTILLE & EASTERN PARIS (11TH & 12TH ARRONDISSEMENTS)

This is a nice part of town for aimless wandering, especially if you are a) in search of youth-oriented nightlife, b) in search of youth-oriented clothing shops, or c) a history buff. The French Revolution was brewed in the workshops of the **Faubourg St-Antoine** and ignited at the **place de la Bastille.**

Parc Zoologique de Paris ★★ ZOO   After 6 years of reconstruction, the Paris Zoo finally reopened in 2014, to the delight of children and parents of all stripes. Little remains of the old-fashioned zoo that once was; today a lush, ecologically correct animal reserve invites visitors to five regions of the world, from the plains of Sudan to Europe, via Guyana, Patagonia and Madagascar. Going for quality, instead of quantity, the new zoo may not have room for elephants and bears, but it does introduce visitors to animals they might not be familiar with, like the fossa, a catlike carnivore from Madagascar, or the capybara, a giant South American rodent. There is still a good sampling of zoo favorites like lions, baboons, penguins, and a troupe of giraffes—if you are lucky you can get an up close look while the latter get lunch in the giraffe house. The enclosures are well adapted to their inhabitants, so much so that at times it's hard to see them. But if you are patient you'll see wolves peeking out of the foliage, or a bright red tomato frog griping a vine. There are over 1,000 animals in all, yet the zoo is human-sized—you can see the whole thing in a couple of hours. Don't miss the huge aviaries, one of which is home to a huge flock of flamingos.

Parc de Vincennes, 12th arrond., www.parczoologiquedeparis.fr. ℰ **01-44-75-20-10.** 22€ adults, 17€ students 12–25, 14€ children 3–11, free ages 2 and under. Mid-Oct to mid-Mar daily 10am–5pm, mid-Mar to mid-Oct Mon–Fri 10am–6pm, Sat–Sun and school holidays 9:30am–7:30pm.

Place de la Bastille ★ PLAZA   The most notable thing about this giant plaza is the building that's no longer here: the Bastille prison. Now an enormous traffic circle where cars careen around at warp speed, this was once the site of an ancient stone fortress that became a symbol for all that was wrong with the French monarchy. Over the centuries, kings and queens condemned rebellious citizens to stay inside these cold walls, sometimes with good reason, other times on a mere whim. By the time the Revolution started to boil, though, the prison was barely in use; when the angry mobs stormed the walls on July 14, 1789, there were only seven prisoners left to set free. Be that as it may, the destruction of the Bastille came to be seen as the ultimate revolutionary moment; July 14 is still celebrated as the birth of the Republic. Surprisingly, the giant bronze column in the center honors the victims of a different revolution, that of 1830.

12th arrond. Métro: Bastille.

Cimetière du Père-Lachaise, Paris, with tombs of very famous people.

BELEVILLE, CANAL ST-MARTIN & LA VILLETTE (10TH, 19TH & 20TH ARRONDISSEMENTS)

One of the most picturesque attractions in this area is the **Canal St-Martin** itself, which crosses a formerly working-class neighborhood that is now peopled by an arty mix of regular folk and *bobos* (bourgeois bohemians). The Belleville neighborhood is home to one of the city's bustling **Chinatowns,** as well as many artists' studios.

Cimetière du Père-Lachaise ★★★ CEMETERY   It's hard to believe that a cemetery could be a top tourist attraction, but this is no ordinary cemetery. As romantic and rambling as a 19th-century English garden, this hillside resting place is wonderfully green, with huge leafy trees and narrow paths winding around the graves, which include just about every French literary or artistic giant you can imagine, plus several international stars. Proust, Moliére, La Fontaine, Colette, Delacroix, Seurat, Modigliani, Bizet, and Rossini are all here, as well as Sarah Bernhardt, Isadora Duncan, Simone Signoret, and Yves Montand (buried side by side, of course), not to mention Oscar Wilde, whose huge stone monument is usually covered with lipstick kisses. Even the Lizard King, Jim Morrison, is here. Though the grave itself is unexceptional, the tomb of the '60s rock star is possibly the most visited in the cemetery. In 1971, battling drug, alcohol, and legal problems, the singer/musician came to Paris; 4 months later, he was found dead in a Parisian bathtub, at age 27.

Celebrity graves can be hard to find, so a map is essential. You can find one at the newsstand across from the main entrance; on the website; or on the Paris municipal site (www.paris.fr; search for "Père Lachaise").

16 rue de Repos, 20th arrond. www.pere-lachaise.com. No telephone number. Free admission. Mon–Fri 8am–6pm; Sat–Sun 8:30am–6pm (closes at 5pm Nov to early Mar). Métro: Père-Lachaise or Philippe Auguste.

Parc des Buttes Chaumont ★ PARK   Up until 1860, this area was home to a deep limestone quarry, but thanks to Napoléon III, the gaping hole was turned into an unusual park, full of hills and dales, rocky bluffs, and cliffs. It took 3 years to make this romantic garden; more than a thousand workers and a hundred horses dug, heaped, and blasted through the walls of the quarry to create green lawns, a cool grotto, cascades, streams, and even a small lake. By the opening of the 1867 World's Fair, the garden was ready for visitors. The surrounding area was, and still is, working-class; the Emperor built it to give this industrious neighborhood a green haven and a bit of fresh air. There are **pony rides** for the kids on weekends and Wednesdays, plus a **puppet theater**, a **carousel**, and **two playgrounds.**

Rue Botzaris, 19th arrond. May 1–Sept 30 7am–11pm; Oct 1–Apr 30 7am–8pm. Métro: Botzaris or Buttes Chaumont.

The Left Bank
LATIN QUARTER (5TH & 13TH ARRONDISSEMENTS)

What's so Latin about this quarter? Well, for several hundred years, the students that flocked here spoke Latin in their classes at the **Sorbonne** (founded in the 13th c.) and other nearby schools. The students still flock and the Sorbonne is still in business, and though classes are now taught in French, the name stuck. Intellectual pursuits aside, this youth-filled neighborhood is a lively one, packed with cinemas and cafes. History is readily visible here, dating back to the Roman occupation: The **rue St-Jacques** and **boulevard Saint-Michel** mark the former Roman cardo, and you can explore the remains of the **Roman baths** at the **Cluny Museum.**

Institut du Monde Arabe ★ MUSEUM   In an age when Arab culture is all over the headlines, this is a good place to come to find out what the phrase actually means. The building alone is almost worth the price of admission, designed by architect Jean Nouvel in 1987. The south facade is covered by a metallic latticework echoing traditional Arab designs, with 30,000 light-sensitive diaphragms that open and close according to how bright it is outside. The collection emphasizes the diversity of peoples and cultures in the Middle East, reminding us, among other things, that it was the birthplace of all three major Western religions. While intellectually stimulating, if art is what you are after, the Islamic Art section of the Louvre will be more satisfying. There's a terrific view from the rooftop restaurant, Le Zyriab.

1 rue des Fossés St-Bernard, 5th arrond. www.imarabe.org. ⓒ **01-40-51-38-38.** Admission 8€, 4€ ages 12–26, free 11 and under. Tues–Thurs 10am–6pm, Fri 10am–9:30pm, Sat–Sun 10am–7pm. Métro: Jussieu, Cardinal Lemoine, Sully-Morland.

Jardin des Plantes ★★ GARDENS   This delightful botanical garden, tucked between the Muséum National d'Histoire Naturelle (see below) and the Seine, is one of my favorite picnic spots. Created in 1626 as a medicinal plant garden for King Louis XIII, in the 18th century it became an internationally famed scientific institution thanks to naturalist, mathematician, and biologist Georges-Louis Leclerc, Count of Buffon, with the help of fellow naturalist Louis-Jean-Marie Daubenton. Today the museums are still part academic institutions, but you certainly don't need to be a student to appreciate the lush grounds.

The garden also harbors a small, but well-kept zoo, the **Ménagerie du Jardin des Plants** (ℂ **01-40-79-56-01;** 13€ adults, 9€ students 18–26 and children 4–16, free under 4; daily 9am–5pm, until 6pm in summer). Created in 1794, this is the oldest zoo in the world. Because of its size, the zoo showcases mostly smaller species, in particular birds and reptiles, but it also has a healthy selection of mammals, including rare species like red pandas, Przewalski horses, and even Florida pumas.

36 rue Geoffroy-St-Hilaire, 5th arrond. www.jardindesplantes.net. ℂ **01-40-79-56-01.** Free admission to gardens; 8am–dusk; Métro: Gare d'Austerlitz.

Musée National d'Histoire Naturelle ★★ MUSEUM

This natural history museum was established in 1793 under the supervision of two celebrated naturalists, the Count of Buffon and Louis Jean-Marie Daubenton. Originally (and still) an academic research institution, this temple to the natural sciences contains a series of separate museums, each with a different specialty. The biggest draw is no doubt the **Grande Galerie de l'Evolution,** where a sort of Noah's ark of animals snakes its way around a huge hall filled with displays that trace the evolution of life and man's relationship to nature. Another interesting hall, the **Galerie de Minérologie et de Géologie,** includes a room full of giant crystals. For dinosaurs, saber-toothed tigers, ancient humans, and thousands of fossilized skeletons, repair to the **Galeries de Paléontologie et d'Anatomie Comparée.** A new **Galerie des Enfants** has hands-on interactive displays for the little tykes. Except for the Grande Galerie, which has a joint ticket deal with the Galerie des Enfants, you'll have to pay for each Galerie separately.

36 rue Geoffrey, 5th arrond. www.mnhn.fr. ℂ **01-40-79-54-79.** Admission to each galerie 6€–11€ adults; 4€–9€ students, seniors 60 and older, and children 4–13, free 3 and under. Wed–Mon 10am–6pm. Métro: Jussieu or Gare d'Austerlitz.

Musée National du Moyen Age/Thermes de Cluny (Musée de Cluny) ★★ MUSEUM

Ancient Roman baths and a 15th-century mansion set the stage for a terrific collection of medieval art and objects at this museum. Built somewhere between the 1st and 3rd centuries, the baths (visible from bd. St-Michel) are some of the best existing examples of Gallo-Roman architecture. They are attached to what was once the palatial home of a 15th-century abbot, whose last owner, a certain Alexandre du Sommerard, amassed a vast array of medieval masterworks. When he died in 1842, his home was turned into a museum and his collection put on display. Sculptures, textiles, furniture, and ceramics are shown, as well as gold, ivory, and enamel work. There are several magnificent tapestries, but the biggest draw is the late-15th-century **"Lady and the Unicorn"** series, one of only two sets of complete unicorn tapestries in the world (the other is in New York City).

Among the many sculptures displayed are the famous severed heads from the facade of Notre-Dame. Knocked off of their bodies during the furor of the Revolution, 21 of the heads of the Kings of Judah were found by chance in 1977 during repair work in the basement of a bank. Other treasures include Flemish retables, Visigoth crowns, bejeweled chalices, stained-glass windows, and beautiful objects from daily life, like hair combs and game boards. Best to visit in the afternoon; school groups abound in the morning.

6 place Paul Painlevé, 5th arrond. www.musee-moyenage.fr. (€) **01-53-73-78-00.** Admission 8€ adults, 6€ ages 18–24, free 17 and under; 1€ supplement during temporary exhibits. Wed–Mon 9:15am–5:45pm. Métro/RER: Cluny–La Sorbonne or St-Michel.

Panthéon ★ MAUSOLEUM High atop the "montagne" (actually a medium-sized hill) of St-Geneviève, the dome of the Panthéon is one of the city's most visible landmarks. This erstwhile royal church has been transformed into a sort of national mausoleum—the final resting place of luminaries such as Voltaire, Rousseau, Hugo, and Zola. Initially dedicated to St-Geneviève, the church was commissioned by a grateful Louis XV, who attributed his recovery from a serious illness to the saint. The work of architect Jacques-Germain Soufflot, who took his inspiration from the Pantheon in Rome, the original interior must have been magnificent. However, during the Revolution, its sacred mission was diverted towards a new god—the Nation—and it was converted into a memorial and burial ground for Great Men of the Republic. This meant taking down the bells, walling up most of the windows, doing away with religious statuary, and replacing it with works promoting patriotic virtues. The desired effect was achieved—the enormous empty space, lined with huge paintings of great moments in French history, resembles a cavernous tomb. Though the building is of architectural interest, unless you're a fan of one of the men (or women) who are buried under the building (a staircase leads down to the actual crypt), it's probably best admired from the outside. *Note:* The building is undergoing a major restoration, so don't be alarmed to see it swathed in scaffolding; the monument is still open to the public.

Place du Panthéon, 5th arrond. www.monuments-nationaux.fr. (€) **01-44-32-18-00.** Admission 7.50€ adults, 4.50€ ages 18–25, free for children 17 and younger. Apr–Sept daily 10am–6:30pm; Oct–Mar daily 10am–6pm. Métro: Cardinal Lemoine, RER: Luxembourg.

St-Etienne-du-Mont ★★ CHURCH One of the city's prettiest churches, this ecclesiastical gem is a joyous mix of late Gothic and Renaissance styles. The 17th-century facade combines Gothic tradition with a dash of classical Rome; inside, the 16th-century chancel sports a magnificent **rood screen** (an intricately carved partition separating the nave from the chancel) with decorations inspired by the Italian Renaissance. Book-ended by twin spiraling marble staircases, this rood screen is the only one left in the city. Among the church's riches are sumptuous 16th- and 17th-century stained glass. A pilgrimage site, this church was once part of an abbey dedicated to St-Geneviève (the city's patron saint), and stones from her original sarcophagus lie in an ornate shrine here. That's about all that is left of her—the saint's bones were burned during the Revolution and their ashes thrown in the Seine. The remains of two other great minds, Racine and Pascal, are buried here.

1 place St-Geneviève, 5th arrond. www.saintetiennedumont.fr. ℰ **01-43-54-11-79.** Free admission. Tues–Fri 8:45am–7:45pm, Sat–Sun 8:45am–noon and 2–7:45pm. Métro: Cardinal Lemoine or Luxembourg.

ST-GERMAIN-DES-PRÉS & LUXEMBOURG (6TH ARRONDISSEMENT)

In the 20th century, the St-Germain-des-Prés neighborhood became associated with writers like Jean-Paul Sartre, Simone de Beauvoir, Albert Camus, and the rest of the intellectual bohemian crowd that gathered at **Café de Flore** or **Les Deux Magots** (p. 73). But back in the 6th century, a mighty abbey founded here ruled over a big chunk of the Left Bank for 1,000 years. The French Revolution put a stop to that, and most of the original buildings were pulled down. Remains of both epochs can still be found in this now-tony neighborhood, notably at the 10th-century church **St-Germain-des-Prés** and the surviving bookstores and publishing houses that surround it.

Jardin du Luxembourg ★★★ GARDENS   Rolling out like an Oriental carpet before the Italianate Palais du Luxembourg (the seat of the French Senate since 1958, not open to the public), this vast expanse of fountains, flowers, lush lawns, and shaded glens is the perfect setting for a leisurely stroll, a relaxed picnic, or a serious make-out session, depending on who you're with. At the center of everything is a fountain with a huge basin, where kids can sail toy wooden sailboats (2.50€ for a half-hour) and adults can sun themselves in the green metal chairs at the pond's edge. Sculptures abound: At every turn there is a god, goddess, artist, or monarch peering down at you from their pedestal. The most splendid waterworks is probably the Médici Fountain (reached via the entrance at place Paul Claudel behind the Odéon), draped with lithe Roman gods sculptured by Auguste Ottin, and topped with the Médici coat of arms, in honor of the palace's first resident, Marie de Médici.

Attention Bored Kids & Tired Parents

Frazzled parents take note: There are lots of activities in the Jardin de Luxembourg for kids who need to blow off steam. First off, there is the extra-large **playground** (1.20€ adults, 2.50€ under 12) filled with all kinds of things to climb on and play in. Then there are the wonderful wooden **sailboats** (2.50€ per half-hour) to float in the main fountain, as well as an ancient **carousel** (1.50€, next to the playground). At the **marionette theater** (4.80€ each for parents and children; Wed, Sat, Sun, and school vacation days; shows usually start after 3pm, Sat–Sun additional shows at 11am, for schedule visit www.marionnettesdu luxembourg.fr), you can see Guignol himself (the French version of Punch) in a variety of puppet shows.

In 1621, the Italian-born French queen, homesick for the Pitti Palace of her youth, bought up the grounds and existing buildings and had a Pitti-inspired palace built for herself as well as a smaller version of the sumptuous gardens. During the Revolution, it was turned into a prison. American writer Thomas Paine was incarcerated there in 1793 after he fell out of favor with Robespierre; he narrowly escaped execution. On the plus side, the Revolutionaries increased the size of the garden and made it a public institution. In the southwest corner, visitors can visit a horticulture school where pear trees have been trained into formal, geometric shapes, as well as beehives (yes, beehives) that are maintained by a local apiculture association.

Entry at Place Edmond Rostand, place André Honnorat, rue Guynemer, or rue de Vaugirard, 6th arrond. www.senat.fr/visite/jardin. 8am–dusk. Métro: Odéon; RER: Luxembourg.

Musée Zadkine ★★ MUSEUM   You could easily miss the alleyway that leads to this tiny museum in the small but luminous house where Ossip Zadkine lived and worked from 1928 to his death in 1967. A contemporary and neighbor of artists such as Brancusi, Lipchitz, Modigliani, and Picasso, this Russian-born sculptor is closely associated with the Cubist movement; his sober, elegant, "primitive" sculptures combine abstract geometry with deep humanity. Dozens of examples of his best works, like a superb 9-ft plaster sculpture of biblical Rebecca carrying a water pitcher, or a vaguely African head of a woman in limestone are displayed in small, light-filled rooms. Be sure to visit the artist's workshop, tucked behind the tranquil garden. *Note:* Due to the museum's small size, during temporary exhibits you'll have to pay to enter even the permanent collection (which is usually free).

100 bis rue d'Assas, 6th arrond. www.zadkine.paris.fr. © **01-55-42-77-20.** Free admission to permanent collections. Tues–Sun 10am–6pm. Tues–Sun 10am–6pm. Métro: Notre-Dame des Champs or Vavin.

St-Germain-des-Prés ★★ CHURCH   The origins of this church stretch back over a millennium. First established by King Childebert in 543, who constructed a basilica and monastery on the site, it was built, destroyed, and rebuilt several times over the centuries. Nothing remains of the original buildings, but the bell tower dates from the 10th century and is one of the oldest in France. The church and its abbey became a major center of learning and power during the Middle Ages, remaining a force to be reckoned with up until the eve of the French Revolution. Once the monarchy toppled, however, all hell broke loose: The abbey was destroyed, the famous library burned, and the church vandalized. Restored in the 19th century, the buildings have regained some of their former glory, though the complex is a fraction of its original size.

Much of the interior is painted in a range of greens and golds—one of the few Parisian churches to retain a sense of its original decor. The paint, however, is in a sorry state; the interior should be restored during 2016. The heart of King Jean Casimir of Poland is buried here, as are the ashes of the body of

René Descartes (his skull is in the collections of the Musée de l'Homme). On the left as you exit you can peek inside the **chapel of St-Symphorien,** where during the Revolution over 100 clergymen were imprisoned before being executed on the square in front of the church. The chapel was restored in the 1970s and decorated by contemporary artist Pierre Buraglio in 1992.

3 place St-Germain-des-Prés, 6th arrond. www.eglise-sgp.org. ℂ **01-55-42-81-10.** Free admission. Mon–Sat 8am–7:45pm; Sun 9am–8pm. Métro: St-Germain-des-Prés.

St-Sulpice ★★ CHURCH   The majestic facade of this enormous edifice looms over an entire neighborhood. Construction started in the 17th century over the remains of a medieval church; it took over a hundred years to build, and one of the towers was never finished. Inside, the cavernous interior seems to command you to be silent; several important works of art are tucked into the chapels that line the church. The most famous of them are **three masterpieces by Eugène Delacroix,** "Jacob Wrestling with the Angel," "Heliodorus Driven from the Temple," and "St-Michael Vanquishing the Devil" (on the right just after you enter the church). Jean-Baptiste Pigalle's statue of the "Virgin and Child" lights up the Chapelle de la Vierge at the farthest most point from the entrance. A bronze line runs north–south along the floor; this is part of a **gnomon,** an astronomical device set up in the 17th century to calculate the position of the sun in the sky. A small hole in one of the stained glass windows creates a spot of light on the floor; every day at noon it hits the line in a different place, reaching a gold disk on top of an obelisk at the winter equinox.

Place St-Sulpice, 6th arrond. www.paroisse-saint-sulpice-paris.org. ℂ **01-42-34-59-98.** Free admission. Daily 7:30am–7:30pm. Métro: St-Sulpice.

View of the Eiffel Tower from the River Seine.

EIFFEL TOWER & LES INVALIDES (7TH ARRONDISSEMENT)

Eiffel Tower ★★★ MONUMENT In his wildest dreams, Gustave Eiffel probably never imagined that the tower he built for the 1889 World's Fair would become the ultimate symbol of Paris and, for many, of France. Originally slated for demolition after its first 20 years, the Eiffel Tower has survived more than a century and is one of the most visited sites in the nation. No less than 50 engineers and designers worked on the plans, which resulted in a remarkably solid structure that despite its height (324m/1,063 ft., including the antenna) does not sway in the wind.

A Workout & a Bargain at the Eiffel Tower

No need to go to the gym after marching up the 704 steps that lead you to the first and second floors of the Eiffel Tower. Not only will you burn calories, but you'll save money: At 5€ adults, 4€ ages 12 to 24, and 3.50€ ages 4 to 11, this is the least expensive way to visit. Extra perks include an up-close view of the amazing metal structure and avoiding long lines for the elevator.

But while the engineers rejoiced, others howled. When the project for the tower was announced, a group of artists and writers (including Guy de Maupassant and Alexandre Dumas, fils) published a manifesto that referred to it as an "odious column of bolted metal." Others were less diplomatic: Novelist Joris-Karl Huysmans called it a "hole-riddled suppository." Despite the objections, the tower was built—over 18,000 pieces of iron, held together with some 2.5 million rivets. In this low-tech era, building techniques involved a lot of elbow grease: The foundations, for example, were dug entirely by shovel, and the debris was hauled away in horse-drawn carts. Construction dragged on for 2 years, but finally, on March 31, 1889, Gustave Eiffel proudly led a group of dignitaries up the 1,710 steps to the top, where he unfurled the French flag for the inauguration.

Over 100 years later, the tower has become such an integral piece of the Parisian landscape that it's impossible to think of the city without it. Over time, even the artists came around—the tower's silhouette can be found in the paintings of Seurat, Bonnard, Duffy, Chagall, and especially those of Robert Delaunay, who devoted an entire series of canvases to the subject. It has also inspired a whole range of stunts, from Pierre Labric riding a bicycle down the stairs from the first level in 1923 to Philippe Petit walking a 700m-long (2,296-ft.) tightrope from the Palais de Chaillot to the tower during the centennial celebration in 1989. Eiffel performed his own "stunts" towards the end of his career, using the tower as a laboratory for scientific experiments. By convincing the authorities of the tower's usefulness in studying meteorology, aerodynamics, and other subjects, Eiffel saved it from being torn down.

The most dramatic view of the tower itself is from the wide esplanade at the Palais de Chaillot (Métro: Trocadéro) across the Seine. From there it's a short walk down through the gardens and across the Pont d'Iena to the base of the tower. Though several tower elevators whisk visitors skyward, they do take time to come back down, so be prepared for a wait. The first floor has just had a makeover, with a new restaurant, displays and a bit of glass floor, so you can pretend you are walking on air. Personally, I think the view from the second level is the best; you're far enough up to see the entire city, yet close enough to clearly pick out the various monuments. But if you are aching to get to the top, an airplanelike view awaits. The third level is,

4

mercifully, enclosed, but thrill-seekers can climb up a few more stairs to the outside balcony (entirely protected by a grill).

Champ de Mars, 7th arrond. www.tour-eiffel.fr. © **01-44-11-23-23.** Lift to 2nd floor 9€ adults, 7€ ages 12–24, 4.50€ ages 4–11; Lift to 2nd and 3rd floors 16€ adults, 14€ ages 12–24, 11€ ages 4–11; stairs to 2nd floor 5€ adults, 4€ ages 12–24, 3.50€ ages 4–11. Free admission for children 3 and under. Mid-June to Aug daily 9am–midnight, Sept to mid-June daily 9:30am–11pm; Sept to mid-June stairs open only to 6pm. Métro: Trocadéro or Bir Hakeim. RER: Champ de Mars–Tour Eiffel.

Hôtel des Invalides/Napoléon's Tomb ★★ MUSEUM This grandiose complex houses a military museum, church, tomb, hospital, and military ministries, among other things. Commissioned by Louis XIV, who was determined to create a home for soldiers wounded in the line of duty, it was built on what was then the outskirts of the city. The first war veterans arrived in 1674—between 4,000 and 5,000 soldiers would eventually move in, creating a mini-city with its own governor. An on-site hospital was constructed for the severely wounded, which is still in service today.

As you cross the main gate, you'll find yourself in a huge courtyard (102×207m, 335×207 ft.), the *cour d'honneur,* once the site of military parades. The surrounding buildings house military administration offices and the recently renovated **Musée de l'Armée,** one of the world's largest military museums, with a vast collection of objects testifying to man's capacity for self-destruction. The most impressive section is **Arms and Armor,** a panoply of 13th- to 17th-century weaponry. Viking swords, Burgundian battle axes, 14th-century blunderbusses, Balkan *khandjars,* Browning machine guns, engraved Renaissance serpentines, musketoons, grenadiers—if it can kill, it's enshrined here. There is also a huge wing covering the exploits of everyone from **Louis XIV** to **Napoléon III,** another on the two **World Wars,** starting with the lead up to the *Grande Guerre* (1914–18) through the final chapter of WWII (1939–45) in the Pacific.

The **Eglise du Dôme** is split in two, the front half being the light-filled "Soldier's Church," decorated with magnificent chandeliers and a collection of flags of defeated enemies. On the other side of the glass partition the **Tomb of Napoléon** lies under one of the most splendid domes in France. Designed by Hardouin-Mansart, it took over 2 decades to build. The interior soars 107m (351 ft.) up to a skylight, which illuminates a brilliantly colored cupola. Ethereal light filters down to an opening where you can look down on the huge porphyry sarcophagus, which holds the emperor's remains, encased in five successive coffins (one tin, one mahogany, two lead, and one ebony). Surrounding the sarcophagus are the tombs of two of Napoléon's brothers, his son, and several French military heroes. Don't blame the over-the-top setting on Napoléon; the decision to transfer his remains to Paris was made in 1840, almost 20 years after his death. Tens of thousands crowded the streets to pay their respects as the coffin was carried under the Arc de Triomphe and down the Champs-Elysées to Les Invalides, where it waited another 20 years until the tomb was finished.

Place des Invalides, 7th arrond. www.invalides.org. ℮ **01-44-42-37-72.** Admission to all the museums, the church, and Napoléon's Tomb: 9.50€ adults, free 17 and younger. Apr–Oct 10am–6pm, Nov–Mar 10am–5pm. Métro: Latour-Maubourg, Varenne, Invalides; RER: Invalides.

Musée d'Orsay ★★★ MUSEUM What better setting for a world-class museum of 19th-century art than a beautiful example of Belle Époque architecture? In 1986, the magnificent Gare d'Orsay train station, built to coincide with the 1900 World's Fair, was brilliantly transformed into an exposition space. The huge, airy central hall lets in lots of natural light, which is artfully combined with artificial lighting to illuminate a collection of treasures.

The collection spans the years 1848 to 1914, a period that saw the birth of many artistic movements, such as the Barbizon School and Symbolism, but today it is best known for the emergence of Impressionism. All the superstars of the epoch are here, including Monet, Manet, Degas, and Renoir, not to mention Cézanne and Van Gogh.

The top floor is now the home of the most famous Impressionist paintings, like Edouard Manet's masterpiece, "Le Déjeuner sur l'Herbe." Though Manet's composition of bathers and friends picnicking on the grass draws freely from those of Italian Renaissance masters, the painting shocked its 19th-century audience, which was horrified to see a naked lady lunching with two fully clothed men. Manet got into trouble again with his magnificent "Olympia," a seductive odalisque stretched out on a divan. There was nothing new about the subject; viewers were rattled by the unapologetic look in her eye—this is not an idealized nude, but a real woman, and a tough cookie to boot.

The middle level is devoted to the post-Impressionists, with works by such artists as Gauguin, Seurat, Rousseau, and Van Gogh, like the latter's "Church at Auvers-sur-Oise," an ominous version of the church in a small town north of Paris where he moved after spending time in an asylum in Provence. This was 1 of some 70 paintings he produced in the 2 months leading up to his suicide.

Gallery in Musée d'Orsay.

A few other standouts:

RENOIR'S "DANCE AT LE MOULIN DE LA GALETTE, MONT-MARTRE": The dappled light and the movement of the crowd in this painting are such that you wonder if it's not going to suddenly waltz out of its frame. The blurred brushstrokes that created this effect rankled contemporary critics.

MONET'S "LA GARE ST-LAZARE": Here is another train station when steam engines were still pulling in on a regular basis. The metallic roof of the station frames an almost abstract mix of clouds and smoke; rather than a description of machines and mechanics, this painting is a modern study of light and color.

GAUGUIN'S "THE WHITE HORSE": The horse isn't even really white, but you don't care when you gaze at Gauguin's Tahitian version of paradise. Not everyone was charmed by the artist's vibrant colors: The pharmacist who commissioned the painting refused it because the horse was too green.

1 rue de la Légion d'Honneur, 7th arrond. www.musee-orsay.fr. ⓒ **01-40-49-48-14.** Admission 11€ adults, 8.50€ ages 18–25, free ages 17 and younger. Tues–Wed and Fri–Sun 9:30am–6pm; Thurs 9:30am–9:45pm. Métro: Solférino. RER: Musée d'Orsay.

Musée du quai Branly ★★★ MUSEUM   It's just a few blocks from the Eiffel Tower, but this museum's wildly contemporary design has forever changed the architectural landscape of this rigidly elegant neighborhood. Its enormous central structure floats on a series of pillars, under which lies a lush garden, separated from the noisy boulevard out front by a huge glass wall. However you feel about the outside, you cannot help but be impressed by the inside: The vast space is filled with exquisite examples of the traditional arts of Africa, the Pacific Islands, Asia, and the Americas. Designed by veteran museum-maker Jean Nouvel, this intriguing space makes an ideal showcase for a category of artwork that too often has been relegated to the sidelines of the museum world.

This magnificent collection is displayed in a way that invites you to admire the skill and artistry that went into the creation of these diverse objects. Delicately carved headrests from Papua New Guinea in the form of birds and crocodiles and intricately painted masks from Indonesia vie for your attention. Look at and listen to giant wooden flutes from Papua New Guinea, displayed with an on-going recording. A selection of "magic stones" from the island nation of Vanuatu includes smooth abstract busts reminiscent of Brancusi sculptures. A fascinating collection of Australian aboriginal paintings segues into the Asian art section, and the journey continues into Africa, starting with embroidered silks from Morocco and heading south through magnificent geometric marriage cloths from Mali and wooden masks from the Ivory Coast. The Americas collection includes rare Nazca pottery and Inca textiles, as well as an intriguing assortment of North American works, like Haitian voodoo objects and Sioux beaded tunics.

37 quai Branly and 206 and 218 rue de Université, 7th arrond. www.quaibranly.fr. © **01-56-61-70-00.** Admission to permanent exhibitions 9€ adults, free children 17 and younger. Tues–Wed and Sun 11am–7pm; Thurs–Sat 11am–9pm. Métro: Alma-Marceau. RER: Pont d'Alma.

Musée Rodin ★★★ MUSEUM   The grounds of this splendid museum are so lovely that many are willing to pay 2€ just to stroll around. Behind the Hôtel Biron, the mansion that houses the museum, is a formal garden with benches, fountains, and even a little cafe. Of course, it would be foolish *not* to go inside and drink in some of the 6,600 sculptures in this excellent collection (don't worry, not all are on display), but it would be equally silly not to take the time to admire the large bronzes in the garden, which include some of Rodin's most famous works. Take, for example, "The Thinker." Erected in front of the Panthéon in 1906 during a political crisis, Rodin's first public sculpture soon became a Socialist symbol and was quickly transferred here by the authorities, under the pretense that it blocked pedestrian traffic. Other outdoor sculptures include the "Burghers of Calais," "Balzac," and the "Gates of Hell," a monumental composition that the sculptor worked on throughout his career.

Indoors, marble compositions prevail, although there are also works in terra-cotta, plaster, and bronze, as well as sketches and paintings on display.

The most famous of the marble works is "The Kiss," which was originally meant to appear in the "Gates of Hell." In time, Rodin decided that the lovers were too happy for this grim composition, and he explored it as an independent work. As usual with Rodin's works, the critics were shocked by the couple's overt sensuality, but not as shocked as they were by the large, impressionistic rendition of "Balzac," exhibited at the same salon, which critic Georges Rodenbach described as "less a statue than a strange monolith, a thousand-year-old menhir." The museum holds hundreds of works, many of them legendary, so don't be surprised if after a while your vision starts to blur. That'll be your cue to head outside and enjoy the garden.

79 rue de Varenne, 7th arrond. www.musee-rodin.fr. © **01-44-18-61-10.** Admission 7€ adults, 5€ ages 18–25, free children 17 and younger. Tues and Thurs–Sun 10am–5:30pm, Wed 10am–8:30pm. Métro: Varenne or St-Francois-Xavier.

The famous marble statue "The Kiss" in Musée Rodin.

MONTPARNASSE (14TH & 15TH ARRONDISSEMENTS)

Even though it had its heart ripped out in the early 1970s when the original 19th-century train station was torn down and the Tour Montparnasse, an ugly skyscraper, was erected, this neighborhood still retains a redolent whiff of its artistic past. Back in the day, artists like Picasso, Modigliani, and Man Ray hung out in cafes like **Le Dôme, La Coupole, La Rotonde,** and **Le Select** as did a "Lost Generation" of English-speaking writers like Hemingway, Fitzgerald, Faulkner, and Joyce. Today the famous cafes are mostly filled with rich tourists, but you can still find quiet corners.

Les Catacombes ★ CEMETERY/HISTORIC SITE   The bones of millions of ex-Parisians line the narrow passages of this mazelike series of tunnels. In the 18th century, the Cimetière des Innocents, a centuries-old, over-packed cemetery near Les Halles, had become so foul and disease-ridden that it was finally declared a health hazard and closed, and the bones of its occupants were transferred to this former quarry, until it was closed in 1814. That's when the quarry inspector got the novel idea of organizing the bones in neat stacks and geometric designs, punctuating the 2km (1¼ miles) with sculptures and pithy sayings carved into the rock. The one at the entrance sets the tone: STOP—HERE IS THE EMPIRE OF DEATH. The visit will be fascinating for some, terrifying for others; definitely not a good idea for claustrophobics or small children. You'll want to wear comfortable shoes and bring a sweater of some sort, as it's cool down here (around 57°F/14°C).

1 avenue du Colonel Henri Rol-Tanguy, 14th arrond. www.catacombes-de-paris.fr. ✆ **01-43-22-47-63.** Admission 10€ adults, 8€ ages 18–26, free ages 17 and under. Tues–Sun 10am–8pm (last entry 7pm). Métro: Denfert-Rochereau.

SHOPPING IN PARIS

Like us, most Parisians can't actually afford to buy the French luxury brands so revered around the world—and yet they manage to look terrifically put together. What's their secret? Read on as I attempt to shed some light on this puzzling mystery; the shops and services listed below will give you a good point of departure for your Parisian shopping adventure.

Business Hours

In general, shops are open from 9 or 10am to 7pm; many are closed on Monday, and most are closed on Sunday. Unfortunately, that means that the stores are jam-packed on Saturday, so don't say I didn't warn you.

Some smaller, family-run operations sometimes still close between noon and 2pm for lunch, but most stores stay open all day. Many larger stores and most department stores stay open late (that is, until 9pm) 1 night a week (called a *nocturne*). For food and toiletry emergencies, tiny minimarkets (called *alimentations*) stay open late into the night 7 days a week. *Note:* Many shops close down for 2 or 3 weeks in July or August, when the vacation exodus empties out major portions of the city.

Great Shopping Areas

STREETS FOR BARGAIN HUNTING

You can find clothes and knickknacks at significantly reduced prices at discount shops, which tend to conglomerate on certain streets. **Rue d'Alésia** (14th arrond.; Métro: Alésia) is lined with outlet stores (*déstock*) selling discounted wares, including designer labels like Sonia Rykiel; and **Rue St-Placide** (6th arrond.; Métro: Sèvres-Babylone) has both outlet stores and discount shops like **Mouton à Cinq Pattes** (p. 114).

MIDRANGE SHOPPING HUBS

Several areas have high concentrations of chain and other midrange stores where you can get a lot of shopping done in a small geographic area. They are **Rue de Rennes** (6th arrond.; especially near the Tour Montparnasse); **Les Halles** (1st arrond.; the Forum des Halles underground mall is still open during the reconstruction of Les Halles above; don't ignore the many nearby shops above); **Rue de Rivoli** (1st arrond., btw. rue du Pont Neuf and Hotel de Ville); and **Grands Magasins** (9th arrond.)—be sure look in the little streets that weave around the Printemps and Galeries Lafayette department stores (see below).

CHIC BOUTIQUE-ING

Paris has an endless number of darling boutiques, ranging from funky to fantastic. A few of the best streets for boutique shopping or simply *lèche-vitrine* (window shopping) are **Rue des Abbesses** (18th arrond.; Métro: Abbesses), for affordable chic and the shops of hip, young startup designers; **Rue de Charonne** (11th arrond.; Métro: Bastille), a youth-oriented street that has recently taken a turn upscale with a dose of tony boutiques; **Rue des Francs Bourgeois** (4th arrond.; Métro: St-Paul), for a cornucopia of fashionable/cool/hip stores, most of which are open on Sunday; and **Rue Etienne Marcel** (2nd arrond.; Métro: Etienne Marcel), next to the hip Montorgueil pedestrian zone, with stylish boutiques galore.

THE SKY'S THE LIMIT

If you don't look at price tags, Paris does not disappoint. For centuries, Paris has been the capital of luxury goods, many of them for sale on **Avenue Montaigne** (8th arrond.; Métro: Franklin D. Roosevelt), with breathtakingly expensive designer flagships like Dior and Chanel; the **Place Vendôme** (1st arrond.; Métro: Concorde or Tuileries), with eye-popping jewelry shops (Cartier, Boucheron, and so on); and **Rue du Faubourg St-Honoré** (8th arrond.; Métro: St-Philippe du Roule), where deeply elegant boutiques are filled with choice morsels of designer goods.

Markets: Food & Flea

Marchés (open-air or covered markets) are small universes unto themselves where nothing substantial has really changed for centuries. These markets are great local spots to hunt for fresh food or browse flea market finds.

FOOD MARKETS

Paris's food markets are noisy, bustling, joyous places where you can buy fresh, honest food. Following is a short list of food *marchés;* you can find more on the municipal website (www.paris.fr; search for "Marché"). *Note:* Unless you see evidence to the contrary, don't pick up your own fruits and vegetables with your hands. Wait until the vendor serves you.

Marché Batignolles ★★ (bd. Batignolles, btw. rue de Rome and Place Clichy, 17th arrond.; Sat 9am–3pm; Métro: Rome): A terrific, all-organic Saturday market with fresh regional produce and close proximity to pretty sidewalk cafes for an after-marché coffee.

Marché d'Aligre ★★★ (also called Marché Beauveau, place d'Aligre, 12th arrond.; outdoor market Tues–Fri 7:30am–1:30pm, Sat–Sun 7:30am–2pm, covered market Tues–Sat 9am–1pm and 4–7:30pm, Sun 9am–1:30pm; Métro: Ledru Rollin or Gare de Lyon): One of the city's largest markets, this sprawling affair invades a whole neighborhood, with both outdoor stalls and a covered market.

Marché Raspail ★★ (bd. Raspail, btw. rue de Cherche-Midi and rue de Rennes, 6th arrond.; Tues and Fri 7am–2:30pm; organic Sun 9am–3pm; Métro: Rennes): Stretching several blocks down the center divider of a wide avenue, this outdoor market makes a delicious gourmet stroll.

FLEA MARKETS

Marché aux Puces de la Porte de Vanves ★★ (Av. Georges-Lafenestre, 14th arrond.; www.pucesdevanves.typepad.com; Sat and Sun 7am–2pm; Métro: Porte de Vanves): This weekend event sprawls along two streets and is the best flea market in Paris—dealers swear by it. Look for old linens, vintage Hermès scarves, toys, ephemera, costume jewelry, perfume bottles, and bad art. Get there early—the best stuff goes fast.

Marché aux Puces de Paris St-Ouen–Clignancourt ★ (Porte de Clignancourt, 18th arrond.; www.marcheauxpuces-saintouen.com; Sat–Mon 10am–1pm and 2pm–5:30pm; Métro: Porte de Clignancourt): At the northern edge of the city, this claims to be the largest antiques market in the world. It was once a bargain-hunter's dream, but prices now often rival those of regular antiques dealers. Still, hard-core browsers will get a kick out of wandering the serpentine alleyways of this Parisian medina. *Note:* Beware of pickpockets.

Shopping A to Z

ANTIQUES & COLLECTIBLES

L'Objet qui Parle ★★   This delightful and quirky shop sells a jumble of vintage finds, including framed butterflies, teapots, furniture, chandeliers, crockery, hunting trophies, religious paraphernalia, and old lace. Great for souvenir shopping. 86 rue des Martyrs, 18th arrond. ℂ **06-09-67-05-30.** Métro: Abbesses.

Village St-Paul ★★   When you pass through an archway on rue St-Paul, you come upon a lovely villagelike enclosure, the remnant of a centuries-old hamlet that was swallowed up by the city. Today, it's a village of antiques dealers and design shops, selling everything from old bistro chairs and vintage lingerie to Brazilian eco-furniture and Iranian kilim rugs. www.levillagesaint paul.com. No phone. Métro: St-Paul.

BEAUTY & PERFUME

The Different Company ★★   This independent perfume house makes its own unique fragrances with mostly natural materials. Signature scents include Osmanthus, Sel de Vétiver, and Rose Poivrée, but let your nose lead the way when you visit the store. 10 rue Ferdinand Duval, 4th arrond. www.the differentcompany.com. ⓒ **01-42-78-19-34.** Métro: St-Paul.

Make Up Forever ★   This French cosmetics company, which trains professional makeup artists, also runs this boutique where you can buy products and get a **makeup lesson** (25 min. for 25€, 60 min. for 60€; call to reserve). A second location is at 5 rue de la Boétie in the 8th arrondissement. 5 rue des Francs Bourgeois, 4th arrond. www.makeupforever.fr. ⓒ **01-42-71-23-19.** Métro: St-Paul.

BOOKS

San Francisco Book Company ★★   Since new books in English can be very expensive in Paris, there's a steady traffic in used ones in the expatriate community, with a couple of bookstores devoted to the task. This centrally located shop has a good stock of both hardback classics and paperback airplane reading, as well as rare and out-of-print editions. 17 rue Monsieur Le Prince, 6th arrond. www.sanfranciscobooksparis.com. ⓒ **01-43-29-15-70.** Métro: Odéon.

Shakespeare & Company ★★★   This venerable shrine is a must on any Parisian literary tour. Run by George Whitman for some 60 years before he passed away in 2011 at 98, today it is helmed by his daughter, Sylvia, who was named for Sylvia Beach (who founded the original bookshop in 1919). Many a legendary writer has stopped in over the decades for tea; many an aspiring author has camped out in one of the back rooms (Whitman liked to think of his store as a "writer's sanctuary"). Today, Whitman's presence is still felt at this historic bookshop, which sells used

---

Sale Mania

Despite a loosening of the laws that restricted sales to certain times of the year, stores still follow the traditional sale (*soldes*) seasons. Two times a year, around the second week in January and the second week in July (specific dates are plastered all over the city and on store websites), retailers go hog-wild and slash prices as far as they want.

However, with the increase in off season reductions and Internet pre-sales, opening day is now both mobbed and anticlimactic. Not only is a lot of the good stuff already gone, but the initial reductions are minimal. That said, if you are patient, there are good deals to be had, but try to avoid the first days of havoc and especially the weekends.

and new books. Check the website for ongoing readings and other events. 37 rue de la Bûcherie, 5th arrond. www.shakespeareandcompany.com. ℰ **01-43-25-40-93.** Métro/RER: St-Michel–Notre-Dame.

CLOTHING & ACCESSORIES

Abou d'Abi Bazar ★★　Here's a store with mostly casual clothes, multiple brands and rotating collections—in other words, great one-stop boutique shopping. There are two other locations: 33 rue de Temple in the Marais, and 15 rue Soufflot, near the Panthéon in the 5th. 125 rue Vieille du Temple, 3rd arrond. www.aboudabibazar.com. ℰ **01-42-71-13-26.** Métro: Saint-Sébastien-Froissart.

Antoine & Lili ★★　Hot pink is the signature color at this wacky store, where the gaily painted walls are hung with oodles of colorful objects from around the world. The women's clothes are innovative and fresh yet wearable, and come in a range of bright colors. It has five other branches in town; check the website for addresses. 95 quai de Valmy, 10th arrond. www.antoineetlili.com. ℰ **01-40-37-41-55.** Métro: Jacques-Bonsergent.

Children

Lilli Bulle ★★　If you are looking for something a little different and original, this is a good place to start. These cool and colorful clothes will make your kids look like they live in this fun and funky neighborhood. 3 rue de la Forge Royale, 11th arrond. www.lillibulle.com. ℰ **01-43-73-71-63.** Métro: Faidherbe-Chaligny.

Marie Puce ★★　A little softer and gentler than Lilli, Marie offers easy elegance for tots who need to dress up (at least a little) but can't stand frills. Most of the clothing here is 100% Made in France. 60 rue du Cherche Midi, 6th arrond. www.mariepuce.com. ℰ **01-45-48-30-09.** Métro: Sèvres-Babylone or St-Placide.

Discount

Mouton à Cinq Pattes ★　Sift through the packed racks of designer markdowns and you just might find Moschino slacks or a Gaultier dress at a fabulous price. If you do, grab it fast—it might not be there tomorrow. The store at No. 8 is women's apparel only; No. 18 serves both sexes, and a third store at 138 bd. St-Germain is just for men. 8 and 18 rue St-Placide, 6th arrond. www.moutonacinqpattesparis.com. ℰ **01-45-48-86-26.** Métro: Sèvres-Babylone.

Lingerie

Orcanta ★　This chain has a great selection of name brands (such as Lise Charmel, Chantal Thomas, and Huit) and usually at least a rack or two of discounted items. More locations on the website. 60 rue St-Placide, 6th arrond. www.orcanta.fr. ℰ **01-45-44-94-44.** Métro: St-Placide.

GIFTS & SOUVENIRS

Finding something to take home that is both different and definitely French is not always an easy task. Here are a few places that will widen your options.

Colette ★★　What can you say about a store that sells both Hermès scarves and knitted hot dogs? This shopping phenom offers both high style and high concept—basically, if it's cool and happening, they sell it. Karl

Lagerfeld jeans, heart-shaped sunglasses, psychedelic nail polish, designer toilet brushes, and so forth. 213 rue St-Honoré, 1st arrond. www.colette.fr.© **01-55-35-33-90.** Métro: Tuileries.

La Tuile à Loup ★★ Dedicated to promoting (and selling) authentic handicrafts from the provinces of France, this cozy shop has a stock that includes handwoven baskets, cutlery, woodcarvings, and pottery. They have a particularly good collection of ceramics, in both traditional styles and works by contemporary artists. 35 rue Daubenton, 5th arrond. www.latuilealoup.com. © **01-47-07-28-90.** Métro: Censier-Daubenton.

Tout S'arrange ★ This tiny boutique is filled with unique, off-the-wall gifts that will make you smile. Goofy masks, bicycle sunglasses, peanut-shell figurines, and hand-made jewelry and bags that appeal to the kid in everyone. 27 rue Delambre, 14th arrond. www.tousarrange.fr. © **01-43-26-44-68.** Métro: Edgar Quinet.

DEPARTMENT STORES

Galeries Lafayette ★★ This emblematic *grand magasin* (department store) sports an over-the-top Art Nouveau dome under which oodles of fashionable goodies are displayed for style-conscious shoppers. A bit less expensive than its more glamorous rival next door (see Printemps, below), it's also so huge that you can usually find just what you are looking for. It has everything from luxury labels to kids' stuff, not to mention books, stationary, wine, and a gourmet shop. 40 bd. Haussmann, 9th arrond. www.galerieslafayette.com. © **01-42-82-34-56.** Métro: Chausée d'Antin-Lafayette.

Le Bon Marché ★★★ Founded in the mid-1800s, this was the one of the world's first department stores. Despite its name (*bon marché* means affordable), this is the most expensive of Paris' *grand magasins.* It is also the most stylish, with beautiful displays and fabulous clothes of every imaginable designer label, both upscale and midrange. Right next door is its humongous designer supermarket, **La Grande Epicerie** (see "Specialty Groceries," below). 24 rue de Sèvres, 7th arrond. www.lebonmarche.com. © **01-44-39-80-00.** Métro: Sèvres–Babylone.

Printemps ★★ The glistening domes of this 19th-century building bring to mind a grand hotel on the French Riviera. High fashion gets priority here; four of the seven floors of women's wear are devoted to designer labels. If you can't handle the crowds inside, you can always enjoy the famed *vitrines,* or **window displays,** outside. Better yet, ride to the top of Printemps Beauté/Maison and enjoy the splendid **panoramic view;** it even has a cafe at the top where you can lunch. 64 bd. Haussmann, 9th arrond. www.printemps.com.© **01-42-82-50-00.** Métro: Havre-Caumartin or St-Lazare.

FOOD & DRINK
Chocolate
Michel Chaudun ★★★ If you are looking for a chocolate cellphone, look no further. Or how about chocolate pliers or Ping-Pong paddles? Known for his sculpting skills, Chaudun is also renowned for the exquisite taste of his

masterworks. Be sure to try the pavés—melt-in-your-mouth little squares of chocolate ganache made to resemble cobblestones. 149 rue de l'Université, 7th arrond. ☏ **01-47-53-74-40.** Métro: Invalides.

Patrick Roger ★★   This cutting-edge chocolate boutique could easily be mistaken for a jewelry shop. Here you can sample chocolates with names like "Insolence" (almond and chestnut) and "Zanzibar" (thyme and lemon), as well as candied fruits, nougat, and other delicacies. Five other stores in the city. 108 bd. St-Germain, 6th arrond. www.patrickroger.com. ☏ **09-63-64-50-21.** Métro: Odéon.

Specialty Groceries

Fauchon ★   Some (like me) find it overhyped and overpriced; others think it's heaven on Earth. Founded in 1886, this tea-room-cum-luxury-food-emporium has been wowing the crowds for over a century, and the crowds are certainly still coming. In 2004, the establishment received a shocking pink makeover and expanded exponentially—now you can find Fauchon from Hamburg to Ho Chi Min City. 26 and 30 place de la Madeleine, 8th arrond. www.fauchon.com. ☏ **01-70-39-38-00.** Métro: Madeleine.

La Grande Epicerie Paris ★★   This humongous gourmet grocery mecca, an outgrowth of Le Bon Marché department store (see above) stocks every imaginable gourmet substance you could possibly imagine, and many that you couldn't. Sculpted sugar cubes, designer mineral waters, truffled balsamic vinegar, pink salt from the Himalayas—need I go on? It also has an excellent (if expensive) takeout department for picnic items. 38 rue de Sèvres, 7th arrond, www.lagrandeepicerie.fr. ☏ **01-44-39-81-00.** Métro: Sèvres-Babylone.

Wines

Before you start planning to stock your wine cellar back home, consider this sad truth: Most non-E.U. countries won't let you bring back much more than a bottle or two. Your best bet is to drink up while you're here.

Legrand Filles et Fils ★★   More than just a wine store, this is a place where you can learn everything there is to know about the sacred grape. 1 rue de la Banque, 2nd arrond. www.caves-legrand.com. ☏ **01-42-60-07-12.** Métro: Bourse.

Les Domaines Qui Montent ★   This association of some 150 wine producers offers a vast selection of wines that come from small, independent vineyards where the emphasis is on quality and *terroir,* not quantity. An on-site wine bar also serves meals. There is a second location at 136 bd. Voltaire in the 11th arrondissement and a third on the corner of rue Ballu and rue Vintimille in the 9th. 22 rue Cardinet, 17th arrond. www.lesdomainesquimontent.com. ☏ **01-42-27-63-96.** Métro: Courcelles or Wagram.

JEWELRY

Bijoux Blues ★★   Hand-crafted, unique jewelry at reasonable prices made in an atelier in the Marais—who could ask for more? Designs are fun and funky, yet elegant. Pieces can be custom-designed. 30 rue St-Paul, 4th arrond. www.bijouxblues.com. ☏ **01-48-04-00-64.** Métro: St-Paul.

White Bird ★ If you are looking for a unique engagement ring or present for your sweetheart, this is a good bet. It has a terrific selection of jewelry made by talented, independent craftspeople/designers. 38 rue du Mont Thabor, 1st arrond. www.whitebirdjewellery.com. ℰ **01-58-62-25-86.** Métro: Concorde.

STATIONERY

L'Art du Papier ★★ This delightful stationery store has a fabulous selection of colored papers and envelopes, as well as ink-stamps, sealing wax, and the essentials for hobbies like calligraphy and "le scrapbooking." It has three other locations: 16 rue Daunou in the 2nd, 197 bd. Voltaire in the 11th, and 17 av. de Villiers in the 17th. 48 rue Vavin, 6th arrond. www.art-du-papier.fr. ℰ **01-43-26-10-12.** Métro: Vavin.

ENTERTAINMENT & NIGHTLIFE

While simply walking around town and gaping at the beautifully illuminated monuments can be an excellent night out, Paris is also a treasure trove of rich evening offerings: bars and clubs from chic to shaggy, sublime theater and dance performances, top-class orchestras, and scores of cinemas and art-film houses.

Finding Out What's On

For dates and schedules for what's happening in music, theater, dance, and film, pick up the **weekly listing magazines "Pariscope"** or **"l'Officiel des Spectacles"** (both .70€) the Parisian bibles for weekly events. Both come out on Wednesdays and are available at any newsstand.

With few exceptions, the city's major concert halls and theaters are in action between September and June, taking off during the summer months during the annual vacation exodus. Summer is the season for wonderful music festivals, including the **Festival Chopin** and **Jazz à La Villette** (p. 23), many of which take place in Paris's lovely parks and gardens.

GETTING TICKETS You can get tickets in person at **FNAC,** the giant bookstore/music chain that has one of the most comprehensive box offices in the city (follow the signs to the "Billeterie"). You can also **order your tickets online in English** at www.fnactickets.com or by phone at ℰ **08-92-68-36-22** (.34€ per min.). **Ticketmaster.fr** offers a similar service where you can buy tickets either online (www.ticketmaster.fr) or by phone (ℰ **08-92-39-01-00;** .34€ per min.).

Discount hunters can stand in line at one of the city's three **half-price ticket booths,** all run by **Le Kiosque Théâtre** (www.kiosquetheatre.com; Tues–Sat 12:30–8pm, Sun 12:30–4pm). There's one in front of the Montparnasse train station; a second is on the west side of the Madeleine; and a third in the center of Place des Ternes (17th arrond.). Half-price tickets for same-day performances go on sale here at 12:30pm. You can also find plenty of ticket discounts online at **BilletRéduc** (www.billetreduc.com, in French).

THEATER

Paris has hundreds of theaters, many of which have nightly offerings. Although most of it is in French, you can find a few English-language shows (see "Belly Laughs in English," below). Of course, avant-garde shows combining dance, theater, and images really need no translation.

Comédie-Française ★★ Established by Louis XVI in 1680, this legendary theater is the temple of classic French theater (Corneille, Racine, Molière), though in recent decades, the troupe has branched out into more modern territory. In addition to the gorgeous just-restored main theater **(Salle Richelieu),** the company presents its offerings in its two other theaters: the medium-size **Théâtre du Vieux Colombier** (21 rue du Vieux Colombier, 6th arrond.; ℭ **01-44-39-87-00;** Métro: St-Sulpice or Sèvres–Babylone) and the smaller **Studio-Théâtre** (Galerie du Carrousel du Louvre, under the Pyramid, 99 rue de Rivoli, 1st arrond.; ℭ **01-44-58-98-58;** Métro: Palais Royal–Musée du Louvre). Place Colette, 1st arrond. www. comedie-francaise.fr. ℭ **08-25-10-16-80** (.15€ per min). Métro: Palais-Royal–Musée du Louvre.

> ### Belly Laughs in English
>
> English-language shows are rare, and comics even more so, but a long-standing gig in town is worth a detour. At press time, the best place to go for a good giggle was **"How to Become a Parisian in One Hour"** (playing at Théâtre des Nouvautés; details at www. oliviergiraud.com), a terrific one-person show written by Olivier Giraud, a Frenchman who spent several years in the U.S.

Théâtre National de Chaillot ★★ Dance and theater are on equal footing at this beautiful Art Deco theater in the Palais de Chaillot, where contemporary choreographers and theater directors share a jam-packed program. There is a lot of blurring of lines here between the two disciplines; dance programs often include video and text, and theater productions often incorporate the abstract. 1 place du Trocadéro, 16th arrond. www.theatre-chaillot.fr. ℭ **01-53-65-30-00.** Métro: Trocadéro.

OPERA, DANCE & CLASSICAL CONCERTS

Opéra de Paris ★★★ This mighty operation includes both the **Palais Garnier** (place de l'Opéra, 9th arrond.; see p. 85), an attraction in itself, and the **Opéra Bastille** (2 place de la Bastille, 12th arrond.) a slate-colored behemoth that has loomed over the place de la Bastille since 1989. The company has since split its energies between the two venues. In theory, more operas are performed at the Bastille, which has more space and top-notch acoustics, and the Garnier, home of the **Ballet de l'Opèra de Paris,** focuses on dance, but you can see either at both. www.operadeparis.fr. ℭ **08-92-89-90-90** (.34€ per min.), from outside France 01-71-25-24-23.

Philharmonie de Paris ★★★ Hovering over La Villette like a visiting spaceship, this spanking new mega-venue seats 2,400 spectators and serves as the new home of the Orchestre de Paris. This silvery apparition also encompasses the institute, museum, and performance spaces in the **Cité de la Musique** (now called **Philharmonie 2**) as well as a nifty cafe and restaurant. In keeping with La Villette's policy of making culture accessible to one and all, the season includes concerts specially designed for young people, families, and audiences that don't usually find themselves in concert halls. 221 ave. Jean-Jaurès, 19th arrond. www.philharmoniedeparis.com. ℂ **01-44-84-44-84.** Métro: Porte de Pantin.

CABARET

Some visitors feel they simply haven't had the true Paris experience without seeing a show at the Moulin Rouge or the Lido, even though there is nothing particularly Parisian, or even French, about them these days. Today's audiences are more likely to arrive in tour buses than touring cars, and the shows are more Vegas than Paris. What you will see here is a lot of scenic razzmatazz and many sublime female bodies, mostly *torse nue* (topless).

Moulin Rouge ★ When it opened in 1889, the Moulin Rouge was the talk of the town, and its huge dance floor, multiple mirrors, and floral garden inspired painters like Toulouse-Lautrec. Times have changed—today's Moulin Rouge relies heavily on lip-synching and pre-recorded music, backed up by dozens of be-feathered Doriss Girls, long-legged ladies who prance about the stage. Be prepared for lots of glitz and not much else. 82 bd. Clichy, place Blanche, 18th arrond. www.moulinrouge.fr. ℂ **01-53-09-82-82.** 92€–201€ show alone; 165€–215€ show with dinner. Métro: Blanche.

The Crazy Horse ★ This temple to "The Art of the Nude" presents an erotic dance show with artistic aspirations. Be advised that unlike the other shows, this one is known for what the girls *aren't* wearing. The performers, who slither, swagger, and lip-synch with panache, have names like Zula Zazou and Nooka Karamel. Note that while it has no dining onsite, it has dinner-show packages with nearby restaurants. 12 av. George V, 8th arrond. www.lecrazyhorseparis.com. ℂ **01-47-23-32-32.** Show standing at the bar 40€–50€ ages 18–20, 65€–85€ 21 and over; 105€–165€ show seated; show plus dinner packages start at 185€. Métro: George V or Alma Marceau.

JAZZ CLUBS

Paris has been a fan of jazz from its beginnings, and many legendary performers like Sidney Bechet and Kenny Clark made the city their home. Still a haven for jazz musicians and fans of all stripes, Paris offers dozens of places to duck in and listen to a good set or two. Here are a few of the best:

Caveau des Oubliettes ★ There are not too many jazz clubs in the world where you can both listen to music and admire an authentic, French Revolution–era guillotine. Located in the Latin Quarter, just across the river from Notre-Dame, this underground nightspot was once a medieval prison. Today patrons laugh, drink, talk, and flirt in the narrow passageways and listen to jazz in the lounge. 52 rue Galande, 5th arrond. www.caveaudesoubliettes.fr. ℂ **01-46-34-23-09.** Free cover, 1 drink min. (from 6€). Métro: St-Michel.

Le Sunset/Le Sunside ★★ One of several famous jazz clubs on the rue des Lombards (and it's a short street!), this one has a split personality. Le Sunset Jazz, is dedicated to electric jazz and international music, whereas Le Sunside is devoted to acoustic jazz for the most part. Some of the hottest names in French jazz appear here regularly (Jacky Terrasson, Didier Lockwood) along with a new crop of international stars. 60 rue des Lombards, 1st arrond. www.sunset-sunside.com. ℰ **01-40-26-46-60.** Tickets 16€–30€. Métro: Châtelet.

New Morning ★★★ If you are looking for big names and hot acts, look no further. This place has incredible lineups, including jazz giants, pop legends, and international superstars, as well as top-grade local talent. This relatively large club (the room holds 300) fills up quick, and no wonder: This truly is one of the best jazz venues in town, and the top ticket price is only around 30€. 7 rue des Petites-Ecuries, 10th arrond. www.newmorning.com. ℰ**01-45-23-51-41.** Cover 20€–30€. Métro: Château-d'Eau.

The Bar Scene

Paris may not be the 24-hour party city some other international capitals claim to be, but it has plenty of places to sip, flirt, and be merry. In general, bars stay open until around 2am.

Chez Jeannette ★ This old bar was revamped by a young hip bunch, who had the good sense to preserve its old, kitschy decor. Located on a somewhat scruffy stretch of rue du Faubourg St-Dennis, it seems out of place on its block, but that's part of what makes the place cool. Hot meals also served here. 47 rue du Faubourg Saint-Denis, 10th arrond. www.chezjeannette.com. ℰ**01-47-70-30-89.** Métro: Château d'Eau.

Experimental Cocktail Club ★ If you're looking for a sophisticated setting to spot stars, you've come to the right place. Known, not surprisingly, for its gourmet cocktails, this cosmopolitan lounge has the feel of a retro speakeasy. 37 rue St-Sauveur, 2nd arrond. www.experimentalcocktailclub.com. ℰ**01-45-08-88-09.** Métro: Sentier.

Le Bar du Plaza Athénée ★★ Knock yourself out and order a shockingly expensive drink at this classy, historic joint, which simply drips with glamour and fabulousness. The bar (and the entire hotel) has had an in-depth overhaul, and sports a transparent bar and extra posh cocktails. Hotel Plaza-Athénée, 25 av. Montaigne, 8th arrond. www.plaza-athenee-paris.fr. ℰ**01-53-67-66-65.** Métro: Alma-Marceau.

WINE BARS

5e Cru ★ Offering a multitude of the best and the brightest French wines, this trendy spot also tickles the taste buds with a terrific lunch menu. At night, there are cheese and charcuterie platters as well as frequent themed wine tastings. 7 rue du Cardinal Lemoine, 5th arrond. www.5ecru.com. ℰ **01-40-46-86-34.** Métro: Jussieu.

Le Baron Rouge ★   This neighborhood institution spills out onto a corner that it shares with the sprawling Marché d'Aligre, a giant outdoor and covered market. It only has a few tables, but most people stand at the counter or outside, glass in hand, especially during market hours. It's a little rough-and-tumble getting your drink order in at the bar. 1 rue Théophile Roussel, 12th arrond. ✆ **01-43-43-14-32.** Métro: Ledru-Rollin.

The Club Scene

If you want to go out to a *boîte de nuit* (nightclub), you'll have plenty to choose from in Paris. Keep in mind that the French love their fashion, so dressing to impress is obligatory—sneakers will rarely get you past the line outside. Most clubs don't really get going until at least 11pm, if not later.

NIGHTCLUBS

Batofar ★★   For more than 15 years, this bright red boat has been the site of music and dancing and general good times. Docked on the quai François Mauriac, this multifunctional floating venue includes a dance club, a bar, a restaurant, and a terrace for cocktails hour and low-key soirees. On good nights, hundreds of gyrating dancers move in rhythm to house, garage, techno, and live jazz music. Facing 11 quai François Mauriac, 13th arrond. www.batofar.org. ✆ **01-53-60-17-00.** Métro: Quai de la Gare.

Nouveau Casino ★★   This former movie theater is now a giant dance club with live music, a huge bar that vaguely resembles an iceberg, hanging chandeliers, and a terrific program that includes all sorts of avant-garde dance music and name bands in the concert space. 109 rue Oberkampf, 9th arrond. www.nouveaucasino.net. ✆ **01-43-57-57-40.** Métro: St-Maur, Parmentier, or Ménilmontant.

GAY & LESBIAN BARS & CLUBS

Paris has a vibrant gay nightlife scene, primarily centered around the **Marais.** Pick up one of the magazines devoted to the subject—like **"Qweek"** (www.qweek.fr)—for free in gay bars and bookstores. Also look for **"Têtu"** magazine at newsstands—it has special nightlife sections.

Le 3w Kafe ★   The most popular lesbian bar in the Marais, this is a good place to come to find company. Downstairs, a DJ spins on weekends, when there's dancing. Men can only enter the premises if accompanied by a woman. 8 rue des Ecouffes, 4th arrond. ✆ **01-48-87-39-26.** Métro: St. Paul.

Le Cox ★   You'll know it when you get here; it's where the crowd is spilling out onto the sidewalk. This place still gets big crowds, even though it's been here for years; people come for the bar as well as the great DJs. The clientele is a pleasant mix, everything from hunky American tourists to sexy Parisians. 15 rue des Archives, 4th arrond. www.cox.fr. ✆ **01-42-72-08-00.** Métro: Hôtel de Ville.

Open Café ★   More relaxed and more diverse than neighboring Le Cox, this cafe-bar has a busy sidewalk terrace that's usually full both day and night.

Everyone from humble tourists to sharp-looking businessmen to TV stars hang out here. 17 rue des Archives, 4th arrond. www.opencafe.fr. ℰ **01-42-72-26-18.** Métro: Hôtel-de-Ville.

DAY TRIPS FROM PARIS

Many visitors (and Parisians, for that matter) make the mistake of thinking that Paris is France, but the minute you disentangle yourself from the city and its suburbs, another country appears: a gentle rural landscape dotted with small towns, not-so-small castles, and other fascinating sites, some of the best of which you can reach without a car.

Versailles ★★★

21km (13 miles) SW of Paris, 71km (44 miles) NE of Chartres

The grandeur of the Château of Versailles is hard to imagine until you are standing before it. Immediately, you start to get an idea of the power (and ego) of the man behind it, King Louis XIV. One of the largest castles in Europe, it is also forever associated with another, less fortunate king, Louis XVI and his wife, Queen Marie Antoinette, who were forced to flee when the French Revolution arrived at their sumptuous doorstep. The palace's extraordinary gardens, designed by the legendary landscape architect André Le Nôtre, are worth a visit all on their own.

ESSENTIALS

ARRIVING   Take the **RER C** (www.transilien.fr; 30 min. from the Champs de Mars station) to **Versailles Château—Rive Gauche.** *Important:* Make sure the final destination for your train is Versailles Château—Rive Gauche, *not* Versailles Chantier, which actually runs in the opposite direction, touring all around Paris before arriving at Versailles, which will add an hour or so to your journey. It's about a 5-minute walk from the Versailles Rive Gauche train station to the château—don't worry, you can't miss it. For a little more (4.35€ adults), you can also take the **SNCF** Transilien suburban train (www.transilien.fr; 40 min;) from the Gare St-Lazare station to **Versailles-Rive Droite,** and then walk 10 minutes to the château (around 45 min. total).

Unless you have a **Paris Visite** or other pass that includes zones 1–4, you will need to buy a special ticket for the RER C (one-way fare 3.55€ adults, 1.75€ 4–10, free under 4); a regular Métro ticket will not suffice. You can buy a ticket from any Métro or RER station; the fare includes a free transfer to the Métro.

TICKETS   The all-inclusive **Château Passeport** grants you access to the main chateau, the gardens, the Trianon Palaces, and the Marie Antoinette Estate (Nov–Mar 18€ adults; Apr–Oct 25€ includes Les Grandes Eaux; free 17 and under). You can also buy a **ticket to just the Palace** (15€; free 17 and under) or **just the Trianons and Marie Antoinette's Estate** (10€). The under-18 crowd (who get in free) will have to buy a ticket to get into the gardens (9€) from April to October. You can avoid some of the long lines at the entrance by purchasing you tickets online. A **Paris Museum Pass** will get you into everything except Les Grandes Eaux musicales (Apr–Oct).

VISITOR INFORMATION Château de Versailles: ✆ **01-30-83-78-00;** www.chateauversailles.fr; **Versailles Tourist Office:** 2 bis av. de Paris; www. versailles-tourisme.com; ✆ **01-39-24-88-88.**

THE CHATEAU OF VERSAILLES: THE BACKSTORY

Back in the 17th century, after having been badly burned by a nasty uprising called Le Fronde, Louis XIV decided to move his court from Paris to Versailles, a safe distance from the intrigues of the capital. He also decided to have the court move in with him, where he could keep a close eye on them and nip any new plots or conspiracies in the bud. This required a new abode that was not only big enough to house his court (anywhere from 3,000–10,000 people would be palace guests on any given day), but also one that would be grand enough to let the world know who was in charge.

Louis, otherwise known as the "Sun King," brought in a flotilla of architects, artists, and gardeners to enlarge the existing castle and give it a new look. Meanwhile, legendary garden designer André Le Notre was carving formal gardens and a huge park out of what had been marshy countryside. Harmonious geometric designs were achieved with flower beds, hedges, canals, and pathways dotted with sculptures and fountains.

Construction, involving as many as 36,000 workers, ground on for years; in 1682 the King and his court moved in, but work continued well into the reign of Louis XV. Louis XVI and his wife, Marie Antoinette, made few changes, but history made a gigantic one for them: On October 6, 1789, an angry mob of hungry Parisians marched on the palace, forcing the royal couple to return to Paris. Versailles would never again be a royal residence. The palace was ransacked during the Revolution, and in the years after it fell far from its original state of grace. Napoléon and Louis XVIII did what they could to bring the sleeping giant back to life, but by the early 1800s, during the reign of Louis-Philippe, the castle was slated for demolition. Fortunately, this forward-thinking king decided to invest his own money to save Versailles for future generations, and in 1837 the vast structure became a national museum.

TOURING THE PALACE

Designed to impress, the main bulk of the tour includes the **Grand Apartments,** used primarily for ceremonial events (a daily occurrence), the **Queen's Apartments,** and the **Hall of Mirrors.** These, along with the **King's Apartments** and the **Chapel,** are must-sees. If you have time and fortitude, you can take a **guided tour** of the royal family's **private apartments** (16€; some in English) for a more intimate look at castle life.

Each room in the **Grand Apartments ★★★** is dedicated to a different planet (circling the sun, as in Sun King), and each has a fabulous painting on the ceiling depicting the god or goddess associated with said heavenly sphere. The first and most staggering, painting-wise, is in the **Salon d'Hercule ★★**, holding an enormous canvas by Paolo Veronese, "Christ at Supper with

Apollo Fountain in the gardens of Versailles Palace.

Simon," as well as a splendid, divinity-bedecked ceiling portraying Hercules being welcomed by the gods of Olympus by Antoine Lemoyne. At 480 sq. m (5,166 sq. ft.), it's one of the largest paintings in France. The **Salon d'Apollon** ★, not surprisingly, was the throne room, where the Sun King received ambassadors and heads of state.

The ornate **Salon de Guerre** ★ and **Salon de Paix** ★ bookend the most famous room in the place, the **Hall of Mirrors** ★★★, which reopened in 2007 following a 3-year restoration. Louis XIV commanded his painter-in-chief, Charles Le Brun, to paint the 12m-high (40-ft.) ceiling of this 73m-long (240-ft.) gallery with representations of his accomplishments. This masterwork is illuminated by light from the 17 windows that overlook the garden, which are matched on the opposite wall by 17 mirrored panels. Add to that a few enormous crystal chandeliers, and the effect is dazzling. This splendid setting was the scene of a historic event in a more recent century: In 1919, World War I officially ended when the Treaty of Versailles was signed here.

A gorgeous bedroom with silk hangings printed with lilacs and peacock feathers in the **Queen's Apartments** ★★ looks exactly as it did in 1789, when Marie Antoinette was forced to flee revolutionary mobs through a secret door (barely visible in the wall near her bed). The **King's Apartments** ★★★ are even more splendiferous, though in a very different style: Here the ceilings have been left blank white, which brings out the elaborate white and gold decoration on the walls. The **King's Bedroom** ★★★, hung from top to bottom with gold brocade, is fitted with a banister that separated the King from the 100 or so people who would come to watch him wake up in the morning.

The **Chapel** ★★★, where the kings attended Mass, is a masterpiece of light and harmony by Jules Hardouin Mansart. This lofty space (the ceiling is more than 25m/82 ft. high) reflects both Gothic and Baroque styles, with a vaulted roof, stained glass, and gargoyles with columns and balustrades typical of the early 18th century.

TOURING THE DOMAINE DE MARIE ANTOINETTE

Northwest of the fountain lies the **Domaine de Marie Antoinette ★★★**. (If you don't have a château passport or museum pass, you'll need a separate ticket to get in.) It was here that the young queen sought refuge from the strict protocol and infighting at the castle. She transformed the **Petit Trianon ★★**, a gift from her husband and the small manor that Louis XV used for his trysts, into a stylish haven. When the queen had finished decorating the manor in the latest fashions, she set to work creating an entire world around it, including a splendid **English garden ★**, several lovely pavilions, a jewel-like **theater ★★**, and even a small **hamlet ★**, complete with a working farm and a dairy, where she and her friends would play cards and gossip or just go for a stroll in the "country." The **Grand Trianon ★** is also worth a brief visit. Built by Louis XIV as a family retreat, this small marble palace consists of two large wings connected by an open columned terrace from which there is a **view ★** of the gardens.

TOURING THE GARDENS & PARK

The entire 800-hectare (2,000-acre) park is laid out according to a precise symmetrical plan. From the terrace behind the castle, there is an astounding **view ★★★** that runs past two parterres, down a central lawn (the Tapis Vert), down the **Grand Canal ★★**, and seemingly into infinity. Le Nôtre's masterpiece is the ultimate example of the French-style garden: geometric, logical, and all in perfect harmony, a reflection of the divine order of the cosmos. Given that the Sun King was the star of this particular cosmos, a solar theme is reflected in the statues and fountains along the main axis of the perspective; the most magnificent of these is the **Apollo Fountain ★★★** where the sun god emerges from the waves at dawn on his chariot. Today, you can **picnic, bike ride** (bikes can be rented next to the restaurant), or even **row a boat** in the canal west of the Apollo Fountain on a sunny day.

Place d'Armes. www.chateauversailles.fr. *C* **01-30-83-78-00.** Palace 15€ adults; free children 18 and under. Marie Antoinette's Domaine 10€ adults; everything free children 17 and younger. Palace Apr–Oct Tues–Sun 9am–6:30pm; Nov–Mar Tues–Sun 9am–5:30pm. Marie Antoinette's Estate Apr–Oct Tues–Sun noon–6:30pm; Nov–Mar Tues–Sun noon–5:30. Park daily dawn–dusk.

Chartres ★★★

97km (60 miles) SW of Paris, 76km (47 miles) NW of Orléans

You'll see it long before you see the actual town: the spire of the cathedral of Chartres rising above a sea of wheat fields. You can easily visit the church and its inspiring stain-glassed windows and still have time to wander the narrow streets of the old town.

ESSENTIALS

ARRIVING   From Paris's Gare Montparnasse, **trains** run directly to Chartres, taking about an hour (16€ one-way). For information visit www.voyages-sncf.com or call *C* 3635. If **driving,** take A10/A11 southwest and follow signs to Le Mans and Chartres. (The Chartres exit is clearly marked.)

VISITOR INFORMATION The **Office de Tourisme** in the Maison du Saumon, 8 rue de la Poissonerie (www.chartres-tourisme.com; ✆ **02-37-18-26-26**).

EXPLORING THE CATHEDRAL

With its carved portals and three-tiered flying buttresses, this would be a stunning sight even without its legendary **stained-glass windows**—though the world would be a far drearier place. For these ancient glass panels are truly glorious, a kaleidoscope of colors so deep, so rich, and so bright, it's hard to believe they are some 700 years old.

A Romanesque church stood on this spot until 1194, when a fire burned it virtually to the ground. All that remained were the towers, the Royal Portal, and a few remnants of stained glass. The locals were so horrified that they sprung to action; in only 3 decades a new cathedral was erected, which accounts for its remarkably unified Gothic architecture. The new cathedral was dedicated in 1260

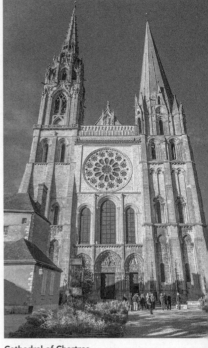

Cathedral of Chartres.

and has miraculously survived the centuries with relatively little damage. The cathedral was somehow spared during the French Revolution; during World War I and World War II, the precious windows were carefully dismounted piece by piece and stored in a safe place in the countryside.

Before you enter the church, take in the **facade ★★**, a remarkable assemblage of religious art and architecture. The base of the two towers dates from the early 12th century (before the fire). The tower to your right (the **Old Tower,** or South Tower) is topped by its original sober Romanesque spire; that on your left (the **New Tower,** or North Tower) was blessed with an elaborate Gothic spire by Jehan de Beauce in the early 1500s, when the original burned down. Below is the **Royal Portal ★★★**, a masterpiece of Romanesque art. Swarming with kings, queens, prophets, and priests, this sculpted entryway tells the story of the life of Christ. The rigid bodies of the figures contrast with their lifelike faces; it is said that Rodin spent hours here contemplating this stonework spectacle. You can **climb to the top of the New Tower** to take in the **view ★**; just remember to wear rubber-soled shoes—the 300 steps are a little slippery after all these centuries.

Once inside the cathedral, you'll really understand what all the fuss is about. The dimness is pierced by the radiant colors of the **stained-glass windows ★★★**, which shine down from all sides. Three windows on the west side of the building, as well as the beautiful rose window to the south called **Notre Dame de la Belle Verièrre** ★, date from the earlier 12th-century structure; the rest, with the exception of a few modern panels, are of 13th-century origins.

Another indoor marvel is the **chancel enclosure** ★★★, which separates the chancel (the area behind the altar) from the ambulatory (the walkway that runs around the outer chapels). Started in 1514 by Jehan de Beauce, this intricately sculpted wall depicts dozens of saints and other religious superstars. Back in the ambulatory is the Chapel of the Martyrs, where the cathedral's cherished **relic** resides: a piece of cloth that the Virgin Mary apparently wore at the birth of Christ, a gift of Charles the Bald in 876.

Note: The cathedral asks that visitors not talk or wander around during Mass, generally held in the late morning and early evening. You are welcome to sit in on services, of course.

16 Cloître Notre-Dame. www.cathedrale-chartres.monuments-nationaux.fr. ⊘ **02-37-21-22-07.** General admission to the cathedral is free; admission to the towers 5.50€ adults; 4.50€ adults 18–25; free children 17 and under. Cathedral open daily Sept–May 8:30am–7:30pm, Jun–Aug 8:30am–10pm.

NORMANDY

by Mary Novakovich

Normand landscape that gives little clue to the region's long and turbulent history. Look a little closer, however, and you see haunting reminders of some of the Second World War's most dramatic battles.

The Allied landings on Normandy's beaches in June 1944 changed the course of the Second World War. Although the embarkation beaches teem with visitors in the summer, they remain living memorials to bravery, determination, and ingenuity.

But these sights don't exclusively define the region. Fashionable Deauville and its family-friendly neighbor Trouville have been drawing sun-seekers since the 19th century. Bayeux attracts lovers of history and art, many to see the extraordinary tapestry documenting another history-changing event: the Norman Conquest of England. Honfleur is a place of arty pilgrimage, and Rouen's history and bustling restaurant scene attract foodies hungry for culture. Mont-St-Michel has stood guard for a millennium.

Head inland to savor the cream of Normandy produce: namely, the pungent cheeses from Camembert, Pont l'Évêque, Livarot, and Neufchâtel. Take a tour of Normandy's apple orchards that produce the region's renowned cider and Calvados brandy.

ROUEN ★★

135km (84 miles) NW of Paris; 89km (55 miles) E of Le Havre

Normandy's historical capital buzzes from dawn 'til dusk, thanks to its busy port and lively university. Its agreeable atmosphere invites leisurely strolls along medieval lanes, where some of Normandy's most delicious produce sits temptingly in shop windows. Former celebrated residents of Rouen include writer Gustave Flaubert, Claude Monet, who endlessly painted Rouen's Cathédrale de Notre-Dame, and Joan of Arc, who met her tragic fate in the place du Vieux Marché, the Old Marketplace, in 1431.

Rouen suffered greatly during World War II when half of it was destroyed, but the old quarter has been reconstructed. Today its metropolitan area is home to half a million people, with about 100,000 clustered in the large center.

Normandy

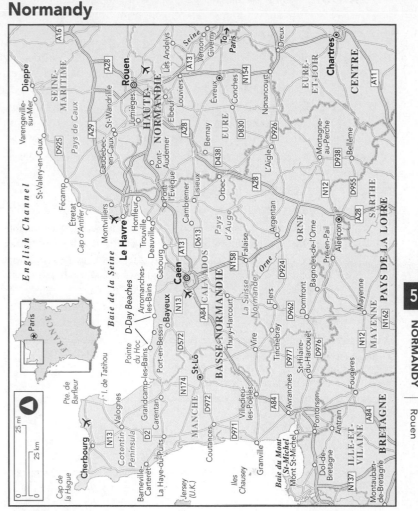

Essentials

ARRIVING   From Paris's Gare St-Lazare, **trains** leave for Rouen about once an hour (trip time: 1½ hr.). The one-way fare is 23€, but you can get deals online for as little as 10€. For rail information, visit www.voyages-sncf. com or call ✆ **36-35.** To **drive** from Paris, take A13 northwest to Rouen (trip time: 1½ hr.).

VISITOR INFORMATION   The **Office de Tourisme** is at 25 place de la Cathédrale (www.rouentourisme.com; ✆ **02-32-08-32-40**).

CITY LAYOUT   As in Paris, the Seine splits Rouen into **Rive Gauche** (Left Bank) and **Rive Droite** (Right Bank). The old city is on Rive Droite.

Getting Around

ON FOOT   Rouen's old town is compact and best navigated on foot, as many of its medieval streets are pedestrianized. The Tourist Office offers free maps marked with walking tours.

BY BICYCLE   Like many French cities, Rouen has its own bike-sharing scheme, **Cy'clic** (http://cyclic.rouen.fr). You can register online or at one of Rouen's 22 bike stands; fees range from 1€ for 1 day to 5€ for a week.

BY CAR   **Rouen Park** (www.rouenpark.com) details the city's five central public parking lots, with information on locations, spaces, and prices.

BY TAXI   **Les Taxis Blancs** (✆ **02-35-61-20-50**).

BY PUBLIC TRANSPORT   Rouen's **Métro** (www.reseau-astuce.fr) has one line running north-south through the city, underground on Rive Droite and at street level on Rive Gauche. The most central stations in Rive Droite are Théâtre des Arts, Palais de Justice, and the train station, Gare-Rue Verte. Tickets cost 1.60€ and are on sale at automatic kiosks at each station.

[FastFACTS] ROUEN

ATMs/Banks   Banks are all around the city center, with 11 along rue Jeanne d'Arc.

Business Hours   As in most of France, shops are closed from about noon until at least 2pm, 3pm, or even 4pm. They might open on Sunday mornings, and most will be closed for a day early in the week, usually a Monday or a Tuesday.

Doctors & Hospitals   **Centre Hospitalier Universitaire de Rouen** (www.chu-rouen.fr; ✆ **02-32-88-89-90**).

Emergencies   The Tourist Office lists a full range of emergency contacts on its website (www.rouentourisme.com). Click on "General Information," then "Emergency Numbers."

Mail & Postage   **La Poste,** 112 rue Jeanne d'Arc (✆ **36-31**).

Pharmacies   **Grande Pharmacie du Centre,** 29 place Cathédrale (✆ **02-35-71-33-17**).

Where to Stay

Hotel de Bourgtheroulde ★★   Just steps from place du Vieux-Marché and rue de l'Horologe is Rouen's only five-star hotel and prettiest hideaway. When you walk into the ornate 16th-century courtyard, the last thing you expect to see when you enter this historic mansion is a screamingly chic and modern galleried restaurant and bar, where locals meet for an after-work drink. Each elegant room is a one-off—some contemporary, others more classic— with interesting features such as exposed stone walls and beams, wood paneling, and bathrooms tiled in chunky, earthy mosaics. At the **Spa du Drap d'Or,** Normandy's largest indoor pool awaits after a day of sightseeing.

15 place de la Pucelle. www.hotelsparouen.com. ✆ **02-35-14-50-50.** 78 units. 270€– 330€ double; 450€–550€ suite. Parking 18€. **Amenities:** 2 bars; indoor swimming pool; 2 restaurants; spa; free Wi-Fi.

Hôtel de la Cathédrale ★ This incredibly charming hotel is one of Rouen's most appealing affordable options. The location—just off a pedestrian street midway between the cathedral and the Eglise St-Maclou—is unbeatable. Guestrooms are simple, but each has its own character, with quirky wallpaper, plump leather armchairs or wooden beamed ceilings. In summertime, a buffet breakfast is served in the cobbled courtyard.

12 rue St-Romain. www.hotel-de-la-cathedrale.fr. ℰ **02-35-71-57-95.** 26 units. 90€–120€ double; 140€ triple; 160€ quadruple. Public parking 11€ nearby. **Amenities:** Breakfast room; free Wi-Fi.

Where to Eat

Don't be surprised to find plenty of fresh, seafood in France's fourth-largest port. Rouen lives up to its status as Normandy's historical capital in offering a superb selection of restaurants serving Norman cuisine. Restaurants are dotted all around the city, with many in the antiques quarter near Eglise St-Maclou and, inevitably, in the old market square. Key local ingredients include fresh fish, cheese, butter, and apples, which are on tantalizing display in the **daily market,** place du Vieux Marché (Tues–Sun 7am–1:30pm). A much larger **food market** is in the more workaday place St-Marc east of the cathedral (Tues, Fri, Sat 6am–6pm, Sun 6am–1:30pm).

La Couronne ★★★ NORMAN It's easy to feel cocooned in the cozy half-timbered interior of France's oldest *auberge,* which has been feeding travellers since 1345. Photos of the great and the good cover the entrance and the upper floor, and a few have left their mark on the menu too. One is Julia Child, whose first-ever French lunch menu in 1948—oysters and *sole meunière*—you can have for 65€). Another menu replicates some of the dishes enjoyed by the Impressionists (35€), including pigs' cheeks that have been braised seemingly forever and are, frankly, sublime.

31 place du Vieux Marché. www.lacouronne.com.fr. ℰ **02-35-71-40-90.** Reservations recommended. Main courses 25€–48€; fixed-price lunch menu 25€–75€; fixed-price dinner menu 35€–75€. Daily noon–2:30pm and 7–10:30pm.

Minute et Mijoté ★★ FRENCH You won't be able to take your eyes off the wonderfully retro decor of this tiny bistro near the Vieux Marché. Practically every collector's item from the 1950 and '60s is crammed into this adorably kitsch space. Start with a creamy foie gras flan in cider sauce, or grilled jumbo shrimp with chorizo risotto. The house specialty, slow-cooked lamb shoulder wrapped in savoy cabbage, just melts in the mouth.

58 rue de Fontenelle. http://minutemijote.canalblog.com. ℰ **02-32-08-40-00.** Reservations recommended. Fixed-price menu 21€–31€. Mon–Sat noon–2pm and 7:30–10pm.

Exploring Rouen

The city's main sights—and the old town—are on the Right Bank of the Seine. Visitors usually make a beeline for **place du Vieux Marché.** Their first impression is often one of bafflement when they see the giant modernist Church of Ste-Jeanne in the place where Joan of Arc was executed for heresy on May 30, 1431. Surrounded by medieval half-timbered restaurants and shops, the church's 1970s architecture comes as a bit of a shock. But it somehow works, with its enormous stained-glass windows and a swirling roof that nudges the neighboring market stalls. A simple sign in the church's garden marks the spot where France's greatest heroine was burnt at the stake.

The pedestrianized "Street of the Great Clock"—**rue du Gros Horloge**—runs between Rouen's cathedral and place du Vieux Marché and is one of the hubs of the city. It's named for an ornate gilt Renaissance clock mounted on an arch over the street and is connected to a bell tower, which you can climb for views of the old town. Open Tuesday to Sunday 10am to 1pm and 2pm to 7pm from April to October, and from

Inside the Cathédrale Notre-Dame de Rouen, Normandy.

2pm to 6pm November to March. Admission 6€ for adults and 3€ for under 18s, including audio guide.

Cathédrale Notre-Dame de Rouen ★★★ CATHEDRAL   Monet immortalized Rouen's cathedral in more than 30 paintings. Consecrated in 1063, this symphony of lacy stonework was reconstructed after World War II. Two towers distinguish it: **Tour de Beurre** was financed by the faithful who paid for the privilege of eating butter during Lent. Containing a carillon of 56 bells, the 1877 **Tour Lanterne** reaches nearly 150m (492 ft.), making its spire the tallest in France.

Inside, the cathedral's choir is a masterpiece, with 14 soaring pillars. Particularly interesting is the **Chapelle de la Vierge,** adorned with Renaissance tombs of the cardinals of Amboise. Also entombed here is the heart of Richard the Lion-Hearted. Along the south-facing side of the cathedral is an entrancing collection of statues of saints that had previously adorned the exterior.

For a bird's-eye view, visit **Le Balcon** (admission 2€; accessed via the Tourist Office), a top-floor viewing platform that tells the story of the cathedral.

Place de la Cathédrale. www.cathedrale-rouen.net. (℡ **02-35-71-51-23.** Free admission. Apr–Oct Mon 2–7pm; Tues–Sat 9am–7pm; Nov–Mar Mon 2–6pm, Tues–Sat 9am–noon and 2–6pm; Sun and holidays year round 8am–6pm. Closed during Mass and some holidays.

Eglise St-Maclou ★★ CHURCH   St-Maclou was built in the Flamboyant Gothic style with a step-gabled porch and cloisters. It's known for the

16th-century panels on its doors; look out for the Portail des Fontaines on the left. The church was built in 1200, rebuilt in 1432, and consecrated in 1521. Its lantern tower is from the 19th century.

Well worth a peek is the nearby **Aître Saint-Maclou,** 184 rue Martainville (*✆* **02-76-08-81-13**). Half-timbered buildings, decorated with creepy skull motifs, mark the site of a cemetery dedicated to victims of the 1348 Great Plague. Open daily 9am until 6pm. Admission is free.

3 place Barthélémy. *✆* **02-32-08-13-90.** Free admission. Apr–Oct Sat–Mon 10am–noon and 2–6pm; Nov–Mar Sat–Mon 10am–noon and 2–5:30pm.

Historial Jeanne d'Arc ★ MUSEUM   The story of France's most tragic heroine is told in this new state-of-the-art exhibition, it's housed in the reopened **Archbishop's Palace,** in the Salle de l'Officialité where Joan of Arc was tried and sentenced to death in 1431. In the same room 25 years later, a new trial declared her innocent. This multimedia exhibition, in atmospheric rooms in the palace, takes visitors back to the 15th century through a series of films, recalling the trial as well as exploring the myths surrounding the Maid of Orléans. Visits are timed to catch each segment, so book ahead for the most suitable time slot. The whole visit lasts about 90 minutes.

Rue Saint-Romain. www.historial-jeannedarc.fr. *✆* **02-35-52-48-00.** Admission 9.50€ adults, 6.50€ students and children 6–17, free for children under 6. Oct–May Tues–Sun 9:45am–7:45pm (until 8:45pm June–Sept).

Musée de la Céramique ★ MUSEUM   Rouen has been an important center for ceramics and pottery production since the 16th century. This small museum highlights local treasures, from reddish-hued 17th- and 18th-century Rouen *faïence* (opaquely glazed earthenware) to two rooms dedicated to 19th- and 20th-century Sèvres porcelain.

1 rue Faucon. www.rouen-musees.com. *✆* **02-35-07-31-74.** Admission 3€ adults, 2€ students, free for children 17 and under. Wed–Mon 2–6pm.

Musée des Beaux-Arts ★★ MUSEUM   More than 8,000 artworks ranging from medieval primitives to contemporary paintings are housed in this imposing 19th-century edifice. You'll find paintings by Ingres, Géricault, Veronese, Velázquez, Caravaggio, Rubens, Poussin, Fragonard, Corot, Renoir, and Sisley, as well as several of Monet's paintings of the cathedral.

Esplanade Marcel Duchamp. www.rouen-musees.com. *✆* **02-35-71-28-40.** Admission 5€ adults, 3€ students. Wed–Mon 10am–6pm.

Panorama XXL ★ MUSEUM   The development of Rouen's Seine riverside continues with the construction of this 35m-high (115-ft.) rotunda, exhibiting enormous circular paintings by the German artist Yadegar Asisi. Three separate platforms give different perspectives of the 360-degree paintings, which change every 6 months or so. Amazonia is the theme until March 2016, followed by an exhibition visualizing Gothic Rouen.

Quai de Boisguilbert. www.panoramaxxl.com. *✆* **02-35-52-95-29.** Admission 9.50€ adults, 6.50€ students. Oct–Apr Tues–Sun 10am–6pm; May–Sep 10am–7pm.

On Normandy's Cider & Calvados Route

In the rolling hills of the Pays d'Auge east of Caen, producers open their half-timbered farms (mostly by appointment) to thirsty tourists eager to try different varieties of apple nectar. Some of the region's most delightful villages lie on this 40km (25-mile) Route du Cidre (www.larouteducidre.fr), notably Cambremer and Beuvron-en-Auge (www.beuvroncambremer.com).

Shopping

Browse the selection of *faïence de Rouen* at **Faïencerie Augy,** 26 rue St-Romain (✆ **02-35-88-77-47**). Rouen also has dozens of **antiques** vendors in the Old Town. The best hunting ground is along **rue Damiette** and **rue St-Romain.** A **flea market** joins the food stalls in place St-Marc on Fridays and Saturdays. Other antiques shops worth visiting are **Galerie Bertran,** 108 rue Molière (✆ **02-35-98-24-06**), with a good selection of 18th- and 19th-century paintings; and the antique books at **Librairie Bertran,** 110 rue Molière (✆ **02-35-70-79-96**).

Chocolate lovers are spoiled for choice, with delectable treats at **Le Cacaotier,** 5 rue Guillaume le Conquérant (www.lecacaotier.com; ✆ **02-35-62-71-06**), and **Auzou,** 163 rue du Gros Horloge (www.auzouchocolat.fr; ✆ **02-35-70-59-31**).

Nightlife

Opéra de Rouen, 7 rue du Docteur Rambert (www.operaderouen.fr; ✆ **02-35-98-74-78**), has ballet, opera, and classical music. At the former hangar **Le 106,** quai Jean de Béthancourt (www.le106.com; ✆ **02-32-10-88-60**), there's a jam-packed lineup of pop and rock shows. Check the Tourist Office's website for the latest events.

Le Vicomté, rue de la Vicomté (✆ **02-35-71-24-11**), attracts everyone from the after-work crowd to clubbers, with five levels devoted to fun and food. There's a club with live bands and DJs.

HONFLEUR ★★

201km (125 miles) NW of Paris; 63km (39 miles) NE of Caen

This exquisite fishing port dating from the 11th century has been the focus of artists for hundreds of years—native sons Eugène Boudin, Gustave Courbet, and Claude Monet, to name but three. Stroll along the **Vieux Bassin** (old harbor) and you can still see art students trying to capture the enchanting light that dances off the glistening water. Impossibly tall 18th-century townhouses tower over the harbor, where restaurants crowd around the pleasure boats.

It's busy and, yes, full of tourists. But it's such a beguiling place that it's worth putting up with the throngs. If you have lunch a bit early, about noon, you'll have the streets to yourself while everyone else is still eating.

The approach from the east is along the Pont de Normandie bridge that spans the Seine River from Le Havre. And the Côte de Grace—the start of the Côte Fleurie—meanders westwards from here en route to Trouville.

Essentials

ARRIVING   There's no direct **train** service into Honfleur. From Paris, take one of the half-dozen daily trains from Gare St-Lazare to Trouville-Deauville (from 25€ one-way). It's cheaper if booked in advance online. From there, **Bus Verts du Calvados** (www.busverts.fr; ℂ **08-10-21-42-14**) no. 20 makes the 25-minute ride to Honfleur; the one-way fare is 2.50€. From Rouen, take the train to Le Havre (15€ one-way; journey time around an hour) and transfer to bus no. 20, 39 or 50 (4.85€ one-way), for the 30-minute ride to Honfleur. Several buses (no. 20) run daily between Caen and Honfleur (trip time: 2 hr.); the one-way fare is 8.55€.

To **drive** from Paris (trip time: 2–2½ hr.; 20€ in tolls), take A13 west, then the A29 north in the direction of Le Havre.

VISITOR INFORMATION   The **Office de Tourisme** is on quai Lepaulmier (www.ot-honfleur.fr; ℂ **02-31-89-23-30**).

[FastFACTS] HONFLEUR

ATMs/Banks   Half a dozen banks are along rue de la Foulerie, place Pierre Berthelot and rue des Longettes.

Mail & Postage   **La Poste,** 7 cours Albert Manuel (ℂ **36-31**).

Pharmacies   **Pharmacie du Dauphin,** 5 rue Dauphin (ℂ **02-31-89-10-80**).

Where to Stay

La Maison de Lucie ★★   Walk less than 10 minutes from the busy port and step into a tranquil world in this 18th-century townhouse. The incredible warmth comes not only from the roaring fire in the reception room but also from the friendly owners. Pleasingly old-fashioned rooms (but with modern fittings) cluster around the internal courtyard, some of which open directly into this flower-filled space. There's also a separate pavilion that houses one of the hotel's attractive suites. Nip into the vaulted cellar of the main house for a dip in the hot tub.

44 rue des Capucins. www.lamaisondelucie.com. ℂ **02-31-14-40-40.** 12 units. 170€–200€ double; 250€–330€ suite. **Amenities:** Spa 40€; free Wi-Fi; parking 15€.

Les Maisons de Léa Hotel & Spa ★★★   In the bustle of place Sainte-Catherine is this ivy-covered collection of 16th-century buildings that make up one of the region's most appealing hotels. The themes vary in this converted salt warehouse and adjoining houses, from Maison Romance—all pale florals and agreeably overstuffed armchairs—to the nautical tones of the Maison Capitaine. Its intimate **Restaurant de Léa** comes up with some beautiful creations. Try the chestnut soup topped with whipped foie gras, or succulent cod with mushroom risotto. Menus from 30€ to 58€.

Place Sainte-Catherine, Honfleur 14600. www.lesmaisonsdelea.com. ℂ **02-31-14-49-49.** 26 units. 170€–260€ double; 285€–320€ suite. **Amenities:** Restaurant; bar; spa; free Wi-Fi; parking 15€.

Where to Eat

There are numerous mediocre restaurants in Honfleur, especially along the Vieux Bassin, that cater for large groups on day trips. If you want better quality food, check out the back streets.

Le Bistro des Artistes ★★ NORMAN   The back of this friendly restaurant overlooks the harbor, so book ahead if you want one of the two tables with waterside views. Chef/owner Anne Marie Carneiro changes her menu regularly but will usually include such regional classics as veal chops à la normande. Anne Marie dishes out the food herself, so don't be impatient if the service is slow. She also runs an adorable little bed and breakfast, **Logis St-Léonard,** on the southern side of town. There are only three rooms (125€ and 155€), one of which has a lovely terrace.

30 place Pierre-Berthelot. www.logis-saint-leonard.com. ℂ **02-31-89-95-90.** Reservations recommended. Main courses 15€–27€. May–Oct Thurs–Tues noon–3pm and 7:30–10pm, Wed 7:30–10pm; Nov–Apr Thurs–Mon noon–3pm and 7:30–10pm.

Le Hamelin ★ NORMAN   This bustling bistro offers seafood of better quality and value than you're likely to find in the Vieux Bassin around the corner. Giant bowls of mussels, delectable shellfish platters, and poached skate with capers keep fish fans happy, while carnivores can feast on slow-cooked lamb and rosemary or veal tenderloin Vallée d'Auge style with apples and a deliciously rich sauce of butter, cream, and Calvados.

16 place Hamelin. www.restaurantlehamelin.com. ℂ **02-31-89-16-85.** Main courses 7.90€–48€. Fixed-price menu 17€–26€. Daily noon–2:30pm and 7–9:30pm.

Exploring Honfleur

Maps from the Tourist Office show three walking routes, all detailing points of interest around town. Stroll along the scenic quays, past the fishing boats and narrow, slate-roofed houses that line the **Vieux Bassin.** On the north side of the harbor, the former governor's house, the imposing **Lieutenance,** dates from the 16th century. Nearby is France's largest wooden church, the 15th-century **Eglise Ste-Catherine,** place Ste-Catherine (ℂ **02-31-89-11-83**). You'll have to cross the street to visit the church's wooden belfry. The church is open daily from 9am to 7pm.

Boat trips (www.promenade-en-bateau-honfleur.fr; 45–90 min.; 6€–9.50€) depart regularly from jetties east of the Vieux Bassin. The 45-minute ride on *La Calypso* explores the harbors that make up the port of Honfleur, while the 90-minute journey on *La Jolie France* takes you out into the Seine estuary.

Les Maisons Satie ★★ MUSEUM   Erik Satie—composer, painter, friend to the Surrealists and Dadaists—was born in this house in 1866, and it's fitting that the museum paying homage to him is just as wonderfully eccentric as the man himself. The entrance's giant pear sculpture sets the stage for some

Monet's Garden at Giverny

Claude Monet spent the last 43 years of his life in creative contentment in his house and gardens in Giverny 75km (47 miles) northwest of Paris. It's just as enchanting as when he lived there with his wife and eight children, surrounded by colorful gardens and ponds decked with the water lilies and green Japanese bridge seen in so many of his paintings. The house and gardens are open daily from 28 March–1 November, 9:30am– 6pm; admission 9.50€ adults, students 5.50€, children under 7 free. Less than a 5-minute walk away is the Musée des Impressionismes Giverny (www.mdig.fr), which puts on temporary exhibitions inspired by Impressionism. If traveling from Paris, take the train from St-Lazare to Vernon, and catch the shuttle to Giverny. Trains cost from 15€ each way; the shuttle costs 8€ round trip. www.fondation-monet.com.

seriously wacky exhibits, enhanced by a suitably strange audio guide. It might not be to everyone's taste, and it's useful to know even a little about his background. *Tip:* Be prepared to apply a little pedal power to get the most out of the exhibit featuring a bicycle.

67 bd. Charles V. www.musees-honfleur.fr. ℂ **02-31-89-11-11.** Admission 6.20€ adults, 4.60€ ages 10–17, free for children 9 and under. May–Sept Wed–Mon 10am–7pm; Oct–Dec and Feb 16-Apr Wed–Mon 11am–6pm. Closed Jan–Feb 15.

Musée Eugène Boudin ★★ MUSEUM   Located in the former chapel of an Augustinian convent, this museum vividly evokes the reasons why so many painters were drawn to Honfleur over the centuries. The works of Honfleur's native son, Eugène Boudin, form part of a fine collection of artworks including paintings by Dubourg, Monet, Courbet, and Dufy, plus vintage photographs, posters, and antiques. It all gives a visually stimulating potted history of the fishing village.

Rue de l'Homme de Bois. www.musees-honfleur.fr. ℂ **02-31-89-54-00.** Admission 6€ adults, 4.50€ students and children 10 and over. May–Sep Wed–Mon 10am–noon and 2–6pm. Closed Oct–Apr.

NaturoSpace ★★ MUSEUM   France's largest tropical butterfly house is a delight. Thousands of colorful specimens flutter through a greenhouselike labyrinth of exotic foliage. Visit in the morning to watch chrysalises crack open and brand-new butterflies make their first flight.

Bd. Charles V. www.naturospace.com. ℂ **02-31-81-77-00.** Admission 8.70€ adults, 6.70€ students and children 3 to 13, family package 34€. Apr–June and Sept daily 9:30am–1pm and 2–6:30pm; July–Aug daily 9:30am–6:30pm; Oct–Nov and Feb–Mar 9:30am–1pm and 2–5:30pm. Closed Dec and Jan.

DEAUVILLE ★★★

206km (128 miles) NW of Paris; 47km (29 miles) NE of Caen

Deauville has been associated with the rich and famous since the Duc de Morny, Napoleon III's half-brother, founded it as an upscale resort in 1859.

Couple exchanging a kiss in Deauville, Normandy.

In 1913, it entered sartorial history when Coco Chanel launched her career here. Chanel cultivated a tradition of elegance that dominates Deauville. It's classy, and understated—precisely the qualities that have been attracting well-heeled Parisians in numbers ever since. They're the ones who unselfconsciously call Deauville the 21st arrondissement of Paris.

Essentials

ARRIVING   There are five to nine daily **rail** connections from Paris's Gare St-Lazare (trip time: 2 hr., but 3 hr. if changing trains in Lisieux); prices start at 15€ one-way. The rail depot is between Trouville and Deauville, within walking distance of both resorts. **Bus Verts du Calvados** (www.busverts.fr; ⓒ **08-10-21-42-14**) run from Caen to Le Havre. To **drive** from Paris (trip time: 2½ hr.), take A13 west to Pont L'Evêque, and then follow D677 north to Deauville.

VISITOR INFORMATION   The **Office de Tourisme** is at 112 rue Victor Hugo (www.deauville.org; ⓒ **02-31-14-40-00**).

SPECIAL EVENTS   For 10 days in late August/early September, the **Deauville American Film Festival** (www.festival-deauville.com; ⓒ **02-31-14-14-14**) honors movies made in the United States. Actors, producers, directors, and writers, from Brad Pitt to Steven Spielberg, flock here. Unlike many film festivals, Deauville's is open to the public.

[FastFACTS] DEAUVILLE

ATMs/Banks   A half-dozen banks cluster on and around rue Eugène-Colas.

Internet Access Various bars offer free Wi-Fi, including **Le Morny's Café**, 6 place Morny ((℃ **02-31-87-32-06**), as well as the Office de Tourisme.

Mail & Postage **La Poste**, 20 rue Robert Fossorier ((℃ **36-31**).

Pharmacies **Pharmacie de Garde**, 8 rue Désiré Le Hoc ((℃ **02-31-14-61-70**).

Where to Stay

Hôtel Barrière Le Royal Deauville ★★★ No hotel epitomizes the epic grandeur of Deauville like the Royal. Guest rooms and suites are a palatial medley of crushed red velvet, plush carpet, and cool marble. Guests enjoy complimentary access to the Royal's beach club and Olympic-size pool or a golf lesson at the prestigious Golf Barrière Club. **Côte Royal** (set menus 50€) is a temple of inventive seafood gastronomy overseen by chef Eric Provost, a one-time understudy of Alain Ducasse and Joël Robuchon.

Boulevard Eugène Cornuché. www.lucienbarriere.com. (℃ **02-31-98-66-33**. 250 units. 275€–910€ double; 765€–7,100€ suite. Parking 15€. Closed Jan–Feb. **Amenities:** Restaurant; children's dining room; bar; babysitting; exercise room; heated outdoor pool; room service; steam room; 2 tennis courts; free bicycles; free Wi-Fi.

L'Augeval ★ Two Norman-style villas make up this immensely charming three-star hotel near the Hippodrome de Deauville-La Touques. It's less than a 10-minute walk from the center, yet it seems a world away in its calm and friendly atmosphere. Rooms in the Trait de l'Union villa are generally more spacious, and those that aren't tucked in under the mansard roof have a balcony or terrace. All have elegant French furnishings, with sumptuous brocades and comfy furniture. The flower-filled gardens are enhanced by a small but heated swimming pool.

15 av. Hocquart-de-Turtot. www.augeval.com. (℃ **02-31-81-13-18**. 40 units. 89€–285€ double; 169€–395€ suite. Parking 8€. **Amenities:** Bar; babysitting; billiards and darts room; exercise room; sauna and steam room 28€ for 30 minutes; outdoor pool; room service; free Wi-Fi.

Where to Eat

Deauville has its share of fine-dining restaurants as well as those that are touristy and overpriced, particularly along rue Eugène Colas. You pay a premium to sit at one of the restaurants along the promenade Les Planches.

Il Parasole ★ ITALIAN This jolly pizzeria proves that you don't have to spend a fortune in Deauville to have an enjoyable meal. Pizzas have perfectly thin crusts and are generous in size, as are the classic pasta dishes such as seafood spaghetti. It gets busy, especially on the terrace, so you might want to book a few hours ahead. There's another branch just over the Touques River in neighboring Trouville.

6 rue Hoche. www.ilparasole.com. (℃ **02-31-88-64-64**. Main courses 9.50€–24€. Daily noon–3pm and 7–midnight. Open non-stop in July and August.

La Cantine de Deauville ★ FRENCH You won't leave hungry in this lively brasserie with an airy, modern ambience. It's the place to come for hearty plates of beef, notably huge steaks (suitably called "Gargantua"). If you want something a bit lighter, try the cod *meunière*. The two-course lunchtime menu at 17€ is particularly good value. La Cantine is certainly a breath of fresh air among the touristy restaurants along Eugène Colas.

90 rue Eugène Colas. www.lacantinedeauville.fr. ℂ **02-31-87-47-47.** Main courses 17€–32€. Tues–Sun 9am–11pm.

Le Ciro's Barrière ★★★ FRENCH/SEAFOOD   From its excellent vantage point on Les Planches, you get some of Deauville's best people-watching to go with some top-class seafood. It may be pricey, but Norman chef Jérôme Taquet's superb cuisine is worth it. For a luxurious appetizer, try grilled langoustines with foie gras and chestnuts before indulging yourself further with a fricassee and bisque of blue lobster.

Planches de Deauville, boulevard de la Mer. www.lucienbarriere.com. ℂ **02-31-14-31-14.** Reservations required. Main courses 33€–52€. Thurs–Mon noon–2pm (Sat–Sun till 2:30pm) and 7:30–10pm (Sat 10:30pm). Daily July–Aug. Closed 2 weeks in Jan.

Exploring Deauville

Some of the architecture in Deauville looks as if it has stepped out of a gothic fairy tale. The style is ostensibly Norman—lots of half-timbered buildings mostly in muted shades. But then you see turrets sprouting here and there, with gables and balconies wedged into every nook and cranny. It's as if a French version of the Addams Family had a hand in designing some of these glorious confections. The overall effect is delightful, enhanced by the profusion of flowers in the public spaces. Indulge in a bit of people-watching along **rue Eugène-Colas, place Morny,** and **place du Casino.**

Outdoor Activities

BEACHES   Deauville's boardwalk, **Les Planches,** is an impossibly pretty promenade running parallel to the town's 2km (1¼-mile) beach, **Plage de Deauville.** Deauville's distinctive primary-colored parasols dot the sands— even out of season. Visitors parade along the boardwalk past private bathing cabins, each one's entrance stenciled with the names of Hollywood stars who have attended the Deauville American Film Festival.

Access to every beach in Normandy is free, although beach clubs cover some stretches of sand. You can rent a beach umbrella from 11€ a day and a sunlounger for 6€. A bathing cabin costs from 10€–20€ a day. Parking costs from 2€ per hour in the public lots.

The **Piscine Municipale,** boulevard de la Mer (ℂ 02-31-14-02-17), is a large indoor seawater pool. Depending on the season, bathers pay 4.50€ to 5€ per person. Swimming caps are compulsory and, as in every municipal swimming pool in France, men have to wear Speedo-style trunks.

The nearby **Thalasso Deauville,** 3 rue Sem (ℂ 02-31-87-72-00), was recently refurbished and offers plenty of ways to spend a self-indulgent day at the spa. The seawater pool has underwater jets and pulsating fountains, and you'll find private couples' cabins with hot tubs and saunas as well as fitness and steam rooms. Spa access starts at 35€.

A day out IN TROUVILLE

Hugging the eastern bank of the Touques River is Deauville's less fashionable—but no less fascinating—neighbor Trouville. Deauville might have the chic boutiques, but Trouville has the soul of a working fishing port. Cross the Touques at the Pont des Belges and you immediately see the change in atmosphere. The large fish market, **Marché aux Poissons,** teems with stalls and small cafes selling the freshest seafood. More restaurants line the quayside, which becomes even livelier every Wednesday and Sunday during the open-air food market.

The bustle of Trouville's quayside carries on into the narrow alleyways that wind behind the port. It's a pleasure to get lost here among the many restaurants and little shops that somehow squeeze into the haphazard collection of lanes. Eventually you'll come to the grand Victorian villas along **Les Planches,** the first seaside boardwalk on the Normandy coast, dating back to 1867. In those days, artists and writers including Gustave Flaubert, Marguerite Duras, and Claude Monet flocked to Trouville's beach, **Plage de Trouville,**

captivated by the light and air. Nowadays it's a firm favorite with families, with a giant children's play area, donkey rides, and tennis courts. There's also the **Piscine de Trouville – Le Complex Nautique du Front de Mer** (𝄐 02-31-14-48-10), an indoor freshwater pool plus an outdoor pool that's open in July and August. Depending on the season, bathers pay 2.50€ to 5.50€ per person. Open daily July and August 10am to 6:45pm, other months open daily but with varying closing times during lunchtime.

For lunch, browse the Marché aux Poissons' stalls and take your pick of fresh seafood before asking to have your food prepared to eat straight away. Grab a glass of muscadet, then perch at one of the high tables surrounding the market and devour. Pick of the bunch is **Poissonnerie Pillet Saiter,** bd. Fernand Moureaux (www.poissonnerie-pilletsaiter.fr; 𝄐 **02-31-88-02-10**), which also has weekend specials.

Trouville's **Office de Tourisme** is at 32 quai Fernand-Moureaux (www.trouvillesurmer.org; 𝄐 **02-31-14-60-70**).

HORSE RACES/POLO You can watch horses—either racing or competing at polo—most days from late June to early September. The venues are the **Hippodrome de Deauville-La Touques,** 45 av. Hocquart de Turtot (www.france-galop.com; 𝄐 **02-31-14-20-00**), near the Mairie de Deauville (town hall); and the **Hippodrome de Deauville Clairefontaine,** route de Clairefontaine (www.hippodrome-deauville-clairefontaine.com; 𝄐 **02-31-14-69-00**), 2km (1¼ miles) west of the center. Tickets normally cost 5€ for adults, free for those under 18.

Shopping

Luxury boutiques such as Hermès, Ralph Lauren, and Louis Vuitton cluster around the **place du Casino.** For more affordable shops, including the Printemps department store, stroll along **rue Eugène-Colas** and **place Morny.**

To see Norman produce in all its glory, head for the **Marché Publique** (open-air market) in place du Marché beside place Morny. In July and August, it's open daily 8am to 1pm. The rest of the year, market days are Tuesday, Friday, and Saturday, as well as Sunday from February to November.

Nightlife

The **Casino de Deauville,** rue Edmond Blanc (www.lucienbarriere.com; *✆* **02-31-14-31-14**), has been one of France's foremost casinos since it opened in 1912. Within the Belle Epoque structure are a theater, Le Brummel nightclub, three restaurants, two bars, and slot machines *(machines à sous).* There are more formal zones containing such table games *(jeux de table)* as roulette. The slots are open daily 10am to 2am (to 3am Fri and 4am Sat). Table games are open Monday to Thursday 4pm to 2am (to 3am Fri and 4am Sat) and Sunday 2:30pm to 2am. Entrance is free, and you must present a passport or I.D. to enter. No official dress code; just dress smartly.

Clubbers head for **Le Chic,** 14 rue Désiré-le-Hoc (www.lechicdeauville.fr; *✆* **02-31-88-30-91**), a favorite with French actors and off-duty jockeys. Polo players frequent the perennially popular **Brok Café,** 14 av. du Général-de-Gaulle (*✆* **02-31-81-30-81**). Hit this Cuban-style venue before midnight.

Les Planches, Domain du Bois Lauret, Blonville (www.lesplanches.com; *✆* **02-31-87-58-09**), 4km (2½ miles) from Deauville, attracts gilded young Parisians with its world-class DJs, dance floor, and swimming pool next to the indoor/outdoor bar. It's open from 11pm until dawn every Saturday except in January and February and daily in July and August.

CAEN ★

238km (148 miles) NW of Paris; 119km (74 miles) SE of Cherbourg

Situated on the banks of the Orne, the port of Caen suffered great damage in the 1944 invasion of Normandy. Mercifully, though, the twin abbeys founded by William the Conqueror and his wife, Mathilda, were spared. Today much of Caen is cosmopolitan and commercial, with a vibrant, welcoming vibe. The capital of Lower Normandy, it's home to a student population of 30,000 and several great museums, and is a convenient base for the surrounding coast.

Essentials

ARRIVING   From Paris's Gare St-Lazare, between 12 and 15 **trains** a day arrive in Caen (trip time: 2–2½ hr.). The fare is 15€ one-way. One-way fares from Rouen (trip time: 1 hr., 45 min.) start at 10€. To **drive** from Paris, travel west along A13 to Caen (drive time: 2½–3 hr.).

VISITOR INFORMATION   The **Office de Tourisme** is on place St-Pierre in the 16th-century Hôtel d'Escoville (www.caen-tourisme.fr; *✆* **02-31-27-14-14**).

CITY LAYOUT   Downtown Caen stretches from Abbaye aux Dames in the east to Abbaye aux Hommes in the west. The pedestrianized rue St-Pierre bisects the town's main shopping district. The train station is southeast of the city center. The towering ramparts of the hilltop Château de Caen are a useful landmark.

Getting Around

ON FOOT Caen's city center is small and much of it is pedestrianized. It's easy to explore the town on foot.

BY BICYCLE Caen has its own bike-sharing scheme, **V'eol** (www.veol. caen.fr). You can register online (where you can also download a map of the city's bike paths) or at one of 40 bike stands; fees start at 1€ for the first 30 minutes.

BY CAR It's best to park and explore on foot. The Tourist Office website offers a downloadable map (under "Transport"), marked with the major parking lots. Among others, there is one behind the train station, three south of the Château and one underground in front of the Château.

BY TAXI **Taxis Abbeilles,** 54 place de la Gare (www.taxis-abbeilles-caen. com; © **02-31-52-17-89**).

BY PUBLIC TRANSPORT The **Twisto bus and tram network** (www. twisto.fr; © **02-31-15-55-55**) crisscrosses the city. Most useful for visitors is the tram. The north-south two lines (A and B) overlap through the city center, passing all of Caen's major monuments en route. Tickets (1.40€) can be purchased from automatic kiosks at each station.

[FastFACTS] CAEN

ATMs/Banks The city center has plenty of banks, including five on rue Jean Eudes.
Doctors & Hospitals **Centre Hospitalier Universitaire de Caen,** av. de la Côte de Nacre (www.chu-caen.fr; © **02-31-06-31-06**).
Mail & Postage **La Poste,** 2 rue Georges Lebret (© **36-31**).
Pharmacies **Pharmacie du Château,** 27 av. Libération ((© **02-31-93-64-78**).

Where to Stay

Best Western Hotel le Dauphin ★ Three separate buildings—one built on the site of a 15th-century priory—make up this friendly and rather quirky hotel. It's wonderfully central, just steps away from the Château and restaurants and shops. The rooms can be a bit compact but they're full of charm, some with exposed brickwork and cute little alcoves. Ask for a room in the tower, which will give you lovely views of the Château.

29 rue Gémare. www.le-dauphin-normandie.com. © **02-31-86-22-26**. 37 units. 100€– 190€ double. Parking free but limited. **Amenities:** Restaurant; bar; spa; room service; free Wi-Fi.

Le Clos St-Martin ★★ Sylvie and Jean Noël run this intimate, four-room bed and breakfast. The three antique-splashed suites (one of which can be booked as a family room) and one double are set over three floors of a rambling 16th-century mansion near the Abbaye aux Hommes. Breakfast is superb, and often includes Sylvie's baked treats, such as *teurgoule,* Norman rice pudding.

18bis place Saint Martin. www.leclosaintmartin.com. (C) **07-81-39-23-67.** 4 units. 90€– 150€ double and suite, including breakfast. Public parking nearby. **Amenities:** Breakfast room; free Wi-Fi.

Where to Eat

A large student population helps to make Caen's dining scene one of the most dynamic in Normandy. Sidewalk cafes and restaurants line rue du Vaugueux and the surrounding neighborhood.

A Contre Sens ★★ FRENCH/NORMAN   Anthony Caillot's Michelin-starred restaurant soon built up a buzz in Caen after it opened in 2009. And no wonder: This highly inventive chef has put the fun back into dining. You could play it safe and go à la carte, but it's much more rewarding to put yourself in Caillot's hands for the "intuition" menu of five or seven courses (three at lunch). The menu changes constantly, and relies heavily on seasonal market produce, but little Asian touches such as guinea fowl with a hint of curry are inspired. *Note:* The restaurant is tiny, so reservations should be made several weeks in advance.

8 rue des Croisiers. www.acontresenscaen.fr. (C) **02-31-97-44-48.** Reservations required. Main courses 30€–35€; fixed-price lunch 25€–54€; fixed-price dinner 54€–64€. Wed–Sat noon–3:15pm; Tues–Sat 7:30–9:15pm.

Le Bouchon du Vaugueux ★★ FRENCH   Everything comes together perfectly in this lively yet intimate little bistro. Warm and friendly ambience, excellent service and, above all, beautifully prepared and unfussy regional dishes. The seasonal menu changes but could include salmon grilled on a plancha with tomato risotto, pork braised in local beer, and, of course, superb Normandy cheeses. There aren't many tables, so book ahead.

12 rue Graindorge. www.bouchonduvaugueux.com. (C) **02-31-44-26-26.** Reservations highly recommended. Fixed-price lunch 16€–24€; fixed-price dinner 21€–33€. Tues–Sat noon–2pm, Tues–Thurs 7–10pm, Fri–Sat 7–10:30pm. Closed 2 weeks Sept.

Exploring Caen

A fun way to visit Caen's major sites is to follow the self-guided **William the Conqueror Circuit.** Maps can be picked up at the Tourist Office, from where the walking tour departs.

Abbaye aux Dames ★ RELIGIOUS SITE   William the Conqueror's wife Mathilda founded this abbey around 1060, which embraces Eglise de la Trinité and its Romanesque towers. Its spires were destroyed in the Hundred Years' War. The 12th-century choir houses Mathilda's tomb.

Place Reine Mathilde. (C) **02-31-06-98-45.** Free admission. Daily 2–5:30pm. Free guided 1-hr. tour of choir, transept, and crypt (in French) daily 2:30 and 4pm.

Abbaye aux Hommes ★★ RELIGIOUS SITE   Founded by William the Conqueror in 1066 to ensure papal pardon for marrying his distant cousin Mathilda, this abbey is next to the Eglise St-Etienne. During the height of the Allied invasion, residents of Caen fled to St-Etienne for protection. Twin

Romanesque towers 84m-tall (276 ft.) dominate the church, and a simple marble slab inside the high altar marks William's burial place. The hand-carved wooden doors and an elaborate wrought-iron staircase are exceptional.

Esplanade Jean-Marie Louvel. ℂ **02-31-30-42-81.** 4.50€–7€ adults, 3.50€–5.50€ students depending on the season, free for children 17 and under. Obligatory tours (50–90 min.) July–Aug daily 10am, 11am, 12:30pm, 2pm, 3pm, 4pm and 5:30pm (in English Mon–Fri 11am, 1:30pm, and 4pm); Apr–June and Sept daily 10:30am, 2:30pm and 4pm; Oct–Mar Mon–Fri 10:30am and 2:30pm, Sat no tours but cloisters open, Sun tours during French school holidays 10:30am, 2:30pm and 4pm.

Le Château de Caen ★★ CASTLE   This castle complex was built on the ruins of a fortress erected by William the Conqueror in 1060. Climb to the top of the extensive ramparts for sublime views over Caen. Within the medieval compound are two museums. The **Musée de Normandie** (www.musee-de-normandie.caen.fr; ℂ **02-31-30-47-60**) displays local archaeological finds, along with a collection of regional sculpture, paintings, and ceramics. Admission is 3.50€–5.50€ depending on the exhibition, free for under-26s, and it's open daily 9:30am to 6pm (closed Tues Nov–May). The **Musée des Beaux-Arts** (www.mba.caen.fr; ℂ **02-31-30-47-70**) has a collection of Old Masters including Veronese, Tintoretto, and Rubens. Admission is 3.50€/2.50€ for the permanent collection and 5.50€/3.50€ for permanent and temporary exhibitions; free for under-26s. Open Wednesday to Monday 9:30am to 6pm.

Esplanade de la Paix, rue de Geôle, av. de la Libération. www.chateau.caen.fr.

Le Mémorial de Caen (Caen Memorial) ★★★ MONUMENT/ MEMORIAL   This is not a museum to be rushed through, as it explores history from 1918 to the present day in engrossing exhibits. It puts the 20th century in context by starting with the end of the First World War, leading to the horrors of the second and beyond to the Cold War. Temporary exhibits explore current conflicts. Civilian stories are told in heartbreaking detail, along with courageous tales of Allied soldiers. Not surprisingly, there is a large exhibition dedicated to D-Day, as well as the headquarters used by German General Richter during the war. The museum's cafe is a good spot to relax in between exhibits.

Esplanade Général Eisenhower. www.memorial-caen.fr. ℂ **02-31-06-06-44.** Admission 19€ adults, 17€ students and children 10–18; free to World War II veterans, those with war disabilities, war widows, and children 9 and under. Feb 7–Nov 1 daily 9am–7pm; Nov 2–Dec 31 Tues–Sun 9:30am–6pm. Closed Jan.

Shopping

Caen has some excellent boutique-lined shopping streets, including **boulevard du Maréchal-Leclerc, rue St-Pierre,** and **rue de Strasbourg. Antiques** hunters should check out the shops along **rue Ecuyère.** The **market** at place Courtonne on Sunday morning sells secondhand goodies.

For foodie souvenirs, **Hotot Chocolaterie,** 13 rue St-Pierre (ℂ **02-31-86-31-90**), has chocolate products as well as local jams. Find regional items at

Le Comptoir Normand, 7 rue de Geôle (www.lecomptoir-normand.com; ℂ **02-31-86-34-13**), including Calvados and charcuterie products.

Nightlife

Check out the action along rue de Bras, rue St-Pierre, and rue Vaugueux. Young hipsters go to **Le Chic,** 19 rue des Prairies St-Gilles (ℂ **02-31-94-48-72**), where dance music begins around 11:30pm. For offbeat international gigs, head to **Le Cargö,** 9 quai Caffarelli, Port de Caen (www.lecargo.fr; ℂ **02-31-86-79-31**).

Day Trip from Caen

MONT-ST-MICHEL ★★★

324km (201 miles) W of Paris; 129km (80 miles) SW of Caen; 48km (30 miles) E of St-Malo

A UNESCO World Heritage Site, Mont-St-Michel is one of the most alluring spots on France's northern coast. The fortified island seems to float on a shifting bed of sand and sea. Once a bastion marking the border between Normandy and Brittany, then a place of monastic retreat, this Disney-like castle now attracts 3 million visitors every year. In summer it's exceptionally busy, but enthralling nevertheless.

Essentials

France's biggest tourist attraction outside of Paris has been undergoing major changes over the past few years. Before 2012, the causeway linking the island with the mainland was crammed with parked cars, and the bay was in danger of silting up. To restore Mont St-Michel to its island status, the authorities have built a **new approach** and banished cars to a parking lot by a new visitor center, the **Tourist Information Centre,** Lieu-dit le Bas Pays, 50170 Beauvoir (www.bienvenueaumontsaintmichel.com; ℂ **02-14-13-20-15**). Free shuttle buses take visitors to the island 2.5km (1½ miles) away. Parking costs 13€ for 24 hours, free for stays of less than 30 minutes. Driving time from Paris is about 3½ hours.

It's a 50-minute hike to the island across the shifting sands. Those with their own bike can pedal over. During high tide, the island is cut off for about an hour. An additional **Office de Tourisme** is on the island itself, to the left of the gates (www.ot-montsaintmichel.com; ℂ **02-33-60-14-30**). Both tourist centers are open daily year round.

There are no direct **trains** between Paris and Mont-St-Michel. One option is to take a local TER train from Paris's Gare Saint-Lazare to Caen (www.voyages-sncf.com; ℂ **36-35**), then another local TER train to Pontorson, where a 3.20€ shuttle bus ferries passengers directly to the visitor center. Another is to take a TGV (fast train) from Paris to Rennes in Brittany, from where a coach takes you to Mont St-Michel for 10€ each way.

Exploring Mont-St-Michel

Once you reach the island, you'll have a steep climb up Grande Rue, lined with 15th- and 16th-century houses and souvenir shops, to reach its **abbey**

Abbey in Mont-St-Michel.

(http://mont-saint-michel. monuments-nationaux.fr; ℭ **02-33-89-80-00**). Ramparts encircle the church and a three-tiered ensemble of 13th-century buildings called **La Merveille** (The Wonder) that rise up to the abbey's pointed spire. This terraced complex is one of Europe's most important Gothic monuments. On the second terrace of La Merveille is one of Mont-St-Michel's largest and most beautiful spaces, a 13th-century hall known as the **Salle des Chevaliers.** Crowning the mount's summit is the spellbinding **Eglise Abbatiale** church.

The abbey is open daily May to August 9am to 7pm, and September to April 9:30am to 6pm. Entrance includes an English-language group tour when available, but you can also explore on your own. Admission is 9€ adults, 7€ for non-European Union nationals aged 18 to 25, and free for European Union nationals aged 18 to 25 and children 17 and under.

Most visitors are content to wander around the medieval ramparts. There is also the **Musée de la Mer,** Grande Rue (ℭ **02-33-60-85-12**), which showcases marine crafts throughout history and the ecology of the local tidal flats. Another museum worth visiting is the **Logis Tiphaine,** Grande Rue (ℭ **02-33-89-02-02**), a 14th-century home originally under the control of the Duguesclin family. Both museums are open daily from 9.30am to 5pm, and cost 9€ for adults, free for children 18 and under. You can buy a pass for 18€ that covers the cost of four museums.

For a different perspective, join one of the guided walks from the mainland to the island, tracing the original pilgrim route. **Chemins de la Baie** (www. cheminsdelabaie.com; ℭ **02-33-89-80-88**) takes groups on various barefoot walks across the sands. Some include picnics and a return via bicycle, and others have a commentary in English but need a minimum number of participants.

Where to Stay & Eat

If you plan to stay overnight on the island, be prepared to pay a premium. And **travel light:** The hotels are a long, uphill walk on cobblestoned streets from where the shuttle bus drops you off. **Auberge Saint-Pierre,** Grand Rue (www.auberge-saint-pierre.fr; ℭ **02-33-60-14-03**), has small but charming double rooms from 217€. On the same winding street, **Crêperie La Sirène** (ℭ **02-33-60-08-60**) makes an appealing stop for lunch of the savory buckwheat crêpe known as galettes, stuffed with gooey cheese and ham, followed by a sweet crêpe for dessert.

BAYEUX ★★

267km (166 miles) NW of Paris; 25km (16 miles) NW of Caen

Bayeux's medieval heart was spared bombardment in 1944, and was the first town to be liberated—the day after D-Day, in fact. Its half-timbered houses, stone mansions, cobblestoned streets, and ancient watermills have remained more or less intact, making this pleasant town a joy to explore. It does get busy in the summer—with the double whammy of the D-Day beaches and the extraordinary historical document that is the Bayeux Tapestry.

Essentials

ARRIVING   Nine **trains** depart daily from Paris's Gare St-Lazare, with most changing in Caen. The 2½-hour trip to Bayeux costs from 22€. Travel time between Caen and Bayeux is about 15–20 minutes and costs 6.80€. To **drive** to Bayeux from Paris (trip time: 3 hr.), take A13 to Caen and E46 west to Bayeux.

VISITOR INFORMATION   The **Office de Tourisme** is at Pont St-Jean (www.bessin-normandie.com; ℭ **02-31-51-28-28**).

SPECIAL EVENTS   The town goes wild on the first weekend in July during **Fêtes Médiévales** (www.fetesmedievales.bayeux.fr; ℭ **02-31-92-03-30**); the streets fill with market stalls, costumes, and themed treats during 2 days of medieval revelry. In mid-June, Bayeux is the finishing point for the annual **Tour de Normandie** (www.tourdenormandie.com; ℭ **06-28-33-00-75**), a classic car race that winds through the countryside in elegant style.

[FastFACTS] BAYEUX

ATMs/Banks   There are banks throughout town, particularly along rue Saint-Malo.

Internet Access   **Médiathèque Municipale,** Centre Guillaume Le Conquérant, rue aux Coqs (ℭ **02-31-51-20-20**), has Internet access and Wi-Fi.

Mail & Postage   **La Poste** rue Larcher (ℭ **36-31**).

Pharmacies   **Pharmacie St-Martin,** 20 rue St-Martin (ℭ **02-31-92-00-22**).

Where to Stay

Villa Lara ★★★   In a dreamy spot by the watermills of the Aure River is what is probably the best hotel in Bayeux. Four-star Villa Lara has been open only since 2012, but it has already built up a dedicated following. Its spacious rooms—some with balconies and views of Bayeux's cathedral—have sumptuous and classic French furnishings of velvet and brocade, complemented by modern marble bathrooms. Its contemporary exterior is subtle and classy enough not to stand out like a sore thumb among its medieval neighbors. You'll find it hard to tear yourself away from the cozy lounge, but when you do, you'll find a welcoming staff eager to organize tours to the D-Day beaches and Mont St-Michel.

6 place de Québec. www.hotel-villalara.com. © **02-31-92-00-55.** 28 units. 180€–350€ double; 290€–520€ suite. Free parking. **Amenities:** Breakfast room; gym; free Wi-Fi. Closed Dec–Feb.

Where to Eat

Bayeux has plenty of informal cafes offering quick snacks for visitors touring the D-Day beaches or seeing the tapestry. There are, however, a couple of special places worth checking out.

Le Pommier ★ NORMAN   Around the corner from the town's cathedral, this cozy restaurant with a big fireplace stands out. Its owners Thierry and Isabelle champion Norman cuisine and make superb use of local ingredients such as pork, seafood and even the famous *tripes à la mode de Caen.*

38–40 rue des Cuisiniers. www.restaurantlepommier.com. © **02-31-21-52-10.** Reservations recommended. Fixed-price menus 21€–25€. Daily noon–2:30pm and 7–9:30pm (closed Sun Nov–Mar).

Le Volet qui Penche ★★ NORMAN   Pierre-Henri Lemessier's wine shop doubles as a wine bar and bistro with a very limited menu. It's a picky eater's nightmare, and a delight for everyone else who enjoys beautifully cooked regional cuisine matched with expertly chosen wines in a convivial atmosphere. The menu depends on what Pierre-Henri has picked up at the market; he certainly knows his wines and will suggest the perfect match for your tastes—and budget.

3 impasse de l'Islet. www.levoletquipenche.com. © **02-31-21-98-54.** Fixed-price menus 9.50€–18€. Tues–Fri 9am–8pm, Sat 5–8pm, after 8pm reservations required.

Exploring Bayeux

This compact town is best explored on foot. At its heart in rue du Général de Dais is **Cathédrale Notre-Dame de Bayeux,** a Norman medieval structure consecrated in 1077 in the presence of William the Conqueror. It's open daily 8:30am to 7pm. Admission is free. Guided tours cost 5€ for adults and 3€ students and children 11 to 17 (free for under 11s) and include visits to the Treasure Room and the Chapter House.

Musée d'Art et d'Histoire Baron Gérard (MAHB) ★ MUSEUM

This airy museum is set within the town's ancient bishop's palace, much of it constructed during the Middle Ages. Exhibitions range from local archaeological finds to regional lacework and delicate porcelain, as well as more than 600 regional artworks created between the 15th and 20th centuries.

Bayeux Tapestry.

37 rue du Bienvenu. www.bayeuxmuseum.com. ℂ **02-31-92-14-21.** Admission 7€ adults, 5.50€ students, 4€ children, free for children 9 and under. May–Sept daily 9:30am–6:30pm; Oct–Apr daily 10am–12:30pm and 2–6pm. Closed Jan–Feb 15.

Musée de la Tapisserie de Bayeux ★★★ MUSEUM   This, arguably the most famous tapestry in the world, is actually an elaborate embroidery on linen, measuring 69m (226 ft.) long and 50cm (20 in.) wide. It depicts 58 scenes in eight colors and was likely created in Kent between 1066 and 1077.

Housed in a 270-degree glass case that sweeps along a low-lit tunnel-like room, this masterpiece tells the story of the conquest of England by William the Conqueror. Make certain you use the free and informative audio guide: It really brings the story to life. And don't ignore the detail in the motifs at the top and bottom of the cloth: Some of them will surprise you. A separate section is dedicated to the creation of the tapestry, and also evokes life in the Middle Ages through scale models and maps.

Centre Guillaume le Conquérant, 13 bis rue de Nesmond. www.bayeuxmuseum.com. ℂ **02-31-51-25-50.** Admission 9€ adults, 4€ students, free for children 9 and under. Mar–Oct daily 9am–6:30pm (May–Aug until 7pm); Nov–Dec daily 9:30am–12:30pm and 2–6pm. Closed 3 weeks in Jan.

Musée Memorial de la Bataille de Normandie ★ MUSEUM   In this low-slung bunkerlike building are window displays of military history, details of the beach landings, and examples of the tanks and weapons used to win the battle. Across from the museum, the **Commonwealth Cemetery** contains 4,144 graves of British Commonwealth soldiers who were killed during the Battle of Normandy.

Bd. Fabian Ware. www.bayeuxmuseum.com. $\textcircled{C}$ **02-31-51-46-90.** Admission 7€ adults, 4€ students and children, free for children 9 and under. May–Sept daily 9:30am–6:30pm; Oct–Apr daily 10am–12:30pm and 2–6pm. Closed Jan–Feb 15.

THE D-DAY BEACHES

A visit to the beaches where the greatest invasion force of all time landed is a must for anyone visiting Normandy's north coast. The 70th anniversary of the invasion in 2014 was the occasion for new events and museum openings to mark this momentous battle.

It was a rainy week in early June 1944 when the greatest armada ever assembled along the southern coast of England. A full moon and cooperative tides were needed for the cross-Channel invasion. Britain's top meteorologist for the USAAF and RAF—Sir James Stagg—forecast a small window in the inclement weather. Over in France, Nazi officers drifted home for the weekend, thinking that no landing could take place soon.

Supreme Allied Commander Dwight D. Eisenhower believed Stagg's reports. With the British invasion commander, Field Marshal Montgomery, Eisenhower made the ultimate call. At 9:15pm on June 5, the BBC used coded messages to announce to Normandy's French Resistance that the invasion was imminent.

Before midnight, Allied planes began bombing the Norman coast. By 1:30am on June 6 ("the Longest Day," and what the French call *Jour-J*), members of the 101st Airborne were parachuting to the ground on German-occupied French soil. At 6:30am, the Americans began landing on the beaches, code-named Utah and Omaha. An hour later, British and Canadian forces made beachheads at Juno, Gold, and Sword, swelling the number of Allied troops in Normandy to a massive 135,000. The push to Paris—and Berlin—had begun.

Transport & Accommodations

A **car** is practically essential to explore the D-Day Beaches at leisure. Each monument, museum, and beach has plenty of parking. **Bus Verts** (www.busverts.fr; $\textcircled{C}$ **08-10-21-42-14**) runs buses from Bayeux to Arromanches (no. 74) and from Bayeux to Omaha Beach and the American Cemetery (no. 70) every few hours for 2.50€ per trip. Several group tours also cover the D-Day Beaches. From Bayeux, **Normandy Tours,** Hotel de la Gare (www.normandy-landing-tours.com; $\textcircled{C}$ **02-31-92-10-70**), runs a 4-hour tour (in English) to Arromanches, Omaha Beach, the American Military Cemetery, and Pointe du Hoc for 62€ adults and 55€ students and seniors. From Caen, the **Caen Memorial Museum,** Esplanade Général Eisenhower (www.memorial-caen.fr; $\textcircled{C}$ **02-31-06-06-45**), conducts full-day (117€) tours, including lunch and access to Caen's museum. A half-day trip costs 65€ or 82€, depending on departure time.

Although the D-Day beaches are easily visited on a day trip, there are numerous countryside B&Bs and hotels. In the pretty village of Port-en-Bessin, midway between Colleville and Arromanches, the **Mercure Omaha Beach,** Chemin du Colombier (www.omaha-beach-hotel.com; ✆ **02-31-22-44-44**), is a convenient base for exploring the sites. Double rooms start at 120€.

Reliving the Longest Day

Few places in the world have a more concentrated—or more moving—selection of sights than Normandy's D-Day Beaches. More than 30 memorials, cemeteries, and museums are spread out along this 50km (31-mile) stretch of coast. The most spellbinding site for all nationalities is the **Normandy American Visitor Center ★★★**, behind Omaha Beach at Colleville-sur-Mer (www.abmc.gov; ✆ **02-31-51-62-00**). The graves of 10,000 Allies who liberated mainland France lie within 70 hectares (173 acres) of grounds above the cliffs. The visitor center retells the dramatic story of the landings on the morning of June 6, 1944. Most dramatic of all are the personal tales. Leave enough time for a good look at the exhibitions; they really are captivating. Admission is free. The cemetery is open daily 9am to 6pm from April 14–Sept 15, and until 5pm the rest of the year. Visitors may also wander down to Omaha Beach itself and explore the bunkers. At 4:30pm, you can watch the Lowering of the Colors, where the American flag is lowered in a poignant ritual.

The **Overlord Museum,** Colleville-sur-Mer (www.overlordmuseum.com; ✆ **02-31-22-00-55**), is half a mile uphill from the Normandy American Visitor Center. More than 10,000 pieces of *matériel* and 35 military vehicles are showcased in D-Day dioramas around a great hall. Admission is 7.50€ adults and 5.50€ students and children; free for children under 10. Open daily 10am–5pm Feb, Nov, Dec; 10am–6pm Mar–May and Oct; 9:30am–7pm June–Aug; 9:30am–6pm Sept; closed Jan–Feb.

Farther west along the coast, you'll see the jagged lime cliffs of the **Pointe du Hoc.** A cross honors a group of American Rangers who scaled the cliffs to get at the gun emplacements. The pockmarked landscape has a lunar look, with giant craters showing where the bombs fell. Farther along the Cotentin Peninsula is **Utah Beach,** where the 4th U.S. Infantry Division landed at 6:30am. A U.S. monument commemorates their heroism.

Eastward along the coast in the British invasion sector is the seaside resort of **Arromanches-les-Bains.** A deep-water port was deemed essential to Allied success, so in June 1944, two mammoth prefabricated ports known as Mulberry Harbours were towed across the Channel. The one that landed in Arromanches was nicknamed Port Winston; its wreckage is still visible just off the beach. Arromanches's **Plage Musée du Débarquement,** place du 6-Juin (www.musee-arromanches.fr; ✆ **02-31-22-34-31**), illuminates the scale of the D-Day landings through maps, models, a cinema, photos, and a diorama of the landing beaches. Admission is 7.90€ adults and 5.80€ students

Graves at the Normandy American Visitor Center.

and children. May to August, hours are daily 9am to 7pm (Oct–Mar daily 10am–12:30pm and 1:30pm–5pm; Apr and Sept till 6pm; closed Jan).

Less than a 10-minute walk uphill from the museum is **Arromanches 360 Circular Cinema,** chemin du Calvaire (www.arromanches360.com; ✆ **02-31-06-06-45**), which relives the Normandy invasion in a compelling film shown on nine high-definition screens. Admission is 5€ adults and 4.50€ for students and children aged 10 to 17. Open daily April to May and Sept 10:10am to 6:10pm; other times vary; closed Mon in early February and late November. Films are shown at 10 and 40 minutes past each hour.

Eastward again through the British and Canadian invasion sectors is **Musée Gold Beach ★★**, 2 place Amiral Byrd, Ver-sur-Mer (www.goldbeachmusee.fr; ✆ **02-31-22-58-58**). The museum focuses on the heroism of Britain's RAF and Royal Navy. Admission is 4.50€ adults and 2.50€ students and children. From April to October, hours are daily 10:30am to 5:30pm (closed Tues Apr–June and Sept–Oct); open November to March only by prior appointment.

Just eastward along the coast in Courseulles-sur-Mer is the **Centre Juno Beach ★★**, voie des Français Libres (www.junobeach.org; ✆ **02-31-37-32-17**). This gem of a museum details Canada's war effort. Outside is a stark memorial to the Canadian dead of D-Day, their names inscribed simply on blue towers. Walk towards the beach and pause in front of the sculpture with the words to Paul Verlaine's poem "Chanson d'Automne": This was the code the BBC used to alert the French Resistance on June 5. Admission is 7€ adults and 5.50€ students and children, with reduced rates for visits only to the park or temporary exhibits. From April to September, hours are daily 9:30am to 7pm (Mar, Oct 10am–6pm; Feb, Nov–Dec 10am–5pm; closed Jan).

THE LOIRE VALLEY

by Lily Heise

Just 2 hours south of Paris, the Loire Valley enchants visitors with a stunning landscape of castles and vineyards straight out of a fairy tale. King François I and his Renaissance court left a spectacular cultural legacy, earning the entire valley a place on the World Heritage Site list.

As its name would imply, the region's rolling hills and forests hug the winding Loire River, encompassing 800 sq. km (308 sq. miles) of land south of Île-de-France, from the city of Orléans and extending west to Nantes on the Atlantic coast. Most visitors use Tours or Orléans as their starting point; however, the towns of Blois, Amboise, or Saumur make excellent bases for exploring the region.

Most visitors to the Loire arrive via Paris; there are about six direct trains daily from the TGV station at Charles de Gaulle airport to the Tours TGV station Saint-Pierre (1 hr., 40 min; 37€–70€ one-way). At least one high-speed train (TGV) an hour runs to both Orléans and Tours, convenient starting points for anyone not renting a car directly in Paris.

The Loire Valley has **two regional tourist offices** that can help you plan your stay in advance: **Comité Régional de Tourisme Val de Loire,** 37 av. de Paris, Orléans 45000 (www.visaloire.com; ✆ **02-38-79-95-28**), and **SEM Régionale des Pays de la Loire,** 1 place de la Galarne, BP 80221, Nantes 44202 Cedex 2 (www.westernloire.com; ✆ **02-40-48-24-20**). Local tourist offices are listed throughout the chapter.

ORLÉANS ★

119km (74 miles) SW of Paris; 72km (45 miles) SE of Chartres

Ever since **Joan of Arc** relieved the besieged city from the Burgundians and the English in 1429, the city has honored the "Maid of Orléans." This deliverance is celebrated every year on May 8, the anniversary of her victory, but even if you aren't in town for the celebration, it's impossible to overlook the city's affection for the warrior, her name adorning everything from streets and cafes to chocolates and candies. Though suffering damage in World War II,

The Loire Valley

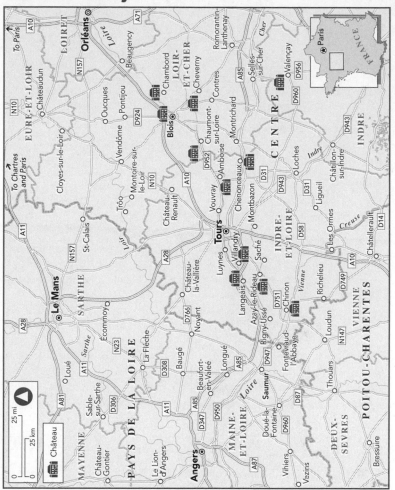

the city's downtown still remains quaint; however, it has gradually been losing its regional prominence to the more prosperous Tours. That said, with several recent urban initiatives from the Turbulences art center to the renovated riverside with walkways and cycle paths, Orléans is developing a 21st-century contemporary flare.

Essentials

GETTING THERE   About two **trains** per hour arrive from Paris's Gare d'Austerlitz (1 hr., 10 min; 17€–25€ one-way); there are also a dozen connections from Tours (50–70 min.). The one-way fare from Tours to Orléans is

biking YOUR WAY THROUGH THE LOIRE

Trains serve some towns, but the best way to see this relatively flat region is by car or bike. The vast program called **La Loire à Vélo** (www.cycling-loire.com; **"The Loire on a Bike"**) has completed the 800km-long (496-mile) **Loire à Vélo trail,** meaning you can now safely pedal from Sancerre to the sea on a dedicated bike path past châteaux, villages, and natural areas or easily bike from one château to another. Relatively flat, the path was designed primarily for low-key cycling with family and friends and is linked to cycling-friendly hotels and bike-rental outfits along the way (look for the ACCUEIL VÉLO signs). More paths are added every year, and the trail will hook up to an even more massive project called **EuroVelo 6,** a cycling path that leads all the way to the Black Sea.

La Loire à Vélo has partnered with various tourist offices and travel agencies to offer a range of bike-trip packages that include hotel, meals, bike rental, and baggage transport (very important if you don't want to haul extra weight). For more information, visit **www.cycling-loire.com**, or one of the two regional tourist offices (listed above). The website also has detailed information on dozens of bike-rental outfits along the route, as well as brochures and links to guide-books on various sections of the path.

One of the better-known outfitters is **Detours de Loire,** 35, rue Charles Gille, Tours (www.locationdevelos.com; ℂ **02-47-61-22-23**), which has three other shops in Blois, Saumur, and Nantes, as well as 20 or so associated outlets up and down the Loire à Vélo circuit. This means that you can pick up your bike in one town and leave it in any partner outlet along the way without having to worry about returning the bike to the place you rented it from. If you are arriving in the Loire Valley by train, the four main shops are all located close to the town station. Prices for all-purpose bikes run from 15€ to 22€ per day, with discounts for multi-day rentals. A 300€ deposit (usually a credit card imprint) is required. Detours de Loire can also organize hotel-bike packages, deliver your bike to your accommodations, and store your baggage while you are out pedaling. *Note:* Most outlets are open only from April to October.

about 20€. Orléans lies on the road between Paris and Tours. If you're **driving** from Paris, take A10 south; from Tours, take A10 north.

VISITOR INFORMATION The **Office de Tourisme** is at 2 place de L'Etape (www.tourisme-orleans.com; ℂ **02-38-24-05-05**).

Sleep Like a King (or Queen)

As one of the most visited regions of France, it's not surprising to find a great variety of accommodation options. Sleep like a king or queen in one of the Loire's many châteaux hotels, from the medieval **Hostellerie Gargantua** (p. 187) to the opulence of the **Château d'Artigny** (p. 177) or the **Chateau de Marçay** (p. 186). The valley is dotted with thousands of unique *gîtes* (B&Bs) including medieval towers, houseboats, and even troglodyte caves. For details and reservations, go to http://en.gites-de-france.com.

Getting Around

ON FOOT   Orléans's city center is small and many streets are pedestrianized. For short stays, it's easiest to explore the town on foot.

BY BICYCLE   Orléans has a Paris style bike-sharing scheme, **Vélo'+** (www.agglo-veloplus.fr). There are 350 bikes available at 33 stations around the city. You can register online (where you can also download a map of the city's bike stations) or directly at one of eight bike stands where credit cards are accepted; fees are 1€ per day.

BY CAR   Since all the sites in the city can be explored on foot it's easier to park if you have a car. Underground parking is well sign-posted; there are convenient lots beside the Hotel de Ville, the Cathedral, and near the river at Place du Châtelet.

BY TAXI   Taxis Orléans (www.taxis-orleans.fr; ✆ **02-38-53-11-11**) can be found throughout the city. They can be ordered or there are ranks in front of the train station and at the corner of rue Royal and place du Martroi.

BY PUBLIC TRANSPORT   Orléans has both buses and trams that snake through the city run by the **TAO** (www.reseau-tao.fr; ✆ **08-00-01-20-00**). Trams will serve your visit best; line A reaches the train station whereas line B goes by the cathedral. Tickets (1.50€) can be purchased from automatic kiosks at the Tram station, or for the bus directly from the driver, they are 1.60€.

[FastFACTS] ORLÉANS

ATMs/Banks   The city center has plenty of banks, especially around shopping hub Place du Châtelet.

Doctors & Hospitals   **Centre Hospitalier Régionale d'Orléans,** 1 rue Porte Madeleine (www.chu-orleans.fr; ✆ **02-33-51-44-44**).

Internet Access   **Mondial Phone,** 84 rue des Carmes (✆ **02-38-72-17-52**), has computers with internet and international phone call services.

Mail & Postage   **La Poste,** 19 rue Royale (✆ **36-31**).

Pharmacies   **Pharmacie du Châtelet,** 38 Place du Châtelet (✆ **02-38-53-34-50**).

Where to Stay

Hôtel de l'Abeille ★★   If you're taking some time to get to know Orléans before embarking on château country, this is the city's most charming hotel. Stepping into the foyer, you will be instantly transported back to the 19th century; in fact the hotel dates from 1903 and has been run for four generations by the same family. The cozy Belle Époque feel flows over into the guest rooms, each individually decorated with colorful vintage prints and antiques. Throughout the building are ornamental nods to both Napoleon, whose symbol was the bee and the namesake of the hotel, and Joan of Arc, the celebrated liberator of Orléans. Take a late afternoon break or morning coffee on its peaceful rooftop terrace.

64 rue Alsace-Lorraine. www.hoteldelabeille.com. ℗ **02-38-53-54-87**. 27 units. 120€–145€ double; 185€–195€ family suite. Parking 12€. **Amenities:** Bar; room service; TV, hair dryer, free Wi-Fi.

Where to Eat

Chez Jules ★★ TRADITIONAL FRENCH Yvan and Isabelle Cardinaux take the idea of "chez" to a whole new level with the warm welcome and delectable dishes at one of the best restaurants in town. Service and quality prevail; don't expect fine crystal and a maitre d'. The extremely reasonable menu features seasonal refined dishes such as veal sweetbreads with horseradish and half roasted pigeon with ginger. To finish we loved the Saint-Nectaire cheese *tartine* with roasted apricots and the crispy chocolate and banana cake served with vanilla ice cream and caramel sauce.

136 rue de Bourgogne. www.chezjulesorleans.fr. ℗ **02-38-54-30-80**. Reservations highly recommended. Main courses 16€–25€; fixed-price lunch 19€, dinner 23€–37€. Tues–Sat noon–2pm and 7–9:30pm. Closed 2–3 weeks in July and Dec 24–Jan 2.

La Vieille Auberge ★ MODERN FRENCH Take a trip to the French countryside in the heart of the city at this charming restaurant housed in a 17th-century building. Dine inside in a stylish room or, on sunny days, enjoy your creative creations in a lovely garden. The menu changes with the season to take advantage of the freshest available ingredients and may start with young pigeon with vanilla-infused cabbage, before moving on to turbot fish with truffle cream and candied fingerling potatoes—and dare to finish off with the pistachio "mystery" with lychees.

2 rue du Faubourg St-Vincent. www.lavieilleauberge45.com. ℗ **02-38-53-55-81**. Main courses 26€–28€; fixed-price lunch 25€, dinner 35€–49€. Mon–Thurs noon–2pm and 7–9:30pm; Fri–Sat noon–2pm and 7–10pm; Sun noon–2pm.

Exploring the Town

Orléans, pop. 116,000, is the chief town of Loiret, on the Loire, and beneficiary of many associations with the French aristocracy. It gave its name to the dukes and duchesses of Orléans. Wander the narrow lanes of the city center to get the feel for what the city might have been like during Joan of Arc's time. Note the equestrian statue of Jeanne d'Arc on place du Martroi. From the square, you can drive past the elegant arched galleries on rue Royal (rebuilt in 18th-c. style) across pont George-V (erected in 1760). A simple cross marks the site of the Fort des Tourelles, which Joan of Arc and her men captured.

Cathédrale Ste-Croix ★★ CATHEDRAL Begun in 1287, after an earlier Romanesque church here collapsed from old age, the cathedral was burned by the Huguenots in 1568. Henri IV laid the first stone of the present building in 1601, and work continued until 1829. The cathedral boasts a 17th-century organ and woodwork from the early 18th century in its chancel, the masterpiece of Jules Hardouin-Mansart and other artists associated with Louis XIV.

Cathédrale Ste-Croix.

Place Ste-Croix. ☏ **02-38-77-87-50.** Free admission. May–Sept daily 9:15am–6pm; Oct–Apr daily 9:15am–noon and 2–6pm.

Eglise St-Aignan ★ CHURCH One of the most frequently altered churches in the Loire Valley, St-Aignan was consecrated in 1509 in the form you see today. It possesses one of France's earliest vaulted hall crypts, complete with polychromed capitals. Scholars of pre-Romanesque art are interested in its rare 10th- and 11th-century aesthetics. Above ground, the church's Renaissance-era choir and transept remain, but the Protestants burned the nave during the Wars of Religion. In a wood-carved shrine are the remains of the church's patron saint.

Place St-Aignan. No phone. Crypt can be visited only on a guided tour; sign up at the tourist office.

Hôtel Groslot ★ HISTORIC HOME This brick Renaissance mansion was begun in 1550 and embellished in the 19th century. François II (the first husband of Mary, Queen of Scots) lived here during the fall of 1560 and died on December 5. It was here that his brother and successor Charles IX met his lovely Marie Touchet. Between the Revolution and the mid-1970s, it functioned as the town hall. Marriage ceremonies, performed by the town's magistrates, are still held here. The statue of Joan of Arc praying was the work of Louis Philippe's daughter, Princesse Marie d'Orléans. In the garden, you can see the remains of the 15th-century Chapelle St-Jacques.

Place de l'Etape (northwest of the cathedral). Free admission. ☏ **02-38-79-22-30.** July–Sept Mon–Fri and Sun 9am–6pm, Sat 5–8pm; Oct–June Mon–Fri and Sun 10am–noon and 2–6pm, Sat 5pm–7pm (occasionally closed Sat for weddings).

Les Turbulences – FRAC Centre ★ MUSEUM The landscape of Loire castles has been shaken up by the creative storm of Les Turbulences. Opened in 2013, this exciting regional art center, designed by award-winning architects Jakob+MacFarlane, has quickly earned a place among the world's most innovated contemporary museums. Its exhibits take visitors on a turbulent trip through artistic, architectural, and urban experiments from the 1950s to today. Like any good journey, take a pit stop at its excellent cafe with a creative menu using local ingredients.

88 rue du Colombier. www.frac-centre.fr. ℂ **02-38-62-52-00.** Admission 4€ adults, 2€ students, free for children 18 and under and for all visitors on 1st Sun of each month; Wed–Sun noon–7pm.

Musée des Beaux-Arts ★★ MUSEUM   The best classical art museum in the region, the fairly large collection is made up of mostly French, but also Italian, Dutch, and Flemish works from the 15th to 20th century. It includes some impressive treasures by Tintoretto, Boucher, Van Dyke, and Vélasquez as well as a variety of portraits, including one of Mme. de Pompadour by Drouais. The museum also holds one of the country's best collections of pastels with works by Quentin de la Tour and Chardin.

Place Saint-Croix. www.coeur-de-france.com/orleans-beauxarts.html. ℂ **02-38-79-21-55.** Admission 4€ adults, 2€ students, free for children 18 and under and for all visitors on 1st Sun of each month; Tues–Sun 10am–6pm.

BEAUGENCY

150km (93 miles) SW of Paris; 85km (53 miles) NE of Tours

On the right bank of the Loire, the charming town of Beaugency boasts many medieval sites including a long 12th-century bridge with 23 arches, said to have been built by the Devil himself.

Essentials

GETTING THERE   If you're **driving** from Blois to Beaugency, take N152 northeast. About 20 **trains** per day run between Beaugency and either Blois or Orléans; each trip takes about 20 minutes, and the one-way fare is 7€. For railway information, visit www.voyages-sncf.com or dial ℂ **36-35.** From Orléans, about four to eight **buses** a day go to Beaugency. For bus schedules and information, visit www.ulys-loiret.com or contact the tourist office (see below).

Where to Eat & Stay Nearby

For lunch in the center of Beaugency, the **Relais du Ch**âteau (8 rue du Pont; ℂ **02-38-44-55-10**), at the foot of the castle, serves up satisfying traditional dishes and lunch menus from 16€.

La Tonnellerie ★★   Situated a short drive south of Beaugency, this 19th-century manor house makes for the perfect restful stay in the immediate area. This isn't one of the region's grand château-hotels; nevertheless, rooms have been recently refurbished and are tastefully appointed with reproduction antiques and period prints. Your experience is complete lounging in the luxuriant garden with a period book by Balzac or Flaubert. The restaurant serves regional classics (main courses from 20€) and is open to non-guests, though reservations are required.

12 rue des Eaux-Bleues, Tavers, Beaugency 45190. http://latonnelleriehotel.com. ℂ **02-38-44-68-15.** 20 units. 95€–115€ double; 155€–190€ suite, several family rooms available. Closed Dec 15–Jan 31. Take A10, exit at Beaugency, and then take N152 to Beaugency/Tavers. **Amenities:** Restaurant; bar; outdoor pool; bike rental; prepared picnics; TV; hair dryer; free Wi-Fi.

Princess de la Loire Youth Hostel ★ The best bargain for bikers on a budget, this youth hostel near Beaugency offers the most reasonable accommodation in the whole of the Loire. Clean and bright, the hostel has dormitories with four to six beds, a common kitchen, and laundry facilities. Share your Loire touring routes with other travelers at the sociable barbecue and picnic areas. Bike rentals are available directly from the hostel or in town at the Détours shop near the train station.

152 rue de Châteaudun (2km from Beaugency on the D925). www.hihostels.com. 116 beds. ℂ **02-38-44-61-31.** 16€ shared dormitory. A Hostelling International card is required. Closed mid-Nov to mid-Mar. **Amenities:** Shared kitchen; laundry room; barbecue and picnic area; bike rental; free Wi-Fi.

Exploring the Town

A major medieval event took place here: the 1152 annulment of the marriage of Eleanor of Aquitaine and her cousin, Louis VII. She then married Henry II of England, bringing southwestern France as her dowry, an act that set off the Hundred Years War. This remarkable woman was the mother of Richard the Lion-Hearted. (The film "The Lion in Winter" dramatizes her life.)

The 15th-century **Château Dunois** (www.chateau-de-beaugency.com) has recently reopened after extensive renovations. The château is brooding and impressive, its historical links stretching back to almost-mystical medieval antecedents. The current castle was built by Jean d'Orléans, who fought alongside Joan of Arc in the siege of Orléans, on the foundations of an earlier 10th-century fortress that belonged to the lords of Beaugency, whose feudal power extended throughout the region. Astride the street (la rue du Pont) that leads to one of the château's secondary entrances, the **Voûte St-Georges (St. George's Vault)** is an arched gateway from the earlier château. You can tour various rooms of the castle's interior, admire period artifacts and furniture, and in summer, enjoy reenactments by actors in historic costumes. Tickets are 8.50€ adults, 7€ students, 5.50€ children 7–15 and free for children 6 and under. It is open June through August daily 10am–7pm; May, September and October 2–6pm and around public holidays the rest of the year.

More medieval moodiness is on hand at **La Tour César,** a 36m-tall (118-ft.) castle keep that is all that remains of an 11th-century citadel. It's a fine example of Romanesque military architecture, but the interior is in ruins.

Eglise Notre-Dame, place Saint-Fermin, a 12th-century abbey, was rebuilt after it was burned during the Wars of Religion (1562–98). You can still see traces of its original Romanesque architecture in the chancel and transept. Nearby, the 16th-century **Tour St-Fermin,** a bell tower with a panoramic view of the valley, is famous for bells that ring out a traditional tune three times a day.

The 10th-century **Eglise St-Etienne,** place du Martroi, is one of the oldest churches in France. Now deconsecrated, it is owned by the municipality and is open only for temporary exhibitions of painting and sculpture.

BLOIS

180km (112 miles) SW of Paris; 60km (37 miles) NE of Tours

The star attraction in this town of 52,000 is unquestionably the **Château de Blois,** but if time remains after a château visit, you may want to wander around the quaint historic core to get a feel for a real Loire Valley town.

Essentials

GETTING THERE   A dozen or so **trains** run from Paris's Gare de Austerlitz every day (1 hr., 45 min.; 29€ one-way), and several others depart from the Gare Montparnasse, which involves a change in Tours (around 1 hr., 50 min.; 35€–76€). From Tours, trains run almost every hour (trip time: 40 min.), at a cost of 11€ one-way. For information and schedules, visit www.voyages-sncf.com or dial ℂ **36-35.** From June to September, you can take a **bus** (www.tlcinfo.net; ℂ **02-54-58-55-44**) from the Blois train station to tour châteaux in the area, including Chambord, Chaumont, Chenonceau, and Amboise. If you're **driving** from Tours, take RN152 east to Blois, which runs along the Loire; if you want to get there fast, take the A10 autoroute. If you'd like to explore the area by **bike,** check out **Traineurs de Loire,** 1 rue Chemonton (www.traineursdeloire.com; ℂ **02-54-79-36-71**). Rentals start at 10€ half day, 15€ full day, open April to September.

VISITOR INFORMATION   The **Office de Tourisme** is at 23 place du Château (www.bloispaysdechambord.com; ℂ **02-54-90-41-41**).

Where to Stay & Eat

Côté Loire–Auberge Ligérienne ★   Even though its decor is akin to a seaside resort, you won't feel lost at sea staying at this quaint hotel on the banks of the Loire. Only a 5-minute walk from the château, it's a great option for travelers touring the region without a car. There is plenty of character at this B&B-like inn from the vintage maritime posters, pillows with sailboat motifs, and ancient building features from the 12th, 15th, and 16th centuries. Most rooms are rather large for the size of the establishment; though beware of the narrow staircase. A tiny restaurant on the ground floor is open to outside guests, with one of the owners doing double duty as chef. His love of the region shines through in such culinary creations as savory blancmange with goat cheese and tomatoes confit or local Sandre fish with butter sauce.

2 place de la Grève. www.coteloire.com. ℂ **02-54-78-07-86.** 8 units. 59€–97€ double. Restaurant fixed-price menu 31€, main course 19€. Open Tues–Sat. **Amenities:** Bar; restaurant; TV; hair dryer; free Wi-Fi. Closed Jan to mid-Feb.

Le Médicis ★★ TRADITIONAL FRENCH   It's worth the short 1km (½ mile) trip from the center of town to dine at this 1 Michelin-starred restaurant and inn. The discerning taste of the Garanger family is evident in both the dining room and the bedrooms. It will be hard to choose from their original dishes of lobster in puff pastry with Thai-style shrimp spring rolls, bass fish suprême with vegetable wasabi puree, and their specialty of veal sweetbreads with spinach ravioli. Even more difficult will be selecting an accompanying bottle from its extensive wine list of over 300 labels. The inn has 10 elegant rooms with air-conditioning, TV, minibar, and hair dryer. Double rates start from 79€.

2 allée François 1er. www.le-medicis.com. ℗ **02-54-43-94-04.** Reservations required. Main courses 20€–30€; fixed-price menu 27€–75€. Daily noon–1:15pm and 7–9pm. Closed Jan and Sun night and Mon. Bus: 2.

Where to Eat

L'Orangerie du Château ★★★ TOURAINE   The king's blessing has been bestowed on this wonderful restaurant located in a former outbuilding of the castle, the perfect majestic lunch spot after a morning inside the château. The classic dining room is also bustling with local fans of chef Jean-Marc Molveaux. He passionately prepares prawn and celery root ravioli, wild bass with cauliflower and comté cheese sauce, and filet of beef with mushroom tortellini and Jerusalem artichoke *mousseline.* There's even a special children's menu for *petits gourmands.* Your regal feast is made complete in summer when you can dine on the outdoor terrace facing the castle.

1 av. Jean-Laigret. www.orangerie-du-chateau-fr. ℗ **02-54-78-05-36.** Main courses 25€–40€; fixed-price menu 38€–83€; children's menu 15€. Tues–Sat noon–1:30pm and 7:15–9:15pm. Closed mid-Feb to mid-Mar.

Exploring the Town & the Château

Blois is a piece of living history, with cobblestone streets and restored white houses with slate roofs and redbrick chimneys. Some of its "streets" are mere alleyways originally laid out in the Middle Ages or lanes linked by a series of stairs. If you have time for **shopping,** head for the area around **rue St-Martin** and **rue du Commerce** for high-end items such as clothing, perfume, shoes, and jewelry. On Saturday, a daylong **food market** is on place Louis XII and place de la République, lining several blocks in the center of town at the foot of the château.

Lights, Sound, Action!

Many of the Loire châteaux present *son-et-lumière* (sound and light) shows on summer nights. The **Château de Blois** hosts one of the best nightly from April to September (around 10–10:30pm). As a taped lecture plays (audioguide available in English), colored lights and readings evoke the age in which the château was built. Admission 8€ adults, 6.50€ students, 5€ children 6 to 17, and free for children 5 and under, or you can save money by purchasing a joint chateau-light show ticket (www.chateaudeblois.fr).

Château de Blois ★★★ CASTLE A wound in battle earned Henri I, the duc de Guise, the name Balafré (Scarface), but he was quite a ladies' man. In fact, on the misty morning of December 23, 1588, he had just left a warm bed of one of Catherine de Médicis' ladies-in-waiting. His archrival, King Henri III, had summoned him, but when the duke arrived, only the king's minions were about. The guards approached with daggers. Wounded, the duke made for the door, where more guards awaited him. Staggering, he fell to the floor in a pool of his own blood. Only then did Henri emerge from behind the curtains. "Mon Dieu," he reputedly exclaimed, "he's taller dead than alive!" The body couldn't be shown: The duke was too popular. Quartered, it was burned in a fireplace.

Château de Blois.

If you stand in the courtyard, you'll find that the château is like an illustrated storybook of French architecture. The Hall of the Estates-General is a beautiful 13th-century work; Louis XII built the Charles d'Orléans gallery and the Louis XII wing from 1498 to 1501. Mansart constructed the Gaston d'Orléans wing between 1635 and 1637. Most remarkable is the François I wing, a French Renaissance masterpiece containing a spiral staircase with ornamented balustrades and the king's symbol, the salamander.

41000 Blois. www.chateaudeblois.fr. ℂ **02-54-90-33-33.** Admission 10€ adults, 7.50€ students, 5€ children 6–17, free for children 5 and under. Additional fees for light shows and special events. July–Aug daily 9am–7pm; Apr–June and Sept daily 9am–6:30pm; Oct daily 9am–6pm; Nov–Mar daily 9am–12:30pm and 1:30–5:30pm.

CHAMBORD ★★★

91km (118 miles) SW of Paris; 18km (11 miles) E of Blois

The Château de Chambord, the grandest of the region's castles, is the culmination of François I's two biggest obsessions: hunting and architecture. It's a must for any Loire castle itinerary.

Essentials

GETTING THERE It's best to **drive** to Chambord. Take D951 northeast from Blois to Saint Dyé, turning on to the rural road to Chambord. You can also rent a **bicycle** in Blois and ride the 18km (11 miles) to Chambord, or take a **tour** to Chambord from Blois in summer. From May to September,

Transports du Loir et Cher (www.tlcinfo.net; © **02-54-58-55-44**) operates bus services to Chambord.

Exploring the Château

The Château de Chambord ★★★ CASTLE   Built as a "hunting lodge," this colossal edifice is a masterpiece of architectural derring-do. Some say Leonardo da Vinci had something to do with it, and when you climb the amazing double spiral staircase, that's not too hard to believe. The staircase is superimposed upon itself so that one person may descend and a second ascend without ever meeting. While da Vinci died a few months before construction started in 1519, what emerged after 20 years was the pinnacle of the French Renaissance, the largest château in the Loire Valley. The castle's proportions are of an exquisite geometric harmony, and its fantastic arrangement of turrets and chimneys makes it one of France's most recognizable châteaux.

Four monumental towers dominate Chambord's facade. The three-story keep has a spectacular terrace from which the ladies of the court watched the return of their men from the hunt. While many of the vast rooms are empty, several have been restored and filled with an impressive collection of period furniture and objects, giving an idea of what the castle looked like during the periods when parts of it were occupied. The château lies in a park of more than 5,260 hectares (12,992 acres), featuring miles of hiking trails and bike paths, as well as picnic tables and bird-watching posts.

www.chambord.org. © **02-54-50-40-00.** Admission 11€ adults, 9€ students and free 17 and under accompanied by an adult. Daily Apr–Sept 9am–6pm and Oct–Mar 9am–5pm.

Family rowing a boat on a canal in front of the Château de Chambord.

CHEVERNY ★

192km (119 miles) SW of Paris; 19km (12 miles) SE of Blois

Unlike most of the Loire castles, Cheverny is the residence of the original owner's descendants, offering a rare glimpse into the normally very private life of French aristocrats.

Essentials

GETTING THERE Cheverny is 19km (12 miles) south of Blois, along D765. It's best reached by **car** or on a **bus tour** (Apr–Aug only) from Blois with **TLC Transports du Loir et Cher** (www.tlcinfo.net; ℂ **02-54-58-55-44**). Bus no. 4 leaves from the railway station at Blois once or twice per day; see the TLC website for the schedule. You can also take a **taxi** (ℂ **02-54-78-07-65**) from the railway station at Blois.

Where to Eat & Stay

The **Orangerie** on the castle grounds is also a nice option for a quick bite, serving a variety of snacks, lunch, and teatime fare.

St-Hubert ★ TRADITIONAL FRENCH If you can't get invited to lunch by the château owners, your appetite can be pleasantly satisfied at this nearby excellent value inn. It offers fixed-price menus of regional specialties such as duck *rillettes* (potted meat); local free-range Touraine Géline chicken with *pommes darphin* (thick potato pancake), crispy roasted cod on a bed of seasonal vegetables, and for "dessert" Ste. Maure goat cheese or homemade *tarte tatin* (apple pie). While it's a far cry from the luxurious bedrooms of the castle, the St-Hubert offers economic **lodging** with 20 conservatively decorated rooms for 68€ to 78€ for a double.

122 rte. Nationale. www.hotel-sthubert.com. ℂ **02-54-79-96-60.** Main courses 17€–22€; fixed-price menu 22€–34€; children's menu 12€. Daily noon–2pm and 7–9pm. Closed Sun night off-season.

Exploring the Château

Château de Cheverny ★ CASTLE The family of the vicomte de Sigalas can trace its lineage from Henri Hurault, the son of the chancellor of Henri III and Henri IV, who built the château in 1634. Designed in classic Louis XIII style, it is resolutely symmetrical, with square pavilions flanking the central pile. Its elegant lines and sumptuous furnishings provoked the Grande Mademoiselle, otherwise known as the Duchess of Montpensier, to proclaim it an "enchanted castle."

You, too, will be impressed by the antique furnishings, tapestries, and *objets d'art*. A 17th-century French artist, Jean Mosnier, decorated the fireplace with motifs from the legend of Adonis. The Guards' Room contains a collection of medieval armor; also on display is a Gobelin tapestry depicting the abduction of Helen of Troy. In the king's bedchamber, another Gobelin traces the trials of Ulysses. Most impressive is the stone stairway of carved fruit and flowers. To complete the regal experience, your arrival or departure from the chateau might be heralded by red-coated trumpeters accompanied by an enthusiastic pack of hunting hounds.

www.chateau-cheverny.fr. © **02-54-79-96-29.** Admission 10€ adults, 7€ students under 25 and children 7–18, and free children 6 and under (additional fee for exhibits), boat and golf cart rentals also available. Daily Nov–Mar 9:45am–5pm; Apr–June and Sept 9:15am–6:15pm; July–Aug 9:15am–6:45pm; and Oct 9:45am–5:30pm.

VALENÇAY ★★

233km (144 miles) SW of Paris; 56km (35 miles) S of Blois

One of the Loire's most handsome Renaissance châteaux, Valençay combines the wonders of châteaux-hopping and family fun, and even has a special museum for car lovers.

Essentials

GETTING THERE If you're **driving** from Tours, take A85 east, turning south on D956 (exit 13 to Selles-sur-Cher) to Valençay. From Blois, follow D956 south.

Exploring the Château & Park

Château de Valençay ★★ CASTLE   Talleyrand acquired it in 1803 on the orders of Napoleon, who wanted his minister of foreign affairs to receive dignitaries in style. The d'Estampes family built Valençay in 1520. The dungeon and west tower are of this period, as is the main body of the building, but other wings were added in the 17th and 18th centuries. The effect is grandiose, all domes and turrets. The apartments are sumptuously furnished, mostly in the Empire style, but with Louis XV and Louis XVI trappings as well. A star-footed table in the main drawing room is said to have been the one on which the final agreement of the Congress of Vienna was signed in June 1815 (Talleyrand represented France).

After your visit to the château, take a walk through the garden and deer park. There are plenty of activities here for kids, including a giant labyrinth, a miniature farm, a playground, a golf cart circuit through the forest, and, in high season, historic reenactments (at 3, 4, and 5pm). A few nights each summer the château and its grounds return to the Renaissance, decked out with thousands of candles, costumed performers, and musical entertainment (see website for details).

Classic car enthusiasts' motors can get revved up at the **Musée de l'Automobile de Valençay,** situated 200m (656 ft.) from the château. It showcases an extensive collection started by a mechanic in 1906. The exhibit shows the evolution of the automobile with over 60 antique vehicles, including a rare tandem style pulley-operated Bédélia (ca. 1914).

2 rue de Blois. www.chateau-valencay.fr. © **02-54-00-10-66.** The Automobile Museum is located at 12 av. de la Résistance (www.musee-auto-valencay.fr; © **02-54-00-07-74**). Admission for castle, automobile museum, and park 13€ adults, 9.50€ students, 4.50€

children 4–6, and free ages 3 and under. Daily Apr 10:30am–6pm; May, Sept 10am–6pm; June 9:30am–6:30pm; July–Aug 9:30am–7pm; Oct–mid-Nov and over Christmas 10:30am–5:30pm,weekends 10:30am–5:30pm mid-Nov–mid-Dec.

AMBOISE ★★

219km (136 miles) SW of Paris; 35km (22 miles) E of Tours

Amboise is on the banks of the Loire in the center of vineyards known as Touraine-Amboise. The good news: This is a real Renaissance town. The bad news: Because it is so beautiful, tour buses overrun it, especially in summer. Other than the myriad of notable royal residences, the town has also played host to Leonardo da Vinci, who spent his last years here, and more recently, royal rocker Mick Jagger, lord of a nearby château.

Essentials

GETTING THERE   About a dozen **trains** per day leave from both Tours and Blois. The trip from Tours takes 20 minutes and costs 5.70€ one-way; from Blois, it takes 20 minutes and costs 7.20€ one-way. Several conventional trains a day leave from Paris's Gare d'Austerlitz (trip time: about 2 hr., 15 min.), and several TGVs depart from the Gare Montparnasse, with a change to a regular train at St-Pierre-des-Corps, next to Tours (trip time: 1 hr., 30 min.). Fares from Paris to Amboise start at 24€. For information, visit www.voyages-sncf.com or call ✆ **36-35.**

If you prefer to travel by bus, **Fil Vert Buses** (www.tourainefilvert.com), which operates out of Gare Routière in Tours, just across from the railway station, runs about six to eight **buses** every day between Tours and Amboise. The one-way trip takes about 45 minutes and costs 2€.

If you're **driving** from Tours, take the D751, following signs to Amboise.

VISITOR INFORMATION   The **Office de Tourisme** is on quai du Général-de-Gaulle (www.amboise-valdeloire.com; ✆ **02-47-57-09-28**).

Where to Eat & Stay

Le Choiseul ★★★   Composed of three mansions dating from the 15th through 18th centuries and nestled on the banks of the Loire River, Le Choiseul is the best hotel in Amboise and serves its best cuisine. Its rooms are opulent with traditional charm and all the modern comforts of a luxury hotel. Be sure to explore the grounds, where an outdoor pool is surrounded by Italian sculptures; ask the staff about visiting the impressive "Greniers de César" troglodyte caves nearby. Chef Mickaël Renard brings his creativity and savoir-faire to its elegant restaurant **Le 36** overlooking the river (open to non-guests). His refined menu of beautifully presented dishes might include fillet of brill with Touraine saffron, sweet potatoes purée and clementines or roasted local "Roi Rose de Touraine" pork chop, served with polenta topped with truffle, mushrooms, and nashi. Lunch ranges from 30€ to 37€, with dinner going for 51€ to 85€.

36 quai Charles-Guinot. www.le-choiseul.com and www.le36-amboise.fr (restaurant).
② **02-47-30-45-45.** 32 units. 204€–330€ double; 390€ suite. **Amenities:** Restaurant; bar; bicycles; outdoor pool; room service; A/C, TV; hair dryer; minibar; free Wi-Fi.

Le Fleuray ★★ The welcome couldn't be warmer at this lovely ivy-covered manor house run by a family of English expatriates, a short drive from Amboise. With their cross-cultural approach, the Newingtons turned a rundown farmhouse into the perfect mélange of Anglo-Saxon comfort and French sophistication. This attention to detail is evident from the intimate foyer to the spacious guest rooms; several of which have private terraces. With peaceful surroundings and plenty to do on the extensive grounds, this is an excellent base for château touring and some family fun. The hotel also has an excellent restaurant serving food infused with regional and international flavors. Items on the fixed-price menus (29€–39€) might include filet of John Dory, sweet potato and ginger puree, with a coconut and combawa sauce, glazed duck breast with Sancho pepper, red cabbage, a vegetable and orange maki, or vegetarian-friendly wild mushroom risotto topped with baby glazed onions and mature parmesan shavings.

Route D74, near Amboise. www.lefleurayhotel.com. ② **02-47-56-09-25.** 24 units. 98€–162€ double. Free parking. From Amboise, take the D952 on the north side of the river, following signs to Blois; 12km (7½ miles) from Amboise, turn onto D74, in the direction of Cangey. **Amenities:** Restaurant; bar; free bikes; golf course; Jacuzzi; massage; outdoor pool; room service; tennis court; TV; hair dryer; free Wi-Fi

Le Manoir Les Minimes ★★ In the shadow of the looming castle is this welcoming and reasonably priced hotel, set in a magical restored 18th-century mansion. Built on the foundations of an ancient convent, the hotel is made up of the main building, draped in wisteria, and a small annexed cottage, centered by a tranquil garden, equipped with outdoor seating. Once inside, you feel like you've entered a fine aristocratic home, with tasteful furnishings and decorations chosen with a careful eye to detail. The most charming rooms are in the main building, especially those in the attic with their beautiful exposed beams (although tall guests might have trouble with the slanted ceilings). The rooms in the annex aren't as quaint, but are more spacious. Many second and third floor rooms open to views of the Loire or the château. Some rooms only have a bathtub (with a shower head), which may not appeal to all guests.

34 quai Charles Guinot. www.manoirlesminimes.com. ② **02-47-30-40-40.** 15 units. 139€–225€ double; 305€–530€ suite. **Amenities:** Parking, Breakfast room; A/C; TV; minibar; free Wi-Fi.

Where to Eat

For finer dining, the restaurants at the hotels **Le Choiseul** and **Le Fleuray** (see above) are excellent.

Chez Hippeau Brasserie de l'Hotel de Ville ★ FRENCH If you need a quick lunch in the town's historic core, this bustling Paris-style brasserie is a good option, particularly in pleasing hungry little bellies. And the city ambience is what you'll get with busy waiters and packed tables, yet the wide menu and the speed will refuel you for the rest of your day of touring. On the menu are the usual suspects of standard steak-frites, grilled salmon with vegetables and canard confit with honey and rosemary—as well as a range of lighter salads, croque monsieurs, and omelets.

1 and 3 rue François 1er. ℰ **02-47-57-26-30.** Main courses 8€–20€; fixed-price menu 12€–23€; children's menu 7.90€. Daily 11am-11pm.

Exploring the Town

Château d'Amboise ★★ CASTLE On a rocky spur above the town, this medieval château was rebuilt in 1492 by Charles VIII, the first in France to reflect the Italian Renaissance.

Visitors enter on a ramp that opens onto a panoramic terrace fronting the river. At one time, buildings surrounded this terrace, and fêtes took place in the enclosed courtyard. The castle fell into decline during the Revolution, and today only about a quarter of the once-sprawling edifice remains. You first come to the Flamboyant Gothic **Chapelle de St-Hubert,** distinguished by its lacelike tracery, which holds the **tomb of Leonardo da Vinci,** who died in Amboise. Tapestries cover the walls of what's left of the château's grandly furnished rooms, which include **Logis du Roi (King's Apartment).** The vast **Salle du Conseil,** book-ended by a Gothic and a Renaissance fireplace, was once the venue of the lavish fêtes. Exit via the **Tour des Minimes** (also known as the Tour des Cavaliers), noteworthy for a ramp up which horsemen could ride. The other notable tower is the Heurtault, which is broader than the Minimes, with thicker walls.

www.chateau-amboise.com. ℰ **02-47-57-00-98.** Admission 11€ adults, 9.40€ students, 7.30€ ages 7–14, free children 7 and under. Daily Jan 9am–12:30pm and 2–4:45pm; Feb 9am–12:30pm and 1:30–5pm; Mar 9am–5:30pm; Apr–June 9am–6:30pm; July–Aug 9am–7pm; Sept–Oct 9am–6pm; Nov 2–15 9am–5:30pm; Nov 16–Dec 31 9am–12:30pm and 2–4:45pm.

Château d'Amboise.

Château du Clos-Lucé ★ HISTORIC HOME/MUSEUM   Within 3km (1¾ miles) of the base of Amboise's château, this brick-and-stone building was constructed in the 1470s. Bought by Charles VII in 1490, it became the summer residence of the royals and also served as a retreat for Anne de Bretagne, who, according to legend, spent a lot of time praying and meditating. Later, François I installed "the great master in all forms of art and science," Leonardo himself. Da Vinci lived here for 3 years, until his death in 1519. Today the site functions as a small museum, where you can step back into the life and imagination of da Vinci. The manor contains furniture from his era; examples of his sketches; models for his flying machines, bridges, and cannon; and temporary exhibits; plus an annual Renaissance musical festival late September (a nod to da Vinci's musical talents).

2 rue de Clos-Lucé. www.vinci-closluce.com. *©* **02-47-57-00-73.** Mar–Nov 15 admission 14€ adults, 10€ students, 9.50€ children 6–18, 39€ family ticket (2 adults, 2 children), free children 5 and under. Jan daily 10am–6pm; Feb–June daily 9am–7pm; July–Aug daily 9am–8pm; Sept–Oct daily 9am–7pm; Nov–Dec daily 9am–6pm.

CHENONCEAUX ★★★

224km (139 miles) SW of Paris; 26km (16 miles) E of Tours

Chenonceau is one of the most remarkable castles in France. Its impressive setting, spanning a whole river, along with an intriguing history and renowned residents, make it many visitors' favorite château in the whole country. (*Note:* The village, whose year-round population is less than 300, is spelled with a final *x*, but the château isn't.)

Essentials

GETTING THERE   About a dozen daily **trains** run from Tours to Chenonceaux (trip time: 30 min.), costing 6.80€ one-way. The train deposits you at the base of the château; from there, it's an easy walk. For information, visit www.voyages-sncf.com or call *©* **36-35.** If you're **driving,** from the center of Tours follow the signs to the D40 east, which will take you to the signposted turnoff for Chenonceaux.

Where to Eat

From March to November a gourmet lunch can be enjoyed at the **Orangerie** of the château, there is also a tea salon, a snack bar, and picnic areas on the grounds.

Au Gâteau Breton ★ TRADITIONAL FRENCH   A brief jaunt from the château, this restaurant is ideal for a casual lunch or tea. Don't be deceived by its name; this is not a creperie, but the pretty 18th-century inn was formerly a grocery store run by natives of neighboring Brittany. The shady terrace offers ample outdoor dining or cozy up over their hardier dishes in the rustic interior. Worthwhile dishes include homey favorites like local andouillette sausage, coq au vin, and their specialty poulet Tourangelle (sautéed chicken with mushroom and cream sauce).

16 rue du Dr. Bretonneau. ℂ **02-47-23-90-14.** Main courses 15€–22€; fixed-price menus 18€–30€. Apr–Sept daily noon–2:30pm, daily 7–10pm; Nov–Mar daily noon–2:30pm.

Exploring the Château, Museum & Gardens

Château de Chenonceau ★★★ CASTLE   A Renaissance masterpiece, the château is best known for the dames de Chenonceau, who once occupied it. Built first for the French noblewoman Katherine Briçonnet, the château was bought in 1547 by Henri II for his mistress, Diane de Poitiers. For a time, this remarkable woman was virtually queen of France, infuriating Henri's dour wife, Catherine de Médicis. Diane's critics accused her of using magic to preserve her celebrated beauty and keep Henri's attentions from waning. Apparently, Henri's love for Diane continued unabated, and she was in her 60s when he died in a jousting tournament in 1559.

When Henri died, Catherine became regent (her eldest son was still a child), and one of the first things she did was force Diane to return the jewelry Henri had given her and abandon her beloved home. Catherine added her own touches, building a two-story gallery across the bridge—obviously inspired by her native Florence. The gallery, which was used for her opulent fêtes, doubled as a military hospital in World War I. It also played a crucial role in World War II, serving as the demarcation line between Nazi-occupied France and the "free" zone.

Gobelin tapestries, including one depicting a woman pouring water over the back of an angry dragon, and several important paintings by Poussin, Rubens, and Tintoretto adorn the château's walls. The chapel contains a marble Virgin and Child by Murillo, as well as portraits of Catherine de Médicis in black and white. There's even a portrait of the stern Catherine in the former bedroom of her rival, Diane de Poitiers. In François I's Renaissance bedchamber, the most interesting portrait is that of Diane as the huntress Diana.

The women of Chenonceau are the subject of the **Musée de Cire (Wax Museum),** located in a Renaissance-era annex a few steps from the château.

The château boasts vast grounds that include a maze, a vegetable garden, and a beautiful *jardin à la française,* open on summer evenings for an illuminated "night walk" accompanied by Italian classical music (weekends in June; nightly July–Aug 9:30–11:30pm).

Château de Chenonceau.

www.chenonceau.com. ✆ **02-47-23-90-07.** Admission 13€ adults and 9.50€ students and children 7–17; combination ticket château, wax museum and audio-guide 17€ adults, 14€ children 7–17, free 6 and under; admission for evening garden light show 5€ adults, free children under 7. Daily 9am–8pm July–Aug; 9am–7pm for the last 2 weeks of March; 9am–7:30pm June and Sept; 9am–6pm Oct; 9am–5pm rest of the year.

CHAUMONT-SUR-LOIRE ★★

200km (124 miles) SW of Paris; 40km (25 miles) E of Tours

The connections of this lesser-visited castle to Diane de Poitiers make it an excellent château to pair with a visit to the Château de Chenonceau (see above). It is also a wonderful stop for garden enthusiasts.

Essentials

GETTING THERE Several **trains** a day travel to Chaumont from Blois (trip time: 10–15 min.) and Tours (about 40 min.). The one-way fare is 3.60€ from Blois, 8.60€ from Tours. The railway station serving Chaumont is in Onzain, a nice 1½-mile walk north of the château. For train schedules and ticketing information, visit www.voyages-sncf.com or call ✆ **36-35.**

Where to Eat & Stay Nearby

From April to October the château grounds are home to four places where you can dine or obtain snacks; the best being the **Grand Velum** restaurant with refined dishes mainly using local or organic ingredients.

Le Domaine des Hauts de Loire ★★ A 3km (1¾ miles) drive from the Château de Chaumont, is one of the finest château-hotels on the eastern Loire circuit. Perched on the north side of the Loire, this estate house was built by the owner of a Paris-based newspaper in 1840. He referred to it as his "hunting lodge," much in the lines of Louis XIII and his grand Versailles. Rooms are decorated in Louis Philippe or Empire style, each with its own individual touches such as vintage tiles or rustic wooden beams. Most are quite large; though those in the half-timbered annex (originally the stables) are less coveted. The large park is perfect for a sunset stroll.

Its Michelin-two-starred restaurant is definitely a highlight. The creative menu may offer the lighter "Bouillabaisse Ligérienne" (stew of fishes from the Loire River) or the decadent wild boar with truffle cream and quince purée. Main courses range from 55€ to 80€, with fixed-price menus ranging from 79€.

Rte. d'Herbault. www.domainehautsloire.com. ✆ **02-54-20-72-57.** 31 units. 250€–395€ double; 610€–890€ suite. Closed mid-Dec and 2 weeks in Jan. **Amenities:** Restaurant; bar; outdoor pool; room service; TV; hair dryer; minibar; free Wi-Fi.

Exploring the Château & Garden

Château de Chaumont ★★ CASTLE On the morning when Diane de Poitiers first crossed the drawbridge, the Château de Chaumont looked grim. Henri II, her lover, had recently died. The king had given her Chenonceau, but

Château de Chaumont.

his angry widow, Catherine de Médicis, forced her to trade her favorite château for Chaumont, a comparatively virtual dungeon for Diane, with its medieval battlements and pepper-pot turrets and position perched high above the Loire.

The château belonged to the Amboise family for 5 centuries. In 1465, when one of them, a certain Pierre, rebelled against the rule of Louis XI, the king had the castle burned to the ground as a punishment. Pierre and his descendants rebuilt for the next few decades. The castle's architecture spans the period between the Middle Ages and the Renaissance, and the vast rooms still evoke the 16th and 17th centuries. In the bedroom occupied by Catherine de Médicis, you can see a portrait of the Italian-born queen. The superstitious Catherine housed her astrologer, Cosimo Ruggieri, in one of the tower rooms (a portrait of him remains). He reportedly foretold the disasters awaiting her sons.

The château passed through the hands of various owners and was eventually acquired and restored by the eccentric Marie Say and Amédée de Broglie in the late 18th century, who also added elaborate stables, a farm, and gardens. Since 1992, the latter has hosted the **International Garden Festival,** a world-renowned gathering of cutting-edge landscape designers that lasts from mid-April to November and is open to the public. Each year, a dozen different gardens are created, using thousands of different plants and innovative garden designs. The château also hosts renowned French and international contemporary art and photography exhibits; check the website for this year's program.

www.domaine-chaumont.fr. ✆ **02-54-51-26-26.** Admission 11€ adults, 6.50€ children 12–18, 4€ children 6-11, free ages 5 and under. Full pass including the festival 17€ adults, 11€ children 12–18, 5:50€ children 6–11, free 5 and under. Daily Nov–Mar 10am–5pm; Apr–June 10am–6:30pm; July–Aug 10am–7pm; Sept 10am–6:30pm; and Oct 10am–6pm.

TOURS ★

232km (144 miles) SW of Paris; 113km (70 miles) SW of Orléans

Though it doesn't have a major château, Tours (pop. 137,000), at the junction of the Loire and Cher rivers, is known for its food and wine. Many of its buildings were bombed in World War II, and 20th-century apartment towers have taken the place of castles. But the downtown core is quite charming, and because Tours is at the doorstep of some of the most magnificent châteaux in France, it makes a good base from which to explore.

Essentials

GETTING THERE As many as 14 high-speed TGV **trains** per day depart from Paris's Gare Montparnasse and arrive at St-Pierre des Corps station, 6km (3¾ miles) east of the center of Tours, in an hour. Free *navettes,* or shuttle buses, await your arrival to take you to the center of town (the Tours Centre train station). A limited number of conventional trains also depart from Gare d'Austerlitz and arrive in the center of Tours, but these take twice as long (about 2¼ hr.). One-way fares range from 27€ to 54€. For information, visit www.voyages-sncf.com or call ☎ **36-35.** If you're **driving,** take highway A10 to Tours.

VISITOR INFORMATION The **Office de Tourisme** is at 78–82 rue Bernard-Palissy (www.ligeris.com; ☎ **02-47-70-37-37**).

TOURS SUR LOIRE FESTIVAL Take a relaxing break from sightseeing and mingle with the locals during this annual summer festival. Much like Paris Plages, the Tours riverside, next to the Pont Wilson, becomes a summer *fête* with an outdoor restaurant, concerts, dancing, cinema, and activities for families. Open daily with a rotating agenda of events from mid-May to end of September (www.tours.fr/453-tours-sur-loire.htm).

Getting Around

ON FOOT Besides the TGV train station, which is in the suburb of St-Pierre des Corps, most other sites of interest in Tours are accessible on foot.

BY BICYCLE There are safe and extensive bike paths in Tours. You can rent a bike at **Detours de Loire,** 35 rue Charles Gilles (www.locationdevelos.com; ☎ **02-47-61-22-23**), at a cost of 15€ per day. A deposit is required.

BY CAR If you have a car for exploring the Loire, you can find a number of underground parking garages downtown. There is a convenient one at the Tours Centre train station and another at rue Nationale and rue de la Préfecture. You can rent a car at **Avis** (www.avis.fr; ☎ **02-47-20-53-27**), located in the Tours Centre station, or **Europcar,** at the St-Pierre des Corps station (www.europcar.fr; ☎ **02-47-63-28-67**).

BY TAXI The most extensive taxi network is **Taxis Tours** (www.taxis-tours.fr; ☎ **02-47-20-30-40**). Their hotline has some English speaking operators or you can usually find one in front of the train.

BY PUBLIC TRANSPORT   Tours has both buses and one brand-new tram line, a network called **Le Fil Bleu,** 9 rue Michelet (www.filbleu.fr; ☎ **02-47-66-70-70**). Tickets (1.50€) can be purchased from automatic kiosks at a Tram station, from bus drivers or from their office.

[FastFACTS] TOURS

ATMs/Banks   The city center has plenty of banks, especially around Place Gaston Paillhou or along rue Nationale.

Doctors & Hospitals   **Centre Hospitalier Régionale de Tours,** 2 bd. Tonnellé (www.chu-tours.fr; ☎ **02-47-47-47-47**).

Mail & Postage   **La Poste,** 17 rue Nationale (☎ **36-31**).

Pharmacies   **Pharmacie du Centre,** 28 rue des Halles (☎ **02-47-05-65-20**).

Where to Stay

Most visitors use Tours as a starting point for their Loire exploration, staying in a small town or the countryside is ideal for discovering the region, see the suggestions throughout the chapter.

Best Western Le Central ★   If you're spending more time touring the sites of Tour or taking in an evening in town, this central hotel is a good headquarters. Despite being walking distance from the station and the cathedral, the surrounding greenery gives it an almost country feel. Parts of the building face a leafy garden, reducing street traffic noise, though it makes the hotel a little tricky to find. Many of its rooms have been recently refurbished decor remains classic and conservative, though a big plus are their size, generous for French standards.

21 rue Berthelot, Tours 37000. www.bestwesterncentralhoteltours.com. ☎ **800/528-1234** in the U.S. and Canada, or 02-47-05-46-44. 37 units. 89€–190€ double; 250€–350€ suite. Parking 10€. **Amenities:** Bar; babysitting; room service; A/C; TV; hair dryer; minibar; free Wi-Fi.

Hôtel de l'Univers ★★   This grand old 19th-century hotel has recently undergone a well needed facelift returning its former grandeur as top hotel in town. Its star-studded line of guests has included Rockefeller, Churchill, and Hemingway. Its midsize rooms are decorated in a conservative contemporary style in beiges and creams accented with splashes of vibrant color. The bathrooms have also been renewed with shower/tubs, some with Jacuzzi functions. Its restaurant serves a good quality and value menu at 28€ if you don't adventure out into the city. On weekdays, the hotel is popular with business travelers; thus on most weekends it offers greatly reduced rates.

5 bd. Heurteloup, Tours 37000. www.oceaniahotels.com. ☎ **02-47-05-37-12.** 85 units. 200€–245€ double; 210€–300€ suite. Parking 15€ must reserve in advance. **Amenities:** Restaurant, bar, room service, A/C, TV, hair dryer, minibar, free Wi-Fi.

Where to Eat

Restaurants in Tours can be pricey, but you can keep costs low by dining at **La Souris Gourmande,** 100 rue Colbert (http://lasourisgourmande.com; ℂ **02-47-47-04-80**), where the chef is respected for the diversity of his cheese selection. Try it in a half-dozen fondues. You may be asked to join a communal table. Main courses cost 10€ to 17€ and the fixed-price menu is 20€. At the raffish but cheerful bistro **Le Lapin qui Fume,** 90 rue Colbert (www.aulapinquifume.fr; ℂ **02-47-66-95-49**), a fixed-price menu costs 13€ to 16€ at lunch and 23€ to 28€ at dinner and features standard bistro fare and, as the name suggests, rabbit.

La Roche le Roy ★★ MODERN FRENCH   Serious gastronomes need not tour the Tours dining scene, head straight to this tasty and tasteful restaurant. Alain Couturier's culinary finesse is accentuated by the picturesque setting of this charming 18th-century manor south of the center. Couturier's repertoire includes sandre fish in a gingerbread crust served with a leak fondue, Brittany "pearl" oysters baked in cheese and champagne, and his masterpiece of "Apicius" suprême of Racan pigeon. For dessert, the warm orange soufflé flavored with Grand Marnier is a must.

55 rte. St-Avertin. www.rocheleroy.com. ℂ **02-47-27-22-00.** Main courses 25€–38€, lunch menu 35€, dinner menu 58€–75€. Tues–Sat noon–1:30pm and 7:30–9:30pm. Closed 2 weeks in Feb and 3 weeks in Aug. From the center of town, take av. Grammont south (follow signs to St-Avertin–Vierzon).

La Table du Grand Marché ★ MODERN FRENCH   This little gem in the heart of Tours is an excellent value, creative bistro. The booths of its simple yet appealing dining room are packed with locals who come back time and time again for its refined seasonal menu. Chef Flavien Lelong gathers inspiration from near and far with such dishes as frogs' legs with broccoli *mousseline,* three fish trio with grilled vegetables and lemon cream, or the gamey doe in a macadamia nut crust with butternut squash and foie gras purée.

25 rue du Grand Marché. www.la-table-du-grand-marche.com. ℂ **02-47-64-10-62.** Main courses 18€–27€; fixed-price menu lunch 17€–20€, dinner 29€–38€. Tues 7:00–10pm Wed–Sat 12:30pm–2pm and 7:00–10pm, Sun 12:30pm–2pm.

Where to Stay & Eat near Tours

Château d'Artigny ★★★   If you want to have the utmost castle experience, this is the glitziest château-hotel in the valley. Nestled in a thick forest 1.5km (1 mile) west of the hamlet of Montbazon and 15km (9¼ miles) south of Tours, the château is newer than it looks, commissioned in 1912 for the perfume and cosmetics king François Coty, and he spared no cost in creating his perfect architectural beauty. Much of this character was retained when it was converted into a hotel in 1961 with fine antiques, Louis XV–style chairs, and various bronze and marble statuary. Only 31 units are in the main building; the others are in four annexes: a former chapel, gatehouse, mill, and staff dormitory, which have their own charm, yet might not be what you're expecting, so be careful when booking. Complete your château experience at the Artigny's regal restaurant **L'Origan** (fixed-price menus from 35€–88€).

Rte. des Monts (D17). www.artigny.com. 📞 **02-47-34-30-30.** 65 units. 180€–440€ double; 550€–790€ junior suite. From Tours, take N10 south for 11km (6¾ miles) to Montbazon, and then take D17 1.5km (1 mile) southeast. **Amenities:** Restaurant; bar; babysitting; exercise room; outdoor pool; room service; sauna; spa; 2 tennis courts; A/C; TV; hair dryer; minibar; free Wi-Fi.

Exploring the City

Pilgrims en route to Santiago de Compostela in northwest Spain once stopped here to pay homage at the tomb of St-Martin, the "Apostle of Gaul" and bishop of Tours in the 4th century. One of the most significant conflicts in European history, the 732 Battle of Tours, checked the Arab advance into Gaul. In the 15th century, French kings set up shop here, and Tours became the capital of France, a position it held for more than 100 years.

Most Loire Valley towns are rather sleepy, but Tours is where the action is, where streets and cafes bustle with a large student population. The heart of town is **place Jean-Jaurès.** The principal street is **rue Nationale,** running north to the Loire River. Head west along rue du Commerce and rue du Grand-Marché to Vieux Tours/Vieille Ville (old town). If you turn left on rue du Commerce toward the old town center, you can explore the streets and courtyards for regional specialties, books, toys, and crafts. A hotbed for antiques is east of rue Nationale (toward the cathedral), along **rue de la Scellerie.** Up rue Nationale toward the river are more shops and upscale boutiques and a small mall with chain stores.

Place Plumereau (often shortened to "place Plume"), a square of medieval buildings, houses a concentration of restaurants and bars. In the warmer months, the square explodes with tables that fill with people who like to people-watch (and be watched themselves). This is a good place to start if you're going out in the evening; otherwise venture to the trendy bars on **rue Colbert,** which lies in the heart of Tours, midway between place Plumereau and the cathedral. Allow a morning, afternoon, or evening to see Tours.

Cathédrale St-Gatien ★ CATHEDRAL   This cathedral honors a 3rd-century evangelist and has a Flamboyant Gothic facade flanked by towers with bases from the 12th century. The lanterns date from the Renaissance. The choir is from the 13th century, with new additions built in each century through the 16th. Sheltered inside is the handsome 16th-century tomb of Charles VIII and Anne de Bretagne's two children. Some of the glorious stained-glass windows are from the 13th century.

5 place de la Cathédrale. 📞 **02-47-70-21-00.** Free admission. Daily 9am–7pm.

Musée des Beaux-Arts ★ ART MUSEUM   For an art fix in Tours, stop by this provincial museum, worth visiting to see the lovely rooms and gardens of the former Archbishop's palace, parts dating from the 12th century. Hanging

If you aren't renting a car, several tour companies in Tours arrange full- and half-day visits to nearby castles, and three of them offer minibus tours that leave daily from the tourist office. **Acco-Dispo** (www.accodispo-tours.com; ℂ **06-82-00-64-51**), **Saint-Eloi Excursions** (http://saint-eloiexcursions.com; ℂ **06-70-82-78-75**), and **Quart de Tours** (www.quartde tours.com; ℂ **06-30-65-52-01**) all offer minibus tours that depart around 9am; you can reserve on the tourist office website (www.visaloire.com) or directly on the company websites. Costs range from 23€ to 55€ per person. The price usually does not include meals or admission to the châteaux, but participation in the tour qualifies you for reduced group rates. Most companies also offer custom tours and car services on request. Keep in mind that less is sometimes more when it comes to castle viewing; after two or three, you may not be able to remember which was which.

on the walls are works by Rubens, Delacroix, Rembrandt, and Boucher whereas the sculpture collection spans from Roman busts to moody Rodin. 18 place François Sicard. www.mba.tours.fr. ℂ **02-47-05-68-73.** Admission 5€ adults, 2:50€ seniors and students, free for children 12 and under. Wed–Mon 9am–12:45pm and 2pm–6pm. Bus: 3.

VILLANDRY ★★★

253km (157 miles) SW of Paris; 32km (20 miles) NE of Chinon; 18km (11 miles) W of Tours; 8km (5 miles) E of Azay-le-Rideau

The Renaissance Château de Villandry should be top of the list for any garden lover. Its 16th-century-style *jardins* are celebrated throughout Touraine and amaze visitors from around the world with their beauty and faithful historic preservation.

Essentials

GETTING THERE Three daily **buses** operate from Tours from July to October only; the trip takes about 30 minutes and costs 2€. For bus information, visit www.tourainefilvert.com or call ℂ **02-47-05-30-49.** Villandry has no train service. The nearest connection from Tours is in the town of Savonnières; the trip takes around 15 minutes and costs 3.50€ one-way. For information, visit www.voyages-sncf.com or call ℂ **36-35.** From Savonnières, you can walk along the Loire for 4km (2½ miles) to reach Villandry, rent a **bike** at the station, or take a **taxi.** You can also **drive,** following D7 from Tours.

Where to Eat & Stay

Le Cheval Rouge ★ MODERN FRENCH Next to the château, this is a surprising country restaurant serving up sophisticated versions of French classics. The bright dining room is welcoming or there is a large enclosed terrace with individual tables shaded with umbrellas. The chef carefully prepares foie gras profiteroles with fig jam; bass poached in sparkling Vouvray wine; and

Opulent room in Château de Villandry.

rump steak with goat cheese sauce. On a hot day, finish off with the frozen soufflé with Cointreau. The inn also rents 41 renovated rooms, decorated with modern appeal and furnishings. A double is 70€; the hotel also has several family rooms renting for 80€ to 100€.

9 rue Principale. www.lecheval-rouge.com. ℗ **02-47-50-02-07.** Main courses 13€–19€; fixed-price menu 24€–36€. Daily noon–2:30pm and 7–9pm.

Exploring the Gardens & Château

Château de Villandry ★★★ CASTLE/GARDENS Every square of the gardens is like a geometric mosaic. Designed on a trio of superimposed cloisters with a water garden on the highest level, the gardens were restored by the Spanish doctor and scientist Joachim Carvallo, great-grandfather of the present owner. The grounds contain 17km (11 miles) of boxwood sculpture, which the gardeners cut to style in only 2 weeks each September. The borders symbolize the faces of love: tender, tragic (represented by daggers), and crazy (with a labyrinth that doesn't get you anywhere). The vine arbors, citrus hedges, and walks keep six men busy full-time. The French vegetable garden is being reverted to all-organic.

A feudal castle once stood at Villandry. In 1536, Jean le Breton, François I's Finance Minister and former Ambassador to Italy, acquired the property and built the present château with strong influences of the Italian Renaissance. The buildings form a U and are surrounded by a moat. Near the gardens is a terrace from which you can see the small village and its 12th-century church. A tearoom on-site, **La Doulce Terrasse** (www.chateauvillandry.com; ℗ **02-47-50-02-10;** closed mid-Nov to mid-Feb), serves regional cuisine, including vegetables from the garden, fresh-baked bread, and homemade ice cream. For a more gourmet meal, try **Le Cheval Rouge** (p. 179).

www.chateauvillandry.com. ℗ **02-47-50-02-09.** Admission to gardens and château 10€ for adults, 6.50€ children 8 to 18, and free for children 7 and under, entrance to gardens only 6.50€ adults and 4.50€ for children 8 to 18. Gardens daily 9am–5 or 7:30pm, depending on the hour of sunset; château daily 9am–5:30 or 6:30pm, depending on a complicated seasonal schedule.

LANGEAIS ★

259km (161 miles) SW of Paris; 26km (16 miles) W of Tours

Dominating the town on a steep slope, this medieval fortress is one of the few châteaux actually on the Loire. Crossing over its drawbridge and through its massive towers takes you back 500 years to the start of the golden age of the Loire.

Essentials

GETTING THERE Several **trains** per day stop here en route from Tours or Saumur. The one-way fare from Saumur is 8.10€; the one-way fare from Tours 5.60€. Transit time from both cities is around 20 minutes. For schedules and information, visit www.voyages-sncf.com or call 𝄐 **36-35.** If you're **driving** from Tours, take D952 southwest to Langeais.

Exploring the Château

Château de Langeais ★★ CASTLE   On December 6, 1491, 15-year-old Anne de Bretagne was wed to Charles VIII at Langeais, permanently attaching Brittany to France. The original castle was built in the 10th century when Fulk III (972–1040), count of Anjou, sometimes called the "Black Falcon," seized Langeais from the Count of Blois. He erected the first keep, the ruins of which can still be seen. The present structure was built in 1465 in the late medieval style. The interior is well preserved and furnished, thanks to Jacques Siegfried, who not only restored it over 20 years, but also bequeathed it to the Institut de France in 1904.

The rooms re-create the ambience of a regal residence of the late Middle Ages, rich with ornamental fireplaces and tapestries. A remarkable 15th-century millefleurs tapestry decorates the Chambre de la Dame, and

Panoramic view of castle, garden and Langeais town.

seven superb tapestries known as the "Valiant Knights" cover the walls of the Salle des Preux.

The Banquet Hall features a mantelpiece carved to resemble a fortress, complete with crenellated towers. The Wedding Hall includes a re-creation of the marriage of Anne de Bretagne and Charles VIII with lavishly costumed wax figures. In the Luini Room is a large 1522 fresco by that artist, removed from a chapel on Lake Maggiore, Italy. It depicts Saint Francis of Assisi and Saint Elizabeth of Hungary with Mary and Joseph. Kids can learn medieval castle construction with interactive displays, or have some fun exploring the treehouse and the two playgrounds.

www.chateau-de-langeais.com. ⓒ **02-47-96-72-60.** Admission 9€ adults, 7.50€ students and ages 18–25, 5€ for children 10–17, free for 9 and under. Daily Apr–June and Sept to mid-Nov 9:30am–6:30pm; mid-Nov to Jan 10am–5pm; Feb–Mar 9:30am–5:30pm; July–Aug 9am–7pm.

AZAY-LE-RIDEAU ★★

261km (162 miles) SW of Paris; 21km (13 miles) SW of Tours

With its idyllic location and fairy-tale turrets, the Renaissance Château d'Azay-le-Rideau was deemed by neighboring writer Honoré de Balzac to be "a facetted diamond set in the Indre."

Essentials

GETTING THERE   To reach Azay-le-Rideau, take the **train** from Tours or Chinon. From either starting point, the trip time is about 30 minutes; the one-way fare is 5.10€ from Chinon, 5.80€ from Tours. For the same fare, the SNCF railway also operates a bus between Tours and Azay; the trip takes 50 minutes. For schedules and information, visit www.voyages-sncf.com or call ⓒ **36-35.** If you're **driving** from Tours, take D751 southwest to Azay-le-Rideau.

Where to Eat

L'Aigle d'Or ★★ TRADITIONAL FRENCH   In this practically one-horse town this isn't merely a watering hole. The tiny town of Azay holds one of the area's best value gastronomic gems. It might not look very special from the outside, which helps keep away the masses; however, the dining room's toasty fireplace and its rustic wooden beams reveal its true character. For decades now chef Jean Luc Fèvre has been wowing guests with his signature filet of beef Chinon and his seasonal creations such as quail with buttery cabbages, sandre fish stew with local Azay wine, or baked apple with local artisanal ice cream. Treat yourself to the wine pairing menu, a steal at only 72 euros and featuring wines produced in the vicinity of the château.

10 av. Adélaïde-Riché. www.laigle-dor.fr. ⓒ **02-47-45-24-58.** Main courses 15€–28€; fixed-price menus lunch 21€-30€, dinner 30€–58€. Mon–Tues and Thurs–Sat noon–1:30pm and 7:30–9pm Sun noon–1:30pm, closed Jan to mid-Feb.

Château d'Azay-le-Rideau.

Château d'Azay-le-Rideau ★★

CASTLE Its machicolated towers and blue-slate roof pierced with dormers give it a medieval air; however, its defensive, fortresslike appearance is all for show. The château was actually commissioned in the early 1500s for Gilles Berthelot, François I's finance minister, and his wife, Philippa, who supervised its construction.

Before you enter, circle the château and note the perfect proportions of the crowning achievement of the Renaissance in the Touraine. Check out its most fancifully ornate feature, the bay enclosing a grand stairway with a straight flight of steps. From the second-floor Royal Chamber, look out at the gardens. This lavish bedroom housed Louis XIII when he came through in 1619. The private apartments are lined with rich tapestries dating from the 16th and 17th centuries and feature examples of rare period furniture, like the Spanish *bargueno,* a carved wooden chest that held writing materials. Azay hosts a sound-and-light show most nights in July and August (details below).

http://azay-le-rideau.monuments-nationaux.fr. © **02-47-45-42-04.** Admission 8.50€ adults, 5.50€ youth 18-25, and free 17 and under. Daily July–Aug 9:30am–7pm; Apr–June and Sept 9:30am–6pm; and Oct–Mar 10am–12:30pm and 2–5:15pm. Admission to the evening sound-and-light show 9€ adults, 4€ children 5–12, free 4 and under; show is nightly mid-July to late Aug 8:30pm–midnight.

SAUMUR

299km (185 miles) SW of Paris; 53km (33 miles) SE of Angers

Saumur lies in a region of vineyards, where the Loire separates to encircle an island. It makes one of the best bases for exploring the western Loire Valley. A small but thriving town, it doesn't entirely live off its past: Saumur produces some 100,000 tons per year of the mushrooms the French adore. Balzac left us this advice: "Taste a mushroom and delight in the essential strangeness of the place." The cool tunnels for the *champignons* also provide the ideal resting place for the region's celebrated sparkling wines. Enjoy both of these local favorites at a neighborhood cafe.

As you drive along the Loire something other than castles may catch your eye along the riverbanks. The region of Anjou holds the largest concentration of troglodyte caves in all of France. The beige limestone of the area was put to good use building the many châteaux, and the empty caverns from the excavated stone were not left abandoned. Not surprisingly, the caves were first used to store bottles of the region's bubbly wine; more recently, however, many have been converted into homes, art galleries, and even restaurants. For a true troglodyte experience, stop in at the bustling and mainly underground artist town of **Turquant,** 10km (6 miles) east of Saumur (www.turquant.fr).

Essentials

GETTING THERE **Trains** run frequently between Tours Centre and Saumur. Some 20 trains per day arrive from Tours (trip time: 30–40 min.); the one-way fare is 12€. From the station, take bus A into town. For schedules and information, visit www.voyages-sncf.com or call ⓒ **36-35.** If you're **driving** from Tours, follow D952 or the A85 autoroute southwest to Saumur.

VISITOR INFORMATION The **Office de Tourisme** is on place de la Bilange (www.ot-saumur.fr; ⓒ **02-41-40-20-60**).

Where to Stay

Hôtel St-Pierre ★ Sophisticated Saumur style shines through at this reasonably priced hotel. In the shadows of the Eglise St-Pierre, you'll enjoy ambling the neighboring maze of historic city-center streets. The 500-year-old building has been brought up to 21st-century standards with creative care to every last detail. Guest rooms have been uniquely decorated with artistic touches and many showcase their architectural aspects such as stone fireplaces or thick wooden beams; the prestige rooms are the best and well worth the splurge. The small French town ambience is complete listening to the tolling church bells while relaxing in the garden terrace.

Rue Haute-Saint-Pierre. www.saintpierresaumur.com. ⓒ **02-41-50-33-00.** 14 units. 120€–20€ double, suite 250€. **Amenities:** Free parking; babysitting; room service; A/C; TV; hair dryer; minibar; free Wi-Fi.

Where to Eat

If you're just breezing through town or looking for a casual bite, try **Les Tontons** (www.bistrotlestontons-saumur.blogspot.fr; ⓒ **02-41-59-59-40**), a welcoming English-friendly bistro with great-value daily lunch specials and a fabulous local wine list. If you're visiting the equestrian center, you can rub shoulders with the riders at nearby **Le Carrousel** (www.le-resto-du-carrousel. com; ⓒ **02-41-51-00-40**), showcasing regional cuisine for 13€ for lunch and from 20€ at dinner.

Le Gambetta ★★ MODERN FRENCH For cuisine as chic as the city of Saumur, book a table at this avant-garde address. The contemporary decor matches the inventive menu of Michelin-starred chef Mickael Pihours. He takes French cuisine far afield with offerings such as Saint-Pierre fish, sprinkled with Yuzu shavings, served with pomegranate, quinoa and Japanese Enokis mushrooms; Peking style pork with mint flavored semolina and chickpea naans; and adventurous desserts, such as Valrhona grand cru chocolate and black-tea infused yoghurt and mandarins.

12 rue Gambetta. www.restaurantle gambetta.com. *C* **02-41-67-66-66.** Main courses 20€–30€; lunch menu 26€, dinner menu 32€–99€. Tues and Thurs–Sun noon–2pm; Tues and Thurs–Sat 7–9pm. Closed 2 weeks in Jan, 3 weeks end of Jul–Aug.

Exploring the Area

Old Town of Saumur with its château.

Of all the Loire cities, Saumur remains the most bourgeois; perhaps that's why Balzac used it for his classic characterization of a smug little town in "Eugénie Grandet." Saumur is also famous as the birthplace of the *couturière* Coco Chanel.

The *Saumuriens* are among the best equestrians in the world. Founded in 1768, the city's riding school, **Cadre Noir de Saumur ★**, avenue de l'Ecole Nationale d'Equitation (www.cadrenoir.fr; *C* **02-41-53-50-50**), is one of the grandest in Europe, rivaling Vienna's, enough so to be deemed a UNESCO World Heritage Site in 2011. The stables house some 350 horses. Mid-February to October, 1-hour tours (8€ adults, 6€ children) run from 10am to 11am and 2pm to 4pm from Monday afternoon to Saturday afternoon. Tours depart about every 20 minutes. Some 48km (30 miles) of specialty tracks wind around the town—to see a rider carry out a curvet is a thrill. The performances peak during the **Carrousel de Saumur ★★** on the third weekend in July.

After lengthy restoration work, the **Château de Saumur** (www.chateau-saumur.com; *C* **02-41-83-31-31**) has reopened to the public. The 12th-century château was the royal residence of Philippe II in the early 13th century and hasn't changed much since being immortalized in the September scene of the famous illuminated manuscript "Les Très Riches Heures" in 1410. The interior of the castle has displays recounting the history of the château as well as examples of tapestries, porcelain, furniture, and other decorative arts. An evening equestrian-and-light show is held in July and August in front of the château (Thurs–Sat; admission 19€ adult, 15€ children). Admission to the château museum from June to September is 7€ adult, 5€ children 7–16, free under 7; spring and autumn 6€ adult, 4€ children (daily Apr to mid-June and mid-Sept to Oct 10am–1pm and 2pm–5:30pm; mid-June to mid-Sept 10am–6:30pm; closed Nov–Mar).

The area surrounding the town has become famous for its delicate sparkling wines. In the center of Saumur, you can wander the many aisles of **La Maison du Vin,** 7 quai Carnot (www.vinsvaldeloire.fr; ℂ **02-41-38-45-83**), and choose from a large stock direct from the many surrounding vineyards.

An alternative is to travel east of Saumur to the village of **St-Hilaire,** where you'll find a host of vineyards. One of the better ones is **Veuve Amiot,** 21 rue Jean-Ackerman (www.veuveamiot.fr; ℂ **02-41-83-14-14**), where you can tour the wine cellars, taste different vintages, and buy bottles right in the showroom (daily except Sun in Jan and Feb).

Mushrooms enthusiasts can learn about the cultivation of the local fungi first-hand at the **Musée du Champignon** (www.musee-du-champignon.com; ℂ **02-41-50-31-55**). Don't miss the annual mushroom festival in October. Admission to the museum is 8.20€ adult, 6€ under 18 (daily Feb to mid-Nov 10am–6pm and until 7pm Apr–Sept).

CHINON ★★

283km (175 miles) SW of Paris; 48km (30 miles) SW of Tours; 31km (19 miles) SW of Langeais

In the film "Joan of Arc," Ingrid Bergman identified the dauphin as he tried to conceal himself among his courtiers. This took place in real life at the Château de Chinon, one of the oldest fortress-châteaux in France. Charles VII centered his government at Chinon from 1429 to 1450. In 1429, with the English besieging Orléans, the Maid of Orléans prevailed upon the dauphin to give her an army. The rest is history. The seat of French power stayed at Chinon until the end of the Hundred Years' War.

Essentials

GETTING THERE   The SNCF runs about seven **trains** and four **buses** every day to Chinon from Tours (trip time: 45 min. by train; 1 hr., 15 min. by bus); the one-way fare is 9.90€. For schedules and information, visit www.voyages-sncf.com or call ℂ **36-35.** Both buses and trains arrive at the train station, which lies at the edge of the very small town. If you're **driving** from Tours, take D751 southwest through Azay-le-Rideau to Chinon.

VISITOR INFORMATION   The **Office de Tourisme** is at place Hofheim (www.chinon-valdeloire.com; ℂ **02-47-93-17-85**).

Where to Eat & Stay

Château de Marçay ★★★   Fairytale dreams come true without breaking the bank at this unique château-hotel. The reverie begins as you drive through the gate onto the grounds of this imposing medieval fortress surrounded by vineyards. The 21st century has made it to the interior, with all the modern comforts. Guest rooms feature vintage floral prints and most rooms have massive exposed beams to augment its castle charm; the less expensive

IN PURSUIT OF grape

Chinon is famous for its wines, which crop up on prestigious lists around the world. Supermarkets and wine shops throughout the region sell them; families that have been in the business longer than anyone can remember maintain the two most interesting stores. At **Caves Plouzeau,** 94 rue Haute-St-Maurice (www.plouzeau.com; ✆ **02-47-93-32-11**), the 12th-century cellars were dug to provide building blocks for the foundations of the château. The present management dates from 1929; bottles of red or white wine cost from 6€ to 12€. You're welcome to climb down to the cellars (open for visits and wine sales Apr–Sept

Tues–Sat 11am–1pm and 3–7pm and Oct–Mar Thurs–Sat 2–6pm, Sat 11am–1pm and 3–8pm).

The cellars at **Couly-Dutheil,** 12 rue Diderot (www.coulydutheil-chinon.com; ✆ **02-47-97-20-20**), are suitably medieval; many were carved from rock. This company produces largely Chinon wines (mostly reds); the popularity of its Bourgueil and St-Nicolas de Bourgueil has grown in North America in recent years. Tours of the caves and a *dégustation des vins* (wine tasting) require an advance call and cost 4€ to 6€ per person. Visits are conducted year-round 8am to noon and 1:45 to 5:45pm.

rooms are located in the Pavillon des Vignes annex. The restaurant is one of the best in the region where you can dine on regional seasonal specialties accompanied by the château's own wine (fixed-price menus at lunch 30€–35€ and dinner 48€–85€). Try your hand at creating the same dishes during one of the chef's cooking classes (70€ person).

Marçay. www.chateaudemarcay.com. ✆ **02-47-93-03-47.** 30 units. 120€–235€ double; 265€–325€ suite. Closed mid-Jan to mid-Mar. Take D116 for 7km (4¼ miles) southwest of Chinon. **Amenities:** Restaurant; bar; outdoor pool; room service; tennis court; TV; hair dryer; minibar; free Wi-Fi.

Hostellerie Gargantua ★   This is the one of the most original economic hotels in all of the Loire. Located in the heart of town at the foot of the Château de Chinon, the castlelike 15th-century building used to be a courthouse where the father of writer François Rabelais (see "Musée Rabelais–La Devinière," below) worked as a lawyer. A highlight is its early Renaissance spiral staircase. The hotel definitely has its quirks, but these are over-ruled by the large high ceilinged guest rooms; most have canopy beds and some stone fireplaces and/or views of the castle. Dine in its medieval hall, where you can sample some tasty local freshwater *sandre* prepared with Chinon wine or duckling with dried pears and smoked lard.

73 rue Haute St. Maurice. www.hotel-gargantua.com. ✆ **02-47-93-04-71.** 7 units. 59€–89€ double. Closed Dec. **Amenities:** Restaurant; bar; TV; free Wi-Fi.

Where to Eat

Les Années 30 ★ FRENCH   Tucked away on the oldest street in Chinon is the town's most cutting-edge cuisine. Set in an appealing 16th-century building, the interior is decorated with paintings and photos from the 1930s, hence the restaurant's name. Its excellent-value menu could include such dishes as snails from nearby Mouliherne in wild mushroom cream or braised veal sweetbreads with caramelized artichokes drizzled in lime. The passion fruit *crème brulée* with ginger ice cream is the perfect way to end a summertime lunch on its vine-draped terrace.

78 Rue Haute St Maurice. www.lesannees30.com. © **02-47-93-37-18.** Reservations recommended. Main courses 16€–28€; fixed-price lunch menu during the week 18€, dinner menus 26€–45€. Thurs–Mon 12:15–2:00pm; Tues 7:30–10pm in July–Aug, closed mid-June to July 1, mid-Nov to early Dec.

Exploring the Town & the Château

On the banks of the Vienne, the winding streets of Chinon are lined with many medieval turreted houses, built in the heyday of the court. The most typical street is **rue Voltaire,** lined with 15th- and 16th-century townhouses. At no. 44, Richard the Lion-Hearted died on April 6, 1199, from a wound suffered during the siege of Chalus in Limousin. The Grand Carroi, in the heart of Chinon, was the crossroads of the Middle Ages. For the best view, drive across the river and turn right onto quai Danton. From this vantage point, you'll be able to see the castle in relation to the town and the river.

Chinon is known for its delightful red wines. After you visit the attractions, stop for a glass on one of Chinon's terraced cafes or visit a few local vineyards.

Château de Chinon ★★ CASTLE   The château, which was more or less in ruins, has undergone a massive excavation and restoration that started in 2003 and so far has resulted in beautifully restored ramparts, castle keep, and royal apartments, which now look more or less as they did in the good old days. After being roofless for 200 years, the apartments sport pitched and gabled slate roofs and wood floors, and the keep is once again fortified. The restoration, while not exact (due to the state of the original building), gives the overall impression of what the castle looked like around the time of Joan of Arc's visit, an era brought to life for children through their interactive exhibits and games.

Btw. rue St-Maurice and av. Francois Mitterrand. www.forteressechinon.fr. © **02-47-93-13-45.** Admission 8.50€ adults, 6.50€ students, free for children 12 and under. Daily May–Aug 9:30am–7pm; Mar–Apr and Sept 9am–6pm; Oct–Feb 9:30am–5pm.

Musée Rabelais–La Devinière ★ MUSEUM   The most famous son of Chinon, François Rabelais, the earthy humanist Renaissance writer, lived in town on rue de la Lamproie. (There's a plaque marking the spot where his father practiced law and maintained a home and office.) The museum in his honor, just outside the hamlet of Seuilly, 5.5km (3½ miles) west of Chinon, was an isolated cottage at the time of his birth. Spending the early years of his life here profoundly affected the writer, and the area served as inspiration for parts of his most famous work, "Gargantua." Exhibits are spread out on the three floors of the main building, the dovecote, and the wine cellars, each area dedicated to an aspect of Rabelais, his times, and his role in Chinon. It is still an active vineyard, producing 4,000 bottles of excellent wine that would do the writer proud.

La Devinière, just outside of Seuilly off the N751. www.monuments-touraine.fr. ℭ **02-47-95-91-18.** Admission 5.50€ adults, 4.50€ students, free for children 11 and under. Daily Apr–June 10am–12:30pm and 2–6pm; July–Aug 10am–7pm; Sept 10am–12:30pm and 2–6pm; Oct–Mar Wed–Mon 10am–12:30pm and 2–5pm. From Chinon, follow the road signs pointing to Saumur and the D117.

USSE ★

295km (183 miles) SW of Paris; 14km (8¾ miles) NE of Chinon

The Château d'Ussé is truly a fairy-tale castle. At the edge of the dark forest of Chinon in Rigny-Ussé, it was the inspiration for Perrault's legend of "The Sleeping Beauty" ("La Belle au Bois Dormant").

Essentials

GETTING THERE   The château is best visited by car or on an organized bus tour from Tours. If you're driving from Tours or Villandry, follow D7 to Ussé.

Exploring the Château

Château d'Ussé ★ CASTLE   Conceived as a fortress in 1424, this complex of steeples, turrets, towers, and dormers was erected at the dawn of the Renaissance on a hill overlooking the Indre River. The terraces, laden with orange and lemon trees, were laid out by the royal gardener Le Nôtre. When the need for a fortified château passed, the north wing was demolished to open up a greater view. The château was later owned by the duc de Duras and then by Mme. de la Rochejacquelin; its present owner, the marquis de Blacas, has opened many rooms to the public, most recently the private dining room and the dungeon.

www.chateaudusse.fr. ℭ **02-47-95-54-05.** Admission 14€ adults, 4€ students and children 8–16, and free children 7 and under. Daily mid-Feb to Mar 10am–6pm; Apr–Aug 10am–7pm; and Sept–mid-Nov 10am–6pm; closed the rest of the year.

FONTEVRAUD-L'ABBAYE ★★

304km (188 miles) SW of Paris; 16km (10 miles) SE of Saumur

The Plantagenet dynasty is buried in the Abbaye Royale de Fontevraud. The kings, whose male line ended in 1485, were also the comtes d'Anjou, and they wanted to be buried in their native soil. This regal patronage led to the building of one of Europe's largest medieval monastery complexes.

Essentials

GETTING THERE   If you're **driving,** take D147 about 4km (2½ miles) from the village of Montsoreau. In season, you can take a **bus** (Line 1) from

Saumur; schedules vary according to school holidays—visit the bus company's website, www.agglobus.fr, to download the schedule or call (℗ **02-41-51-11-87**). The one-way fare for the 30-minute trip is 1.50€.

Where to Eat

La Licorne ★ MODERN FRENCH   Luckily the frugal monks' lifestyle of the Fontevraud Abbey isn't replicated at this nearby popular dining spot. Located on a walkway between the abbey and the parish church, this 18th-century bourgeois home exudes the grace of the *ancien régime*. However, the service isn't quite as regal and can be somewhat slow. So sit back and relax in its walled garden; the excellent-value menu is certainly worth the wait. It includes refined dishes such as filet of local Féra freshly caught from lake Léman in a white wine sauce; royal Maine d'Anjou pigeon *confit* served with a cauliflower flan, roasted *magret de canard* in a red wine reduction. Go all out with the profiteroles of goat cheese or the poached pear with absinthe ice cream.

Allée Ste-Catherine. www.restaurant-gastronomique-licorne.fr. ℗ **02-41-51-72-49.** Main courses 15€–30€; fixed-price menu 19€–65€, child menu 17€. Nov–Apr Tues–Sun noon–2pm; Tues and Thurs–Sat 7–9pm; May–Oct daily noon–2pm and 7–9pm. Closed 2 last weeks of Dec.

Exploring the Abbey

Fontevraud-l'Abbaye ★★ ABBEY   In this 12th-century Romanesque church—with four Byzantine domes—lie the remains of two English kings or princes, including Henry II of England, the first Plantagenet king, and his wife, Eleanor of Aquitaine, the most famous woman of the Middle Ages. Their crusading son, Richard the Lion-Hearted, is also entombed here. The Plantagenet line ended with the death of Richard III at the 1485 Battle of Bosworth. The tombs fared badly during the Revolution, when mobs desecrated the sarcophagi and scattered their contents on the floor.

More intriguing than the tombs is the octagonal **Tour d'Evraud,** the last remaining Romanesque kitchen in France. Dating from the 12th century, it contains five of its original eight *apsides* (half-rounded indentations originally conceived as chapels), each crowned with a conically roofed turret. A pyramid tops the conglomeration, capped by an open-air lantern tower pierced with lancets. Robert d'Arbrissel, who spent much of his life as a recluse, founded the abbey in 1101. Aristocratic ladies occupied one part; many, including discarded mistresses of kings, had been banished from court. The four youngest daughters of Louis XV were educated here. Since 1975, the abbey has also functioned as a cultural center, offering expositions, concerts, and seminars.

www.abbaye-fontevraud.com. ℗ **02-41-51-73-52.** Admission 10€ adults, 7€ students, free 8 and under. Daily Apr–June and Sept–Oct 9:30am-6pm; daily July–Aug 9:30am–7pm; daily Nov–Dec 10am–5:30pm; and Feb–Mar Tues–Sun 10am–5:30pm; closed Jan.

PROVENCE

by Kathryn Tomasetti

The ancient Greeks left their vines, the Romans their monuments, but it was the 19th-century Impressionists who most shaped the romance of Provence today. Cézanne, Gauguin, Chagall, and countless others were drawn to the unique light and vibrant spectrum brought forth by what van Gogh called "the transparency of the air."

Provence, perhaps more than any other part of France, blends past and present with an impassioned pride. It has its own language and customs, and some of its festivals go back to medieval times. The region is bound on the north by the Dauphine River, on the west by the Rhône, on the east by the Alps, and on the south by the Mediterranean. In chapter 8, we focus on the part of Provence known as the Côte d'Azur, or the French Riviera.

AVIGNON ★★★

691km (428 miles) S of Paris; 83km (51 miles) NW of Aix-en-Provence; 98km (61 miles) NW of Marseille

In the 14th century, Avignon was the capital of Christendom. What started as a temporary stay by Pope Clement V in 1309, when Rome was deemed too dangerous even for clergymen, became a 67-year golden age. The cultural and architectural legacy left by the six popes who served during this period makes Avignon one of Europe's most alluring medieval destinations.

Today this walled city of some 95,000 residents is a major stop on the route from Paris to the Mediterranean. In recent years, it has become known as a cultural center, thanks to its annual international performing-arts festivals and wealth of experimental theaters and art galleries.

Essentials

ARRIVING Frequent TGV **trains** depart from Paris's Gare de Lyon. The ride takes 2 hours and 40 minutes and arrives at Avignon's modern TGV station, located 6 minutes from town by a speedy rail link. The one-way fare is around 57€–95€ depending on the date and time, although it can also be as cheap as 19€ if booked well in advance. TGVs also arrive from Marseille (trip time: 35 min.; 30€ one-way), and Aix-en-Provence (trip time: 20 min.; 25€ one-way).

Town walls and fortifications, Avignon.

Regular trains, leaving from the Avignon Centre station, depart for Arles every hour or so (trip time: 20min.; 7.70€ one-way). For rail information, visit www.voyages-sncf.com or call ✆ **36-35**. The regional **bus** routes (www.info-ler.fr; ✆ **08-21-20-22-03**) go from Avignon to Arles (trip time: 1 hr., 10 min.; 7.10€ one-way) and Aix-en Provence (trip time: 1 hr., 15 min.; 17€ one-way). The bus station at Avignon is the **Gare Routière, 5 av. Monclar** (✆ **04-90-82-07-35**). If you're **driving** from Paris, take A6 south to Lyon, and then A7 south to Avignon.

VISITOR INFORMATION   The **Office de Tourisme** is at 41 cours Jean-Jaurès (www.avignon-tourisme.com; ✆ **04-32-74-32-74**).

CITY LAYOUT   Avignon's picturesque Old Town is surrounded by 14th-century ramparts. Within the walls is a mix of winding roads, medieval townhouses, and pedestrianized streets. To the west of the city is the Rhône River, and beyond, Villeneuve les Avignon. Just south of the Old Town sits the Gare d'Avignon Centre train station.

SPECIAL EVENTS   The international **Festival d'Avignon** (www.festival-avignon.com; ✆ **04-90-14-14-14**), held for 3 weeks in July, focuses on avant-garde theater, dance, and music. Companies from around the world come here to strut their latest stuff in the "On," or official, festival. Tickets, which range from 17€ to 47€, are snapped up quickly; visit the website for info on advanced sales. An edgier (and cheaper) alternative festival, the **Avignon OFF** (www.avignonleoff.com; ✆ **04-90-85-13-08**), takes place almost simultaneously in July, with hundreds of theater companies performing short pieces in various improbable venues. From morning to midnight, the streets are packed with theater lovers and actors hawking their shows; be sure to pick up a program to see what's on.

From mid-August through mid-October, the Palais des Papes' cour d'Honneur is illuminated by **Les Luminessences d'Avignon** (www.leslum inessences-avignon.com), a total-immersion 3-D light and sound show. Shows

Provence

Map labels:

ALPES-MARITIMES

Grasse

St-Raphaël
Ste-Maxime
St-Tropez

D562
Le Muy
Fréjus

Castellane

Barrême

ÎLES D'HYÈRES
Île du Levant
PORT-CROS
NATIONAL PARK
Île de
Port-Cros

D559

D98

D900

N85

Digne

ALPES-DE-
HAUTE-
PROVENCE

Lac de
Ste-Croix

D952

Riez

Draguignan

VAR

Barjols

Hyères

Île de Porquerolles

Sisteron

Volonne

Peyruis

A51

Oraison

Manosque

Rians

St-Maximin-
la-Ste-Baume

Brignoles

Cuers

Pierrefeu

Le Beausset

Toulon

A57

Forcalquier

Mt. du Lubéron

PROVENCE-ALPES-
CÔTE-D'AZUR

A8

A50

Bandol
Sanary

Mt. Ventoux

Apt

Gordes

Bonnieux

Cadenet

Durance

**Aix-en-
Provence**

A51

A52

Aubagne

Marseille

A7

A55

Château d'If
Îles du Frioul

Cassis

La Ciotat

Cap Croisette
Île de Riou

Carpentras

VAUCLUSE

Cavaillon

D900

D973

Salon-de-Provence

A7

Étang de
Berre

Istres

Golfe
de Fos

MEDITERRANEAN SEA

D938

Châteauneuf-
du-Pape

Orange

A7

Rhône

A9

St-Rémy-de-
Provence

Les Baux

Fontvieille

Arles

A54

BOUCHES-DU-RHÔNE

N568

Fos-sur-Mer

Martigues

Pt-St-
Louis

Grand Rhône

Bagnols-sur-Cèze

D6

Uzès

LANGUEDOC-
ROUSSILLON

Beaucaire
Tarascon

GARD

Gard

N106

Nîmes

A9

A54

St-Gilles

N572
Vauvert

Aigues-
Mortes

Petit Rhône

Étang de
Vaccarès

CAMARGUE

D570

Stes-Maries-
de-la-Mer

Beauduc

FRANCE
Paris

20 mi
20 km

in English are held at 10:15pm on Mondays, Wednesdays, and Fridays. Admission is 10€; 8€ for students, seniors over 60, and children from 8 to 17 years old; and free for children 7 and under.

Getting Around

ON FOOT   All of Avignon's major sights—as well as its infinitely enchanting back streets—are easily accessible on foot. The helpful tourist office's free maps are marked with four easy walking routes, ideal for getting a feel for the city.

BY BICYCLE & MOTOR SCOOTER   The **Vélopop** bicycle-sharing scheme (www.velopop.fr; from 1€ per day) lets registered riders borrow any of the city's 200 bikes for up to 30 minutes at a time for free. To get out of town and explore the surrounding countryside, **Provence Bike,** 7 av. St-Ruf (www.provence-bike.com; ℂ **04-90-27-92-61**), rents different models for around 12€ to 40€ per day. It's possible to reserve a bike online. Alternatively, new outfit **Daytour,** Île de la Barthelasse (www.daytour.fr; ℂ **04-90-80-63-50**), rents standard and electric bikes (from 18€ for 2 hr.). A free app is included in the rental fee, detailing various self-guided tours around the region, including routes through the nearby Châteauneuf-du-Pape vineyards.

BY CAR   Traffic and a labyrinthine one-way system means it's best to park once you've arrived in Avignon's town center. Seven fee-paying parking lots and two free ones are dotted around the city. See the Avignon tourist office website for details.

BY TAXI   **Taxis Avignon** (www.taxis-avignon.fr; ℂ **04-90-82-20-20**).

BY PUBLIC TRANSPORT   Eco-friendly **Baladine** vehicles (www.tcra.fr; Aug–June Mon–Sat 10am–12:30pm and 2–6pm; July daily same hours) zip around within the city walls for 0.50€ per ride. Avignon is also currently undergoing extensive roadwork for the construction of a citywide tram system. It's due to begin service around town in 2018.

[FastFACTS] AVIGNON

ATMs/Banks   Avignon's town center is home to banks aplenty, including three on or nearby rue de la République.

Doctors & Hospitals   **Hôpital Général Henri Duffaut,** 305 rue Raoul Follereau (www.ch-avignon.fr; ℂ **04-32-75-33-33**).

Internet Access   The Avignon municipality is in the process of installing free Wi-Fi in public areas around town. It's currently available in **square Perdiguier,** just behind the Tourist Office. However, to get online, you'll need to register a French cell phone number in order to receive an access code by text message. Don't have one to hand? Head a block eastwards to **Milk Shop,** 26 place des Corps Saints (www.milkshop.fr; ℂ **09-82-54-16-82**), a little cafe that offers its patrons free Wi-Fi.

Mail & Postage   **La Poste,** 4 cours Président Kennedy (ℂ **36-31**).

Pharmacies   **Pharmacie des Halles,** 48 rue Bonneterie (ℂ **04-90-82-54-27**).

Avignon

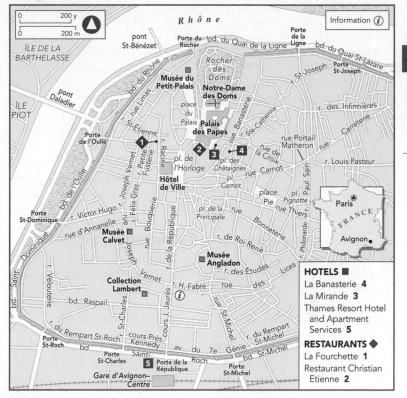

HOTELS ■
La Banasterie **4**
La Mirande **3**
Thames Resort Hotel
and Apartment
Services **5**

RESTAURANTS ◆
La Fourchette **1**
Restaurant Christian
Etienne **2**

Where to Stay

For travelers on a budget, the friendly **Hôtel Le Colbert** (www.avignon-hotel-colbert.com) is an excellent town center option.

La Banasterie ★   This pretty B&B is situated in a 16th-century property just opposite the Palais des Papes. It's owned by gregarious chocolate lovers Françoise and Jean-Michel Rivière—and their candy-fueled passion permeates throughout. The traditionally decorated bedrooms (exposed stone walls, sumptuous fabrics) are named for varieties of chocolate bean, and decadent cups of cocoa are offered at bedtime. The indulgent breakfast alone (included in the rate) makes this spot unmissable. Note there is no elevator.

11 rue de la Banasterie. www.labanasterie.com. © **06-87-72-96-36.** 5 units. 100€–145€ double; 145€–190€ suite. Parking 10€. **Amenities:** Free Wi-Fi.

La Mirande ★★★   La Mirande was once a 14th-century cardinal's palace from the adjoining Palais des Papes. It now boasts an additional 7 centuries of fixtures and features in one gloriously palatial package. The hotel's owners are not from the hotel industry, and it shows. Guestrooms are no-expense-spared collections of locally sourced antique furniture, Carrara marble, authentic Chinoiserie, and Murano chandeliers. The courtyard chairs, for example, used to belong in the Musée d'Orsay in Paris. La Mirande's gourmet restaurant and **Le Marmiton,** a classic French cooking school, are headed by chef Séverine Sagnet. Both take an environmentally friendly approach to their creations, using seasonal and organic ingredients sourced from local producers. All-organic afternoon tea—featuring homemade madeleines, thick hot chocolate, and Kombucha—is served daily on the patio or terrace.

4 place de l'Amirande. www.la-mirande.fr. ✆ **04-90-14-20-20.** 27 units. 370€–690€ double; 810€–1,715€ suite. Parking 25€. **Amenities:** Restaurant; bar; boutique; concierge; room service; free Wi-Fi. Restaurant closed in January.

ALTERNATIVE ACCOMMODATIONS

Thames Resort Hotel and Apartment Services ★★ This handful of suites and superbly equipped apartments (formerly named the Thames Résidences) lies a short stroll from both the train station and Avignon's city center. Decor is Provençal-themed, and each one boasts either its own private balcony or panoramic views over the town's medieval ramparts. As well as free satellite television, speedy Wi-Fi, and unlimited free telephone calls abroad, some of the well-equipped residences also possess kitchenettes and sleek Nespresso Pixie espresso machines.

36 bd. Saint Roch. www.thames-residences.com. ✆ **04-32-70-17-01.** 8 units. 129€–214€ 2-person apartments (4th night free Oct–Mar). Free parking. **Amenities:** Free Wi-Fi.

Where to Eat

La Fourchette ★★ PROVENÇAL Set a block back from the bustling place de l'Horloge, this upscale bistro has been a local favorite since it opened its doors in 1982. Philippe Hiély, the sixth generation in his family's long line of chefs, dishes up a cuisine that's sophisticated yet hearty: Think saffron-infused salt cod *brandade* served with crusty bread, or seared scallops atop fennel purée. Walls are adorned with an eclectic collection of antique cutlery (*la fourchette* translates as "the fork").

17 rue Racine. www.la-fourchette.net. ✆ **04-90-85-20-93.** Reservations recommended. Main courses 20€; fixed-price menu 35€. Mon–Fri 12:15–1:45pm and 7:15–9:45pm. Closed 3 weeks in Aug.

Restaurant Christian Etienne ★★★ PROVENÇAL This Michelin-starred temple of gastronomy is perched atop a 12th-century stone edifice—complete with 15th-century frescoes—just next door to the Palais des Papes. Avignon-born Chef Etienne is wildly innovative, and many of his dishes have a more than a hint of molecular influence. Fixed-price menus are themed around single ingredients such as duck, lobster, truffles, or (summertime only) heavenly heirloom tomatoes.

10 rue de Mons. www.christian-etienne.fr. ✆ **04-90-86-16-50.** Reservations required. Fixed-price lunch 35€, dinner 80€–150€. Tues–Sat noon–1:15pm and 7:30–9pm. Closed 2 weeks in Nov.

Medieval bridge, Pont St-Bénézet, in Avignon.

Exploring Avignon

Avignon is undoubtedly one of the prettiest towns in France. From its impressively imposing skyline to the verdant Île de la Barthelasse, it's a delight to simply amble along aimlessly, perhaps stopping at a sidewalk cafe or two en route. Countless hidden gems crop up along the way, including 50 or so trompe-l'œil frescoes that decorate many of Avignon's city center facades. Painted by artists Dominique Durand and Marion Pochy, each one depicts a highlight from past editions of the Avignon Festival. Be sure to keep an eye out for the sun-dappled courtyard of the **Hôtel d'Europe** (www.heurope. com). This luxury hotel has been in operation since 1799, welcoming luminaries from Charles Dickens to Jacqueline Kennedy.

And then there's that bridge they all sing about. The star of "Sur le Pont d'Avignon" is actually a bridge called the **Pont St-Bénézet ★★** (www. avignon-pont.com; ℰ **04-32-74-32-74**). Constructed between 1177 and 1185, it once spanned the Rhône, connecting Avignon with Villeneuve-lèz-Avignon. Today it is a ruin, with only 4 of its original 22 arches remaining (half of it fell into the river back in 1669). The remains of the bridge have the same opening hours as those of the Palais des Papes (see below). Admission is 5€ adults, 4€ seniors and ages 8–17, and free children 7 and under.

Collection Lambert ★★ MUSEUM This contemporary art space is housed within an 18th-century private home that once belonged to collector and gallery owner Yvon Lambert. It stages three groundbreaking exhibitions each year. Works may range from video and photography to conceptual installations. Major artists such as Anselm Kiefer, Jenny Holzer, and Cy Twombly have all featured. After a lengthy renovation project, Collection Lambert more than doubled its size, reopening in July 2015 with the exhibition "An Imaginary Museum," dedicated to the work of opera, film, and theatre director Patrice Chéreau.

5 rue Violette. www.collectionlambert.fr. ℰ **04-90-16-56-20.** Admission changes according to exhibition, free for children 5 and under. July–Aug daily 11am–7pm; Sept–June Tues–Sun 11am–6pm.

Musée Angladon ★★ MUSEUM Haute-couture designer Jacques Doucet (1853–1929) didn't limit himself to the appreciation of finely cut fabrics. His former home is now a showcase for the international artworks that he and his wife collected over their lifetimes—from 16th-century Buddhas and Louis XVI chairs to Degas's famous dancers and canvases by Cézanne, Sisley, and Modigliani.

5 rue Laboureur. www.angladon.com. ℰ **04-90-82-29-03.** Admission 6.50€ adults, 4.50€ seniors, 3€ students and children 13–17, 1.50€ children 7–12, free for children 6 and under. Tues–Sun 1–6pm. Closed Tues in winter.

Musée du Petit-Palais ★ MUSEUM An ideal complement to the Palais des Papes' architectural austerity, this museum's artworks were originally part of a collection belonging to 19th-century art lover Giampietro Campana. Today this museum's collection focuses on paintings from the Italian and Provençal schools of the 13th to 16th century, in particular the "Avignon School" an artistic movement that was a product of the city's golden age, when the Pope lived in the palace next door. The collection's star attraction is Botticelli's "Madonna with Child."

Palais des Archevêques, place du Palais des Papes. www.petit-palais.org. ℰ **04-90-86-44-58.** Admission 6€ adults, 3€ students, seniors and ages 12–18, free for children 11 and under. Wed–Mon 10am–1pm and 2–6pm.

Palais des Papes ★★★ PALACE Dominating Avignon from a hilltop is one of the most famous, or notorious, palaces in the Christian world. Headquarters of a schismatic group of 14th-century cardinals who came close to destroying the authority of the popes in Rome, this fortress is the city's most popular monument. The gargantuan palace, one of the largest Gothic buildings in Europe, was home to seven popes, a huge library, and the administrative offices of all Christendom for 67 years.

Because of the Palais des Papes' massive size, you may be tempted to opt for a guided tour—but these can be monotonous. The detailed audioguide, which now includes cutting-edge 3-D animation and is included in the price of admission, will likely suffice.

A highlight is the **Chapelle St-Jean,** known for its frescoes of John the Baptist and John the Evangelist, attributed to the school of Matteo Giovanetti and painted between 1345 and 1348. The **Grand Tinel (Banquet Hall)** is about 41m (134 ft.) long and 9m (30 ft.) wide; the pope's table stood on the south side. The walls of the **Pope's Bedroom,** on the first floor of the Tour des Anges, are painted with foliage, birds, and squirrels. The **Studium (Stag Room)**—the study of Clement VI—was frescoed in 1343 with hunting scenes. The **Grande Audience (Great Receiving Hall)** contains frescoes of the prophets, also attributed to Giovanetti and painted in 1352.

Note that the 12th-century **Cathédrale Notre-Dame des Doms cathedral,** just next door on the main square, contains the elaborate tombs of popes Jean XXII and Benoît XII.

Place du Palais des Papes. www.palais-des-papes.com. ℰ **04-32-74-32-74.** Admission (including audioguide) 11€ adults, 9€ seniors, students and ages 8–17, free for children 7 and under. Daily Nov–Feb 9:30am–5:45pm; Mar 9am–6:30pm; Apr–June and Sept–Nov 9am–7pm; July 9am–8pm; Aug 9am–8:30pm

Organized Tours

Avignon's Office de Tourisme organizes a range of themed tours around the city, in particular the excellent **"Secret Palace" tour,** an access-all-areas ramble around the Palais de Papes. You'll wind your way through the Palace's private apartments, hidden passageways, and secret gardens (25€ including refreshments, in English Apr–May and Sept–Oct Sat at 10am), areas that few visitors can claim to have seen.

For epicureans, Jean-Claude Altmayer (formerly of La Mirande, p. 195) now offers cooking ateliers in French and English at the brand-new **Maison de Fogasses,** 7 rue des Fourbisseurs (www.maison-de-fogasses.com; © **04-90-87-25-02**). Courses may take in a trip to the market, or are centered on a certain skill, such as sauce-making or vegetarian cuisine. From 135€ per person, followed by tasting and wine.

Avignon is also the capital of the Côtes du Rhône appellation. François Marcou at **Avignon Wine Tour** (www.avignon-wine-tour.com; © **06-28-05-33-84**) offers five different wine-tasting itineraries, from exploring Châteauneuf-du-Pape to dropping into domaines located in the Luberon, and includes introductory lessons on how to taste wine. Tours are an all-day affair, taking place from 9am to 5pm. Each one costs from 95€ per person.

Shopping

The chain boutique **Souleiado,** 19 rue Joseph-Vernet (© **04-90-86-32-05**), sells reproductions of 18th- and 19th-century Provençal fabrics by the meter or made into clothing and linens.

Hervé Baume, 19 rue Petite Fusterie (www.herve-baume.com; © **04-90-86-37-66**), is the place to buy a Provençal table. A massive inventory includes French folk art and hand-blown hurricane lamps.

Pâtisserie Mallard, 32 rue des Marchands (www.patisseriemallard.fr; © **04-90-82-42-38**), makes the hard-to-find local specialty *les papalines d'Avignon.* Dark chocolate is coated in a pink, "thistle"-like pink chocolate, then filled with Origan du Comat liquor, the latter created from 60 local plants and produced by Maison Blachère, Provence's oldest distillery.

Pick up Rhône Valley wines at **Le Carré du Palais,** 1 place du Palais (www.carredupalaisavignon.com; © **04-90-27-24-00**). Occupying the 17th-century Hôtel Calvet de la Palun, this complex—which opened at the end of 2015—is dedicated to all things wine, from promoting local vintages to offering its own multi-lingual workshops at the on-site L'École des Vins du Rhône.

A covered market with 40 different merchants is **Les Halles,** place Pie (www.avignon-leshalles.com), open Tuesday through Sunday (6am–1:30pm). Local chefs—some of them Michelin-starred—offer free cooking demonstrations here every Saturday morning at 11am (except Aug). The **flower market** is on place des Carmes on Saturday (8am–1pm), and the **flea market** occupies the same place each Sunday morning (6am–1pm).

Nightlife

Start your evening at **Avitus Bar à Vin,** 11 rue du Vieux Sextier (www.avitus lacave.com; ✆ **09-84-27-57-97**), a cozy wine bar offering a wide range of local wines by the glass. Avignon's beautiful people continue on to **Les Ambassadeurs,** 27 rue Bancasse (www.clublesambassadeurs.fr; ✆ **04-90-86-31-55**), an upscale dance club.

Behind the Hôtel d'Europe, disco-bar **L'Esclave,** 12 rue du Limas (www. esclavebar.com; ✆ **04-90-85-14-91**), is a focal point of the city's gay scene.

DAY TRIP FROM AVIGNON

Orange ★

31km (19 miles) N of Avignon

Antiquities-rich Orange was not named for citrus fruit, but as a dependency of the Dutch House of Orange-Nassau during the Middle Ages. It is home to two UNESCO World Heritage sites: Europe's third-largest **triumphal arch** and its best-preserved **Roman theater.** Louis XIV, who once considered moving the theater to Versailles, claimed: "It is the finest wall in my kingdom." The Théâtre Antique is now the site of **Les Chorégies d'Orange** (www.choregies. fr), a summertime opera and classical music festival.

Just 10km (6 miles) south along the D68 is **Châteauneuf-du-Pape,** a prestigious appellation known for its bold red wines. Spend an afternoon visiting the village's numerous tasting rooms, winding your way up to the ruins of a castle that served as a summer residence for Pope John XXII.

ESSENTIALS

Frequent **trains** (trip time: 20 min.; 6.40€ one-way) and **buses** (www.sudest-mobilites.fr; ✆ **04-32-76-00-40;** trip time: 1 hr.; 2€ one-way) connect

Roman theater in Orange.

Avignon and Orange. If you're **driving** from Avignon, take A7 north to Orange. The **Office de Tourisme** is at 5 cours Aristide-Briand (www.ot orange.fr; ✆ **04-90-34-70-88**).

EXPLORING ORANGE & AROUND

The carefully restored **Théâtre Antique** ★★★, rue Madeleine Roch (www. theatre-antique.com; ✆ **04-90-51-17-60**), dates from the days of Augustus. Built into the side of a hill, it once held 9,000 spectators in tiered seats. Nearly 105m-long (344 ft.) and 37m high (121 ft.), it's open daily November to February 9:30am to 4:30pm; March and October 9:30am to 5:30pm; April, May, and September 9am to 6pm; and June to August 9am to 7pm. Admission (which includes a free audioguide) is 9.50€ adults, 7.50€ students and children 7 to 17, and free children 6 and under.

The imposing **Arc de Triomphe** ★, avenue de l'Arc-de-Triomphe, comprises a trio of arches held up by Corinthian columns embellished with military and maritime emblems. Also built during the reign of Augustus, it was once part of the original town's fortified walls.

WHERE TO EAT

At **Au Petit Patio,** 58 cours Aristide Briand (✆ **04-90-29-69-27**), contemporary Provençal cuisine is served on a petite outdoor terrace. Sample honey-glazed sea bass or summery strawberry tartare.

GORDES ★★★

720km (446 miles) S of Paris; 38km (24 miles) E of Avignon; 77km (48 miles) N of Aix-en-Provence; 92km (57 miles) N of Marseille

Hilltop Gordes is a supremely chic rocky outcrop deep in Provence. From afar, this gorgeous *village perché* (perched village) is a pastiche of beiges, grays, and terra cotta that blushes golden at sunrise and sunset.

Essentials

ARRIVING   Gordes is difficult to reach via public transportation. The closest **train** station is Cavaillon, where trains arrive from Avignon's central station (trip time: 35 min.; 7.20€ one-way). From here, bus nr. 15.3 departs two to three times daily for place du Château in Gordes (www.sudest-mobilites.fr; trip time: 35 min.; 2€ one-way). Alternatively, you could take a 1-day **coach tour** such as the one offered by the Aix-en-Provence tourist office (www.aixenprovencetourism.com; ✆ **04-42-16-11-61;** from 65€ per person), or departing from Avignon with **Provence Panorama** (www. provence-panorama.com; ✆ **04-90-22-02-61;** from 65€ per person). For a view that's totally different, **Provence Vue Avion,** Aéroport d'Avignon (www.provence-vue-avion.com; ✆ **04-90-92-22-84**) organizes year-round flights over Gordes and the region from 58€ per person. By **car,** Gordes is a 38km (24-mile) drive east of Avignon via D900, or a 75km (48-mile) drive north of Aix-en-Provence via the A7.

VISITOR INFORMATION The
Office de Tourisme is at Le Château
(www.gordes-village.com; 📞 **04-90-
72-02-75**).

[FastFACTS]
GORDES

Gordes, medieval village.

Mail & Postage **La Poste,** place du
Jeu de Boules (📞 **36-31**). Note that the
post office also offers an ATM.

Pharmacies **Pharmacie de Gordes,** 2
rue de l'Eglise (📞 **04-90-72-02-10**).

Where to Stay

La Ferme de la Huppe ★★
This combination bed-and-breakfast,
and its superb Provençal restaurant
(also open to nonguests), spills over a
pristinely renovated 18th-century
farmhouse. Country-style guest
rooms are named after their former
functions, such as Hay Loft or Wine
Cellar, and all boast cute modern
bathrooms. An abundant buffet breakfast (croissants, fresh juices, local
cheeses) is served on the poolside
terrace. La Ferme's location, just down the road from Gordes itself, makes it
perfectly positioned for exploring the wider Luberon region.

R.D. 156, Les Pourquiers. www.lafermedelahuppe.com. 📞 **04-90-72-12-25.** 10 units.
116€–225€ double, breakfast included. Half-board available for guests staying 7 nights
or longer. Free parking. **Amenities:** Restaurant, outdoor pool; free Wi-Fi. Closed Nov
to Feb.

Where to Eat

For a splurge-worthy occasion, head to **Bastide de Gordes,** rue de la Combe
(www.bastide-de-gordes.com; 📞 **04-90-72-12-12**), where the newly refurbished restaurant has been headed up by one of France's most famous chefs,
Michelin-starred chef Pierre Gagnaire, since it reopened in mid-2015.

L'Artegal PROVENÇAL A standout venue among Gordes' handful of
eateries, this family-run restaurant prides itself on its creative local cuisine.
Well-conceived dishes include lentil and salmon tartare, rich lamb *navarin*
stew, and the restaurant's own generous adaptation of duck-heavy *salade
Landaise.* Tucked into the shadow of the Château de Gordes, L'Artegal is a
romantic spot to dine, particularly in the evening.

Place du Château. ⓒ **04-90-72-02-54.** Main courses 16€–26€; fixed-price lunch 22€; fixed-price dinner 36€. Thurs–Tues noon–2pm; Thurs–Mon 7:15–9pm. Closed mid-Jan to mid-Mar.

Exploring Gordes

Gordes is best explored on foot. Its primarily pedestrianized streets unwind downhill from the Château de Gordes, the Renaissance rehabilitation of a 12th-century fortress. Its windows still bear grooves from bows and arrows used to protect Gordes during Gallo-Roman times, when it was a border town. Today Gordes is more likely to be invaded by easels. Its austere beauty has drawn many artists, including Marc Chagall and Hungarian painter Victor Vasarely, who spent summers here gathering inspiration for his geometric abstract art.

Caves du Palais St. Firmin ★ RUINS Steep Gordes lacks an abundance of surface area, so early settlers burrowed into the rock itself, creating an underground network of crude rooms and stairways over seven levels. Over the centuries, these rooms have housed the village's production of olive oil and grain. Though the tunnels are adequately lit, children are provided with a small headlamp to let them feel like true explorers.

Rue du Belvédère. www.caves-saint-firmin.com. No telephone. Admission 6€ adults, 4.50€ seniors, students, and children 5–17, free for children 4 and under. Free audioguide. Mid-Apr–mid-Oct daily 10am–6pm. Mid-Oct–mid-Apr by reservation only.

Château de Gordes ★ HISTORIC HOME/ART MUSEUM Access to the ancient château is reserved for visitors of its small museum, previously dedicated to contemporary Flemish painter Pol Mara (1920–98), a former resident of Gordes. Since 2014, the museum has been given over exclusively to short-term temporary shows, such as a recent exhibition by National Geographic photographer, Reza.

Place Genty Pantaly. ⓒ **04-90-72-98-64.** Admission 4€ adults, 3€ children 10–17, free for children 9 and under. Daily 10am–1pm and 2–6:30pm.

Outlying Attractions

Gordes is part of the **Parc Naturel Régional du Luberon** (www.parcdulu beron.fr), made up of three mountain ranges and their common valley. Author Peter Mayle brought attention to the area with his "A Year in Provence" series extolling the virtues of villages such as Bonnieux, Lourmarin, and Ménerbes. The latter, where Mayle restored his first French home, was home to Picasso and his (then) muse Dora Maar. Most of these are within 12km (7½ miles) of each other, making the Luberon well worth an afternoon's exploration.

For avid cyclists, **Vélo Loisir en Luberon** (www.leluberonavelo.com; ⓒ **04-90-76-48-05**) has marked hundreds of kilometers of bike routes throughout the region's vineyards and lavender fields. See the website for maps and bicycle rental agencies, as well as suggestions of bucolic dining spots and spots to bed down en route.

Abbaye Nôtre Dame de Sénanque ★★★ MONASTERY One of the prettiest sights in the Luberon—indeed, in all of Provence—is the Abbaye

Abbaye Nôtre Dame de Sénanque.

Nôtre Dame de Sénanque. And even more so when the lavender is in bloom. Five kilometers (3 miles) down the road from Gordes, it was built by Cistercian monks in 1148. Just a handful of monks continue to live on the premises today. The structure is noted for its simple architecture—though standing in a sea of lavender purple, from June to late July, it's dramatic indeed. The abbey is open daily to visitors, either in the morning for a self-guided wander (except Sun), or throughout the day via guided tours in French only. A gift shop sells items made by the resident monks, including lavender honey.

D177. www.senanque.fr. ⓒ **04-90-72-05-86.** Admission 7.50€ adults, 5€ students and ages 18–25, 3€ children 6–17, free children 5 and under. Hours vary; see website for details.

Village des Bories ★ RUINS   Bories are beehive-shaped dwellings made of intricately stacked stone—and not an ounce of mortar. They date back as far as the Bronze Age and as recently as the 18th century in Provence. An architectural curiosity, the thick walls and cantilevered roofs beg the question: How did they do that? The Village des Bories is the largest group of these structures in the region, comprising 30 huts grouped according to function (houses, stables, bakeries, silkworm farms, and more). Traditional tools are on display, along with an exhibit on the history of dry-stone architecture in France and around the world.

1.5km (1 mile) west of Gordes on the D15. ⓒ **04-90-72-03-48.** Admission 6€ adults, 4€ children 12–17, free children 11 and under. Daily 9am to sundown.

ST-RÉMY-DE-PROVENCE ★

710km (440 miles) S of Paris; 24km (15 miles) NE of Arles; 19km (12 miles) S of Avignon; 10km (6¼ miles) N of Les Baux

Though the physician and astrologer Nostradamus was born here in 1503, most associate St-Rémy with Vincent van Gogh, who committed himself to a local asylum in 1889 after cutting off his left ear. "Starry Night" was painted during this period, as were many versions of "Olive Trees" and "Cypresses."

Come to sleepy St-Rémy not only for its history and sights, but also for an authentic experience of local life. The town springs into action on Wednesday mornings for its weekly **Grand Marché Provençal,** when stalls bursting with the region's bounty, from wild-boar sausages to olives, elegant antiques to bolts of French country fabric, huddle between the sidewalk cafes.

Essentials

ARRIVING   A regional **bus** (line 57) runs four to nine times daily between Avignon's Gare Routière and St-Rémy's place de la République (trip time: 45 min.; 3.60€ one-way). For bus information, see www.lepilote.com or call © **08-10-00-13-26.** The St-Rémy Tourist Office also provides links to up-to-date bus schedules on their website (see below). If **driving,** head south from Avignon along D571.

VISITOR INFORMATION   The **Office de Tourisme** is on place Jean-Jaurès (www.saintremy-de-provence.com; © **04-90-92-05-22**).

[Fast FACTS] ST-RÉMY-DE-PROVENCE

ATMs/Banks   **Société Marseillaise de Crédit,** 10 bd. Mirabeau (© **04-90-92-74-00**).

Mail & Postage   **La Poste,** 5 rue Roger Salengro (© **36-31**).

Pharmacies   **Pharmacie Lafayette,** 20 rue Lafayette (© **04-90-92-11-21**).

Where to Stay

Château des Alpilles ★★★   A former castle situated at the heart of magnolia-studded parkland, Château des Alpilles was constructed by the Pichot family in 1827. Françoise Bon converted the mansion in 1980, creating luxurious double rooms inside the castle itself, with additional private accommodation in the property's former chapel, farm, and washhouse. Decor throughout encompasses a confident mix of antiques (plush upholstery, local artworks) and cool amenities (deep travertine-trimmed bathtubs, iPod docks). It's 2km (1¼ miles) from the center of St-Rémy.

Route de Rougadou. www.chateaudesalpilles.com. © **04-90-92-03-33.** 21 units. 215€–350€ double; 350€–450€ suite; 360€–480€ apartment; 320€–380€ maisonette. Free parking. Closed Jan to mid-Mar. **Amenities:** Restaurant; bar; fitness room; outdoor pool; room service; sauna; 2 tennis courts; free Wi-Fi.

L'Amandière ★   Tucked into the Provençal countryside around 1.5km (1 mile) north of town, this budget bolthole is justly favored by visitors who would rather splurge on the region's gourmet restaurants. L'Amandière's accommodation may be simple, but bedding down here is certainly no hardship. Rooms are spacious, all boast their own balcony or private patio, and there's a large outdoor pool. Breakfast is served under citrus trees in the lavender-trimmed gardens.

Av. Théodore Aubanel. www.hotel-amandiere.com. ✆ **04-90-92-41-00.** 26 units. 80€–99€ double; 99€ triple. Free parking. **Amenities:** Outdoor pool; free Wi-Fi.

Where to Eat

La Maison Jaune ★ FRENCH/PROVENÇAL Within an 18th-century village home in St-Rémy's Old Town, handsome tables spill over two chic dining rooms, as well as a terrace overlooking the neighboring Hôtel de Sade's gardens. It's here that creative chef François Perraud concocts his Michelin-starred cuisine, relying on local ingredients. Mediterranean anchovies may be doused in a parsley pesto, Provençal lamb seared with smoky eggplant, or the darkest chocolate cake paired with frozen lemon parfait.

15 rue Carnot. www.lamaisonjaune.info. ✆ **04-90-92-56-14.** Reservations required. Main courses 38€–44€; fixed-price lunch 32€; fixed-price dinner 42€–72€. Wed–Sat noon–1:30pm; Tues–Sat 7:30–9pm. Closed Nov to Feb.

L'Estagnol ★★ MEDITERRANEAN This popular eatery (which translates as "little pond" in the regional dialect) is owned and operated by the Meynadier family, third-generation restaurateurs. Hearty local cuisine ranges from Camargue bull hamburger topped with goat cheese and eggplant to Provençal gazpacho with basil sorbet. Dining takes place either in the ancient *orangerie* (private greenhouse) or in the sun-dappled courtyard adjacent.

16 bd. Victor Hugo. www.restaurant-lestagnol.com. ✆ **04-90-92-05-95.** Reservations recommended. Main courses 14€–28€; fixed-price lunch 14€, fixed-price dinner 30€. May–Sept Tues–Sun noon–2:30pm and 7:15–10pm; Oct–Jan and Mar–Apr Tues–Sun noon–2:30pm, Tues–Sat 7:15–10pm. Closed Feb.

Exploring St-Rémy

St-Rémy's pale stone Old Town is utterly charming. Scattered among its pedestrianized streets are 18th-century private mansions, art galleries, medieval church towers, bubbling fountains, and Nostradamus's birth home. Note that St-Rémy's two major sites (see below) lie around 1km (½ mile) south of the town center.

Le Site Archéologique de Glanum ★★ RUINS Kids will love a scramble around this bucolically sited Gallo-Roman settlement, which

Corinthian temple in Glanum.

thrived here during the final days of the Roman Empire. Its monuments include a triumphal arch from the time of Julius Caesar, all garlanded with sculptured fruits and flowers. Another interesting feature is the baths, which had separate chambers for hot, warm, and cold. Visitors can stroll around entire streets and see the foundations of private residences from the 1st-century town, plus the remains of a Gallo-Greek town of the 2nd century B.C.

Route des Baux-de-Provence. http://glanum.monuments-nationaux.fr. ℰ **04-90-92-23-79.** Admission 7.50€ adults, 4.50€ ages 18–25, free ages 17 and under. Apr–Aug daily 10am–6:30pm; Sept Tues–Sun 10am–6:30pm; Oct–Mar Tues–Sun 10am–5pm.

Saint Paul de Mausole ★ MONASTERY This former monastery and clinic is where Vincent Van Gogh was confined from 1889 to 1890. It's now a psychiatric hospital for women, which specializes in art therapy. You can't see the artist's actual cell, but there is a reconstruction of his room. The Romanesque chapel and cloisters are worth a visit in their own right, as Van Gogh depicted their circular arches and beautifully carved capitals in some of his paintings. A way-marked path between the town center and the site (east of av. Vincent Van Gogh) is dotted with 21 reproductions of Van Gogh's paintings from the period he resided here.

Chemin Saint-Paul. www.saintpauldemausole.fr. ℰ **04-90-92-77-00.** Admission 4.65€ adults, 3.30€ students, free for children 12 and under. Apr–Sept daily 9:30am–6:30pm; mid-Feb to Mar, Oct–Dec daily 10:15am–5:15pm. Closed Jan–Feb.

Shopping

St-Rémy is a decorator's paradise, with many antiques shops and fabric stores on the narrow streets of the Old Town and surrounding boulevards. **La Brocante de Poun,** 4 rue du Château (ℰ **06-19-75-62-70**), sells everything from architectural salvage to vintage furniture. The town's famous Provençal market is held on Wednesday mornings.

Nightlife

Located in a former Art Deco movie theater, **Le Cocktail Bar,** Hôtel Image, 36 bd. Victor Hugo (ℰ **04-90-92-51-50**), is an unusual destination in this laid-back town. In summertime, it is open Tuesday to Saturday until midnight.

LES BAUX ★★★

720km (446 miles) S of Paris; 18km (11 miles) NE of Arles; 85km (53 miles) N of Marseille

Les Baux de Provence's location and geology are extraordinary. Cardinal Richelieu called the massive, 245m-high (804-ft.) rock rising from a desolate plain "a nesting place for eagles." A real eagle's-eye view of the outcropping would be part moonscape, dotted with archaeological ruins and a vast plateau, and part civilization, with boxy stone houses stacked like cards on the rock's east side.

Baux, or *baou* in Provençal, means "rocky spur." The power-thirsty lords who ruled the settlement took this as their surname in the 11th century, and by

Les Baux, built on a rocky formation.

the Middle Ages had control of 79 other regional fiefdoms. After they were overthrown, Les Baux was annexed to France with the rest of Provence, but Louis XI ordered the fortress demolished. The settlement experienced a rebirth during the Renaissance, when structures where restored and lavish residences built, only to fall again in 1642 when, wary of rebellion, Louis XIII ordered his armies to destroy it once and for all. Today the fortress compound is nothing but ruins, but fascinating ones.

Be sure to time your visit wisely: Because of its dramatic beauty, plus a number of quaint shops and restaurants in the village, during summertime Les Baux is often overrun with visitors at peak times.

Essentials

ARRIVING Les Baux is best reached by car. From St-Rémy, take D27 south; from Arles, D17 east. Alternatively, on weekends in June and September, and every day during July and August, **bus** no. 57 (35 min.; 2.40€ one-way) runs between Arles and St-Rémy, stopping at Les Baux en route. For bus information, see www.lepilote.com or call ✆ **08-10-00-13-26.** You can also book 1-day coach tours through **Provence Panorama** (www.provence-panorama.com; ✆ **04-90-22-02-61;** from 70€ per person) in Avignon or the tourist office in Aix-en-Provence (www.aixenprovencetourism.com; ✆ **04-42-16-11-61;** from 110€ per person).

VISITOR INFORMATION The **Office de Tourisme** (www.lesbaux deprovence.com; ✆ **04-90-54-34-39**) is at Maison du Roy, near the northern entrance to the old city.

FAST FACTS Note that you'll need to head to the nearby town of Maussane-les-Alpilles for access to a bank, pharmacy, or post office.

Where to Stay

Golf aficionados may wish to bed down at the new **Domaine de Manville** (www.domainedemanville.fr), a traditional Provençal sheep farm turned luxury hotel and spa, all sited on an 18-hole eco-friendly golf course.

Le Mas d'Aigret ★ This charming hotel surrounded by olive trees and shady pines is a 5-minute stroll from Les Baux. Guestrooms are simple yet elegant, and almost all have their own terrace or balcony. Two "cave" rooms are built into Les Baux's rock face itself, a neat contrast with the rooms' modern amenities (air-conditioning, flatscreen TVs). An outdoor swimming pool and small *pétanque* (French boules) run are nestled into the hotel's rustic grounds. There's a recommended restaurant on site too. In winter, meals are served in the cavernous dining room with open fireplace; in summertime, the outdoor terrace overlooks Les Baux's valley and Château.

D27A. www.masdaigret.com. ℂ **04-90-54-20-00.** 16 units. 100€–215€ double; 190€–235€ triple; 180€–250€ family room. Breakfast/half-board available. Free parking. **Amenities:** Outdoor pool; restaurant; free Wi-Fi.

Where to Eat

Within Les Baux's old town and near the entrance to the Château, the petite **Les Café des Baux** (www.cafedesbaux.com) makes an excellent lunch stop.

La Cabro d'Or ★★★ PROVENÇAL Under Chef Michel Hulin, the Cabro d'Or delivers intelligent, innovative Provençal cuisine with a lightness of touch on the most bucolic restaurant terrace in southern France. Diners savor the unctuousness of Mediterranean langoustines, the crispness of roasted red mullet, the froth of fresh pea velouté, and the crunch of slow-cooked suckling pig. More important, the restaurant is part of a truly fabulous trio of luxury hotels surrounding Les Baux. Together they form the most magical resort in all Provence. These include the **Hotel Cabro d'Or** (www.lacabrodor.com; ℂ **04-90-54-33-07;** doubles 200€–460€), which has enchanting grounds, an organic garden, and a vast swimming pool; the **Le Manoir** annex next door, which looks like a rural French movie set; and **Oustau de Baumanière**, at the foot of the village (www.oustaudebaumaniere.com; ℂ **04-90-54-33-07;** doubles 200€–630€), which has hosted the likes of HRH Queen Elizabeth II and Johnny Depp, and also purveys an even more acclaimed (and more expensive) restaurant than the Cabro d'Or.

In the Hotel Cabro d'Or, Chemin départemental 27. www.lacabrodor.com. ℂ **04-90-54-33-21.** Reservations recommended. Main courses 55€–58€; fixed-price lunch 58€; fixed-price dinner 83€–130€. Daily midday–2pm and 7:30–10pm. Closed Jan–Feb.

Exploring Les Baux

Les Baux's windswept ruins, **Château des Baux** ★★★ (www.chateau-baux-provence.com; ℂ **04-90-54-55-56**), cover an area of 7 hectares (17 acres), much larger than the petite hilltop village itself. Consider visiting them early in the morning before the sun gets too strong.

The medieval compound is accessed via the 15th-century **Hôtel de la Tour du Brau.** Beyond this building are replicas of wooden military equipment that would have been used in the 13th century. Built to scale—that is to say, enormous—are a battering ram and various catapults capable of firing huge boulders. From April to August, these are fired every day at 11am and 1:30pm, 3:30pm, and 5:30pm, with an extra show during July and August at 6:30pm. Medieval jousting demonstrations (noon, 2:30, and 4:30pm) are held in summer.

Other stopping points include the **Chapel of St-Blaise** (inside which a film of aerial views of Provence is shown), a windmill, the skeleton of a hospital built in the 16th century, and a cemetery. The **Tour Sarrazin,** so named because it was used to spot Saracen invaders coming from the south, yields a sweeping view. Alongside each of the major points of interest, illustrated panels show what the buildings would have originally looked like and explain how the site has evolved architecturally.

Admission to the Château (including audioguide) is 8€ adults, 6€ children 7 to 17 from September to March. The rest of the year, it costs 10€ adults, 8€ children 7 to 17 (daily Apr–June and Sept 9am–7:15pm; July and Aug 9am–8:15pm; Mar and Oct 9:30am–6:30pm; Nov–Feb 10am–5pm).

Carrières de Lumières ★★ MUSEUM   A 10-minute stroll downhill from Les Baux, this temporary exhibition space occupies the site of a former limestone quarry. It's here that images of modern artworks (such as audiovisual exhibitions dedicated to Monet, Renoir, Van Gogh, or Gauguin) are projected against the 7 to 9m (23- to 30-ft.) columns. The museum's Cubist-style entrance featured in Jean Cocteau's final film, "The Testament of Orpheus."

Route de Maillane. www.carrieres-lumieres.com. (*) **04-90-54-47-37.** Admission 11€ adults, 8.50€ children 7–17 and students, free children 6 and under. Daily Apr–Sept 9:30am–7pm; Oct–early Jan and Mar 10am–6pm. Closed Jan–Feb.

ARLES ★★

744km (461 miles) S of Paris; 36km (22 miles) SW of Avignon; 92km (57 miles) NW of Marseille

On the banks of the Rhône River, Arles (pop. 53,000) attracts art lovers, archaeologists, and historians. To the delight of visitors, many of the vistas Vincent van Gogh depicted in his artworks remain luminously present today. Here the artist was even inspired to paint his own bedroom ("Bedroom in Arles," 1888).

Julius Caesar established a Roman colony in Arles in the 1st century. Constantine the Great named it the second capital of his empire in AD 306, when it was known as "the little Rome of the Gauls." The city was incorporated into France in 1481.

Arles's ancient streets are not as pristinely preserved as, say, Avignon's, but are stunningly raw instead, with excellent restaurants and summer festivals to boot. Its position on the river makes it a gateway to the Camargue, giving the town a healthy dose of Spanish and gypsy influence.

Essentials

ARRIVING Trains run almost every hour between Arles and Avignon (trip time: 20 min.; 7.70€ one-way) and Marseille (trip time: 1 hr.; 16€). Be sure to take local trains from city center to city center, not the TGV, which, in this case, takes more time. If **driving**, head south along D570N from Avignon.

VISITOR INFORMATION The **Office de Tourisme** is on bd. des Lices (www.arlestourisme.com; ℰ **04-90-18-41-20**).

SPECIAL EVENTS **Les Rencontres d'Arles** (www.rencontres-arles.com; ℰ **04-90-96-76-06**), held from early July until late September, focuses on contemporary international photography. Tickets range from free to 12€ per exhibition, although passes are also available for 25€ to 37€. A ticket office is located in place de la République for the duration of the festival.

[Fast FACTS] ARLES

ATMs/Banks There are more than a dozen banks in downtown Arles, including three in place de la République.

Internet Access **CyberSaladelle,** 17 rue de la République (www.cybersaladelle.fr; ℰ **04-90-93-13-56**).

Mail & Postage **La Poste,** 5 bd. des Lices (ℰ **36-31**).

Pharmacies **Pharmacie des Arènes,** 17 rue du 4 Septembre (ℰ **04-90-96-02-77**).

Where to Stay

Hôtel Jules César ★★ The colonnaded Hôtel Jules César has long been one of Arles' landmark hotels, with a prestigious guest book that includes Pablo Picasso. The former 17th-century Carmelite convent was entirely renovated, a project undertaken in collaboration with born and bred local designer Christian Lacroix. Reopening its sleek new doors in 2014, the hotel's rooms and suites have been refreshed, with Lacroix focusing on rustic decor inspired by the nearby Camargue region. The top-notch Lou Marquès restaurant, serving classic Provençal cuisine, is also on site.

9 boulevard des Lices. www.hotel-julescesar.fr. ℰ **04-90-52-52-52.** 52 units. 179€–399€ double; 545€–749€ suite. Parking 20€. **Amenities:** Bar, concierge, fitness room, laundry service, outdoor pool, restaurant, room service, spa, free Wi-Fi.

Le Cloître ★★ Perfectly positioned in Arles' Old Town, midway between Les Arènes and place de la République, Le Cloître is a unique medley of ancient stone features and funky 1950s furnishings. Each room is individually decorated in bright tones, with wooden ceiling beams, mosaic floors, and designer knickknacks. Free bikes are available for guest use. Organic breakfast is served up on the rooftop terrace.

18 rue du Cloître. www.hotel-cloitre.com. ℰ **04-88-09-10-00.** 19 units. 96€–185€ double. Parking 11€. **Amenities:** Bar; laundry service; free Wi-Fi.

Where to Eat

Cuisine de Comptoir ★ FRENCH   This superb little lunch spot is tucked just off place du Forum in an ancient boulangerie. Each day, owners Alexandre and Vincent dish up a dozen different *tartines,* or open-faced sandwiches, created using toasted Poilâne bread. Both smoked duck's breast with Cantal cheese and the *brandade* (creamy cod and potato) *tartines* are highly recommended. The laid-back venue hosts a rotating selection of contemporary art.

10 rue de la Liberté. www.cuisinedecomptoir.com. © **04-90-96-86-28.** Main courses 11€–13€; fixed-price lunch 15€. Mon–Sat 8:30am–2pm and 7pm–9pm.

L'Atelier Jean-Luc Rabanel ★★★ MODERN PROVENÇAL   Put simply, this is the finest restaurant that one of the authors of this book ever had the pleasure of experiencing. And that's saying something. Double-Michelin-starred chef Jean-Luc Rabanel pairs organic ingredients from his own garden with locally reared bull, pork, and game (and even herbs, mushrooms, and flowers). Delivery combines the deftness of touch of a Japanese samurai (an Asian influence pervades Rabanel's set menus) with the creative vision of a Parisian fashion designer. A wine-accompaniment option offers a unique and passionate oenophilic tour of France. The chef also purveys two adjoining restaurants. The **Bistro Acote** (www.bistro-acote.com; © **04-90-47-61-13**) is softer on the wallet and serves Provençal classics on a 29€ set menu; and **Iode** (www.iode-rabanel.com; © **04-90-91-07-69**) specializes in "hyper-fresh" crustaceans and shellfish. Wow.

Serious epicureans can now also bed down on site, in one of "Les Confidentielles." This luxury accommodation was designed by chef Rabanel himself. Prices range from 250€ to 295€, with special packages comprising breakfast, dinner and/or lunch also available.

7 rue des Carmes. www.rabanel.com. © **04-90-91-07-69.** Reservations recommended. Fixed-price lunch 85€; fixed-price dinner 125€. Wed–Sun noon–1:30pm and 8pm–9pm.

Exploring Arles

The **Place du Forum,** shaded by plane trees, stands around the old Roman forum. The Terrasse du Café le Soir, immortalized by Van Gogh, is now the square's Café Van Gogh. Visitors keen to follow on in the footsteps of the great artist may pick up a **Van Gogh walking map** (1€), which takes in 10 important sites around the city, from the tourist office. On a corner of place du Forum sits the legendary **Grand Hôtel Nord-Pinus** (www.nord-pinus.com): Bullfighters, artists, and A-listers have all stayed here. Three blocks south, the **Place de la République** is dominated by a 15m-tall (49-ft.) red granite obelisk that once towered above a nearby stadium.

One of the city's great classical monuments is the Roman **Théâtre Antique** ★, rue du Cloître (© **04-90-18-41-20**). Augustus began the theater in the 1st century; only two Corinthian columns remain. The "Venus of Arles"

Les Taureaux

Bulls are a big part of Arlesien culture. It's not unusual to see bull steak on local menus, and *saucisson de taureau* (bull sausage) is a local specialty. The first bullfight, or *corrida*, took place in the amphitheater in 1853. Appropriately, Arles is home to a bullfighting school (the **Ecole Taurine d'Arles**). Like it or loathe it, *corridas* are still held during the Easter Feria and in September, during the Feria du Riz. The bull is killed only during the Easter *corrida;* expect a few protestors. A seat on the stone benches of the amphitheater costs 19€ to 97€. Tickets are usually available a few hours beforehand at the ticket office on **Les Arenes d'Arles** (1 rond-pont des Arènes). For information or advance tickets, go to www.arenes-arles.com or contact ☎ **08-91-70-03-70.**

(now in the Louvre in Paris) was discovered here in 1651. The theater is open May through September daily 9am to 7pm; March, April, and October daily 9am to 6pm; and November through February daily 10am to 5pm. Admission is 8€ adults, 6€ students, and free for children 17 and under. The same ticket admits you to the nearby **Amphitheater (Les Arènes)** ★★, rond-pont des Arènes (same phone number and opening hours), also built in the 1st century. Sometimes called Le Cirque Romain, it seats almost 25,000. For a good view, climb the three towers that remain from medieval times, when the amphitheater was turned into a fortress.

Fondation Vincent Van Gogh Arles ★★ EXHIBITION SPACE   This much-anticipated permanent home for the Van Gogh Foundation (founded more than 3 decades ago) is in the 15th-century private mansion Hôtel Léautaud de Donines. Highlighting the connection between Arles and Van Gogh, it stages seminars, interactive debates, and temporary exhibitions, such as 2015's "Night of Colors," a tribute to Van Gogh by French-Chinese artist Yan Pei-Ming. Check the website for the current program.

35 ter rue du Docteur Fanton. www.fondation-vincentvangogh-arles.org. ☎ **04-90-93-08-08.** Admission 9€ adults, 7€ seniors, 4€ students and children 12–18, free children 11 and under. Admission may vary depending on temporary exhibition. Daily 11am–7pm.

Le Cloître et l'Église St-Trophime ★ CHURCH   This church is noted for its 12th-century portal, one of the finest achievements of the southern Romanesque style. Frederick Barbarossa was crowned king of Arles here in 1178. In the pediment, Christ is surrounded by the symbols of the Evangelists. The pretty cloister, in Gothic and Romanesque styles, possesses noteworthy medieval carvings. During July's Les Rencontres d'Arles festival, contemporary photographs are also exhibited here.

East side of place de la République. ☎ **04-90-18-41-20.** Free admission to church; cloister 4.50€ adults, 3.60€ students, free for children 17 and under. Church daily 10am–noon and 2–5pm; cloister May–Sept daily 9am–7pm; Mar, Apr, and Oct daily 9am–6pm; Nov–Feb daily 10am–5pm.

Les Alyscamps ★ RUINS Perhaps the most memorable sight in Arles, this once-Roman necropolis became a Christian burial ground in the 4th century. Mentioned in Dante's "Inferno," it has been painted by both Van Gogh and Gauguin. Today it is lined with poplars and studded with ancient sarcophagi. Arlesiens escape here with a cold drink to enjoy a respite from the summer heat.

Avenue des Alyscamps. ☎ **04-90-18-41-20.** Admission 3.50€ adults, 2.60€ students, free children 17 and under. May–Sept daily 9am–7pm; Mar, Apr, and Oct daily 9am–noon and 2–6pm; Nov–Feb daily 10am–noon and 2–5pm.

Musée Départemental Arles Antiques ★★ MUSEUM Set within a sleek compound around 1km (½ mile) south of Arles' town center, this archaeological museum hosts finds uncovered throughout the region's rich territories. Vast, airy rooms present Roman sarcophagi, sculptures, mosaics, and inscriptions from ancient times through the 6th century A.D. Temporary shows, such as 2015's major photo exhibition celebrating the museum's 20th anniversary, highlight local history, as well as the regional and Mediterranean landscape. In late 2013, the museum opened a brand-new wing to showcase the 31m (102-ft.) flat-bottomed Roman barge (*chaland*) that was unearthed from the Rhône River in 2010.

Avenue 1ere Division France Libre, presqu'île du Cirque Romain. www.arles-antique. cg13.fr. ☎**04-13-31-51-03.** Admission 8€ adults, 5€ seniors, free children 17 and under. Wed–Mon 10am–6pm.

Musée Réattu ★★ ART MUSEUM Exhibited over the labyrinthine rooms of the 15th-century Grand Priory of the Order of Malta, this museum was opened in 1868 to showcase artworks previously owned by local painter Jacques Réattu. Over the past 150 years, the collection has swollen with donations and annual acquisitions, including dozens of Picasso drawings and close to 4,000 photographs. The building's former archives room is now dedicated to the history of the Order of the Knights Hospitaller. The museum also stages some three temporary exhibitions each year.

10 rue du Grand-Prieuré. www.museereattu.arles.fr. ☎ **04-90-49-37-58.** Admission 8€ adults, 6€ students, free children 17 and under. Tues–Sun Mar–Oct 10am-6pm, Nov–Feb 10am–5pm.

Nightlife

Come evening, Arles' most appealing spot is the organic wine bar–cafe **L'Ouvre-Boîte,** 22 rue du Cloître (☎ **04-88-09-10-10**). Open June to September and December only, it's set under a majestic canopy of trees in one of the Old Town's loveliest squares. **Le Patio de Camargue,** 49 chemin de Barriol (www.patiodecamargue.com; ☎ **04-90-49-51-76**), is a deservedly popular place south of town, spilling over the banks of the Rhône. The venue stages live folk music most nights. It's owned by Chico Bouchikhi, one of the co-founders of the folk band Gipsy Kings.

Mistral, Two Ways

Born just north of Arles, Frédéric Mistral (1830–1914) dedicated his life to defending and preserving the original Provençal language known as Occitan. The poet won the Nobel Prize for his epic work "Mirèio" and his overall contributions to French literature. Mistral joined six other Provençal writers in 1854 to found Félibrige, an association for the promotion of Occitan language and literature. He is the author of "Lo Tresor dóu Félibrige," the most comprehensive dictionary of the Occitan language to this day. Many think Mistral lent his name to the notorious glacial wind that roars through Provence every year. However, in this case, *mistral* is the Occitan word for "master"—and those who experience the phenomenon regularly say it's a cruel one. Tearing through the Rhône River Valley toward the Mediterranean, the mistral reaches speeds of 100km (62 miles) per hour and can blow up to 100 days per year. Most of these occur in winter, but it is also common in the spring and, in unlucky years, can persist until early summer.

AIX-EN-PROVENCE ★★

760km (471 miles) S of Paris; 84km (52 miles) SE of Avignon; 34km (21 miles) N of Marseille; 185km (115 miles) W of Nice

One of the most surprising aspects of Aix is its size. Frequently guidebooks proclaim it the very heart of Provence, evoking a sleepy town filled with flowers and fountains. Which it is—in certain quarters. But Aix is also a bustling university town of nearly 143,000 inhabitants (the Université d'Aix dates from 1413).

Founded in 122 B.C. by Roman general Caius Sextius Calvinus, who conveniently named the town Aquae Sextiae, after himself, Aix originated as a military outpost. Aix's most celebrated son, Paul Cézanne, immortalized the Aix countryside in his paintings. Just as he saw it, the Montagne Ste-Victoire looms over the town today.

Time marches on. Local boy turned superstar soccer player Zinedine Zidane recently opened his **Z5** sports complex (www.z5complexe.fr) in Aix. Last year rumors were rife that actress Jessica Alba was planning to settle down in the nearby town of Éguilles. But there are still plenty of decades-old, family-run shops on the narrow streets of the Old Town. A lazy summer lunch or early evening aperitif at one of the bourgeois cafes on the cours Mirabeau is an experience not to be missed.

Essentials

ARRIVING   **Trains** arrive frequently from Marseille (trip time: 40 min.; 8€ one-way) and Nice (trip time: 3–3½ hr.; 41€ one-way). High-speed TGV trains—from Paris as well as Marseille and Nice—arrive at the modern station near Vitrolles, 18km (11 miles) west of Aix. Bus transfers to the center of Aix cost 4.10€ one-way. There are **buses** from Marseille, Avignon, and Nice; for

A day out IN THE CAMARGUE

A marshy delta south of Arles, the Camargue is located between the Mediterranean and two arms of the Rhône. With the most fragile ecosystem in France, it has been a nature reserve since 1970. You cannot drive into the protected parts, and some areas are accessible only to the Gardians, the local cowboys. Their ancestors may have been the first American cowboys, who sailed on French ships to the port of New Orleans, where they rode the bayous of Louisiana and east Texas, rounding up cattle—in French, no less.

The Camargue is also cattle country. Black bulls are bred here both for their meat and for the regional bullfighting arenas. The whitewashed houses, plaited-straw roofs, plains, sandbars, and pink flamingos in the marshes make this area different, even exotic. There's no more evocative sight than the snow-white horses galloping through the marshlands, with hoofs so tough that they don't need shoes. The breed was brought here by the Arabs long ago, and it is said that their long manes and bushy tails evolved over the centuries to slap the region's omnipresent mosquitoes. Exotic flora and fauna abound. The birdlife here is among the most luxuriant in Europe. Looking much like the Florida Everglades, the area is known for its colonies of pink flamingos (*flamants roses*), which share living quarters with some 400 other bird species, including ibises, egrets, kingfishers, owls, wild ducks, swans, and ferocious birds of prey.

The best place to see flamingo colonies is at the **Parc Ornithologique de Pont de Gau,** route d'Arles (www.parcornithologique.com; ✆ **04-90-97-82-62**), 4km (3 miles), north of Camargue's capital, Stes-Maries-de-la-Mer. For a more general introduction to the region, head to the recently renovated Musée de la Camargue, RD570, Mas du Pont de Rousty (www.parc-camargue.fr; ✆ **04-90-97-10-82**).

You can also explore the Camargue's rugged terrain by boat, bike, jeep, or horse. The latter can take you along beaches and into the interior, fording waters to places where black bulls graze and wild birds nest. Dozens of stables are located along the highway between Arles to Stes-Maries. Virtually all charge the same rate (around 40€ for 2 hr.). The rides are aimed at the neophyte, not the champion equestrian.

For details, visit Arles' Office de Tourisme (see above) or head to the **Office de Tourisme,** 5 av. Van Gogh, Stes-Maries-de-la-Mer (www.saintesmaries.com; ✆ **04-90-97-82-55**).

information, see www.lepilote.com or call ✆ **08-10-00-13-26.** If you're **driving** to Aix from Avignon or other points north, take A7 south to A8 and follow the signs into town. From Marseille or other points south, take A51 north.

VISITOR INFORMATION The **Office de Tourisme** is at Les Allées Provençales, 300 av. Giuseppe Verdi (www.aixenprovencetourism.com; ✆ **04-42-16-11-61**).

CITY LAYOUT Aix's **Old Town** is primarily pedestrianized. To the south, it's bordered by the grand **cours Mirabeau,** which is flanked by a canopy of plane trees. The city was built atop thermal springs, and 40 fountains still bubble away in picturesque squares around town.

SPECIAL EVENTS The **Festival d'Aix,** created in 1948 (www.festival-aix.com; © **08-20-92-29-23**), mid-June through late July, features music and opera from all over the world.

Held for 2 weeks over the Easter holidays, **Festival de Pâques** (www.festivalpaques.com; © **08-20-13-20-13**) is Aix's newest annual festival, celebrating its fourth edition in 2016. Classical concerts from the likes of Yo-Yo Ma and the Philharmonique de Radio France are performed at Aix's Grand Théâtre de Provence and the Théâtre du Jeu de Paume.

[FastFACTS] AIX-EN-PROVENCE

ATMs/Banks There are scores of banks in downtown Aix, including three along cours Mirabeau.

Internet Access **Brasserie Les Deux Garçons,** 53 cours Mirabeau (© **04-42-26-00-51**).

Mail & Postage **La Poste,** place de l'Hôtel de Ville (© **36-31**).

Pharmacies **Pharmacie Victor Hugo,** 16 av. Victor Hugo (© **04-42-26-24-93**).

Where to Stay

In a city where expensive is the norm, the budget option **Hôtel du Globe** (www.hotelduglobe.com) is also recommended.

Hôtel Cézanne ★★ This super-chic—and very friendly—boutique hotel is best suited to guests seeking a more unusual spot to snooze. Conceived by one of the designers of both Villa Gallici and sophisticated *hotel particulier* **28 à Aix** (www.28-a-aix.com), the Cézanne is a mélange of colorful decor and hip designer touches. Baroque furnishings, unique artworks, and an honesty bar all add to the atmosphere. The hotel's location—midway between the train station and Aix's Old Town—makes it ideal for visitors planning day trips farther afield.

40 av. Victor Hugo. www.hotelaix.com. © **04-42-91-11-11.** 55 units. 150€–260€ double; 170€–360€ junior suite; 275€–460€ suite. Parking 17€. **Amenities:** Bar; concierge; fitness room; laundry service; massage; free Wi-Fi.

La Villa Gallici ★★★ This 18th-century Provençal house is one of Aix's most luxurious getaways. It also boasts a 7-acre garden and a gastronomic restaurant on site. It may be just a 5-minute stroll from the town center, yet the countrified ambience makes it feel miles away. Guest rooms are swathed in pastel printed fabrics, while suites have their own private patios. Days may be spent lounging by the terra-cotta-trimmed pool or exploring the French-style gardens; candlelit dinners are served alfresco under the stars. There's also an onsite spa by French skincare specialist Guinot, as well as an extensive Wine Cellar housed in the hotel's 18th-century pavilion (guided tastings available upon request).

Av. de la Violette. www.villagallici.com. © **04-42-23-29-23.** 16 units. 235€–690€ double; 460€–1,030€ suite. Free parking. Closed Jan. **Amenities:** Restaurant; bar; babysitting; outdoor pool; room service; spa; free Wi-Fi.

Aix Through the Eyes of Cézanne

One of the best experiences in Aix is a walk along the well-marked *route de Cézanne*. From the east end of cours Mirabeau, take rue du Maréchal-Joffre across boulevard Carnot to boulevard des Poilus, which becomes avenue des Ecoles-Militaires and D17. The stretch between Aix and the hamlet of Le Tholonet is full of twists and turns where Cézanne used to set up his easel. The route also makes a lovely 5.5km (3½-mile) stroll. Le Tholonet has a cafe or two where you can refresh yourself while waiting for one of the frequent buses back to Aix.

Where to Eat

In addition to the restaurants listed below, tiny Lebanese joint **Sajna,** 8 rue Lieutaud (✆ **07-58-17-07-91**), is perfect for picnics on the go, or alternatively there's just one six-person table for communal dining.

La Fromagerie du Passage ★★ FRENCH   Duck through the tiny entrance to Passage Agard by squeezing through the building where Cézanne's father once owned a hat shop. Then follow the (somewhat strange) sounds of bells and farm animals. It's here that the cheery La Fromagerie—part wine and cheese shop, part restaurant—is dedicated to all things cheese-related. Dine on the tapas menu (8€–28€), or a mixed cheese platter paired with local wines (18€–25€) on the rooftop terrace.

Passage Agard, 55 cours Mirabeau. www.lafromageriedupassage.fr. ✆ **04-42-22-90-00.** Main courses 16€–21€. Fixed-price lunch 20€–25€. Mon–Sat noon–3pm and 6–11pm, Sun brunch 10am–3pm.

Le Mille Feuille ★★ PROVENÇAL   Nestled into a quiet corner of Aix's Old Town, this excellent eatery stands out against the often-average local dining scene. Little surprise, as the restaurant is the brainchild of chef Nicolas Monribot and sommelier Sylvain Sendra, both former staff at the famous l'Oustau de Baumanière in Les Baux (p. 209). The market-fresh menu changes daily but may include yellow and green zucchini crumble with *cœur de bœuf* tomatoes, Sisteron lamb atop wild mushrooms and sautéed potatoes, or a delectable vanilla bourbon *millefeuille* pastry. You can dine either on the small outdoor terrace or indoors, where the classy decor features crimson walls and chartreuse upholstered furnishings.

8 rue Rifle-Rafle. www.le-millefeuille.fr. ✆ **04-42-96-55-17.** Dinner reservations required. Main courses 15€; fixed-price lunch 26€–31€, dinner 37€–43€. Wed–Sat noon–2pm and 8–9:30pm.

Exploring Aix-en-Provence

Aix's main street, **cours Mirabeau** ★, is one of Europe's most beautiful. A double row of plane trees shades it from the Provençal sun and throws dappled daylight onto its rococo fountains. Shops and sidewalk cafes line one side; 17th- and 18th-century sandstone *hôtels particuliers* (private mansions) take

Aix-en-Provence

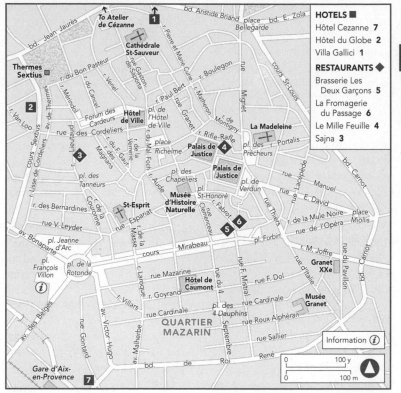

HOTELS ■
Hôtel Cezanne **7**
Hôtel du Globe **2**
Villa Gallici **1**

RESTAURANTS ◆
Brasserie Les
Deux Garçons **5**
La Fromagerie
du Passage **6**
Le Mille Feuille **4**
Sajna **3**

up the other. Stop into **Brasserie Les Deux Garçons,** 53 cours Mirabeau, for a coffee or a glass of rosé. The brasserie was founded in 1792 and frequented by the likes of Emile Zola, Cézanne, Picasso, and Sir Winston Churchill. Or dip just south of here to check out the new **Hôtel de Caumont,** 3 rue Joseph Cabassol (www.caumont-centredart.com), an ornate 18th-century private mansion that was transformed into an exhibition space in mid-2015. Boulevard Carnot and cours Sextius circle the heart of the old quarter (Vieille Ville), which contains the pedestrian-only zone.

One fun way to check out the lay of the land is aboard an eco-friendly **Diabline** (www.la-diabline.fr; Mon–Sat 8:30am–7:30pm; 0.50€/ride). These vehicles operate three routes along cours Mirabeau and through most of the Old Town.

Atelier de Cézanne ★★ MUSEUM   A 10-minute (uphill) stroll north of Aix's Old Town, Cézanne's studio offers visitors a glimpse into the artist's daily life. Because the building remained untouched for decades after Cézanne's death in 1906, the studio has remained perfectly preserved for close to a century. Note the furnishings, vases, and small figurines on display, all of which feature in the modern master's drawings and canvases. Cézanne aficionados will also enjoy **Jas de Bouffan,** the artist's family manor, and the inspirational Cubist landscape of the **Bibémus Quarries** (both www. cezanne-en-provence.com). The **Passeport Cézanne** (15€) allows entry to all three sites.

9 av. Paul-Cézanne. www.atelier-cezanne.com. *©* **04-42-21-06-53.** Admission 6€ adults, 2.50€ students and ages 13–25, free for children 12 and under. July–Aug daily 10am–6pm, English tour at 5pm; Apr–June and Sept daily 10am–noon and 2–6pm, English tour at 5pm; Oct–Feb Mon–Sat 10am–noon and 2–5pm, English tour at 4pm; Mar daily 10am–noon, English tour at 4pm.

Musée Granet ★★ MUSEUM One of the South of France's top art venues, this popular museum displays a permanent collection of paintings and sculpture ranging from 15th-century French canvases and 20th-century Giacometti sculptures to large-scale temporary exhibitions, such as 2015's "American Icons." However, it's Granet XXe, a collection of more than 300 modern artworks, which truly impresses. On long-term loan from the Fondation Jean et Suzanne Planque, the paintings, drawings, and sculptures are on display in the nearby 17th-century Pénitents Blancs Chapel, place Jean-Boyer (same ticket).

Place Saint Jean de Malte. www.museegranet-aixenprovence.fr. *©* **04-42-52-88-32.** Permanent collection: admission 5€ adults, free for students under 26 and all visitors under 18. Additional fee for temporary exhibitions. Tues–Sun mid-July–mid-Oct 10am–7pm; mid-Oct–mid-July noon–6pm.

Organized Tours

Aix's Tourist Office organizes bilingual tours around Aix (*©* **04-42-16-11-61**), including the year-round **tour of the historic city center** (Jan–Mar Sat 10am, Apr–Oct Tues and Sat 10am; 2 hr.; 9€ adults, 5€ seniors, students, and ages 7–25, free under 7), and **"In the Steps of Cézanne"** (Apr–Oct Thurs 10am; 2 hr.; 9€ adults, free under 7).

Shopping

Opened more than a century ago, **Béchard,** 12 cours Mirabeau (*©* **04-42-26-06-78**), is the most famous bakery in town. It specializes in the famous *Calissons d'Aix,* a candy made from ground almonds, preserved melon, and fruit syrup. **Chocolaterie de Puryicard,** 7 rue Rifle-Rafle (www.puyricard.fr; *©* **04-42-21-13-26**), creates sensational chocolates filled with candied figs, walnuts, or local lavender honey.

Founded in 1934 on a busy boulevard just east of the center of town, **Santons Fouque,** 65 cours Gambetta (www.santons-fouque.com; *©* **04-42-26-33-38**), stocks close to 2,000 traditional *santons* (crèche figurines).

For a range of truly useful souvenirs, including copper pots and pocket knives by famous French forgers such as Laguiole, try **Quincaillerie Centrale,** 21 rue de Monclar (*©* **04-42-23-33-18**), a hardware/housewares store that's been offering a little bit of everything since 1959.

To the Markets We Will Go

Aix offers the best markets in the region. Place Richelme holds a **fruit and vegetable market** every morning from 8:30am to 12:30pm. Come here to buy exquisite products such as olives, lavender honey, and regional local cheeses. There's a **flower market** every day, with the same hours, at either place de l'Hôtel de Ville or place des Prêcheurs (the former on Tues, Thurs, and Sat; the latter on Mon, Wed, Fri, and Sun). Place de Verdun is packed with **crafts and collectibles** every Tuesday and Thursday, with stalls selling clothes and linens joining the others on Saturday. And each week on Tuesday and Thursday, cours Mirabeau is lined with a mix of **regional treats,** from lavender honey to unique handbags.

Market in Aix-en-Provence.

Nightlife

Au P'tit Quart d'Heure, 21 place Forum de Cardeurs (www.auptitquart dheure.fr), and next-door's **La Curieuse,** 23 place Forum des Cardeurs (✆ **06-06-66-77-01**), are two of the city's liveliest spots to stop for an early evening aperitif. Expect seasonal happy hours, with prices as low as 1€ for a beer and 2€ per glass of wine. Open daily from 8am until 2am, **La Rotonde,** 2A place Jeanne d'Arc (www.larotonde-aix.com; ✆ **04-28-31-06-62**), is a bar, cafe, and historic hangout.

Under-30s who like thumping beats should head for **Le Mistral,** 3 rue Frédéric Mistral (www.mistralclub.fr; ✆ **04-42-38-16-49**), where techno and house pumps long and loud for a cover charge of around 10€ to 20€. More mature local patrons head to jazzy **Scat Club,** 11 rue de la Verrerie (✆ **04-42-23-00-23**), instead.

MARSEILLE ★★

776km (481 miles) S of Paris; 203km
(126 miles) SW of Nice; 32km (20 miles) S
of Aix-en-Provence

Marseille is the country's oldest
metropolis. It was founded as a port
by the Greeks in the 6th century B.C.
Today it's the second-largest city in
France, as well as one of its most
ethnically diverse, with just over
1.5 million inhabitants.

Author Alexandre Dumas called
teeming Marseille "the meeting place
of the entire world." Never was this
statement truer than in 2013 when
Marseille was designated the prestigious **European Capital of Culture.**
More than 11 million visitors fun-
neled into the city. They took in a new
cultural venues and landmark museums, as well as the completion of
long-term architectural projects, in

Vieux Port in Marseille, with Basilique Notre-
Dame-de-la-Garde on the hilltop.

particular the old docklands neighborhood west of the Vieux Port.

The Capital of Culture crowds may have departed. But its legacy remains.
A handful of Marseille's newest projects only came to fruition in 2014 and
2015, such as the complete renovation of the massive **Stade Vélodrome**
(p. 229) soccer stadium. In fact, the city will soon be taking the mantle as
European Capital of Sport 2017 (www.mpsport2017.com). Therefore
there's never been a better time to visit Marseille than right now. From the
vintage shops that pepper Le Panier's backstreets to the boutique boltholes
that are flinging open their doors, it's evident that France's second city has
finally come of age.

Essentials

ARRIVING   **Marseille-Provence Airport** (www.marseille-airport.com;
© **08-20-81-14-14**), 27km (17 miles) northwest of the city center, receives
international flights from all over Europe. From the airport, shuttle buses
(*navettes;* www.navettemarseilleaeroport.com; *©* **08-92-70-08-40**) make the
trip to Marseille's St-Charles rail station, near the Vieux-Port, for 8.20€, 5.80€
passengers 12 to 26, 4.10€ children 6 to 11, and free for children 5 and under.
The shuttle buses run daily every 15 minutes from 5am until midnight; the trip
takes 25 minutes.

Marseille has **train** connections from all over Europe, particularly to and
from Nice, and on to Italy. It's also linked to Paris via the TGV bullet train,

Marseille

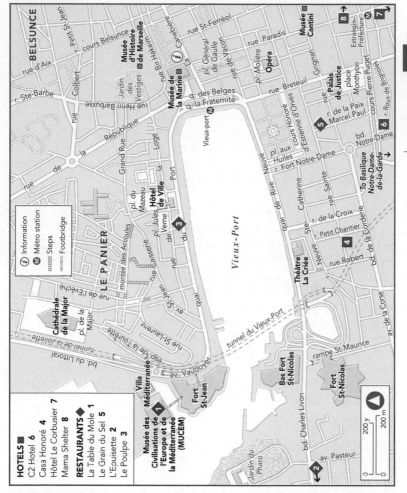

HOTELS ■
C2 Hotel **6**
Casa Honoré **4**
Hôtel Le Corbusier **7**
Mama Shelter **8**
RESTAURANTS ◆
La Table du Mole **1**
Le Grain du Sel **5**
L'Epuisette **2**
Le Poulpe **3**

Information
ⓜ Métro station
::::: Steps
━━ Footbridge

which departs almost every hour from the Gare de Lyon (trip time: 3 hr., 20 min.; 40€–125€ one-way). **Buses** serve the **Gare Routière,** rue Honnorat (www.rtm.fr; ☎ **04-91-08-16-40**), adjacent to the St-Charles railway station. Several buses run daily between Aix-en-Provence and Marseille (trip time: 40 min.; 5.70€ one-way, for schedule visit www.navetteaixmarseille.com). If you're **driving** from Paris, follow A6 south to Lyon, and then continue south along A7 to Marseille. The drive takes about 8 hours. From Provence, take A7 south to Marseille.

VISITOR INFORMATION   The **Office de Tourisme** is at 11 la Canebière (www.marseille-tourisme.com; ☎ **08-26-50-05-00;** Métro: Vieux-Port).

CITY LAYOUT   Marseille is a large, sprawling metropolis. Unlike any of the other towns mentioned in this chapter, if you're keen to explore different parts of the city, you'll probably need to take advantage of its comprehensive public transport.

NEIGHBORHOODS IN BRIEF   The major arteries divide Marseille into 16 *arrondissements*. Like Paris, the last two digits of a postal code tell you within which *arrondissement* an address is located. Visitors tend to spend most of their time in four main neighborhoods. The first is the **Vieux Port,** the atmospheric natural harbor that's a focal point for the city center. From here, the wide La Canebière boulevard runs eastwards, bisected by Marseille's most popular shopping avenues. To the north lies **Le Panier,** the original Old Town, crisscrossed by a pastel network of undulating alleyways. This neighborhood's western edge is trimmed by former docklands, which have been completely redeveloped over the past few years. Southeast of the Vieux Port, the alternative neighborhood around **cours Julien** is home to convivial restaurants and one-off boutiques aplenty. And come summertime, action shifts to the **Plages du Prado,** a strip of beaches due south of the city center.

SPECIAL EVENTS   **Le Défi de Monte-Cristo** (www.defimonte-cristo. com)—also known as the Monte-Cristo Challenge—is inspired by Alexandre Dumas' 19th-century novel, "The Count of Monte Cristo." In late June, hundreds of competitors battle it out to replicate main character Edmond Dantès' 5km (3-mile) swim from Château d'If to the French mainland.

The city's **Festival de Marseille** (www.festivaldemarseille.com), a citywide celebration of music, dance, and arts, is held from mid-June to mid-July. But Marseille's most popular music festival since its inception in 1992 is **Fiesta des Suds** (www.dock-des-suds.org). It's held annually in late October. Live acts include prominent South American and African bands, as well as big international names such as Patti Smith.

Getting Around

ON FOOT   Each of Marseille's neighborhoods is easily navigable on foot. However, unless you're an avid walker, you may want to rely on either the Métro or the tramway (see below) to zip you around town.

BY CAR   Parking and car safety are so problematic that your best bet is to park in a garage and rely on public transport. The website **www.parking-public.fr** lists Marseille's public parking lots and hourly fees.

BY TAXI   **Taxis Radio Marseille** (www.taximarseille.com; ✆ **04-91-02-20-20**).

BY PUBLIC TRANSPORT   **Métro** lines 1 and 2 both stop at the main train station, Gare St-Charles, place Victor Hugo. Line 1 makes a U-shaped circuit from the suburbs into the city and back again; Line 2 runs north and south in the downtown area. Boasting a brand-new third line as of mid-2015, Marseille's tramway services La Canebière and the refurbished Joliette Docks district, as well as linking the latter with place Castellane in the south. Individual tickets are 1.50€; they're valid on Métro, tram, and bus lines for up to

60 minutes after purchase. If you plan to take public transport several times during your stay, buy a **Pass XL,** valid for 1 day for 5.20€ or 3 days for 11€. For more information, visit the city transit authority site: www.rtm.fr.

Alternatively, it's also possible to purchase a 1-day (24€), 2-day (31€), or 3-day (39€) **City Pass** from the Marseille Tourist Office or via their website. The pass covers all public transport, including the round-trip ferry trip to **Château d'If** (p. 229) as well as entrance to more than a dozen of the city's museums and a ride on the *petit-train* (p. 230) up to the **Basilique Notre-Dame de la Garde** (p. 228).

[FastFACTS] MARSEILLE

ATMs/Banks   Marseille's banks are plentiful, including three along La Canebière.

Doctors & Hospitals   **Hopital Saint Joseph,** 26 bd. de Louvain (www.hopital-saint-joseph.fr; ℂ **04-91-80-65-00**).

Embassies & Consulates   **British Consulate Marseille,** 24 av. du Prado (www.gov.uk; ℂ **04-91-15-72-10**); **Consulate General of the United States Marseille,** place Varian Fry (http://marseille.usconsulate.gov; ℂ **01-43-12-48-85**).

Internet Access   There are around 50 free Wi-Fi hotspots dotted throughout Marseille. Central locations (including Jardin du Pharo, the square outside the Hôtel de Ville, and La Vieille Charité) are indicated on the free maps distributed by the tourist office.

Mail & Postage   **La Poste,** 1 cours Jean Ballard (ℂ **36-31**).

Newspapers & Magazines   Bilingual **"COTE Magazine"** (www.cotemagazine.com) offers a good selection of tried-and-true Marseille tips, as well as local interviews and recent openings.

Pharmacies   **Pharmacie Belsunce,** 10 cours Belsunce (ℂ **04-91-90-14-58**).

Safety   As in any big city, it's wise to keep a close eye on your belongings and avoid poorly lit areas at night.

Where to Stay

Although slightly removed from the city center, the iconic **Hôtel le Corbusier** (www.gerardin-corbusier.com) is a must for architecture aficionados. Be sure to pop up to the top floor, where local French designers have transformed the hotel's rooftop gym into a popular contemporary art space, **MAMO** (www.mamo.fr).

C2 Hotel ★★★   The five-star C2 was launched in 2014. Twenty luxurious, light-filled rooms spill over a 19th-century merchant family mansion, each one decked out in exposed brick walls and designer furnishings. Some have a private hammam steam bath. There's a superb Filorga Spa onsite with indoor pool and Jacuzzi, as well as a cocktail bar. But the hotel's *pièce de résistance?* That would have to be C2's beach, located on the private Mediterranean island of Île Degaby. Pack a picnic and cast away.

48 rue Roux de Brignoles. www.c2-hotel.com. ℂ **04-95-05-13-13.** 20 units. 189€–469€ double. Parking 30€. Métro: Estrangin-Préfecture. **Amenities:** Bar; private beach; concierge; spa; free Wi-Fi.

Casa Honoré ★ Interior designer Annick Lestrohan, creator of the Honoré brand of homewares, has transformed this former print shop into an ultra-stylish bed-and-breakfast. Unsurprisingly, guest rooms are decorated with Lestrohan's exquisite creations, from sleek designer furnishings to quality linens (and all are for sale too). An oasis of tranquility just south of Marseille's Vieux Port, the B&B's four rooms all center around a courtyard splashed with tropical foliage and a small swimming pool. Book well in advance.

123 rue Sainte. www.casahonore.com. © **04-96-11-01-62.** 4 units. 150€–200€ double. Minimum 2-night stay. No credit cards. Métro: Vieux-Port. **Amenities:** Outdoor pool; free Wi-Fi.

Mama Shelter ★★ Tucked into the hipster cours Julien district, this unique hotel is the brainchild of designer Philippe Starck. Rooms are bright and contemporary, from the modular furnishings to the wall-mounted iMacs offering dozens of free on-demand movies. Downstairs, Egyptian graffiti artist Tarek has tagged the industrial-chic restaurant's ceiling. And outdoors, Mama Shelter's yellow-striped courtyard hosts a pastis bar where guests can sip their way through more than four dozen variants of the city's beloved anise-flavored tipple. An excellent bet for a true taste of France's second city.

64 rue de la Loubière. www.mamashelter.com. © **04-84-35-20-00.** 127 units. 79€–109€ double; 139€ family room; 189€ suite. Parking 19€. Métro: Notre Dame du Mont. **Amenities:** Restaurant; bar; free Wi-Fi.

Where to Eat

For diners interested in re-creating Marseille's famous *bouillabaisse* fish stew at home, **Miramar Restaurant** (www.lemiramar.fr) offers cooking classes (120€/5-hr. lesson including lunch). Contact the tourist office for details.

La Table du Môle ★★★ MODERN MEDITERRANEAN Triple Michelin-starred-chef Gérard Passédat's newest restaurant, this "chic bistro" is perched atop the MuCEM (p. 228). Much like the MuCEM itself, stellar dishes herald from across the Mediterranean, including seafood tart served with a creamy ginger jus, crab paired with spicy harissa, or grilled turbot with truffled potatoes. All are served against a sweeping backdrop of Marseille's port and the Mediterranean Sea. Note that it's also possible to dine at La Table's lower-key (and cheaper) sister restaurant, **La Cuisine** ★★★ (12:30–3pm, closed Tues), located at the adjacent dining room—no sea views however. The fabulous two-course buffet lunch here is a steal at just 22€. Much of the produce used in both restaurants is sourced from the organic Les Olivades d'Ollioules farm.

MuCEM, 1 esplanade du J4. www.passedat.fr. Reservations required, available via internet only. Main courses 38€; fixed-price lunch 52€; fixed-price dinner 73€. Wed–Mon 12:30–3pm; Wed–Sat and Mon 7:30–10:30pm. Métro: Vieux-Port. Bus: 49, 60, or 82.

Le Grain du Sel ★★ MODERN MEDITERRANEAN Marseille-born chef Pierre Giannetti concocts what many locals consider to be the city's most creative bistro cuisine. Dishes are infinitely innovative, often taking inspiration from Giannetti's years of cooking in Barcelona. Following morning market finds, the daily menu may include Sardinian gnocchi with clams, mussel *escabèche,* or Spanish rice with shellfish harvested from the Camargue seaside town of Saintes-Maries-de-la-Mer. The wine list is carefully considered, and you can dine outside in the petite courtyard.

39 rue de la Paix Marcel Paul. ✆ **04-91-54-47-30.** Reservations recommended. Main courses 13€–28€; fixed-price lunch 22€–26€. Tues–Sat noon–2pm, Fri–Sat 8–10pm. Closed Aug. Métro: Vieux-Port.

L'Epuisette ★★ SEAFOOD/MEDITERRANEAN   This Michelin-starred option is undoubtedly the premier place in Marseille to sample **bouillabaisse** stew. Pack your appetite: Fresh fish is poached in saffron-infused soup; the final product is served as two separate courses, accompanied by *rouille,* a mayonnaise-like sauce flavored with garlic, cayenne pepper, and saffron. L'Epuisette's setting is as sublime as the cuisine: The seaside dining room overlooks Château d'If from the picturesque fishing port of Vallon des Auffes, 2.5km (1½ miles) south of Marseille's Vieux Port.

Vallon des Auffes. www.l-epuisette.fr. ✆ **04-91-52-17-82.** Reservations required. Main courses 45€–58€; fixed-price dinner 70€–145€. Tues–Sat noon–1:30pm and 7:30–9:30pm. Closed Aug. Bus: 83.

Le Poulpe ★★ PROVENCAL/MEDITERRANEAN   This brand-new venue, opened by top Marseillaise chef Michel Portos and his childhood friend Michel Ankri, is firmly focused on the "locatore movement," or eating locally. In fact, all the restaurant's ingredients are proudly sourced from within a maximum of 200km (125 miles). Decor has a 1950s bistro vibe, while the daily menu is short and sweet, with a choice of two appetizers, two main courses, and two desserts. Seasonal dishes may include *panisses* (chickpea flour fritters) salad with chorizo and garlicky aïoli, or traditional slow-cooked octopus *daube* stew.

84 quai du Port. www.lepoulpe-marseille.com. ✆ **04-95-09-15-91.** Main courses 21€–36€; fixed-price lunch 19€–26€. Daily 10am–midnight for snacks, lunch noon–2:30pm, dinner 8–11pm. Métro: Vieux-Port.

Exploring Marseille

Immerse yourself in local life with a wander through Marseille's busy streets, including along the famous **La Canebière.** Lined with hotels, shops, and restaurants, it used to be a very seedy street indeed, saturated with sailors from every nation. With Marseille's ongoing urban regeneration, however, it has become the heart and soul of the city.

La Canebière joins the **Vieux Port** ★★, dominated at its western end by the massive neoclassical forts of St-Jean and St-Nicolas. The harbor is filled with fishing craft and yachts and ringed by seafood restaurants. For a panoramic view, head to the **Jardin du Pharo,** a promontory facing the entrance to the Vieux-Port. From the terrace of the Château du Pharo, built by Napoleon III, you can clearly see the city's old and new cathedrals, as well as the recently redeveloped docklands, now the **Cité de la Méditerranée,** which includes

Fort Saint-Jean and the stunning MuCEM (Museum of European and Mediterranean Civilizations).

North of the old port is **Le Panier,** Marseille's Old Town. Small boutiques and designer ateliers now populate these once-sketchy streets. To the south, the **corniche Président-J.-F.-Kennedy** is a 4km (2½-mile) promenade. You'll pass villas and gardens facing the Mediterranean, before reaching the popular **Plages du Prado.** Patrolled by lifeguards in the summer, these spacious, sandy beaches have children's playgrounds, sunloungers, and waterside cafes. Serious hikers can continue south of here into the **Parc National des Calanques** (www.calanques-parcnational.fr), France's newest national park. This series of impressive limestone cliffs, fjords, and rocky promontories stretches along the coast for 20km (12 miles) southeast of Marseille; the postcard-perfect **Calanque d'En Vau** in particular is well worth seeking out.

Basilique Notre-Dame-de-la-Garde ★ CHURCH This landmark church crowns a limestone rock overlooking the southern side of the Vieux-Port. It was built in the Romanesque-Byzantine style popular in the 19th century and topped by a 9.7m (32-ft.) gilded statue of the Virgin. Visitors come for the views (best at sunset) from its terrace. Spread out before you are the city, the islands, and the shimmering sea.

Rue Fort-du-Sanctuaire. www.notredamedelagarde.com. (℃ **04-91-13-40-80.** Free admission. Daily Apr–Sept 7am–7:15pm, Oct–Mar 7am–6.15pm. Métro: Estrangin-Préfecture. Bus: 60.

MuCEM (Museum of European and Mediterranean Civilizations) ★★ MUSEUM Opened in 2013, the MuCEM is the first national gallery in France to be located outside of Paris. More than 250,000 objects have been collected from throughout the Mediterranean region and are exhibited here, along with local prints, photographs, and historical postcards. The permanent collection is superbly displayed, mixing objects and artworks with video diaries, commissioned cartoons, and enchanting photographs from around the Mediterranean. Architect Rudy Ricciotti designed the museum's contemporary form, which is encased in unique concrete lace. The premises are linked to the 17th-century **Fort Saint-Jean** and its suspended gardens via a panoramic elevated walkway; Michelin-starred-chef Gérard Passédat's two **Le Môle** restaurants (p. 226) are also on site.

1 esplanade du J4. www.mucem.org. (℃ **04-84-35-13-13.** Admission 8€ adults, 5€ ages 18–25 and over 65, 12€ family ticket, free children 17 and under. Additional fee for temporary exhibitions. May–June and Sept–Oct Wed–Thurs and Sat–Mon 11am–7pm, Fri 11am–10pm; Nov–Apr Wed–Mon 11am–6pm, July–Aug Wed–Thurs and Sat–Mon 9am–8pm, Fri 9am–10pm. Métro: Vieux-Port. Bus: 49 or 82.

Musée Cantini ★ ART MUSEUM This 17th-century *hôtel particulier* (private mansion) organizes outstanding modern art exhibitions. Recent shows have been dedicated to Haitian-born French artist Hervé Télémaque and native Marseillaise sculptor César. The museum also houses a permanent

La Marseillaise

Few know that France's national anthem was actually composed in Strasbourg. Originally titled "War Song of the Army of the Rhine," it was written in 1 night by army captain Claude-Joseph Rouget de Lisle in 1792. That same year, revolutionaries from Marseille (who had been given printed copies) marched into Paris singing it. In their honor, the song became known as "La Marseillaise" and was quickly adopted as the rallying cry of the French Revolution. It was officially declared the national anthem of France in 1795, only to be banned by Napoleon during the Empire, Louis XVIII in 1815, and Napoleon III in 1830. The anthem was reinstated for good in 1879.

collection, particularly strong on masterpieces (by Picasso, Dufy, de Staël, Ernst, and others) created during the first half of the 20th century.

19 rue Grignan. http://musee-cantini.marseille.fr. ℰ **04-91-54-77-75.** Admission 5€ adults, 3€ students and seniors, free for children 17 and under. Tues–Sun 10am–6pm. Métro: Estrangin/Préfecture. Bus: 18, 21, 41S, 54, or 221.

Musée des Beaux-Arts ★ MUSEUM   The 150-year-old Museum of Fine Arts is Marseille's oldest exhibition venue. The museum reopened its permanent collection to the public in 2014, after an incredible 9 years of renovations. Exhibits range from 16th-century Italian works to 19th-century French masterpieces, including Rodin's sculpture "La Voix Intérieure" ("The Inner Voice").

Palais Longchamp. http://musee-des-beaux-arts.marseille.fr. ℰ **04-91-14-59-30.** Admission 5€ adults, 3€ students and seniors, free for children 17 and under. Additional fee for temporary exhibitions. Tues–Sun 10am–6pm. Métro: Longchamp. Tram: Longchamp. Bus: 81.

Stade Vélodrome ★ SPORTS STADIUM   The Stade Vélodrome—constructed for the 1938 World Cup and home to local club Olympique de Marseille—has been renovated in its entirety for this year's UEFA Euro 2016 soccer championships. It is now France's second largest sports stadium. For sports enthusiasts, the tourist office offers guided visits of the premises, from the dressing rooms to the press box. Alternatively, catch one of the six international matches taking place here between mid-June and mid-July.

3 boulevard Michelet. www.lenouveaustadevelodrome.com. ℰ **04-13-64-64-71.** Admission 13€ adults, 8€ children 6–12. Family ticket (2 adults + 2 children) 35€. Contact Tourist Office for current tour schedule. Métro: Rond-point du Prado. Bus: 19, 21, 22, 22s, 23, 41, 44, 45, 72, 83, 921.

Outlying Attractions

You can take a 25-minute ferry ride to the **Château d'If** (http://if.monuments-nationaux.fr), a national monument built by François I as a fortress to defend Marseille. Alexandre Dumas used it as a setting for the fictional adventures of "The Count of Monte Cristo." The château is open daily May 16 to September

Château d'If, Marseilles.

16 9:30am to 6:10pm; September 17 to March 31 Tuesday to Sunday 9:30am to 4:45pm; and April 1 to May 31 daily 9:30am to 4:45pm. Entrance to the island is 5.50€ adults, free children 17 and under. Boats leave approximately every 45 to 60 minutes, depending on the season; the round-trip transfer is 11€. For information, contact the **Frioul If Express** (www.frioul-if-express. com; ℭ **04-96-11-03-50;** Métro: Vieux-Port).

Organized Tours

One of the easiest ways to see Marseille's centrally located monuments is aboard the fleet of open-top **L'Open Tour Buses** (www.marseille.opentour. com; ℭ **04-91-91-05-82;** Métro: Vieux-Port). You can hop off at any of 13 different stops en route, and back on to the next bus in the day's sequence, usually arriving between 1 and 2 hours later, depending on the season. The buses run four to eight times a day during each month except January. A 1-day pass costs 19€ adults and 17€ seniors and students; the fare for children ages 4 to 11 is 8€. Two-day passes are also available for just a few euros more.

The motorized **Trains Touristiques de Marseille** (www.petit-train-marseille.com; ℭ **04-91-25-24-69;** Métro: Vieux-Port), or *petit-trains,* make circuits around town too. Year-round, train no. 1 drives a 75-minute round-trip to Basilique Notre-Dame-de-la-Garde and Abbaye St-Victor. From April to mid-November, train no. 2 makes a 65-minute round-trip of old Marseille by way of Cathédrale de la Major, Vieille Charité, and the Quartier du Panier. Both trains make a 30-minute stop for sightseeing en route. The trains depart from the quay just west of the Hôtel de Ville. The fare for train no. 1 is 8€ adults and 4€ children; train no. 2 is 1€ less for both.

Boat tours to the **Parc National des Calanques** are popular. Many tour operators with different prices and formulas (for example, six Calanques in 2 hr./23€; www.croisieres-marseille-calanques.com.) can be found on the quai des Belges at the Vieux-Port.

Shopping

Only Paris and the French Riviera can compete with Marseille for its breadth and diversity of merchandise. Your best bet is a trip to the streets just southeast of the **Vieux-Port,** crowded with stores of all kinds.

The neighborhood around **rue Paradis** and **rue Saint Ferréol** has many of the same upscale fashion boutiques found in Paris, from big name local brands, such as **American Vintage,** 31 rue Francis Davso (www.americanvintage-store.com; ℭ 04-91-33-43-46) and **Le Temps des Cerises,** 9 rue Haxo (www.letempsdescerises.com; ℭ 04-91-33-97-78), to **Galeries Lafayette,** 40 rue St Ferréol (ℭ 04-96-11-35-00), France's largest chain department store. For more bohemian wear, head to **cours Julien** and **rue de la Tour** for richly brocaded and beaded items on offer in North African boutiques.

Le Panier is now home to a vibrant range of unique boutiques. Try **5.7.2,** 23 rue du Panier (www.5-7-2.com; ℭ 06-07-14-62-92), for 1930s to 1970s homewares, or **Les Baigneuses,** 3 rue de l'Eveche (www.lesbaigneuses.com; ℭ 09-52-68-67-64), which sells a gorgeous range of retro-styled swimwear. Wrapping its way around the Cathédrale de la Major, the high-end shops of new **Les Voûtes de la Major,** quai de la Tourette (www.lesvoutes-marseille. fr), are spliced by **Les Halles de la Major** (www.leshallesdelamajor.com), a gourmet market featuring local specialties. Just north of here, brand-new **Les Docks de Marseille,** 10 place de la Joliette (www.lesdocks-marseille.fr; ℭ 04-91-17-34-60), shopping center—with 80 boutiques and restaurants—was inaugurated in late 2015.

Navettes, small cookies that resemble boats, are a Marseillaise specialty. Flavored with secret ingredients that include orange zest and orange flower water, they were invented in 1791 and are still sold at **Le Four des Navettes,** 136 rue Sainte (www.fourdesnavettes.com; ℭ 04-91-33-32-12). In Le Panier, José Orsoni also purveys top-notch *navettes,* as well as other baked goods such as Corsican *canistrelli* (biscuits), at **Navettes des Accoules,** 68 rue Caisserie (www.les-navettes-des-accoules.com; ℭ 04-91-90-99-42).

One of the region's most authentic fish markets at **Quai de la Fraternité** (daily 8am–1pm), on the old port, is partially sheltered under the Norman Foster-designed **L'Ombrière** mirrored canopy. On **cours Julien,** you'll find a market with fruits, vegetables, and other foods (Mon, Tues, Fri, Sat 8am–1pm); exclusively organic produce (Wed 8am–1pm); stamps (Sun 8am–1pm); and secondhand goods (third Sun of the month 8am–1pm).

Nightlife

For an amusing and relatively harmless exposure to the town's saltiness, walk around the **Vieux-Port,** where cafes and restaurants angle their sightlines for the best view of the harbor.

L'Escale Borély, avenue Pierre Mendès France, is 20 minutes south of the town center (take bus no. 83). With a dozen animated bars and cafes, plus restaurants of every possible ethnicity, you'll be spoiled for choice.

Marseille's dance clubs are habitually packed out, especially **Trolley Bus,** 24 quai de Rive-Neuve (www.letrolley.com; ✆ **04-91-54-30-45;** Métro: Vieux-Port), known for techno, house, hip-hop, jazz, and salsa. Equally buzzing is **l'Exit,** 12 quai de Rive-Neuve (✆ **06-42-59-96-24;** Métro: Vieux-Port), a bar/disco with a terrace that profits from Marseille's sultry nights and two floors of seething nocturnal energy (happy hour starts at 5pm and runs all night on Thurs). The **New Can Can,** 3–7 rue Sénac (www.newcancan.com; ✆ **04-91-48-59-76;** Métro: Noailles), is a lively, sprawling bar and disco that identifies itself as a gay venue but attracts many straight folks too. It's open Friday through Sunday midnight until 7am. Sister bar **Le Petit Cancan,** 10 rue Beauvau (www.lepetitcancan.com; ✆ **04-91-33-44-93;** Métro: Vieux-Port), is open daily from 6pm for cocktails and tapas.

For jazz right on the port, head to **La Caravelle,** 34 quai du Port (www.lacaravelle-marseille.com; ✆ **04-91-90-36-64;** Métro: Vieux-Port), an aperitif bar and dinner club that serves a different flavor almost every night, including *manouche,* the French gypsy style most associated with guitarist Django Reinhardt.

ÎLES D'HYÈRES ★★

39km (24 miles) SE of Toulon; 119km (74 miles) SW of Cannes

Bobbing off the French Riviera in the Mediterranean Sea, a small group of islands encloses the eastern boundary of Provence. During the Renaissance, they were coined the Îles d'Or (Golden Islands), named for the glow the rocks give off in sunlight. As might be expected, their location only half an hour from the French coast means the islands are often packed with tourists in summer—but there is still space on its breathtaking beaches for everyone.

If you have time for only one island, choose the beautiful, lively Île de **Porquerolles.** The Île de Port-Cros is quieter—and perhaps better for an overnight stay in order to take advantage of the great hiking, exploring, and snorkeling that would be too rushed for a solitary afternoon. As for the Île du Levant, 80% belongs to the French army and is used for missile testing; the remainder is a nudist colony.

Essentials

GETTING TO ÎLE DE PORQUEROLLES Ferries leave from several points along the Côte d'Azur. The most frequent, cheapest, and shortest trip is from the harbor of La Tour Fondue on the peninsula of Giens, a 32km (20-mile) drive east of Toulon. Depending on the season, there are 5 to 19 departures per day. The round-trip fare for the 15-minute crossing is 20€ adults, 17€ children 4 to 12, 17€ for seniors and students, and free for children 3 and under. For information, contact **TLV-TVM,** La Tour Fondue, Giens 83400 (www.tlv-tvm.com; ✆ **04-94-58-21-81**). **Bateliers de la Côte d'Azur** (www.bateliersdelacotedazur.com; ✆ **04-94-05-21-14**) and **Les Vedettes Île**

d'Or & Le Corsaire (www.vedettesilesdor.fr; © **04-94-71-01-02**) also offer services from La Londe-les-Maures and Le Lavandou respectively.

GETTING TO ÎLE DE PORT-CROS   The most popular ferry route to the island is the 35-minute crossing that departs from Le Lavandou three to seven times daily, depending on the season (28€ adults, 23€ children 4–17 round-trip). For information, contact **Les Vedettes Île d'Or & Le Corsaire** (see above). The **TLV-TVM** and **Bateliers de la Côte d'Azur** (see above) also service Île de Port-Cros. Some of the former's services travel onwards to Île de Levant.

VISITOR INFORMATION   There's a small **Office de Tourisme** (www. porquerolles.com; © **04-94-58-33-76**) near the ferry docks in Porquerolles, as well as a kiosk that distributes brochures and advice near the docks in Port-Cros. For more detailed information, contact the **Office de Tourisme de Hyères,** Rotonde du Park Hôtel, av. de Belgique, Hyères (www.hyerestourisme.com; © **04-94-01-84-50**). Information can also be found at www. portcrosparcnational.fr.

MAIL/POSTAGE & MONEY   The post office, **La Poste,** place d'Armes, Porquerolles (© **36-31**), also has an ATM, but it's best to bring petty cash. Most establishments accept credit cards.

Exploring Île de Porquerolles ★★

Île de Porquerolles is the largest and westernmost of the Îles d'Hyères. It has a rugged south coast, but the northern strand, facing the mainland, boasts a handful of pristine white-sand beaches. The island is about 8km (5 miles) long and 2km (1¼ miles) wide, and is 4.8km (3 miles) from the mainland. The permanent population is only 400.

The island has a history of raids, attacks, and occupation by everyone from the Dutch and the British to the Turks and the Spaniards. Ten forts, some in ruins, testify to its fierce past. The most ancient is **Fort Ste-Agathe,** built in 1531 by François I. In time, it was a penal colony and a retirement center for soldiers of the colonial wars.

In 1971, the French government purchased a large part of Porquerolles and turned it into a national park. Today the landscape—said to receive 275 days of sunshine annually—is one of rocky capes, pine forests twisted by the mistral, sun-drenched vineyards, and pale ochre houses. Indigenous trees such as fig, mulberry, and olive are protected, as well as plants that attract butterflies. The island is best explored on foot or by bike (look for plenty of bike-rental agencies just behind the harbor). The **place d'Armes,** former site of the garrison, is home to several quaint cafes—your best bet for lunch if you're here for a day trip.

For a dose of contemporary culture, the **Fondation Carmignac** (www. fondation-carmignac.com) is opening its **Porquerolles Arts Venue** in 2016. Look out for key works from the Foundation's permanent collection of

20th- and 21st-century paintings, photographs, and sculptures by the likes of Andy Warhol, Roy Lichtenstein, and Cindy Sherman.

WHERE TO EAT & STAY

Hotel et Residence Les Medes (www.hotel-les-medes.fr) also offers good-value guest rooms and apartments.

Mas du Langoustier ★★ This Provençal-style hotel is far and away Porquerolles' most luxurious accommodation. Located on the island's western tip, it's set in a 40-hectare park shaded by eucalyptus and Aleppo pines, and overlooks a lovely pine-ringed bay. Elegant rooms are decorated with classic local textiles; many have their own private patio. And come evening time, there's no need to leave paradise. The onsite **Restaurant L'Olivier** (open to nonguests) is Michelin-starred: Prepare for unique pairings like steamed crayfish and fig ravioli or foie gras with hibiscus jelly.

www.langoustier.com. © **04-94-58-30-09.** 49 units. 300€–660€ double; 690€–760€ suite; 920€–1,200€ family room. Rates include half-board. Closed Oct to late Apr. **Amenities:** 2 restaurants; bar; babysitting; outdoor pool; tennis court; free Wi-Fi.

Exploring Île de Port-Cros ★★

The most mountainous island of the archipelago, Port-Cros has been France's smallest national park since 1963. It's just 5km (3 miles) long and 2km (1¼ miles) wide. It's blanketed with beautiful beaches, pine forests, and subtropical vegetation (birders flock here to observe nearly 100 different species). A hiker's paradise, it has a number of well-marked trails. The most popular and scenic is the easy, 1-hour **sentier des plantes.** The more athletic take the 10km (6¼-mile) **circuit de Port-Man** (and pack their lunch). There is even a 274m (899-ft.) "underwater trail" along the coast where you can snorkel past laminated signs identifying the plants and fish you'll see.

WHERE TO EAT & STAY

Le Manoir de Port-Cros ★★ Port-Cros's only hotel sits within a 19th-century whitewashed building. Accommodation may be simple—crisp white sheets, oversized copper vases, terra-cotta tiled floors—but guests stay here to truly switch off. Paddle in the pool, head out for a hike, or simply amble the surrounding palm and eucalyptus-studded gardens. Rates are half-board, although plenty of day-trippers visit for the restaurant's hearty three-course lunch (60€).

www.hotel-lemanoirportcros.com. © **04-94-05-90-52.** 21 units. 340€–500€ double; 240€–270€ per person in cottages for 4. Closed Oct–Apr. **Amenities:** Restaurant; bar; outdoor pool; room service; free Wi-Fi in common areas.

THE FRENCH RIVIERA

by Tristan Rutherford

The fabled real estate known as the French Riviera, also called the Côte d'Azur (Azure Coast), ribbons for 200km (125 miles) along the sun-kissed Mediterranean. The region has long attracted artists and jetsetters alike with its clear skies, blue waters, and carefree cafe culture. Chic, sassy, and incredibly sexy, the Riviera can be explored by bus, train, boat, bikes, Segway, electric car, SUP paddleboards, or in a dozen novel ways.

A trail of modern artists captivated by the region's light and setting has left a rich heritage: Matisse at Vence, Cocteau at Villefranche, Léger at Biot, Renoir at Cagnes, and Picasso at Antibes and seemingly everywhere else. The finest collection of contemporary artworks is at the Fondation Maeght in St-Paul-de-Vence. New museums dedicated to Jean Cocteau in Menton and Pierre Bonnard near Cannes offer a vivid introduction to the Riviera's storied art scene.

A century ago, winter and spring were considered high season on the Riviera. In recent decades, July and August have become the most crowded months, and reservations are imperative. The region basks in more than 300 days of sun per year, and even December and January are often clement and bright.

The ribbonlike corniche roads stretch across the western Riviera from Nice to Menton, and are scenic stars in scores of films including Cary Grant's "To Catch a Thief" and Robert de Niro's "Ronin." The lower road, the 32km (20-mile) Corniche Inférieure, takes in the resorts of Villefranche, Cap-Ferrat, Beaulieu, Monaco, and Cap-Martin. The 31km (19-mile) Moyenne Corniche (Middle Road) winds in and out of mountain tunnels and takes in the picture-perfect village of Eze. Napoleon built the Grande Corniche—the most panoramic roadway—in 1806. La Turbie is the principal town along the 32km (20-mile) stretch, which reaches more than 480m (1,574 ft.) high at Col d'Eze.

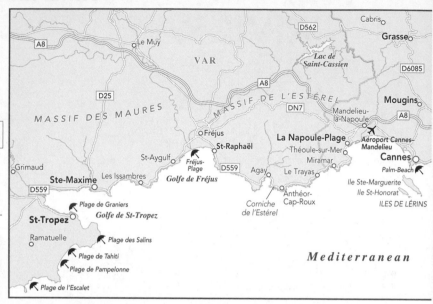

Cabris

Grasse

D562

A8

Le Muy

Lac de
Saint-Cassien

VAR

D6085

D25

MASSIF DE L'ESTÉREL

Mougins

MASSIF DES MAURES

DN7

Mandelieu-
la-Napoule

A8

Fréjus

La Napoule-Plage

Aéroport Cannes-
Mandelieu

St-Raphaël

Théoule-sur-Mer

St-Ayuglf

Fréjus-
Plage

D559

Miramar

Cannes

Grimaud

Les Issambres

Golfe de Fréjus

Agay

Le Trayas

Palm-Beach

Ste-Maxime

Ile Ste-Marguerite
Ile St-Honorat

D559

Anthéor-
Cap-Roux

ILES DE LÉRINS

Plage de Graniers

Golfe de St-Tropez

Corniche
de l'Estérel

St-Tropez

Ramatuelle

Plage des Salins

Mediterranean

Plage de Tahiti

Plage de Pampelonne

Plage de l'Escalet

ST-TROPEZ ★★★

874km (542 miles) S of Paris; 76km (47 miles) SW of Cannes

Cruise ships at St-Tropez.

While this sun-kissed town has a well-known air of hedonism, Trope-zian style is blissfully understated—it's not in-your-face. St-Tropez attracts artists, musicians, models, writers, and an A-lister movie colony each summer, with a flamboyant parade of humanity trailing behind. In winter it morphs back into a boho fishing village, albeit one with modern art galleries and some of the best restaurants along the coast.

The Brigitte Bardot movie "And God Created Woman" put St-Tropez on the tourist map. Droves of decadent tourists baring almost all on the peninsula's white-sand beaches trailed in her wake. In 1995, Bardot

pronounced St-Tropez dead, "squatted by a lot of no-goods, drugheads, and villains." But even she returned, followed in recent years by celebrity A-listers including David Beckham, Paris Hilton, Jay-Z, and Beyoncé.

Essentials

ARRIVING   The nearest rail station is in St-Raphaël, a neighboring coastal resort. **Boats** depart (www.bateauxsaintraphael.com; ℂ **04-94-95-17-46**) from its Vieux Port for St-Tropez (trip time: 1 hr.) five times a day in high summer, reducing to once- or twice-daily sailings in winter. The one-way fare is 15€. Year-round, 10 to 15 Varlib **buses** per day leave from the Gare Routière in St-Raphaël (www.varlib.fr; ℂ **04-94-24-60-00**) for St-Tropez. The trip takes 1½ to 2 hours, depending on the bus and the traffic, which during midsummer is usually horrendous. A one-way ticket is 3€. Buses also run from Toulon train station 56km (35 miles) away.

If you **drive,** note that parking in St-Tropez is tricky, especially in summer. For parking, follow the signs for **Parking des Lices** (ℂ **04-94-97-34-46**), beneath place des Lices, or **Parking du Nouveau Port,** on waterfront avenue Charles de Gaulle (ℂ **04-94-97-74-99**). To get here from **Cannes,** drive southwest along the coastal highway (D559), turning east when you see signs to St-Tropez.

VISITOR INFORMATION   The Office de Tourisme is on quai Jean-Jaurès (www.ot-saint-tropez.com; ℂ **08-92-68-48-28**).

[FastFACTS] ST-TROPEZ

ATMs/Banks   **Crédit Agricole,** 17 place des Lices (✆ **32-25**).

Internet Access   There's free Wi-Fi—as well as a handy table and stools—at the **Casino Supermarket,** av. Genéral Leclerc.

Mail & Postage   **La Poste,** rue de la Poste (✆ **36-31**).

Pharmacies   **Pharmacie du Port,** 9 quai Suffren (✆ **04-94-97-00-06**).

Where to Stay

Hôtel Byblos ★★★   Opened in 1967 on a hill above the harbor, this hamlet of pastel-hued, Provençal-style houses is opulence personified. Inspired by the legendary Phoenician city of the same name, Byblos is favored by visiting celebrities, rock stars, aristocrats, and the über-rich. Its patios and private spaces are splashed with antiques, rare objects, bubbling fountains, and ancient olive trees. Rooms range in size from medium to mega; some units have such special features as four-posters with furry spreads or sunken whirlpool tubs. Also on the premises is Alain Ducasse's superb restaurant **Rivea** (✆ **04-94-56-68-20**). Ingredients, used to create tapas-style sharing dishes, are sourced exclusively from the French and Italian Rivieras. It's the best place to sample Brangelina's exclusive Château Miraval wine, recently ranked by Wine Spectator magazine as "the best rosé in the world."

20 av. Paul Signac. www.byblos.com. ✆ **04-94-56-68-00**. 96 units. 440€–1,225€ double; 875€–3,070€ suite. Parking 35€. Closed Nov to mid-Apr. **Amenities:** 2 restaurants; 1 bar; nightclub; babysitting; concierge; exercise room; massage; outdoor pool; room service; sauna; spa; free Wi-Fi.

Hôtel Les Palmiers ★   In a town packed with pricey accommodation options, this friendly, family-run hotel is a real find. Apart from its fantastic location—directly astride place des Lices in the center of St-Tropez—Les Palmiers boasts compact Provençal-style rooms and a sun-dappled courtyard garden. Part of the hotel dates from the late 18th century and gives the place a cozy, vintage feel.

24–26 bd. Vasserot (place des Lices). www.hotel-les-palmiers.com. ✆ **04-94-97-01-61**. 25 units. 87€–280€ double. **Amenities:** Bar; free Wi-Fi.

Pastis Hôtel-St-Tropez ★★   This portside Provençal house feels more like a sophisticated, eclectic home than a hotel—albeit one decorated with a phenomenal eye for design. British owners John and Pauline Larkin have arranged their private collection of Matisse prints, vintage photographs, 1970s framed album artwork, and Provençal antiques in and around the guest-only lounge and inspired guestrooms surrounding the courtyard swimming pool. Each unique unit is spacious yet intimate and possesses its own balcony or breakfast terrace. Highly recommended.

75 av. du Général Leclerc. www.pastis-st-tropez.com. ✆ **04-98-12-56-50**. 10 units. 225€–750€ double. Free parking. Closed Dec–Jan. **Amenities:** Bar; outdoor pool; free Wi-Fi.

Where to Eat

St-Tropez's dining scene is both expensive and exclusive—particularly during the summer season. Reserve well in advance; alternatively be prepared to dine very early or very late. In addition to the suggestions below, the long-established Moroccan restaurant **Salama,** 1 rue Tisserands (✆ **04-94-97-59-62**), cooks up a fine selection of couscous, pastilla, and tajines; **Chez Madeleine,** 4 place aux Herbes (✆ **04-94-96-59-81**), behind the fish market, serves stellar seafood platters; and **Barbarac,** 2 rue Allard (www.barbarac.fr; ✆ **04-94-97-67-83**), scoops up the finest ice cream in town.

L'Aventure ★ MODERN PROVENÇAL   A backstreet St-Tropez eatery beloved of locals and visitors alike, L'Aventure serves globally inspired market-fresh cuisine: Think snails, Provençal lamb, and harbor-fresh fish alternately laced with pesto, honey, and ginger. Blessedly unpretentious, right down to the authentically battered tables on the petite terrace.

4 rue du Portail-Neuf. ✆ **04-94-97-44-01.** Reservations recommended. Main courses 21€–34€. Tue–Sun 7:30–10pm.

Pizzeria Bruno ★ ITALIAN   Proving that not all good meals in St-Tropez have to break the bank, this casual joint has been turning out thin, crispy, wood-fired pizzas since 1959. Even Bardot was a regular. The menu includes a handful of creative salads, pasta dishes, and grilled meats. Note that the restaurant's copious wood-paneled and overly snug seating isn't the comfiest—but the atmosphere is among the liveliest in town.

2 rue de l'Eglise. ✆ **04-94-97-05-18.** Main courses 12€–20€. Daily noon–2pm and 7–11pm. Closed Oct–Apr.

Exploring St-Tropez

During summertime, St-Tropez's pleasure port is trimmed with superyachts, each one berthing stern-to after a day of hedonistic excess at nearby Plage de Pampelonne. Yacht owners, their lucky guests, spectators, and celebrity-seekers all intermingle along the town's chic quays.

In the Old Town, one of the most interesting streets is **rue de la Miséricorde.** It's lined with stone houses that hold boutiques and evokes medieval St-Tropez better than any other in town. At the corner of rue Gambetta is **Chapelle de la Miséricorde,** with a blue, green, and gold tile roof. Towering above town is the **Citadelle** (✆ **04-94-54-84-14**), a fortified castle complete with drawbridges and stunning views across the Bay of St-Tropez. In 2013, a brand-new **Maritime Museum** opened within the Citadelle, charting famous local historical figures and their travels around the world, including Admiral Suffren, who whupped the British several times during the War of American Independence. From April to September, the entire complex is open daily from 10am to 6:30pm; October through March from 10am to 12:30pm and 1:30pm to 5:30pm. Admission is 3€; entrance is free for those 8 and under.

Musée de l'Annonciade (Musée St-Tropez) ★★★ MUSEUM   Set in a 16th-century chapel just off the harbor, this petite museum showcases a collection of superb post-Impressionist paintings (1890–1950). Many of the artists, including St-Tropez's adopted son, Paul Signac, painted the port of St-Tropez, a backdrop that lies right outside the building. The museum includes such masterpieces as Bonnard's "Nu Devant la Cheminée" as well as artworks by Matisse, Braque, Dufy, Marquet, and Derain. Temporary shows, like recent exhibits showcasing Modigliani drawings or works by 20th-century artists from Marseille (the Ecole Marseillaise), are held on the ground floor.

Place Grammont. ℰ **04-94-17-84-10.** Admission 6€ adults, 4€ children 11 and under. July–Oct Wed–Mon 10am–noon and 2–6pm. Closed Nov.

Organized Tours

This is St-Tropez, darling. Guests keen to be guided around town are handed a **pre-programmed iPod Touch** (3€ per day) and told discreetly to get on with it. The interactive tour takes around 60 minutes. Alternatively, official English-language guided tours of St-Tropez take place every Wednesday at 10am from April to October, departing from in front of the tourist office. Tickets cost 6€, or free for children aged 12 and under.

Outdoor Activities

BEACHES   The hottest Riviera beaches are at St-Tropez. The best for families are closest to the center, including **Plage de la Bouillabaisse, Plage des Graniers,** and **Plage des Salins.** More daring is the 5km (3-mile) crescent of **Plage de Pampelonne,** about 10km (6¼ miles) from St-Tropez. Here around 35 hedonistic beach clubs dot the sand. Overtly decadent is **Club 55** (www.club55.fr; ℰ 04-94-55-55-55), a former Bardot hangout, while the American-run **Nikki Beach** (www.nikkibeach.com; ℰ **04-94-79-82-04**) is younger and more understated, if painfully chic. Gay-friendly **Aqua Club** (ℰ **04-94-79-84-35**) and bare-all **Plage de Tahiti** (www.tahiti-beach.com; ℰ **04-94-97-18-02**) are extremely welcoming.

You'll need a car, bike, or scooter to get from town to Plage de Pampelonne. Parking is around 10€ for the day. More than anywhere else on the Riviera, topless bathing is the norm.

BOATING   In St-Tropez port, **Octopussy** (www.octopussy.fr; ℰ **04-94-56-53-10**) rents boats 5 to 16m (16–52 ft.) long. Larger ones come with a captain at the helm. Prices begin at 350€ per day.

DIVING   Multilingual scuba tuition and equipment hire is available from the **European Diving School** (www.europeandiving.com; ℰ **04-94-79-90-37**), on Plage de Pampelonne. Regular dives, including all equipment, cost 38€.

WINE-TASTING   The St-Tropez peninsula is justly famed for its white and rosé vintages. **Wine Tours Provence** (www.winetoursprovence.com; ℰ **06-17-14-43-41**) organizes half- and full-day expeditions starting in place des Lices and visiting up to 3 local wineries for tastings in the company of an experienced *oenologue*. Call for their bespoke pricing structure.

St-Tropez

HOTELS ■
Hôtel Byblos **8**
Hôtel Les
  Palmiers **7**
Pastis Hôtel-
  St-Tropez **5**

RESTAURANTS ◆
Barbarac **4**
Chez Madeleine **3**
L'Aventure **2**
Pizzeria Bruno **1**
Rivea **8**
Salama **6**

Information ⓘ

Golfe de St-Tropez

Tour du Portalet
Tour Vieille
La Glaye
La Ponche
môle Jean Réveille
quai F. Mistral
Château Suffren
Hôtel de Ville
place du Revelin
place des Remparts
quai Jean Jaurès
rue du Clocher
pl. de l'Ormeau
rue des Remparts
Tour Jarlier
rue du Portail Neuf
Vieux Port
Statue de Suffren
quai G. Péri
quai Suffren
rue Gambetta
rue de la Miséricorde
rue du Petit Bal
Musée de l'Annonciade
Chapelle de la Miséricorde
av. du Maréchal Foch
r. du 11 Nov. 1918
Allard
rue Henri Seillon
rue Général Allard
r. des Etienne Berry
rue des Charrons
rue G. Clémenceau
rue François Sibilli
rue J. Quaranta
rue des Tisserands
bd. Vasserot
place Carnot
place des Lices
place du XVe Corps
av. A. Grangeon
Théâtre
rue de la Ressence
rue du Temple
av. Général Leclerc
bd. Louis Blanc
place de la Croix-de-Fer
av. Paul Roussel
rue du Mortier
rue du Maréchal Memmoz
To Plage de Bouillabaisse
To Chapelle Ste-Anne
To Plages de Pampellone, Tahiti, Moorea, Bora-Bora
montée de la Citadelle
Citadelle & Maritime Museum
montée G. Ringrave
rue Paul Signac
To Plage des Graniers
To Plage des Salins
Paris ⊛
FRANCE
St-Tropez

0 — 100 y
0 — 100 m

Shopping

St-Tropez is awash in stylish shops. The merchandise is Mediterranean, breezy, and sophisticated. Dotted throughout the town's *triangle d'or,* the rough triangle formed by place de la Garonne, rue François Sibilli, and place des Lices, chic labels include Hermès, Sonia Rykiel, and Louis Vuitton. For the past 4 years, a summer pop-up shop has occupied the old Hotel la Mistralée at 1 av. du Général Leclerc, while nearby, Michelin-starred chef Yannick Alléno dishes up delights at **Dior des Lices,** 13 rue François Sibilli, the fashion house's own summertime pop-up eatery. There are also scores of unique boutiques around the Vieille Ville (Old Town), including **Chichou 88,** 27 rue Georges Clémenceau (ⓒ **04-94-96-48-93**), which stocks Indian-inspired homewares and neon handbags; **Truffaux Chapelier,** 44 rue de la Citadelle (ⓒ **04-94-45-33-14**), packed with Panama hats; and **K. Jacques,** 25 rue Allard (www.lestropeziennes.com; ⓒ **04-94-97-41-50**), with its iconic *tropéziennes* sandals. Place des Lices hosts an excellent **outdoor market,** Marché Provençal, with food, clothes, and *brocante* (second-hand goods) on Tuesday and Saturday mornings.

French Boules

A game of *pétanque,* or French boules, is seriously cool for kids. Hop to **Le Café** (www.lecafe.fr; ℰ **04-94-97-44-69**), one of many alfresco bars in place des Lices, and request a handful of *pétanque* boules to toss around the tree-dappled square. The game was created down the coast and is about as Provençal as it gets. Pick up some tips by watching the locals. Games begin with a toss of the jack, or *bouchon.* Teams then take turns to throw. Whoever is farthest away keeps trying to get closest to the *bouchon,* with any remaining balls tossed in at the end. A point is awarded for each steel ball that's closer to the jack than any balls from the opposing team.

Nightlife

On a lower level of the Hôtel Byblos' grounds, **Les Caves du Roy,** 20 avenue Paul-Signac (www.lescavesduroy.com; ℰ **04-94-56-68-00**), is the most self-consciously chic nightclub in St-Tropez. Entrance is free, but drink prices are eye-wateringly high. It's open nightly from Easter to early October from 11:30pm until dawn. Relatively fresh on the scene is **White 1921,** place des Lices (www.white1921.com; ℰ **04-94-45-50-50**), a champagne and cocktail bar set within a jasmine-cloaked courtyard garden. **Le Papagayo,** port de St-Tropez (www.papagayo-st-tropez.com; ℰ **04-94-97-95-95**), is one of the largest nightclubs in town. The decor is inspired by the psychedelic 1960s. Entrance is around 20€ and includes one drink, although those dining at the attached restaurant can routinely sneak in for free. New for summer 2015 was Papagayo's adjoining cabaret bar, **L'Opera** (www.opera-saint-tropez.com; ℰ **04-94-49-51-31**). Adjacent to Le Papagayo is **Le VIP Room,** in the Résidence du Nouveau-Port (www.st-tropez.viproom.fr; ℰ **06-38-83-83-83**), a younger yet similarly chic version of Les Caves du Roy. Paris Hilton and Snoop Dogg have been known to drop by. Cocktails hover around the 20€ mark.

Le Pigeonnier, 19 rue de la Ponche (ℰ **06-38-40-69-22**), rocks, rolls, and welcomes a mostly gay or lesbian crowd between 20 and 50. **L'Esquinade,** 2 rue de Four (ℰ **04-94-56-26-31**), equally gay-friendly, is the habitual sweaty follow-up club.

Below the Hôtel Sube in the port, **Café de Paris** (www.cafedeparis.fr; ℰ **04-94-97-00-56**) is one of the most popular—and friendly—hangouts in town. It has 1900s-style globe lights, masses of artificial flowers, and a long zinc bar. **Café Sénéquier,** quai Jean Jaurès (www.senequier.com; ℰ **04-94-97-20-20**), is historic, venerable, snobbish by day, and off-puttingly stylish by night.

CANNES ★★★

905km (561 miles) S of Paris; 163km (101 miles) E of Marseille; 26km (16 miles) SW of Nice

When Coco Chanel came here and got a suntan, returning to Paris bronzed, she shocked the milk-white society ladies—who quickly began to copy her.

Today the bronzed bodies, clad in nearly nonexistent swimsuits, line the beaches of this chic resort and continue the late fashion designer's example. A block back from the famed promenade de la Croisette are the boutiques, bars, and bistros that make Cannes the Riviera's capital of cool.

Essentials

ARRIVING   By **train,** Cannes is 10 minutes from Antibes, 30 minutes from Nice, and 45 minutes from Monaco. The TGV from Paris reaches Cannes in an incredibly scenic 5 hours. The one-way fare from Paris is 45€ to 129€, although advance purchase bargains can be had for as low as 26€. For rail information and schedules, visit www.voyages-sncf.com or call ☎ **36-35.** **Lignes d'Azur** (www.lignesdazur.com; ☎ **08-10-06-10-06**), line 200, provides bus services from Cannes' Gare Routière (place Bernard Cornut Gentille) to Antibes every 20 minutes during the day (trip time: 25 min.). The one-way fare is 1.50€.

The **Nice International Airport** (www.nice.aeroport.fr; ☎ **08-20-42-33-33**) is a 30-minute drive east. **Bus no. 210** picks up passengers at the airport every 30 minutes during the day (hourly at other times) and drops them at Cannes' Gare Routière. The one-way fare is 20€, round-trip is 30€.

By **car** from Marseille, take A51 north to Aix-en-Provence, continuing along A8 east to Cannes. From Nice, follow A8 or the coastal D6007 southwest to Cannes.

VISITOR INFORMATION   The Office de Tourisme is at 1 bd. de la Croisette (www.cannes-destination.fr; ☎ **04-92-99-84-22**).

SPECIAL EVENTS   Cannes is at its most frenzied in mid-May during the **International Film Festival** (www.festival-cannes.com) at the Palais des Festivals, on promenade de la Croisette. It attracts not only film stars (you can palm the cement molds of their handprints outside the Palais des Festivals), but also seemingly every photographer in the world. You have a better chance of being named prime minister of France than you do attending one of the major screenings, although if you're lucky, you may be able to swing tickets to screenings of one of the lesser films. (Hotel rooms and tables at restaurants are equally scarce during the festival.) But the people-watching is absolutely fabulous!

Getting Around

ON FOOT   Cannes' small town center is a labyrinth of one-ways and serious traffic—which makes it best explored on foot.

BY BICYCLE & MOTOR SCOOTER   Despite the summertime commotion, the flat landscapes between Cannes and satellite resorts such as La Napoule and Juan-les-Pins are well suited for bikes and motor scooters. At **Daniel Location,** 7 rue de Suffern (www.daniel-location-2roues.com; ☎ **04-93-99-90-30**), *vélos tout terrain,* or VTT (mountain bikes), cost 15€ a day. Motorized bikes and scooters cost from 30€ per day. For larger motorbikes, you must present a valid driver's license. Another bike shop is **Mistral Location,** 4 rue Georges Clémenceau (www.mistral-location.com; ✆ **04-93-39-33-60**), which charges 16€ per day.

BY CAR The Cannes Tourist Office website offers a downloadable document (under "Cannes Practical," then "Useful Information") listing all of the town's **public parking lots** and their hourly fees.

BY TAXI **Allô Taxi Cannes** (www.allo-taxis-cannes.com; ✆ **08-90-71-22-27**).

BY PUBLIC TRANSPORT **Bus Azur** (www.busazur.info; ✆ **08-25-82-55-99**) operates all public transport in and around Cannes. There's little need for public transport in the city center—although the open-top no. 8, which runs along the seafront from the port in the west to the Palm Beach peninsula in the east, makes for a fun and scenic ride. Tickets cost 1.50€ and can be purchased directly aboard any bus.

[FastFACTS] CANNES

ATMs/Banks Banks are dotted throughout the city, including more than a dozen along the central rue d'Antibes.

Dentists For emergency dental services, contact **SOS Dentaire** (✆ **04-93-68-28-00**).

Doctors & Hospitals **Hopital de Cannes,** 15 av. Broussailles (www.ch-cannes.fr; ✆ **04-93-69-70-00**).

Internet Access Cannes city council has blanketed the city with free Wi-Fi. Coverage areas include the Jardins de l'Hotel de Ville.

Mail & Postage **La Poste,** 22 rue Bivouac Napoléon (✆ **36-31**).

Pharmacies **Pharmacie du Casino,** 9 bis square Mérimée (✆ **04-93-39-25-48**).

Where to Stay

Five Seas Hôtel ★★ The newest, coolest hotel in Cannes harks back to a Gatsby era of Art Deco furnishings and no-limits lavishness. The style is Louis Vuitton meets vintage liner. The furniture design is based on classic traveling cases, albeit with Apple computers and Nespresso machines thrown into the mix. Popular with both guests and non-residents is the hotel's **Cinq Mondes & Carita Spa.** The top-floor terrace features a small infinity pool, a cocktail bar, and linen-shaded sun loungers. It's also the location of the acclaimed **Sea Sens** modern Mediterranean restaurant (fixed-price dinner 65€–95€ Tues–Sat) under the direction of head chef Arnaud Tabarec. And boy, what a view it has. Desserts come courtesy of 30-year-old World Pastry Champion Jérôme de Oliveira, who also maintains **Intuitions by J** (www.patisserie-intuitions.com), a tea and pastry shop on the ground floor.

1 rue Notre Dame. www.five-seas-hotel-cannes.com. ✆ **04-63-36-05-05.** 45 units. 20€–1,000€ double; from 700€ suite. **Amenities:** Restaurant; bar; concierge; outdoor pool; room service; spa; free Wi-Fi.

Grand Hyatt Hotel Martinez ★★★ The Martinez has been the socialite hub of the South of France for a century. The great and good have marched through its revolving doors including—during the most recent Cannes Film Festivals—Eva Longoria, Nicole Kidman, and Steven Spielberg. This Art Deco masterpiece is more than just an ultra-luxe hotel. Nonguests can mingle with celebrities in the **l'Amiral** cocktail bar, bathe next to A-listers in the **ZPlage** beach club, or dine alongside minor royalty in one of the finest restaurants in the South of France, **La Palme d'Or** (see below). The hotel recently offered super-cool bicycles for guests to peddle around town.

73 bd. de la Croisette. http://cannesmartinez.grand.hyatt.com. ℂ **04-93-90-12-34.** 409 units. 820€–1600€ double; from 3,500€ suite. Parking 40€. **Amenities:** 3 summer restaurants; 2 winter restaurants; bar; babysitting; private beach; free bikes; children's center; concierge; exercise room; outdoor pool; room service; sauna; spa; free Wi-Fi.

Hôtel Pruly ★★ Relatively new on the local scene, this delightful hotel spills from a renovated century-old townhouse. Charming rooms are decorated in bright colors and Provençal textiles; some boast traditional terra-cotta *tomette* floors or private balconies. An afternoon nap on a sun lounger in the hotel's palm-splashed private garden is a welcome respite from Cannes' summertime crowds. It's located just behind the train station.

32 bd. d'Alsace. www.hotel-pruly.com. ℂ **04-93-38-41-28.** 14 units. 65€–115€ double; 90€–150€ triple. **Amenities:** Garden; free Wi-Fi. Closed Jan–Feb.

Where to Eat

Cannes' dining scene is all-encompassing: Expect to stumble across everything from Michelin-starred gastronomy to traditional Provençal peasant cuisine. Restaurants are scattered across the city center, with a particularly heavy concentration around Le Suquet, Cannes' Old Town.

EXPENSIVE

La Palme d'Or ★★★ MODERN FRENCH Double-Michelin-starred chef Christian Sinicropi has presided over this theater of fine dining for more than a decade. Yet his level of innovation knows no bounds. Think algae lollipops, flavored smoke, herb perfume. Guests are greeted at the table by the man himself. Diners are then taken on an intensely seasonal 5- to 10-course gastronomic journey in a dining room so rococo that even Liberace would feel at home. Sinicropi also serves the Cannes Film Festival jury a special set dinner each spring. Spellbinding dishes created for recent festival presidents, like Tim Burton and Woody Allen, can be sampled from the menu. Unforgettable.

In the Grand Hyatt Hotel Martinez, 73 bd. de la Croisette. http://cannesmartinez. grand.hyatt.com. ℂ **04-92-98-74-14.** Reservations required. Jacket and tie recommended. Main courses 75€–144€; fixed-price menu 78€–205€. Wed–Sat 12:30–2pm and 8–10pm. Closed Jan–Feb.

Le Park 45 ★★★ MEDITERRANEAN One of the most inventive—and least expensive—Michelin-starred restaurants on the Riviera is run by one of the coast's youngest chefs, baby-faced Sebastien Broda. Nicknamed the "Petit Prince de la Croisette," Broda scooped up his first Michelin star before the age of 30, after a career at La Palme d'Or in Cannes and L'Amandier in Mougins, two dens of fine Riviera dining. Locally grown vegetables and Atlantic seafood sparkle with additions of yuzu condiment, ponzu cream, Parmesan bouillon, and zingy Granny Smith apple *jus*. Surrounding Le Park 45 is the modernist splendor of **Le Grand Hotel** (www.grand-hotel-cannes.com; ✆ **04-93-38-15-15**). Originally the first hotel on the Croisette, this current 1960s incarnation boasts the best sea views in Cannes and perfectly preserved period features— from funky plastic telephones to Art Deco lampshades. Prices run 144€ to 520€ for a double and from 520€ for a suite, including free Wi-Fi.

In Le Grand Hotel, 45 bd. de la Croisette. www.grand-hotel-cannes.com. ✆ **04-93-38-15-15.** Reservations recommended. Main courses 35€–40€; fixed-price lunch 55€, dinner 55€–120€. Daily midday–2pm and 7:30–10pm.

MODERATE

Restaurant L'Affable ★★ MEDITERRANEAN   Chef Jean-Paul Battaglia's menu may be petite. But his creations are as innovative and as contemporary as can be. The frequently changing selection of dishes may include pumpkin soup with foie gras foam, ceviche "Grenoble-style" drizzled with capers and lime, or tartare of scallops and oysters served with lemon Chantilly cream. Be sure to save space for Battaglia's signature *soufflé au Grand-Marnier.* Note the ambiance is decidedly formal and the service is superb— making L'Affable a good choice for a special occasion. The bargain set lunch is a steal.

5 rue Lafontaine. www.restaurant-laffable.fr. ✆ **04-93-68-02-09.** Reservations recommended. Main courses 36€–42€; fixed-price lunch 24€–28€; fixed-price dinner 44€. Mon–Fri 12:30–2pm, Mon–Sat 7–10pm. Closed Aug.

INEXPENSIVE

Aux Bons Enfants ★ PROVENÇAL   You could easily miss this old-fashioned eatery, tucked among a crowd of mediocre tourist-targeted restaurants. But what an oversight that would be. Family-run for three generations, the authentic Aux Bons Enfants today is headed up by Chef Luc Giorsetti. Dishes are traditional: *daube de canard;* slow-cooked *duck à la niçoise;* zucchini flower fritters; or house-cured salmon gravlax. Seasonal ingredients are sourced each morning from Marché Forville, just around the corner. Note that the restaurant has no telephone and does not accept reservations or credit cards.

80 rue Meynadier. www.aux-bons-enfants.com. No telephone. No reservations. Main courses 16€–23€; fixed-price menu 28€. No credit cards. Tues–Sat noon–2pm and 7–10pm. Closed Dec.

Exploring Cannes

Far and away, Cannes' most famous street is the **promenade de la Croisette**— or simply La Croisette—which curves along the coast. It's lined by grand hotels (some dating from the 19th c.), boutiques, and exclusive beach clubs. It's also home to temporary exhibition space **La Malmaison,** 47 La Croisette (www.cannes.com; ☏ **04-97-06-44-90**), which holds three major modern art shows—featuring artists ranging from Miró to Picasso—each year. It's open daily July to August 11am to 8pm (Fri until 9pm), September 10am to 7pm, and October to April Tuesday to Sunday 10am to 1pm and 2 to 6pm. Admission varies with exhibits. Above the harbor, the Old Town of Cannes sits on Suquet Hill, where visitors can climb the 14th-century **Tour de Suquet.**

Musée Bonnard ★★ ART MUSEUM   The only museum in the world dedicated to the Impressionist painter Pierre Bonnard is located 3km (1¾ miles) north of Cannes, in the suburb of Le Cannet. Portraits, sculptures, and sketches on display in this petite museum were created primarily between 1922 and 1947, the period during which the artist was a local resident.

16 bd. Sidi Carnot, Le Cannet. www.museebonnard.fr. ☏ **04-93-94-06-06.** Admission 5€ adults, 3.50€ ages 12–18, free for children 11 and under. Sept–June Tues–Sun 10am–8pm (Thurs until 9pm); Jul–Aug 10am–8pm (Thurs until 9pm). Bus 1 from Cannes city center.

Musée de la Castre ★ MUSEUM   Perched above Cannes' Old Town within the medieval Château de la Castre, this museum focuses primarily on ethnographic finds from around the world. Spears from the South Seas and Tibetan masks are interspersed with Sumerian cuneiform tablets and 19th-century paintings of the Riviera. Many visitors, however, will be most impressed by the astounding views from the museum's viewing tower—accessed via 109 steeps steps. The shady Mediterranean gardens, just outside the museum's entrance, are a welcome respite for tired sightseers.

Le Suquet. ☏ **04-93-38-55-26.** Admission 6€ adults, 3€ ages 18–25, free for children under 17. July–Aug daily 10am–7pm (Wed until 9pm); Sept and Apr–June Tues–Sun 10am–1pm and 2–6pm (June and Sept Wed until 9pm); Oct–Mar Tues–Sun 10am–1pm and 2–5pm.

Organized Tours

One of the best ways to get your bearings in Cannes is to climb aboard the **Petit Train Touristique de Cannes** (www.cannes-petit-train.com; ☏ **06-22-61-25-76**). The vehicles operate every day from 9 or 10am to between 7 and 11pm, depending on the season. Three itineraries are offered: Modern Cannes, with a ride along La Croisette and its side streets (35 min.); Historical Cannes, which weaves through the narrow streets of Le Suquet (35 min.); or the Big Tour, a combination of the two (1 hr.). All trains depart from outside the Palais des Festivals every 30 to 60 minutes. Shorter tours cost 7€ for adults and 3€ for children aged 3 to 10; the Big Tour costs 10€ for adults and 5€ for children aged 3 to 10.

Outdoor Activities

BEACHES   Beachgoing in Cannes has more to do with exhibitionism than actual swimming. **Plage de la Croisette** extends between the Vieux Port and the Port Canto. The beaches along this billion-dollar stretch of sand are

Plage de la Croisette.

payante, meaning entrance costs between 15€ to 30€. You don't need to be a guest of the Martinez, say, to use the beaches associated with a high-end hotel (see "Where to Stay," above), and Cannes has heaps of buzzing beach clubs dotted around, including sassy **3.14 Beach** (www.314cannes.com; ℗ **04-93-94-25-43**). Why should you pay an entry fee at all? Well, the price includes a full day's use of a mattress, a chaise longue (the seafront is more pebbly than sandy), and a parasol, as well as easy access to freshwater showers. There are also outdoor restaurants and bars (some with organic menus, others with gourmet burgers and sushi) where no one minds if you dine in your swimsuit. Every beach allows topless bathing. Looking for a free public beach without chaises or parasols? Head for **Plage du Midi,** just west of the Vieux Port, or **Plage Gazagnaire,** just east of the Port Canto. Here you'll find families with children and lots of RV-type vehicles parked nearby.

BOATING   Several companies around Cannes's Vieux Port rent boats of any size, with or without a crew, for a day, a week, or even longer. An outfit known for short-term rentals of small motorcraft from 200€ per day is **Boat Evasion,** 110 boulevard du Midi (www.boatevasion.com; ℗ **06-26-59-10-77**). For kayak rental and guided tours of the coastline, including trips into the Esterel natural park by canoe, try **SeaFirst,** Place Franklin Roosevelt (www.seafirst.fr; ℗ **04-93-65-06-14**).

GOLF   Cannes is ringed by 10 golf courses, almost all within a 20-minute drive of the city. The **Old Course,** 265 route de Golf, Mandelieu (www.golfoldcourse.com; ℗ **04-92-97-32-00**), is a leafy gem dating from 1891. Greens fees start at 90€, with big reductions for lunch deals, afternoon tee-offs, and simple Pitch and Putt rounds. The prestigious **Royal Mougins Golf Club,** 424 av. du Roi, Mougins (www.royalmougins.fr; ℗ **04-92-92-49-69**), also boasts a gourmet restaurant and spa. Greens fees start at 180€, including buggy hire; it's half-price for 9 holes.

PADDLEBOARDING   Cannes is nothing if not cutting edge. And like the rest of the world, this city has fallen in love with stand-up paddleboarding

(SUP). Rent your own from **Cannes Standup Paddle Location,** Plage du Mouré Rouge, bd. Gazagnaire, Palm Beach (www.cannesstanduppaddle.fr; ✆ **06-82-17-08-77**). Fees start at 12€ per hour.

TENNIS Some resorts have their own courts. The city of Cannes also maintains 16 synthetic courts and 6 clay-topped ones at the **Garden Tennis Club,** 99 av. Maurice Chevalier (www.cannes-tennis.com; ✆ **04-93-47-29-33**). Court rental costs 17€ per hour.

Shopping

Cannes achieves a blend of resort-style leisure, glamour, and media glitz more successfully than many of its neighbors. You'll see every big-name designer you can think of (Saint Laurent, Rykiel, and Hermès), plus a legion of one-off designer boutiques and shoe stores. There are also real-people shops; resale shops for star-studded castoffs; flea markets for fun junk; and a fruit, flower, and vegetable market.

BOOKS Ciné-Folie, 14 rue des Frères-Pradignac (✆ **04-93-39-22-99**), is devoted entirely to film. Called "La Boutique du Cinema," it is the finest film bookstore in the south of France; vintage film stills and movie posters are also for sale. **Cannes English Bookshop,** 11 rue Bivouac Napoleon (www.cannes englishbookshop.com; ✆ **04-93-99-40-08**), stocks locally based classics from Peter Mayle and Carol Drinkwater, plus bestselling novels, travel guides, and maps.

DESIGNER SHOPS Most of the big names in fashion line promenade de la Croisette, the main drag running along the sea. Among the most prestigious are **Dior,** 38 La Croisette (✆ **04-92-98-98-00**), and **Hermès,** 17 La Croisette (✆ **04-93-39-08-90**). The stores stretch from the Hôtel Carlton almost to the Palais des Festivals, with the top names closest to the **Gray-d'Albion,** 38 rue des Serbes (www.lucienbarriere.com; ✆ **04-92-99-79-79**), both a mall and a hotel (how convenient). Near the train station, department store **Galeries Lafayette** has all the big-name labels crammed into one smallish space at 6 rue du Maréchal-Foch (✆ **04-97-06-25-00**).

Young hipsters should try **Bathroom Graffiti,** 52 rue d'Antibes (✆ **04-93-39-02-32**), for sexy luggage, bikinis, and designer homeware. The rue d'Antibes is also brilliant for big-brand bargains (Zara and MaxMara), as well as one-off boutiques.

FOOD The Marché Forville (see below) and the surrounding streets are unsurprisingly the best places to search for picnic supplies. For bottles of Côtes de Provence, try **Cave du Marché,** 5 place Marché Forville (✆ **04-93-99-60-98**). It also serves up glasses of local rosé and olive crostini on tables outside. **La Compagnie des Saumons,** 12 place Marché Forville (✆ **04-93-68-33-20**), brims with caviar, bottles of fish soup, and slabs of smoked salmon. Local cheese shop **Le Fromage Gourmet,** 8 rue des Halles (✆ **04-93-99-96-41**), is a favorite of celebrated chef Alain

Ducasse. New chocolatier **J.P. Paci,** 20 rue Hoche (℅ **04-93-39-47-94**), molds dark chocolate treats into stiletto heels and other far-out shapes.

MARKETS   The **Marché Forville,** in place Marché Forville just north of the Vieux Port, is a covered stucco structure with a few arches but no walls. From Tuesday to Sunday, 7am to 1pm, it's the fruit, vegetable, and flower market that supplies the dozens of restaurants in the area. Monday (8am–6pm) is *brocante* day, when the market fills with dealers selling everything from Grandmère's dishes and bone-handled carving knives to castaways from estate sales.

Tuesdays to Sundays, 8am to 12:30pm, the small **Marché aux Fleurs** (Flower Market) takes place outdoors along the edges of the allée de la Liberté, across from the Palais des Festivals.

Nightlife

BARS & CLUBS   A strip of sundowner bars stretches along rue Félix Faure. Most are chic, some have happy hour cocktails, and several have DJs after dinner. New tapas bar **Le Bivi,** 7 rue des Gabres (www.lebivi-cannes.com; ℅ **04-93-39-97-90**), is a convivial spot to sample more unusual South of France wines. For an aperitif with history, the **Bar l'Amiral,** in the Hôtel Martinez, 73 La Croisette (℅ **04-93-90-12-34**), is where deals have always gone down during the film festival. The bar comes complete with the nameplates of stars that once propped it up, Humphrey Bogart among them. Alternatively, head to **Le 360,** Radisson Blu 1835 Hotel & Thalasso, 2 bd. Jean Hibert (www.radissonblu.com; ℅ **04-92-99-73-20**), a panoramic rooftop terrace overlooking the port that's idyllic for a cocktail as the sun sets. At **Le Bâoli,** Port Pierre Canto, La Croisette (www.lebaoli.com; ℅ **04-93-43-03-43**), Europe's partying elite, from Prince Albert of Monaco to Jude Law, dance until dawn. Dress to the nines to slip past the über-tight security and into this Asian-inspired wonderland.

CASINOS   Cannes is invariably associated with easygoing permissiveness, filmmaking glitterati, and gambling. If the latter is your thing, Cannes has world-class casinos loaded with high rollers, voyeurs, and everyone in between. The better established is the **Casino Croisette,** in the Palais des Festivals, 1 espace Lucien Barrière (www.lucienbarriere.com; ℅ **04-92-98-78-00**). A well-respected fixture in town since the 1950s, a collection of noisy slot machines it is most certainly not. Its main competitor is the newer **Palm Beach Casino,** place F-D-Roosevelt, Pointe Croisette (www.palmbeach-casino.com; ℅ **04-97-06-36-90**), on the southeast edge of La Croisette. It attracts a younger crowd with a summer-only beachside poker room, a beach club with pool, a restaurant, and a disco that runs until dawn. Both casinos maintain slots that operate daily from lunchtime to 4 or 5am. Smarter dress is expected for the *salles des grands jeux* (blackjack, roulette, craps, poker, and chemin de fer), which open nightly 8pm to 4am. The casino also pulls in daytime visitors with tasty inexpensive lunches and Sunday brunches, both of which come with free gaming chips.

DAY TRIPS FROM CANNES

Îles de Lérins ★★

Short boat ride from Cannes

Floating in the Mediterranean just south of Cannes' southern horizon, the Lérins Islands are an idyllic place to escape the Riviera's summertime commotion. Head for Cannes port's western quai Laubeuf, where ferryboats operated by **Trans-Côte d'Azur** (www.trans-cote-azur.com; ✆ **04-92-98-71-30**) offer access to Île Ste-Marguerite. To visit Île St-Honorat, head for the same quay, to the **Transports Planaria** (www.cannes-ilesdelerins.com; ✆ **04-92-98-71-38**) ferryboats. Both companies offer frequent service to the islands at intervals of between 30 and 90 minutes depending on the season, and operate daily and year-round. Round-trip transport to Île Ste-Marguerite costs 14€ per adult and 8€ for children 5 to 10; round-trip transport to Île St-Honorat costs 17€ per adult and 8.50€ for children 5 to 10 (although discount tickets of 14€ per adult and 7.50€ for children 5–10 are often available if you book in advance online). Travel to both islands is free for children 4 and under. As dining options on the islands are limited, pack up a picnic lunch from Cannes' Marché Forville before you set off.

EXPLORING ÎLE STE-MARGUERITE

Île Ste-Marguerite is one big botanical garden ringed by crystal-clear sea. Cars, cigarettes, and all other pollutants are banned. From the dock, you can stroll along the island to Fort Royal, built by Spanish troops in 1637 and used as a military barracks and parade ground until World War II. The infamous "Man in the Iron Mask" was allegedly imprisoned here, and you can follow the legend back to his horribly spooky cell.

Musée de la Mer, Fort Royal (✆ **04-93-38-55-26**), traces the history of the island, displaying artifacts of Ligurian, Roman, and Arab civilizations, plus the remains discovered by excavations, including paintings, mosaics, and ancient pottery. Temporary exhibitions, often showcasing contemporary French artists, are also held on the premises. The museum is open June to September daily 10am to 5:45pm, and Tuesday to Sunday October to May 10:30am to 1:15pm and 2:15 to 4:45pm (closing at 5:45pm Apr–May). Admission is 6€, 3€ for visitors 25 and under, and free for children 17 and under.

EXPLORING ÎLE ST-HONORAT ★★

Only 1.6km (1 mile) long, the Île St-Honorat is much quieter than neighboring Ste-Marguerite. But in historical terms, it's much richer than its island sibling and is the site of a monastery whose origins date from the 5th century. The **Abbaye de St-Honorat** ★ (www.abbayedelerins.com; ✆ **04-92-99-54-00**) is a combination of medieval ruins and early-20th-century ecclesiastical buildings, and is home to a community of about 25 Cistercian monks. The monks transform the island's herbs, vines, and honey into a wealth of organic products, including lavender oil and wine. All can be purchased in the monastery shop. Since 2015, oenophile monk Brother Marie has welcomed visitors for **tours of the island's sun-kissed vineyards** (www.excellencedelerins. com). For 16 centuries, rare grapes like Provençal Mourvèdre and Turkish-derived Viognier have been cultivated here.

Most visitors content themselves with a wander through the pine forests on the island's western side, a clamber around the ruined monastery on the island's southern edge, and a bathe on its seaweed-strewn beaches.

Grasse ★

18km (11 miles) N of Cannes

Grasse, a 20-minute drive from Cannes, has been renowned as the capital of the world's perfume industry since the Renaissance. It was

Abbey in Île St-Honorat.

once a famous resort, attracting such royals as Queen Victoria and Princess Pauline Borghese, Napoleon's lascivious sister.

Today some three-quarters of the world's essences are produced here from thousands of tons of petals, including violets, daffodils, wild lavender, and jasmine. The quaint medieval town has several free perfume museums where visitors can enroll in workshops to create their own scent.

ESSENTIALS

Trains run to Grasse from Cannes, depositing passengers a 10-minute walk south of town. From here, a walking trail or shuttle bus leads visitors into the center. One-way train tickets cost 4.40€ from Cannes. **Buses** pull into town every 10 to 60 minutes daily from Cannes (trip time: 50 min.), arriving at the Gare Routière, place de la Buanderie (𝄐 **04-93-36-37-37**), a 5-minute walk north of the town center. The one-way fare is 1.50€. Visitors arriving by **car** may follow RN85 from Cannes. The **Office de Tourisme** is at place de la Buanderie (www.grasse.fr; 𝄐 **04-93-36-66-66**).

EXPLORING GRASSE

Musée International de la Parfumerie ★ MUSEUM   This comprehensive museum chronicles both Grasse's fragrant history, as well as worldwide perfume development over the past 4,000 years. Wander among raw materials, ancient flasks (including Marie Antoinette's 18th-c. toiletry set) and scented soaps, all set against a backdrop of contemporary artworks. Kids age 7 and older have their own dedicated pathway, lined with interactive exhibits to touch—and, of course, smell.

2 bd. du Jeu-de-Ballon. www.museesde grasse.com. ℭ **04-97-05-58-00.** Admission (depending on exhibition) 4€—6€ adults, 2€—3€ students, free for children under 18. Apr–Sept daily 10am–7pm; Oct—Mar Wed–Mon 10:30am–5:30pm. Closed Nov.

WHERE TO EAT & SHOP

For light lunch or an afternoon snack, pop into **Le Péché Gourmand,** 8 rue de l'Oratoire (ℭ **06-62-69-61-57**), a combination mini-restaurant, tearoom, and ice cream parlor. Try the goat's cheese and candied tomato crumble, or order up a bowl of the decadent chocolate sorbet.

Both **Parfumerie Molinard,** 60 bd. Victor Hugo (www.molinard. com; ℭ **04-93-36-01-62**), and **Parfumerie Fragonard,** 20 bd. Fragonard (www.fragonard.com; ℭ **04-93-36-44-65**), offer factory tours,

Perfume shop inside Fragonard factory.

where you'll get a firsthand peek into scent extraction and perfume and essential oil production. You can also purchase their products on-site.

Vallauris ★

7km (4½ miles) NE of Cannes

Once simply a stopover along the Riviera, Vallauris's ceramics industry was in terminal decline until it was "discovered" by Picasso just after World War II. The artist's legacy lives on both in snapshots of the master in local galleries and in his awesome "La Paix et La Guerre" fresco.

ESSENTIALS

Envibus **bus** (www.envibus.fr; ℭ **04-89-87-72-00**) connects Cannes' train station with Vallauris every 30 minutes (journey time: 20 min.). Tickets cost 1€ each way. There's an **Office de Tourisme** at 67 ave. George Clemenceau (www.vallauris-golfe-juan.fr; ℭ **04-93-63-82-58**).

EXPLORING VALLAURIS

In Vallauris, Picasso's **"l'Homme au Mouton"** ("Man and Sheep") is the outdoor statue at place Paul Isnard in front of which Prince Aly Kahn and screen goddess Rita Hayworth were married. The local council had intended to enclose this statue in a museum, but Picasso insisted that it remain on the square, "where the children could climb over it and dogs piss against it." Closed for years, you can now enjoy contemporary art at the newly renovated **Galerie Madoura** (www.madoura.com), rue Georges et Suzanne Ramié,

Picasso's former ceramics studio. It is open 10:30am–1pm and 2–5pm Monday to Friday.

Musée Magnelli, Musée de la Céramique & Musée National Picasso La Guerre et La Paix ★★ ART MUSEUM   Three museums in one, this petite cultural center developed from a 12th-century chapel where Picasso painted "La Paix" ("Peace") and "La Guerre" ("War") in 1952. Visitors can physically immerse themselves in this tribute to pacifism. Images of love and peace adorn one wall; scenes of violence and conflict the other. Also on site is a permanent exposition of works by Florentine-born abstract artist Alberto Magnelli, as well as a floor dedicated to traditional and innovative ceramics from potters throughout the region.

Place de la Libération. www.musees-nationaux-alpesmaritimes.fr. © **04-93-64-71-83.** Admission 4€ adults, free for children 15 and under. July–Aug daily 10am–7pm; Sept–June 10am–12:15pm and 2–5pm.

WHERE TO EAT & SHOP

Join the locals for lunch at **Le Café du Coin,** 16 place Jules Lisnard (www.cafe-du-coin.com; © **04-92-90-27-79**), where a small selection of market-fresh specials are scribbled on the chalkboard daily. For souvenirs, head around the corner to avenue Georges-Clemenceau, lined with small shops selling brightly glazed, locally made ceramics.

Mougins ★★

7km (4½ miles) N of Cannes

A fortified hill town, Mougins preserves the quiet life in a postcard-perfect manner. The town's artsy legacy—Picasso, Jean Cocteau, Paul Eluard, Fernand Léger, Isadora Duncan, and Christian Dior were all previous residents—has blessed the town with must-see galleries. Real estate prices are among the highest on the Riviera, and the wealthy residents support a dining scene that also punches well above its weight. The **Etoile des Mougins food festival** (www.lesetoilesdemougins.com), held each September, is a highbrow gastronomic love-in featuring Michelin-starred chefs from across the globe.

ESSENTIALS

From Cannes, the best way to get to Mougins is to **drive** north of the city along D6285. By **bus, Société Tam** (www.cg06.fr; © **08-00-06-01-06**) runs bus no. 600 from Cannes to Val-de-Mougins, a 10-minute walk from the center of Mougins. One-way fares cost 1.50€. The **Office de Tourisme** is at 39 place des Patriotes (www.mougins-tourisme.fr; © **04-92-92-14-00**).

EXPLORING MOUGINS

Picasso discovered Mougins' tranquil maze of flower-filled lanes in the company of his muse, Dora Marr, and photographer Man Ray, in 1935. The Vieux Village's pedestrianized cobblestone streets—each corner prettier than the last—have changed little over the decades since. After the highlights below, it's well worth seeking out the romantic **Chapelle Notre-Dame de Vie,** Chemin de la Chapelle, and its tree-dappled grounds, once painted by Sir Winston Churchill. Just 1.5km (1 mile) southeast of Mougins, it was built in the 12th century and reconstructed in 1646. The priory next door was Picasso's studio and residence for the last 12 years of his life. It's still a private home occupied intermittently by the Picasso heirs.

Musée d'Art Classique de Mougins ★★ MUSEUM   The newest addition to Mougins' art scene is wonderfully quirky: Egyptian, Greek, and Roman artifacts are juxtaposed alongside similarly themed modern artworks, including sculptures, drawings, and canvases from Matisse, Dufy, Cézanne, Dali, and Damien Hirst. A personal favorite pairing matches an ancient statue of Venus with Yves Klein's neon-blue "Venus" sculpture. Some sculpture shows spill out onto Mougin's old village streets.

32 rue Commandeur. www.mouginsmusee.com. ℂ **04-93-75-18-65.** Admission 12€ adults, 7€ students and seniors, 5€ children 10–17, free for children 9 and under. Daily 10am–6pm.

Musée de la Photographie André Villers ★ ART MUSEUM   Picasso's close friend, photographer André Villers, chronicled the artist's Mougins years in black-and-white photos. Images line the walls of an ancient medieval home: Some are hilarious, such as the photo showing Picasso sitting down for breakfast in his trademark Breton shirt, pretending he has croissants for fingers. Additional portraits by Villars—including snaps of Dali, Catherine Deneuve, and Edith Piaf—are frequently on display, along with three major temporary exhibitions each year.

Porte Sarrazine. ℂ **04-93-75-85-67.** Free admission. Daily 10am–12:30pm and 2–6pm. Closed Jan.

WHERE TO EAT
Three acclaimed **cooking schools** are hosted by the three grandest establishments in town: L'Amandier, Moulin de Mougins, and the Michelin-starred Mas Candille.

Le Moulin de Mougins, Notre Dame de Vie (www.moulindemougins. com; ℂ **04-93-75-78-24;** fixed-price lunch 31€–45€, fixed-price dinner 85€–120€), is a place of foodie pilgrimage. Inside an enchanting 16th-century mill, talented chef Erwan Louaisil follows in the footsteps of founder Roger Vergé and previous head chef Alain Llorca with modern twists on culinary traditions from both Provence and his native Brittany. The restaurant is closed Monday and Sunday all day. It also rents six double rooms (150€–200€) and two suites (200€–250€) on site.

On a budget? Try the traditional bistro **Le Resto des Arts,** 2 rue Maréchal Foch (ℂ **04-93-75-60-03;** set-menu 22€), which dishes up hearty specials like basil-spiked *soupe au pistou,* red mullet doused in tomato sauce, or seared steak with morel mushrooms.

JUAN-LES-PINS ★★

913km (566 miles) S of Paris; 9.5km (6 miles) S of Cannes

Just west of the Cap d'Antibes, this Art Deco resort burst onto the South of France scene during the 1920s, under the auspices of American property developer Frank Jay Gould. A decade later, Juan-les-Pins was already drawing a chic summer crowd, as the Riviera "season" flipped from winter respites to the hedonistic pursuit of summer sun, sea, and sensuality. It has been attracting the young and the young-at-heart from across Europe and the U.S. ever since. F. Scott Fitzgerald decried Juan-les-Pins as a "constant carnival." His words ring true each and every summer's day.

Essentials

ARRIVING Juan-les-Pins is connected by **rail** to most nearby coastal resorts, including Nice (trip time: 30 min.; 5.10€ one-way), Antibes, and Cannes. A **bus** (www.envibus.fr; ⓒ **04-89-87-72-00**) leaves for Juan-les-Pins from Antibes' Gare Routière (bus station) daily every 20 minutes and costs 1€ one-way (trip time: 10 min.). To **drive** to Juan-les-Pins from Nice, travel along coastal D6007 south; from Cannes, follow the D6007 north.

VISITOR INFORMATION The Juan-les-Pins **Office de Tourisme** is housed into the new Convention Center at 60 chemin des Sables (www.antibesjuanlespins.com; ⓒ **04-22-10-60-01**).

SPECIAL EVENTS The town offers some of the best nightlife on the Riviera. The action reaches its peak during the annual 10-day **Festival International de Jazz** (www.jazzajuan.com) in mid-July. It attracts jazz, blues, reggae, and world music artists who play nightly on the beachfront Parc de la Pinède. In 2015, the festival's alfresco seaside stage hosted Santana and Lionel Richie. Tickets cost 25€ to 75€ and can be purchased at the Office de Tourisme in both Antibes and Juan-les-Pins, as well as online.

[FastFACTS] JUAN-LES-PINS

ATMs/Banks **BNP Paribas,** 14 av. Maréchal Joffre (ⓒ **08-20-82-00-01**).

Internet Access **Mediterr@net-phone.com,** av. du Dr Fabre (ⓒ **04-93-61-04-03**).

Mail & Postage **La Poste,** 1 av. Maréchal Joffre (ⓒ **36-31**).

Pharmacies **Pharmacie Provençale,** 144 bd. Président Wilson (ⓒ **04-93-61-09-23**).

Where to Stay

Hôtel Belles-Rives ★★★ This luxurious hotel is one of the Riviera's most fabled addresses. It started life in 1925 as a holiday villa rented by Zelda and F. Scott Fitzgerald (as depicted in Fitzgerald's semi-autobiographical novel "Tender Is the Night"). Today, 90 years after her grandparents first opened the Belles-Rives' doors, the elegant Madame Estène-Chauvin owns and oversees this waterside gem. Guestrooms are sumptuous yet eclectic—each one its own unique size and shape. The lower terraces hold garden dining rooms, an elegant bar and lounge, as well as a private jetty. Also on site is the superb **La Passagère** restaurant and a private beach. If you're daring, you can even try waterskiing at the waterside aquatic club where, almost a century ago, the sport was invented.

33 bd. Edouard Baudoin. www.bellesrives.com. ℂ **04-93-61-02-79.** 43 units. 150€–850€ double; 850€–2,000€ suite. Parking 30€. Closed Jan–Feb. **Amenities:** 2 summer restaurants; 1 winter restaurant; 2 bars; private beach; room service; free Wi-Fi.

Hôtel Mademoiselle ★★★   Juan-les-Pins' newest, coolest hotel offers 14 individually styled rooms in the absolute center of town. Decor is seriously funky. We're talking velvet headboards, golden robot statuettes, floral cushions, rocking horses, and a figurine of Her Majesty The Queen. Breakfast, drinks, and afternoon tea are served in the oasis-like rear garden. Homemade cakes and biscuits come under the tutelage of the hotel's young pastry chef, Alexandra. Alas, the Mademoiselle may not be for everyone, as guests step out onto the main boulevard of one of Europe's most liberal resorts. The sandy beach is a 60 second stroll away.

12 avenue Docteur Dautheville. www.hotelmademoisellejuan.com. ℂ **04-93-61-31-34.** 14 units. 102€–189€ double; 142€–229€ suite. **Amenities:** Room service; free Wi-Fi.

Where to Eat

Cap Riviera ★★ FRENCH   One of Juan-les-Pins' most appealing attributes is its endless ripple of beachside restaurants, all peering out over the picturesque Iles de Lérins. And Cap Riviera is undoubtedly one of this resort's finest. Cuisine is classically French. Think shrimp flambéed in pastis, lemon-infused sardine *rillettes,* or *sole meunière;* staff are charming and attentive. It's well worth popping by in advance to select your own special sea-facing table. Each evening the 39€ three-course set menu makes a great bet for a trustworthy splurge. Items may include half-lobster or shellfish cassoulet to start, beef fillet with *morilles* mushrooms or flambéed kidneys for a main course, and rum baba or iced nougat to finish.

13 bd. Édouard Baudoin. www.cap-riviera.fr. ℂ **04-93-61-22-30.** Reservations recommended. Main courses 23€, fixed-price lunch 25€, fixed-price dinner 39€. Daily noon–3pm, Mon-Sat 8–10pm. Closed Nov–mid Dec and Jan.

Le Capitole ★ CLASSIC FRENCH   This restaurant's decor, menu, and service have hardly changed since its inception in the 1950s. And that's no bad thing. Expect impeccable service—with limited English—in a mirrored dining room filled with more lamps, boxes, and *objets d'art* than Gatsby's mansion. Classic French fare is a delight. Menu items may include smoked herrings with potatoes, *steak-frites,* snails in garlic, and crème caramel. Best value of all is the 16€ early dining menu. Arrive for dinner before 8pm for three bargain courses, with coffee and wine included in the deal.

22 av. Amiral Courbet. ℂ **04-93-61-22-44.** Reservations recommended. Main courses 9€–17€; fixed-price lunch 16€; fixed-price dinner 22€–39€. Wed–Sun noon–2pm and 7–10pm.

Exploring Juan-les-Pins

Spilling over from Antibes' more residential quarter, Juan-les-Pins is petite—which makes the resort town best navigated on foot. Be sure to swing by the shady square known as **La Pinède** (square Frank Jay Gould) to check out the legions of local *pétanque* players. Nearby, the town's long-awaited **Palais des Congrès,** or Convention Center (www.antibesjuanlespins-congres.com) opened to much fanfare in 2014. New for 2015 is Juan-les-Pins' **Solex vintage scooter rental** agency (www.so-solex.com; ℂ **06-49-40-52-89**), which operates from the Convention Center's News Caffé. These half-cycle, half-motorbike combos were first built in 1946 and have achieved cult status. Brigitte Bardot was a fan. Rides costs 20€ per person for 2 hours, or 40€ with an accompanying tour guide. Bikes can be delivered anywhere on the French Riviera for a small fee.

Come sunset, stroll the long, beachside promenade to Golfe-Juan, where Napoleon kicked off his march to Paris and famous Hundred Days in power in 1815. Alternatively, pick a beach bar, order a glass of rosé, and watch the sun drop over the Îles de Lérins (p. 251).

Outdoor Activities

BEACHES   Part of the reason people flock to Juan-les-Pins is for the town's wealth of sandy beaches, all lapped by calm waters. The town also basks in a unique microclimate, making it one of the warmest places on the Riviera to soak up the sun, even in winter. **Plage de Juan-les-Pins** is the most central beach, although quieter stretches of sand wrap around the Cap d'Antibes and include family-friendly **Plage de la Salis** and chic **Plage de la Garoupe.** If you do want to stretch out on a sunlounger, go to any of the beach-bar concessions that line the bay, where you can rent a mattress for around 12€ to 20€. Topless sunbathing and overt shows of cosmetic surgery are the norm.

WATERSPORTS   If you're interested in scuba diving, try **Easy Dive,** bd. Edouard Baudouin (www.easydive.fr; ℂ **04-93-61-26-07**). A one-tank dive costs 30€ to 55€, including all equipment. **Sea kayaking, pedalos, parascending,** and **donuts** are available at virtually every beach in Juan-les-Pins. **Waterskiing** was invented at the Hôtel des Belles-Rives in the 1920s, and it's still a great place to try out the sport.

Nightlife

For a faux-tropical-island experience, head to **Le Pam Pam,** 137 bd. Wilson (www.pampam.fr; ℂ **04-93-61-11-05**), a time-honored "rhumerie" where guests sip rum and people-watch while reggae beats drift around the bar. More modern is **La Réserve,** av. Georges Gallice (ℂ **04-93-61-20-06**), where a younger crowd sips rosé on leopard-print seats under a large plane tree. The alfresco terrace of **News Caffé,** 60 chemin des Sables (ℂ **04-89-68-90-55**), is another hip hangout of choice.

If you prefer high-energy partying, you're in the right place. The entire Riviera descends upon Juan-les-Pins' discos every night in summer, and it's best to follow the crowds to the latest hotspot. **Le Village,** 1 bd. de la Pinède (© **04-92-93-90-00**), is one of the more established clubs and boasts an action-packed dance floor with DJs spinning summer sounds from salsa to soul. The cover charge is usually 16€ including one drink; more for themed evenings. For top jazz, head to **Le New Orleans,** 9 av. Georges Gallice (© **04-93-67-41-71**), a relatively new addition to the local live music scene.

ANTIBES & CAP D'ANTIBES ★★

913km (566 miles) S of Paris; 21km (13 miles) SW of Nice; 11km (6¾ miles) NE of Cannes

Antibes has a quiet charm unique to the Côte d'Azur. Its harbor is filled with fishing boats and pleasure yachts. The likes of Picasso and Monet painted its oh-so-pretty streets, today thronged with promenading locals and well-dressed visitors. A pedestrianized town center makes it a family-friendly destination as well, and a perfect place for an evening stroll. An excellent covered market is also located near the harbor, open every morning except Mondays.

Spiritually, Antibes is totally divorced from Cap d'Antibes, a peninsula studded with the villas of the super-rich. But the less affluent are welcome to peek at paradise, and a lovely 6km (3¾ miles) coastal path rings the headland, passing picnic and diving spots en route.

Essentials

ARRIVING **Trains** from Cannes arrive at the rail station, place Pierre-Semard, every 20 minutes (trip time: 15 min.); the one-way fare is 3€. Around

Old town of Antibes.

25 trains arrive from Nice daily (trip time: 20 min.); the one-way fare is 3.70€. The **bus** station, or Gare Routière, place Guynemer (www.cg06.fr or www. envibus.fr; ℰ **04-89-87-72-00**), offers bus services throughout Provence. Bus fares to Nice, Cannes, or anywhere en route cost 1.50€ one-way.

To **drive** to Antibes from Nice, travel along coastal D6007 south; from Cannes, follow the D6007 north. The Cap d'Antibes is clearly visible from most parts of the Riviera. To drive here from Antibes, follow the coastal road south—you can't miss it

VISITOR INFORMATION The **Office de Tourisme** is at 42 avenue Robert Soleau (www.antibesjuanlespins.com; ℰ **04-22-10-60-10**).

[FastFACTS] ANTIBES

ATMs/Banks Among others, there are half a dozen banks dotted along av. Robert Soleau.

Internet Access **Wilson.net,** 74 bd. Wilson (ℰ **04-92-90-25-34**).

Mail & Postage **La Poste,** 2 av. Paul Doumer (ℰ **36-31**).

Pharmacies **Grande Pharmacie d'Antibes,** 2 place Guynemer (ℰ **04-93-34-16-12**).

Where to Stay

Hotel Villa Fabulite ★★ The newest star on the Cap d'Antibes is expertly run by multilingual Franco-Mexican Angelina Framery. Housed in an old scuba diving school 2 minutes from the beach, her 15 rooms are arranged around fragrant gardens stocked with orchids and palms, and an outdoor pool. She even stocks a fleet of free bikes, which guests may use to tour around the Cap. Unlike the surrounding multi-million-dollar villas, the Fabulite is a bargain. The chef Cyrille Chaussade (formerly of La Gavroche in London) serves Asian-inspired beef noodles and local octopus salad for 15€ per main course. Provençal wine is served by the jug. As a final bonus, Framery has links with every boat agency, SUP paddleboard rental, and tour specialist from Antibes to Cannes.

50 traverse des Nielles. www.fabulite.com. ℰ **04-93-61-47-45.** 15 units. 160€–250€ double. Closed mid-Oct to Mar. **Amenities:** Restaurants; babysitting; massage; outdoor pool; room service; boat rental; free Wi-Fi.

Le Relais du Postillon ★ Like Antibes itself, Le Relais is charmingly individualistic with bags of character. It's sited on the town's principal square, with a cafe and terrace right on the action. The interior bar–with cozy fireplace in winter–has toasted a century of local color. Guestrooms aren't exactly the Ritz, but they are tidy, Frenchy, and spotlessly clean. Moreover, they cost under 100€ per night even in high summer. Le Relais also rents a 40-square-metre holiday apartment next door from 600€–900€ per week, or 120€–160€ per night.

8 rue Championnet. www.relaisdupostillon.com. ℰ **04-93-34-20-77.** 16 units. 69€–149€ double. Parking 20€. **Amenities:** Cafe; bar; free Wi-Fi.

Where to Eat

The Zelda and Scott Fitzgeralds of today head for the **Restaurant Eden-Roc** (www.hotel-du-cap-eden-roc.com; ℂ **04-93-61-39-01**) at the Hôtel du Cap-Eden-Roc for grand service and grand cuisine. Alternatively, the excellent **Restaurant de Bacon,** bd. de Bacon (www.restaurantdebacon.com; ℂ **04-93-61-50-02**), has served the best seafood around for more than 6 decades. For light bites and unusual local wines, stop into **Entre 2 Vins,** 2 rue James Close (ℂ **04-93-34-46-93**). Antibes' **Marché Provençal** produce market is a top spot for picnic items. Purchase olives, cheese, or a whole-roast chicken and simply dine on the beach. Thirsty? For the adventurous, the **Balade en Provence,** 25 cours Massena (ℂ **04-93-34-93-00**), is an underground absinthe bar situated in a 9th-century cellar, serving the dangerously alcoholic liqueur over a sugar cube and diluted with a tiny dash of water.

Bistro Le Rustic ★ FRENCH/PIZZA   For hearty local dishes on a budget, it's hard to beat family-run Le Rustic. The menu here focuses on wood-fired pizzas and rich pots of fondue, with plenty of Riviera classics (fish soup, a fresh shrimp platter, slow-roasted duck) thrown in too. The restaurant is located at the heart of Antibes' Old Town, with spacious (and kid-friendly) outdoor seating in the square.

33 place Nationale. ℂ **04-93-34-10-81.** Main courses 10€–18€; fixed-price menu 19€. Daily noon–2.30pm and 6–11pm.

L'Armoise ★★ PROVENÇAL   Talented chef Laurent Parrinello, who honed his skills at Eze's Chèvre d'Or à Eze and the nearby Hôtel du Cap–Eden-Roc, crafts modern adaptations of traditional dishes, such as pesto-drizzled asparagus, fennel, and goat-cheese salad, or sea bream served with curry-infused red cabbage. Fresh ingredients come from Antibes' daily market; cheeses and wines are sourced from local producers. Note that reservations at this tiny restaurant are required in advance.

2 rue de la Tourraque. ℂ **04-92-94-96-13.** Reservations required. Main courses 22€–24€; fixed-price menu 48€–80€. Tues–Sun 7:30–9:30pm, Sat–Sun 12:30–2pm. Closed 2 weeks in July and 2 weeks in Dec.

La Taille de Guepe ★★ PROVENÇAL   For affordable gourmet French classics look no further than this family-run Old Town establishment. It's quirky, kooky, and overwhelmingly friendly. Decor is verdantly tropical with plants and bamboo furniture, and the interior even boasts a gazebo. Most dishes are spotted with edible flowers and chefy touches like foams and emulsions. Slow-cooked Provençal cod comes with an aioli dip and chargrilled asparagus. The house wine is a refreshingly inexpensive delight.

24 Rue de Fersen. ℂ **04-93-74-03-58.** Main courses 10€–18€; fixed-price lunch 16€; fixed-price menu 23€. Tues–Sun 12–2.30pm and 7:30–10:30pm.

Restaurant La Closerie ★ PATISSERIE/FRENCH   Christian Cottard, winner of the prestigious *Meilleur Ouvrier de France* master craftsman award, opened this scrumptious restaurant and cake shop in summer 2014. The tea room offers an early morning sugar rush of patisserie classics like Paris-Brest choux stuffed with Chantilly cream, and Kavelinka cakes laden with Belgian chocolate. In season, lunch is served under the palm trees on the outdoor terrace. Try tomato fondue or chilled heirloom tomato soup. Cottard's cake-making school on the upper floor opened in May 2015. Lessons, from 60€, cover everything from cake design to macaroons.

8 boulevard Dugommier. www.patisserie-cottard-antibes.fr. ℂ **04-93-34-09-92.** Main courses 15€–23€. Mon–Sat 11:30–3pm (tea and patisserie salon open Mon–Sat 9am–6pm).

Exploring Antibes

Antibes' largely pedestrianized Old Town—all pale stone homes, weaving lanes, and window boxes of colorful flowers—is easily explored on foot. A dip into Picasso's former home, now a museum, and a stroll along the bling-tastic pleasure port, where artist Jaume Plensa's giant "Nomad" sculpture shimmers against the night sky, are undoubtedly its highlights.

Antibes' Tourist Office offers a number of different **guided tours.** English language explorations of the historic old town take place every Wednesday at 10am. Prices are 7€ for adults, 3.50€ for children under 16, and free for childen aged 8 and under. French-only tours around Antibes' artist hotspots take place each Friday at 10am for the same prices.

Visitors keen to escape the crowds may head to the Cap d'Antibes' **Espace du Littoral et du Milieu Marin,** bd. J.F. Kennedy (ℂ **04-93-61-45-32**). This small, kid-friendly space showcases a permanent Jacques Cousteau exhibition, and it has a seaside park (which overlooks the grounds of the ultra-exclusive Hôtel du Cap–Eden-Roc!) to explore too. It's open April to mid-September, Tuesday to Saturday 10am to 5:45pm; entrance is free.

Musée Picasso ★★ ART MUSEUM   Perched on the Old Town's ramparts, the 14th-century Château Grimaldi was home to Picasso in 1946, when the Spanish artist lived and worked here at the invitation of the municipality. Upon his departure, he gifted all the work he'd completed to the château museum: 44 drawings and 23 paintings, including the famous "La Joie de Vivre." In addition to this permanent collection, contemporary artworks by Nicolas de Staël, Arman, and Modigliani, among many others, are also on display.

Château Grimaldi, Place Mariejol. ℂ **04-92-90-54-28.** Admission 6€ adults, 3€ students and seniors, free for children 17 and under. Mid-June to mid-Sept Tues–Sun 10am–6pm (July–Aug Wed and Fri until 8pm); mid-Sept to mid-June Tues–Sun 10am–noon and 2–6pm.

DAY TRIPS FROM ANTIBES

Biot ★

6.5km (4 miles) NW of Antibes

Biot has been famous for its pottery since merchants began to ship earthenware jars to Phoenicia and throughout the Mediterranean. Thirty handicraft workshops, many making Biot's famous blown glass and jewelry, are open daily. It's also where color-loving artist Fernand Léger painted until the day he died, leaving a magnificent collection of his work on display just outside town.

ESSENTIALS

Bus lines no. 7 and no. 10 from Antibes's Gare Routière, place Guynemer (© www.envibus.fr; **04-89-87-72-00**), run to Biot's town center. Tickets cost 1€. To **drive** to Biot from Antibes, follow D6007 east, then head west on the D4. Biot's **Office de Tourisme** is at 4 rue Chemin Neuf (www.visit-biot.com; © **04-93-65-78-00**).

EXPLORING BIOT

Exploration of Biot's small historic center begins at **place des Arcades,** where you can see the 16th-century gates and the remains of the town's ramparts. You may also use Biot's Historical Trail app to make a 45-minute navigation of the oh-so-cute town center. The **Musée d'Histoire et Céramique Biotoise,** 8 rue St-Sebastien (www.musee-de-biot.fr; © **04-93-65-54-54**), has assembled the best works from local artists, potters, ceramists, painters, and silver- and goldsmiths. Hours are mid-June to mid-September Tuesday to Sunday 10am to 6pm and mid-September to mid-June Wednesday to Sunday 2 to 6pm. Admission is 4€, 2€ for seniors and students, free ages 16 and under.

Outside of town, the excellent **Musée National Fernand Léger,** 316 chemin du Val de Pôme (www.musees-nationaux-alpesmaritimes.fr/fleger; © **04-92-91-50-20**), displays a comprehensive collection of the artist's colorful creations, from 1930s Cubist ladies to circus scenes of the 1950s. Hours are Wednesday to Monday, May to October 10am to 6pm and November to April, 10am to 5pm. Admission is 5.50€, 4€ for students and seniors, and free for ages 25 and under. There are temporary exhibitions and a cafe garden on site.

WHERE TO EAT & SHOP

For a Provençal take on crêpes—such as summery tomato, olive tapenade with basil or the house specialty, crêpe-pizza—stop in to **Crêperie Auberge du Village,** 29 rue Saint Sébastien (www.creperie-aubergeduvieuxvillage.com; © **04-93-65-72-73**). This low-key lunch spot sits at the northern end of Biot's main shopping street. In the late 1940s, local glassmakers created a bubble-flecked glass known as *verre rustique.* In brilliant cobalts and emeralds, it's displayed in many store windows here.

ESPECIALLY FOR KIDS

Just south of Biot sits a kid-tastic complex of theme parks. **Marineland** (www.marineland.fr) is an ever-popular water park complete with penguins, polar bears, and sharks, although bear in mind that all marine life is kept in captivity. **Aqualand** (www.aqualand.fr) boasts more than 2km (1¼ miles) of waterslides, including toboggan-style Le Draguéro and the Rainbow Cannon. **Adventure Golf** is criss-crossed by two dinosaur-dotted miniature golf courses. **Kid's Island** caters to animal-loving little ones, with pony rides and a petting zoo, plus plenty of jungle gyms and a Magic River. Admission is as follows: Marineland 40€, 32€ children between 3 and 12; Aquasplash 27€, 21€ children between 3 and 12; Adventure Golf 12€, 10€ children between 3 and 12; and Kid's Island 14€, 11€ children between 3 and 12. All are free for children 2 and under; combination entrance tickets are also available. Marineland is open daily July and August 10am to 11pm, mid-April to June and September 10am to 7pm, and mid-March to mid-April 10am to 6pm. Aquasplash, Adventure Golf, and Kid's Island all have varying opening hours. See the Marineland website for further details.

ST-PAUL-DE-VENCE ★★

926km (574 miles) S of Paris; 23km (14 miles) E of Grasse; 28km (17 miles) E of Cannes; 31km (19 miles) N of Nice

Of all the hilltop villages of the Riviera, St-Paul-de-Vence is by far the most famous. It gained popularity in the 1940 and '50s, when artists including Picasso, Chagall, and Matisse frequented the town, trading their paintings for hospitality at the Colombe d'Or inn. Art is now the town's principal attraction, and the winding streets are studded with contemporary galleries and museums. Circling the town are magnificent old ramparts (allow about 30 min. to walk the full loop) that overlook flowers and olive and orange trees.

Essentials

ARRIVING   The nearest **rail** station is in Cagnes-sur-Mer. Some 20 **buses** per day (no. 400) leave from central Nice, dropping passengers off in St-Paul-de-Vence (1.50€ one-way, journey time: 1 hr.), then in Vence 10 minutes later. For information, contact Ligne d'Azur (www.lignesdazur.com; ✆ **08-10-06-10-06**). If you're **driving** from Nice, take either the A8 highway or the coastal route du Bord du Mer west, turn inland at Cagnes-sur-Mer, and follow signs north to St-Paul-de-Vence.

VISITOR INFORMATION   The **Office de Tourisme** is at 2 rue Grande (www.saint-pauldevence.com; ✆ **04-93-32-86-95**).

Getting Around

St-Paul's Old Town is entirely pedestrianized, and most of the narrow streets are paved in cobblestones. Note that driving a car here is prohibited, except to drop off luggage at an Old Town hotel, and by prior arrangement only. The Fondation Maeght is around half a mile out of town.

[FastFACTS] ST-PAUL-DE-VENCE

ATMs/Banks   **BNP Paribas,** rd-pt Sainte Claire (✆ **08-20-82-00-01**).

Mail & Postage   **La Poste,** rd-pt Sainte Claire (✆ **36-31**).

Pharmacies   **Pharmacie Saint Paul,** rd-pt Sainte Claire (✆ **04-93-32-80-78**).

Where to Stay

La Colombe d'Or rents deluxe rooms (see "Where to Eat," below).

La Vague de Saint-Paul ★★★   Here is an affordable hotel for art lovers seeking country tranquility and wow-factor design. The wavelike main hotel building was originally conceived by far-out architect André Minangoy in the 1960s. Color-coded guestrooms now look out onto a vast garden complete with *pétanque* run, tennis court, bar, and pool. The attached restaurant delivers three locally sourced set menus at 18€, 24€ and 29€. The complex sits a short walk from the Fondation Maeght contemporary art museum—and a longer stroll through the forest to St-Paul-de-Vence village via a secret trail. Highly recommended.

Chemin des Salettes. www.vaguesaintpaul.com. ☏ **04-92-11-20-00.** 37 units. 85€–208€ double; 246€–328€ suite. Free parking. **Amenities:** Restaurant; bar; concierge; outdoor pool; room service; spa; tennis; free Wi-Fi. Closed Nov.

Where to Eat

St-Paul's petite size means that dining options are limited and may also be pricey. That said, the views and the ambience of pretty much any local eatery often make up for these shortcomings.

La Colombe d'Or ★★ PROVENÇAL   This celebrated restaurant opened its doors in 1920. At the time it was little more than a scattering of tables overlooking an overgrown artichoke patch. It was Paul Roux, the restaurant's art-adoring owner, who encouraged the era's struggling artists, such as Raoul Dufy, Paul Signac, and Chaime Soutine, to swap a canvas or two for generous room and board. Picasso, Braque, and Miró followed—and today La Colombe d'Or's art collection is one of the finest in the world. For a peek at these masterpieces, you'll need to dine here, either indoors beneath works by the likes of Signac, Matisse, and Braque or outdoors on the fig-trimmed terrace. The house specials include a selection of fresh hors-d'oeuvres (such as *crudités* and *anchoïade,* a traditional anchovy dip), and crispy roast chicken. It also offers 25 luxurious doubles and suites sprawling over the original 16th-century stone house and the two 1950s wings. Prices are 250€ for a double, 430€ for a suite.

1 place du Général-de-Gaulle. www.la-colombe-dor.com. ☏ **04-93-32-80-02.** Reservations required. Main courses 25€–45€. Daily noon–2pm and 7:30–10pm. Closed Nov–mid Dec.

Les Terrasses ★ PROVENÇAL   A few minutes' stroll downhill from the Fondation Maeght, this laidback eatery offers classic regional cuisine and superb views over St-Paul's Old Town. Opt for *aïoli,* steamed vegetables, and cod served alongside a garlic-spiked mayonnaise dip; *secca d' Entrevaux,* a locally cured beef dished up with grilled goat cheese; or one of a dozen different pizzas. Prices are the best in the area, and the atmosphere is convivial—do note, however, that the restaurant is a favorite with large groups.

20 chemin des Trious. www.laterrassesursaintpaul.com. ☏ **04-93-32-85-60.** Main courses 11€–30€; fixed-price menu 29€. Thurs–Tues 9am–10pm. Closed 2 weeks in Nov.

Exploring St-Paul

Perched at the top of the village, the **Collégiale de la Conversion de St-Paul** ★ was constructed in the 12th and 13th centuries and has been much altered over the years. The Romanesque choir is the oldest part, containing some remarkable stalls carved in walnut in the 17th century. Look to the left as you enter: You'll see the painting "Ste-Cathérine d'Alexandrie," which has been attributed to Tintoretto. The **Trésor de l'Eglise** is one of the most beautiful in the Alpes-Maritimes, with a spectacular ciborium. Look also for a low relief of the "Martyrdom of St-Clément" on the last altar on the right. It's open daily 9am to 6pm (to 7pm July–Aug). Admission is free.

Just around the corner is the light-flooded **Chapelle des Pénitents Blanc** (© **04-93-32-41-13**). The artist Jean-Michel Folon, who worked on this unmissable masterpiece until his death in 2005, decorated the church with stained-glass windows, shimmering mosaics, and rainbow-hued frescos. It's open May to September daily 10am to 12:30pm and 2 to 6pm, and October to April daily from 10:30am to 12:30pm to 2 to 4pm. Admission is 4€ adults, 3€ students and children 6 to 18, and free for children 5 and under.

Fondation Maeght ★★★ ART MUSEUM   Established by Parisian art dealers Aimé and Marguerite Maeght in 1964, this avant-garde building houses one of the most impressive modern-art collections in Europe. It was Spanish architect José Luis Sert who designed the pagoda-like exhibition space, ensuring the artwork it displays sits in perfect harmony with the surrounding pine-studded woods. In the gardens, colorful Alexander Calder installations are clustered with skinny bronze sculptures by Alberto Giacometti. A rotating selection of artworks is displayed over the various levels inside, showcasing key pieces by artists like Matisse, Chagall, Bonnard, and Léger. Each summer the museum stages a large seasonal show. There's also a library, a cinema, a cafeteria, and a magnificent museum store on-site.

623 chemin des Gardettes, outside the town walls. www.fondation-maeght.com. © **04-93-32-81-63**. Admission 15€ adults, 10€ students and ages 10–18, free for children 9 and under, 5€ fee for photographs. July–Sept daily 10am–7pm; Oct–June daily 10am–6pm.

Organized Tours

With advance booking, the local tourist office offers 10 different walking tours of the town's historic core and outskirts. **Themed tours** (7€, free for children under 12) last around an hour and a half. They include following in the footsteps of former resident Marc Chagall, trying your hand at the beloved Provençal pastime of *pétanque* (also known as *boules*) under the instruction of accomplished locals, or guided tours of the Fondation Maeght.

In nearby La Colle sur Loup, culinary legends Alain and Jean-Michel Llorca offer cooking workshops for adults and children at their **Ecole de Cuisine** (www.alainllorca.com; 40€–170€ per person). Lessons, which include children's' pastry making and formal gastronomic desserts, are in French and English and are often followed by an informal dinner.

Shopping

The pedestrian-only **rue Grande** is St-Paul's most evocative street, running the length of the town. Most of the stone houses along it are from the 16th and 17th centuries, and several still bear the coats of arms placed there by the original builders. Today many of the houses are antiques shops, arts-and-crafts galleries, and souvenir and gift shops; some are still artists' studios.

Galerie du Vieux Saint-Paul, 16–18 rue Grande (www.galeries-bartoux. com; ✆ **04-93-32-74-50**), is the place to pick up serious art, from sculptures by local artist Arman to bronze works by Salvador Dali. Just down the road, **Galerie Capricorne,** 64 rue Grande (www.galeriecapricorne.com; ✆ **04-93-58-34-42**), offers a colorful array of prints, including a selection by Marc Chagall. Stock up on olive oils, fruit vinegars, and olive-wood chopping boards at **Premier Pression Provence,** 68 rue Grande (www.ppp-olive.com; ✆ **04-93-58-07-69**). It's worth plunging into the town's winding streets, too: **Saint Georges Editions,** 5 montée de l'Eglise (✆ **09-71-57-68-21**), stocks superb, unique handbags, each one created from lengths of unusual antique textiles. Nearby **Atelier Silvia B** (www.silviabertini.com; ✆ **04-93-32-18-13**) is packed with bright collages of St-Paul.

VENCE ★

926km (574 miles) S of Paris; 31km (19 miles) N of Cannes; 24km (15 miles) NW of Nice

Often bypassed in favor of nearby St-Paul-de-Vence, the pretty village of Vence is well worth a detour. Its pale stone Old Town is atmospheric yet untouristy, splashed with shady squares and pavement cafes. The highlight is undoubtedly Matisse's Chapelle du Rosaire, set among a countryside studded with cypresses, olive trees, and oleanders.

Essentials

ARRIVING Frequent **buses** (no. 94 or 400) originating in Nice take 65–80 minutes to reach Vence, passing the nearest **rail** station in Cagnes-sur-Mer, about 10km (6¼ miles) southwest from Vence, en route. The one-way fare is 1.50€. For bus information, contact **Ligne d'Azur** (www.lignesdazur.com; ✆ **08-10-06-10-06**). To **drive** to Vence from Nice, take D6007 west to Cagnes-sur-Mer, and then D36 north to Vence.

VISITOR INFORMATION The **Office de Tourisme** is on place du Grand-Jardin (www.ville-vence.fr; ✆ **04-93-58-06-38**).

[FastFACTS] VENCE

ATMs/Banks Many banks are dotted around Vence, including **BNP Paribas,** 28 place du Grand-Jardin (✆ **08-20-82-00-01**).

Internet Access **La Régence Cafe,** 10 place du Grand-Jardin (www.laregencecafe.com; ✆ **04-93-24-02-10**), on Vence's main square has free Wi-Fi and serves excellent patisserie.

Mail & Postage **La Poste,** place Clemenceau (📞 **36-31**).

Pharmacies **Pharmacie du Grand-Jardin,** 30 place du Grand-Jardin
(📞 **04-93-24-04-07**).

Where to Stay

Note that St-Paul-de-Vence's hotels also make an excellent base for exploring Vence.

l'Auberge des Seigneurs ★★ In the dead center of historic Vence comes this age-old guesthouse. Don't let the low rates put you off—Vence simply isn't an expensive town. Decor in its charm-laden guestrooms hasn't changed since the hotel's inception in 1916: Think hardwood furniture, antique tiles, and no TV. The building itself is a 17th-century castle made of stone. For some guests the best bit is the restaurant. Closed on Sunday and Monday, it offers convivial communal classics like lamb roasted over an open-fire. Set menus range from 23€ to 32€. Highly recommended.

1 rue du Dr Binet. www.auberge-seigneurs.com. 📞 **04-93-58-04-24.** 6 units. 90€–95€ double. **Amenities:** Restaurant; bar; free Wi-Fi.

The Frogs' House ★★ This gem of a B&B is a 10-minute drive from Vence, in the cutesy village of St Jeannet. Renoir used to paint in the charming village and surrounds, which also forms its own AOC wine appellation, one of France's smallest. Bilingual hosts Benoît and Corinne welcome guests to The Frog's shared outdoor terrace. Here is where breakfasts and—to those visitors who desire them—communal dinners are served. Group hikes are also led into the surrounding countryside. Several of the seven simple bedrooms overlook the sea.

35, rue du Saumalier, St Jeannet. www.thefrogshouse.fr. 📞 **06-28-06-80-28.** 7 units. 81€–107€ double. Rates include breakfast. Closed Jan–Feb. **Amenities:** Free Wi-Fi.

Where to Eat

Vence's unpretentious attitude is also evident in the local cuisine. It tends to be traditional and tasty, occasionally Michelin-starred, and often dished up in a sublime setting. For homemade hot chocolate or artisanal sweets, **Entre Mes Chocolats,** 12 av. Marcellin Maurel (www.entre-mes-chocolats.com; 📞 **09-81-82-34-59**), is well worth a visit.

Le Pigeonnier ★ PROVENÇAL One of the Old Town's most welcoming eateries, Le Pigeonnier spills across the dining rooms of a 14th-century building and a sunny square, the latter perfect for people-watching. The restaurant menu is traditional. Linger over slow-cooked *daube* (a classic Niçois beef stew), a generous steak, or fish soup served with garlic croutons and *rouille*, saffron mayonnaise.

3 place du Peyra. 📞 **04-93-58-03-00.** Main courses 11€–20€; fixed-price menu 23€. July–Aug daily noon–2:30pm and 7:30–10pm; Sept–June Tues–Sat noon–2:30pm and 7:30–10pm, Sun noon–2:30pm.

Les Bacchanales ★★ PROVENÇAL   A short stroll from the Chapelle du Rosaire, Les Bacchanales is located inside a century-old villa, overlooking chef Christophe Dufau's enchanting kitchen garden. The creative menu uses almost exclusively local ingredients, transforming them into strikingly innovative versions of traditional Provençal cuisine. Mediterranean bream may be paired with apricots and Italian Taggiasche olives; sweet cantaloupe melon is grilled and served with fresh almonds and Corsican *brousse* cheese. Note that the market-fresh weekly menu is limited: Diners may simply select their preferred number of courses (two at lunch only, five to seven at dinner). The restaurant holds one Michelin star.

247 av. de Provence. www.lesbacchanales.com. © **04-93-24-19-19.** Reservations recommended. Fixed-price menus 32€–95€. Wed–Mon 12:30–2pm and 7:30–9:30pm. Closed last 2 weeks of Dec, 3 weeks in Jan.

Exploring Vence

Vence's medieval **Vieille Ville (Old Town)** is compact, making it easy to explore on foot. A poke around its picturesque squares reveals place du Peyra's bubbling **Vieille Fontaine (Old Fountain),** while nearby the **Chateau de Villeneuve/Fondation Émile Hugues,** 2 place du Frêne (www.musee devence.com; © **04-93-58-15-78**), is a temporary exhibition space dedicated to 20th-century art. Hours are Tuesday to Sunday 10am to 12:30pm and 2 to 6pm. Admission is 7€, 5€ for students, and free for children under 12. Also in the Old Town is **place Godeau,** where the **mosaic** "Moses saved from the Nile" by Marc Chagall adorns the 11th-century **cathedral**'s baptistery (free).

Vence's main draw, however, lies just outside the fortified main town. The Chapelle du Rosaire represents one of Matisse's most remarkable achievements.

Chapelle du Rosaire ★★ RELIGIOUS SITE   From the age of 47, Henri Matisse made Nice his home. But Vence held a special place in the artist's heart: It was his place of residence during World War II, as well as home to Dominican nun Sister Jacques-Marie, Matisse's former nurse and muse. So in 1947, when Matisse discovered that the sisters were planning the construction of a new chapel, he offered not only to design it, but fund the project as well. Matisse was 77 at the time.

The Chapelle du Rosaire was completed in 1951. A beautifully bright space, it offers the exceptional possibility of stepping into a three-dimensional artwork. Matisse described his creation: "What I have done in the chapel is to create a religious space . . . in an enclosed area of very reduced proportions and to give it, solely by the play of colors and lines, the dimensions of infinity."

From the front of the chapel, you may find the structure unremarkable and pass it by—until you spot a 12m (39-ft.) crescent-adorned cross rising from a blue-tile roof. Within, dozens of stained-glass windows shimmer cobalt blue (symbolizing the sea), sapphire green (the landscape), and golden yellow (the sun). Most remarkable are the 14 black-and-white-tile Stations of the Cross, featuring Matisse's self-styled "tormented and passionate" figures.

The bishop of Nice came to bless the chapel in the late spring of 1951; Matisse died 3 years later.

466 av. Henri-Matisse. www.vence.fr. ℭ **04-93-58-03-26.** Admission 6€ adults; contributions to maintain the chapel are welcome. Mon, Wed, and Sat 2–5:30pm; Tues and Thurs 10–11:30am and 2–5:30pm. Closed mid-Nov to mid-Dec.

NICE ★★★

929km (576 miles) S of Paris; 32km (20 miles) NE of Cannes

The largest city on this fabled stretch of coast, Nice is known as the "Queen of the Riviera." It's also one of the most ancient, founded by the Greeks, who called it Nike (Victory). By the 19th century, Russian aristocrats and the British upper class—led by Queen Victoria herself—were sojourning here. These days, however, Nice is not as chichi as Cannes or St-Tropez. In fact, of all the major French resorts, Nice is the most down-to-earth, with an emphasis on fine dining and high culture. Indeed, it has more museums than any other French city outside Paris. In 2013 it inaugurated a new city center urban park, one of the largest public spaces in the South of France. Visit during 2016 when big screens will relay the action from the UEFA Euro soccer championships, of which four matches will be played live in Nice's Allianz-Riviera Stadium.

Nice is also the best place to base yourself on the Riviera, especially if you're dependent on public transportation. You can go to San Remo, a glamorous town over the Italian border, for lunch and return to Nice by nightfall. From Nice airport, the second busiest in France, you can travel by train or bus along the entire coast to resorts such as Antibes, Juan-les-Pins, and Monaco.

Because of its brilliant sunshine and liberal attitude, Nice has long attracted artists and writers, among them Dumas, Nietzsche, Flaubert, Hugo, Sand, and Stendhal. Henri Matisse, who made his home in Nice, said, "Though the light is intense, it's also soft and tender." The city averages 300 sunny days a year.

Essentials

ARRIVING   Trains arrive at the city's main station, Gare Nice-Ville, avenue Thiers. From here you can take trains to Cannes for 7€, Monaco for 3.90€, and Antibes for 4.60€, with easy connections to Paris, Marseille, Avignon, Aix-en-Provence, and anywhere else along the Mediterranean coast.

Buses (www.lignesdazur.com; ℭ **08-10-06-10-06**) to towns east, including Monaco (no. 100) depart from place Garibaldi; to towns west, including Cannes (no. 200) from Jardin Albert I.

Transatlantic and intercontinental flights land at **Aéroport Nice–Côte d'Azur** (www.nice.aeroport.fr; ℭ **08-20-42-33-33**). From there, municipal bus nos. 98 and 99 depart at 20-minute intervals for the port and Gare Nice-Ville, respectively; the one-way fare is 6€. A **taxi** from the airport to the city center costs between 35€ and 40€ each way. Trip time is about 20 minutes.

Nice

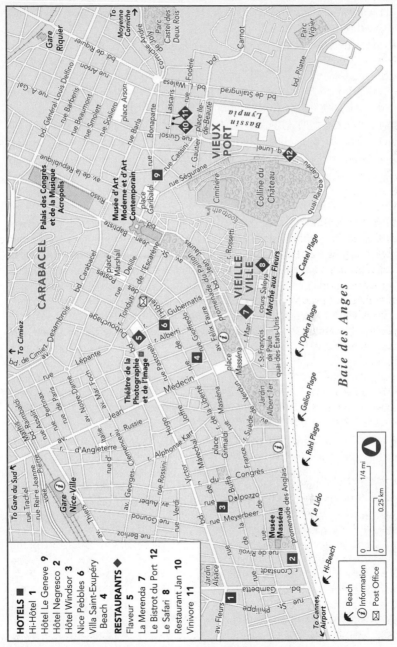

To Moyenne Corniche ↑

Gare Riquier

Parc Castel des Deux Rois

Parc Vigier

To Gare du Sud ↖

Gare Nice-Ville

To Cimiez ↗

CARABACEL

Palais des Congrès et de la Musique Acropolis

Musée d'Art Moderne et d'Art Contemporain

Théâtre de la Photographie et de l'Image

place Arson

place Ile-de-Beauté

VIEUX PORT

Bassin Lympia

Colline du Château

Cimitière

VIEILLE VILLE

Marché aux Fleurs

Musée Masséna

Baie des Anges

↖ Castel Plage
↖ l'Opéra Plage
↖ Galion Plage
↖ Ruhl Plage
↖ Le Lido
↖ Hi-Beach

To Cannes, Airport ↙

HOTELS ■
Hi-Hôtel **1**
Hôtel Le Geneve **9**
Hôtel Negresco **2**
Hôtel Windsor **3**
Nice Pebbles **6**
Villa Saint-Exupéry Beach **4**
RESTAURANTS ◆
Flaveur **5**
La Merenda **7**
Le Bistrot du Port **12**
Le Safari **8**
Restaurant Jan **10**
Vinivore **11**

↖ Beach
ⓘ Information
⊠ Post Office

1/4 mi
0 0.25 km

Ferryboats operated by **Trans-Côte d'Azur** (www.trans-cote-azur.com; ✆ **04-92-00-42-30**), on quai Lunel on Nice's port, link the city with Île Ste-Marguerite (p. 251) from June to September and St-Tropez from June through August.

VISITOR INFORMATION   Nice maintains four **tourist offices.** The largest is at 5 promenade des Anglais, near place Masséna (www.nice tourisme.com; ✆ **08-92-70-74-07**). Additional offices are in the arrivals hall of the Aéroport Nice–Côte d'Azur, in the new Promenade du Paillon public park, and outside the railway station on avenue Thiers.

CITY LAYOUT   The city is divided into five main neighborhoods: the Italianate Old Town; the vintage port; the commercial city center between place Masséna, and the main train station; the affluent residential quarter known as the Carre d'Or, just inland from the promenade des Anglais; and hilltop Cimiez. All are easy to navigate on foot, with the exception of Cimiez. For more, see "Exploring Nice," p. 277.

SPECIAL EVENTS   The **Nice Carnaval** (www.nicecarnaval.com), known as the "Mardi Gras of the Riviera," runs from mid-February to early March, celebrating the return of spring with 3 weeks of parades, *corsi* (floats), *veglioni* (masked balls), confetti, and battles in which young women toss flowers at spectators.

The **Nice Festival du Jazz** (www.nicejazzfestival.fr) runs for a week in mid-July, when jazz, funk, and reggae artists perform in the Jardins Albert I near the seafront. Recent performers have included Herbie Hancock and George Benson.

Getting Around

ON FOOT   Nice is very walkable, and no point of interest downtown is more than a 10-minute walk from place Massena, including the seafront promenade des Anglais, Old Town, and harbor.

BY BICYCLE & MOTOR SCOOTER   Like many French cities, Nice has its own bike-sharing scheme, **Vélo Bleu** (www.velobleu.org). You can register directly at one of Nice's 175 bike stands (difficult) or online (much easier); fees range from 1€ for 1 day to 5€ for a week. Alternatively, you can rent bikes (from 12€ per day) and scooters (from 26€ per day; driver's license and deposit required) from **Holiday Bikes,** 23 rue de Belgique (www.holiday-bikes.com; ✆ **04-93-16-01-62**).

BY CAR   See boxed text.

BY TAXI   **Taxis Niçois Indépendants** (www.taxis-nicois-independants.fr; ✆ **04-93-88-25-82**) will pick up within 5 minutes across town. Alternatively, call a **Cyclopolitain** (http://nice.cyclopolitain.com; ✆ **04-93-81-76-15**), an electronic tricycle for a ride around town (until 7pm, maximum two passengers, from 5€ per ride).

BY PUBLIC TRANSPORT   Most local buses leave from the streets around place Masséna. Municipal buses charge 1.50€ for rides within the entire

Alpes-Maritime province, even as far as Monaco or Cannes. The same ticket can also be used on Nice's tramway, which connects the Old Town with Gare Nice-Ville and northern Nice. Tickets, day passes (5€), and week passes (15€) can be bought directly onboard buses (although not trams) or at electronic kiosks around the city. For further information, see www.lignesdazur.com.

[FastFACTS] NICE

ATMs/Banks   Nice is home to dozens of banks; **LCL Banque,** 15 av. Jean Médecin (*(℃* **04-93-82-84-61**), is one of the most central.

Dentists   **SOS Dentaire** (*℃* **04-93-01-14-14**).

Doctors & Hospitals   **Hôpital Saint-Roch,** 5 rue Pierre Dévoluy (www.chu-nice.fr; *℃* **04-92-03-33-33**).

Embassies & Consulates   **U.S. Consular Agency Nice,** 7 av. Gustave V (*℃* **04-93-88-89-55**); **Consulate of Canada,** 2 place Franklin (*℃* **04-93-92-93-22**).

Internet Access   As of 2013, various public squares and streets (such as the cours Saleya) throughout Nice offer free Wi-Fi. Look for the network "NiceGOWEXFREEWiFi."

Local Information   The **"Riviera Times"** (www.rivieratimes.com) and the **"Riviera Reporter"** (www.rivierareporter.com) both cover news, art, culture, and events in and around Nice. **"Angloinfo French Riviera"** (http://riviera.angloinfo.com) is also an invaluable resource.

Mail & Postage   **La Poste,** 6 rue Louis Gassin (*℃* **36-31**).

Pharmacies   **Pharmacie Masséna,** 7 rue Masséna (*℃* **04-93-87-78-94**).

Safety   Nice is generally a very safe place. However, as in any big city, it's important to keep an eye on your valuables, in particular anywhere that's crowded. Avoid poorly lit streets at night, including in Nice's Old Town.

Where to Stay
EXPENSIVE

Hôtel Negresco ★★   For more than a century, the Negresco has been Nice's most iconic hotel. Its flamingo-pink dome crowns the promenade des Anglais, its Belle Epoque facade turned towards the sea. Guestrooms—a mix of Louis XIV antiques and state-of-the-art wetrooms—have hosted each era's most noted celebrities, from the Beatles and Salvador Dali to Michael Jackson. Public areas are decorated with works from an exceptional collection of private art, which kicks off with the shimmering Nikki de St-Phalle jazz musician welcoming guests at the hotel's entrance. Dining ranges from the exquisite (the double-Michelin-starred **Chantecler** and its 15,000-bottle wine cellar) to the playful (the kooky merry-go-round-style brasserie, **La Rotonde**).

37 promenade des Anglais. www.hotel-negresco-nice.com. *℃* **04-93-16-64-00**. 117 units. 185€–600€ double; 530€–2,700€ suite. Parking 28€. **Amenities:** 2 restaurants; bar; babysitting; exercise room; massage; room service; free Wi-Fi.

MODERATE

Hi-Hôtel ★★   Tucked into a residential neighborhood, yet just minutes from the beach, this seven-story, former 1930s boardinghouse is a tribute to contemporary architecture. Designed by Matali Crasset, a one-time colleague of Philippe Starck, the hotel's 10 high-tech room concepts are utterly unconventional. They range from Indoor Terrasse, a vision of wooden decking and bamboo, to the brand-new Utop-Hi, sleek with polished concrete and a glass cube shower. Onsite there's an organic restaurant, a REN spa, Turkish baths, and a rooftop swimming pool with its own honesty bar. The Hi's nearby beach club, **Hi-Beach** (p. 281), is a hip hangout in its own right.

3 av. des Fleurs. www.hi-hotel.net. © **04-97-07-26-26.** 38 units. 99€–399€ double. Parking 24€. **Amenities:** Restaurant; 24-hr. bar and snack bar; outdoor swimming pool; Turkish bath; free Wi-Fi.

Hôtel Windsor ★★★   The coolest, funkiest, and most friendly hotel in Nice is also one of its best-value lodgings. This *maison bourgeoise* was built by disciples of Gustav Eiffel in the 1890s and has remained a family-run hotel for three generations. Current proprietor Mme Payen-Redolfi has ushered in an artsy era where a different acclaimed artist decorates another guest room each year. As of 2015 the hotel had 32 contemporary-art rooms, including one painted entirely in gold leaf by Claudio Parmigiani. Art and color stream outside into the unkempt bamboo garden—**WiJungle**—where alfresco breakfasts are also served. Back indoors, **WiLounge** serves dinner and chilled rosé. **WiZen** is the fifth-floor health club, hammam, sauna, and meditation zone.

11 rue Dalpozzo. www.hotelwindsornice.com. © **04-93-88-59-35.** 57 units. 81€–260€ double. Parking 15€. **Amenities:** Restaurant; bar; babysitting; health club; outdoor pool; room service; sauna; free Wi-Fi.

INEXPENSIVE

Hôtel Le Geneve ★   The newly hip Garibaldi area, between the Port and Nice Old Town, sorely lacked a good hotel, until this discount gem opened in 2014. Guestrooms are achingly modern, if a touch Spartan. But the French bistro bar and restaurant downstairs—where breakfast is also served—is loads of fun. Nice's MAMAC art museum and gay-friendly rue Bonaparte zone are literally seconds away.

1 rue Cassini. www.hotel-le-geneve-nice.com. © **04-93-56-84-79.** 16 units. 70€–169€ per double. **Amenities:** Bar; restaurant; room service; free Wi-Fi.

Villa Saint Exupéry Beach ★   A "flashpacking" pioneer, based just outside Galeries Lafayette (Nice's answer to Macy's), this upscale hostel makes an ideal base for budget travelers of all ages. Accommodation ranges from dormitory-style beds to private twin rooms, and includes an abundant buffet breakfast. Also onsite is a communal kitchen, gym with sauna, daily happy hour, and quality meals at backpacker prices, including a daily *plat du jour* for 8€ and a bottle of wine for just 6€.

6 rue Sacha Guitry. www.villahostels.com. © **04-93-16-13-45.** 60 units. 25€–80€ per person in a single or twin-bedded room; 16€–40€ per person for dormitory bed. Rates include continental breakfast, sheets and towels. **Amenities:** Bar; cooking facilities; computers; luggage room; TV lounge; free Wi-Fi.

ALTERNATE ACCOMMODATIONS

Nice Pebbles ★★★ A short-term rental of one of these holiday apartments allows you time to truly immerse yourself in local life, from cooking up morning-market bounty to sipping sunset aperitifs on your private terrace. More than 100 carefully selected properties (from studios to 10-bed homes) are dotted throughout the city's central neighborhoods, including the Old Town and harbor and along the promenade des Anglais. Apartments boast first-class amenities (iPod docks, high-def TVs, and designer bathrooms are common), yet weigh in at just a fraction of the price of a hotel room. Demand is high, so book well in advance. Sister agency **Riviera Pebbles** (www.rivierapebbles.com) manages additional properties along the coast.

20 rue Gioffredo. www.nicepebbles.com. ℰ **04-97-20-27-30.** 70€–450€ per apartment per night; 700€–6,000€ per week in high season. **Amenities:** Babysitting; free Wi-Fi.

Where to Eat

The Riviera boasts more Michelin commendations (43 stars over 34 establishments as of 2015) than almost anywhere else on the planet. The regional capital of Nice teems with exquisite restaurants, from the high end to the downright local. Excellent eateries are scattered across the city—although beware of many of the Old Town's careless offerings, keen to lure in tourists for a single night only. The city's hottest dining district is currently a block behind Nice Port in the rue Bonaparte and rue Lascaris areas. Simply wander around and eat—you won't be disappointed. In addition to the suggestions below, the portside **Le Bistrot du Port,** 28 quai Lunel (www.lebistrotduport denice.fr; ℰ **04-93-55-21-70**), is where the Orsini family has been dishing up top-quality fish and creative seafood concoctions for over 30 years.

EXPENSIVE

Flaveur ★★ MODERN FRENCH Brothers Gaël and Mickaël Tourteaux (whose last name, almost unbelievably, translates as "cake") are a pair of very talented chefs. They may be relatively young—38 and 34 respectively—yet they've already spent decades in the kitchens of the Riviera's top restaurants. Little surprise, then, that in 2011 their contemporary bistro, Flaveur, earned its first Michelin star. A childhood growing up on the tropical islands of Réunion and Guadeloupe means their modern French cuisine is laced with exotic flavors: Plump scallops are seasoned with Japanese *gomasio;* artistically displayed lemongrass and bubbles of lemon caviar sit atop risotto. Note that meals are variations on fixed-price menus only; there's no ordering à la carte, although lunchtime menus allow for gourmet bites on a relative budget.

25 rue Gubernatis. www.flaveur.net. ℰ **04-93-62-53-95.** Reservations required. Fixed-price lunch 46€–95€; fixed-price dinner 60€–95€. Tues–Fri noon–2pm and 7:30–10pm; Sat 7:30–10pm. Closed last 2 weeks Aug.

MODERATE

La Merenda ★★★ NIÇOIS Top chef Dominique Le Stanc left the world of *haute cuisine* far behind to take over this tiny, traditional, family-run bistro. And how lucky we all are. La Merenda is now one of most authentic and unpretentious eateries along the French Riviera. Market-fresh specials are scribbled on a small chalkboard; depending on the season, they may include stuffed sardines, tagliatelle drenched in delicious basil pesto, or a delectable *tarte au citron*. Note that the restaurant has no phone, so you'll need to make reservations in person.

4 rue Raoul Bosio. www.lamerenda.net. No phone. Reservations required. Main courses 13€–21€. No credit cards. Mon–Fri noon–2pm and 7:30–10pm.

Le Safari ★ NIÇOIS/PROVENÇAL   You cannot go wrong at Le Safari. A good bet for honest prices and solid cooking, from an establishment that's been in business for over 50 years. Diners can choose the alfresco terrace on the bustling cours Saleya in spring or summer, or they may cozy up inside around the wood-fired oven in winter. Menu items include a pungent *bagna cauda*, which calls for diners to immerse vegetables in a sizzling brew of hot oil and anchovy paste; grilled peppers bathed in olive oil; *daube* (stew) of beef; fresh pasta with basil; and an omelet with *blettes* (tough but flavorful greens). Even the pizzas and bottles of inexpensive house wine are commendable.

1 cours Saleya. www.restaurantsafari.fr. ✆ **04-93-80-18-44.** Main courses 14€–26€; fixed-price menu 25€. Daily noon–3pm and 7–11pm.

Restaurant Jan ★★ MODERN MEDITERRANEAN   This Franco-South African gourmet restaurant was commended by the New York Times in 2014. Both decor and service (under the watchful eye of Maître d' Philippe Foucault, formerly of the Negresco and Grand Hotel du Cap Ferrat) are akin to being a guest in a French Presidential retreat. The inventive cuisine of South African chef Jan Hendrik van der Westhuizen blends regional ingredients (line-caught seabass, Charolais beef) with African spice (Madagascar vanilla, rooibos jelly) and Italian style (Parmesan shavings, prosciutto chips). Dishes may include slow-roasted pork belly with scallops and sweet potato puree, and soya tuna with capers and crispy onion rings.

12 rue Lascaris. www.restaurantjan.com. ✆ **04-97-19-32-23.** Reservations recommended. Main courses 24€–44€; fixed-price menu 69€. Fri noon–3pm, Tues–Sat 7:30–10pm.

INEXPENSIVE

Vinivore ★★ MODERN FRENCH   This vibrant eatery, located just behind the port, mixes fresh Provençal ingredients with Cantonese flair. Each day, Hong Kong–born chef Chun Wong's changing menu features just four appetizers, four main courses, and four desserts. Recent highlights include beef *tataki* with garlic flowers, wild rice risotto with grilled scallops, and vanilla-infused candied pineapple. Québécois sommelier Bonaventure Blankstein has handpicked some 200 vintages—carefully noted on the large chalkboards—from often-organic wineries across southern France. A small **Vinivore wine bar** operates next door to the main restaurant.

10 rue Lascaris. www.vinivore.fr. ✆ **04-93-14-68-09.** Reservations recommended. Main courses 12€–34€; fixed-price menus 39€–41€. Tues–Fri noon–2pm, Tues–Sat 7:30–10:00pm.

Exploring Nice

In 1822, Nice's orange crop had an awful year. The workers faced a lean time, so the English residents employed them to build the **promenade des Anglais ★★**, today a wide boulevard fronting the bay that stretches for 7km (4¼ miles), all the way to the airport. Along the beach are rows of grand cafes, the Musée Masséna, and the city's most glamorous hotels.

People taking a walk on promenade des Anglais, Nice.

Crossing this boulevard in the tiniest bikinis are some of the world's most attractive bronzed bodies. They're all heading for the **beach.** Tough on tender feet, *le plage* is made not of sand, but of pebbles (and not small ones, either).

Rising sharply on a rock at the eastern end of the promenade is the **Colline du Château.** Once a fortified bastion, the hill has since been turned into a wonderful public park complete with a waterfall, cafes, and a giant children's play area, as well as an incredibly ornate cemetery. Head up aboard an elevator from the quai des Etats-Unis; more athletic visitors can walk up one of five sets of steep steps. The park is open daily from 8am to dusk.

Continuing east of the Colline, you reach the **Vieux Port,** or harbor, where the restaurants are filled with locals. While lingering over a drink at a sidewalk cafe, you can watch the ferries depart for Corsica and the yachts for St-Tropez. Just inland, the neighborhood around rue Bonaparte and place Garibaldi has become one of the hippest in town: Head here for authentic eateries, hip bars, and the superb **MAMAC Museum of Contemporary Art,** place Yves Klein (www.mamac-nice.org; *℡* **04-97-13-42-01;** free admission; closed Mon). Your 10€ MAMAC ticket will get you into four other museums (and under 18 gets in free).

The **Vieille Ville ★★**, or Old Town, begins at the foot of the Colline and stretches to place Masséna. Sheltered by red-tiled roofs, many of the Italianate facades suggest 17th-century Genoese palaces, including the free museum **Palais Lascaris,** 15 rue Droite (www.palais-lascaris-nice.org; *℡* **04-93-62-72-40,** 10€ adults, 17 and under free; closed Tues). The Old Town is a maze of narrow streets teeming with local life, flower-strewn squares, and traditional *boulangeries:* Sample a Niçois-style onion pizza *(pissaladière)* here. Many of the buildings are painted a faded Roman gold, and their banners are laundry flapping in the sea breeze.

Nice's municipal museums are now part of a ticket/pass system, which works like this: Your 10€ ticket will get you into one or a themed group of museums for a 48-hour period. For example, you could opt for just the Palais Lascaris or just the Matisse Museum, or you could use your ticket to visit the "Contemporary Art Group" of five museums, including the MAMAC (see below). If you have time and want access to all the municipal museums, invest 20€ in the 7-day museum pass. Students, children under 18, and residents get into all city museums for free.

From Tuesday through Sunday (8am–1pm), the Old Town's main pedestrianized thoroughfare, the **cours Saleya,** is crowded with local producers selling seasonal fruits and vegetables, cured meats, and artisanal cheeses. At the market's western end is the **Marché aux Fleurs.** A rainbow of violets, lilies and roses, the market operates Tuesday to Sunday from 8am to around 6pm. On Monday (8am–6pm), the cours Saleya is occupied by a superb **antiques market,** with vendors carting wares in from across France and Italy.

Nice's centerpiece is **place Masséna,** with rococo buildings and bubbling fountains, as well as the new **Promenade du Paillon** parkway that stretches from the **MAMAC** art museum and the pavement cafes of **place Garibaldi** down to the **Jardin Albert 1** and seafront. With palms and exotic flowers, this pedestrian-only zone is one of the prettiest places in town.

Cathédrale Orthodoxe Russe St-Nicolas à Nice ★ CATHEDRAL Ordered built by none other than Tsar Nicholas II, this recently renovated cathedral is the most beautiful religious edifice of the Orthodoxy outside Russia. It dates from the Belle Epoque, when some of the Romanovs and entourage turned the Riviera into their stomping ground. Everyone from grand dukes to ballerinas arrived on the—recently reinstated—direct train from Moscow, then paraded their tiaras on the promenade. The cathedral is richly ornamented and decorated with icons. You'll spot the building from afar because of its collection of ornate onion-shaped domes.

Av. Nicolas II (off bd. Tzaréwitch). www.cathedrale-russe-nice.fr. ☏ **04-93-83-94-08.** Free admission. Tues–Sun 9am–noon and 2–6pm. From the central rail station, bus nr. 71, or head west along av. Thiers to bd. Gambetta, and then go north to av. Nicolas-II.

Musée Masséna ★★★ MUSEUM Riviera aficionados will adore this astounding history museum. Located within an imposing Belle Epoque villa, it exhibits a quirky range of objects charting local life in Nice and its surrounds, from the first Victorian visitors through the roaring 1920s. Elegantly printed menus, train tickets from London to Nice, period maps, and snapshots of the promenading rich on vacation bring the past to life. Of additional note are the paintings and *objets d'art* donated by the Masséna family, a noble set of locals who constructed the villa. Botanist Edouard Ardre, who also designed the verdant greenery in front of the Casino de Monte-Carlo, land-scaped the museum's neatly manicured gardens.

65 rue de France or 35 promenade des Anglais. www.nice.fr. © **04-93-91-19-10.** 10€ adults, free 17 and under. Wed–Mon 10am–6pm.

Théâtre de la Photographie et de l'Image ★ PHOTOGRAPHY MUSEUM   Nice's most overlooked exhibition space houses world-beating photography displays. Shows are displayed over its six Belle Epoque salons. Recent exhibitions have included homages to Riviera photographer Jean Gil-letta and Paris chronicler Brassaï, as well as images from Nice in the roaring 1920s. The most famous collection is that of Charles Nègre, who photo-graphed the city in its pre-tourism splendor in the 1860s. The Théâtre recently held an acclaimed retrospective of National Geographic photographer Steve McCurry, whose most captivating image is a piercingly green-eyed Afghan refugee girl taken in 1984.

27 bd. Dubouchage. www.tpi-nice.org. © **04-97-13-42-20.** 10€ adults, free 17 and under. Tues–Sun 10am–6pm.

Outlying Attractions in Cimiez

In the once-aristocratic hilltop quarter of Cimiez, 5km (3 miles) north of Nice, Queen Victoria wintered at the Hôtel Excelsior. Half the English court traveled down from Calais with her on a luxurious private train. Be sure to stroll over to the adjacent **Monastère de Cimiez** (Cimiez Convent), which offers panoramic views over Nice and the Baie des Anges; artists Matisse and Dufy are buried in the cemetery nearby. To reach this suburb and its attrac-tions, take bus no. 15 from boulevard Dubouchage.

Musée Matisse ★★ ART MUSEUM   In 1963, this beautiful old Italian villa was transformed into a museum honoring Henri Matisse, one of the 20th century's greatest painters. Matisse came to Nice for the light and made the city his home, living in the Hotel Beau Rivage and on the cours Saleya, and dying in Cimiez in 1954. Most of the pieces in the museum's permanent col-lection—including "Nude in an Armchair with a Green Plant" (1937) and "Blue Nude IV" (1952)—were created in Nice. Artworks are interspersed with Matisse's personal possessions, such as ceramic vases and antique furni-ture, as well as scale models of his architectural masterpiece, Vence's **Chapelle du Rosaire** (p. 269).

164 av. des Arènes de Cimiez. www.musee-matisse.nice.org. © **04-93-81-08-08.** 10€ adults, free 17 and under. Wed–Mon 10am–6pm.

Musée National Message Biblique Marc Chagall ★★ ART MUSEUM   Surrounded by pools and a garden, this handsome museum is devoted to Marc Chagall's treatment of biblical themes. Born in Russia in 1887, Chagall became a French citizen in 1937 and painted with astonishing light and color until his death in St-Paul-de-Vence in 1985. This museum's focal set of artworks—12 large paintings, illustrating the first two books of the Old Testament—was originally created to adorn the central cathedral in

Anyone can Google a car hire deal in advance. Far more fun are Nice's grand selection of cabriolets, classic cars, and all-green wheels. A novel addition to the local transport scene is **Auto Bleue** (www.autobleue.org; ℭ **09-77-40-64-06**). The scheme allows visitors to rent an electric Peugeot car from one of 50 vehicle stands around Nice for 45€ per day, inclusive of electricity, parking, and insurance. Sign up online in advance.

Brand new outfit **Green Rent** (www.greenrent.fr; ℭ **09-83-80-98-16**) offers all-electric Smarts, Toyotas, Twizzys, and scooters from 39€ per day. Want something meatier? **Rent A Classic Car** (www.rentaclassiccar.com; ℭ **09-54-00-29-33**) offers everything from Citroen 2CVs (from 179€ per day) to Porsche 550 Spyders (from 349€ per day) from their base behind Nice's Promenade des Anglais.

Vence. The church's high humidity nixed the artist's original plans, and Chagall assisted in planning this purpose-built space instead. The 200 additional artworks include gouaches, a mosaic, sculptures, and prints.

Av. du Dr. Ménard. www.musee-chagall.fr. ℭ **04-93-53-87-20.** Admission 8€ adults, 6€ students, free for children 17 and under. May–Oct Wed–Mon 10am–6pm; Nov–Apr Wed–Mon 10am–5pm.

Organized Tours

One of the most enjoyable ways to quickly gain an overview of Nice is aboard a **Nice–Le Grand Tour** (www.nicelegrandtour.com; ℭ **04-92-29-17-00**) double-decker bus. Between 10am and 6pm year-round, one of a flotilla of this company's buses departs from a position adjacent to the Jardin Albert I. The panoramic 90-minute tour takes in the harbor, the museums of Cimiez, the Russian church, and the promenade. Per-person rates for the experience are 22€ adults, 18€ students, and 8€ children 4 to 11. Participants can get off at any of 11 stops en route and reboard any other buses, which follow at 30- to 60-minute intervals, depending on the season. Advance reservations aren't necessary, and commentary is piped through to headsets in seven different languages. Tickets are valid the entire day of purchase. Nice's museums, transport routes, rental bikes, and historical buildings are also charted in a series of **free travel apps** (www.nicetourisme.com).

Another easy way to see the city is by the small **Train Touristique de Nice** (www.traintouristiquesdenice.com; ℭ **06-08-55-08-30**), which also departs from the promenade des Anglais, opposite Jardin Albert I. The 45-minute ride passes many of Nice's most-heralded sites, including place Masséna, the Old Town, and the Colline du Château. Departing every 30 minutes, the train operates daily 10am to 5pm (until 6pm Apr–May and Sept, until 7pm June–Aug). The round-trip price is 8€ adults and 4€ children 4 to 12.

Energetic guests may join **Nice Cycle Tours** (www.nicecycletours.com; ℭ **06-19-99-95-22**), 3-hour bike voyages around the city. Tours cost 30€ per person, and the friendly team also runs food tours and cycle expeditions.

Possibly the coolest way to get around Nice is by Segway, the two-wheeled electronic scooters. Bespoke tours are run by **Mobilboard,** 2 rue Halévy (www.mobilboard.com; ✆ **04-93-80-21-27**). Children 14 (minimum age) to 17 must be accompanied by an adult. An hour-long tour of Nice costs 30€ per person.

Outdoor Activities

BEACHES   Along Nice's seafront, beaches extend uninterrupted for more than 7km (4¼ miles), going from the edge of Vieux-Port (the old port, or harbor) to the international airport. Tucked between the public areas are several rather chic private beaches. Many of these beach bars provide mattresses and parasols for 12€ to 22€. The coolest clubs include **Hi-Beach** (www.hi-beach.net; ✆ **04-97-14-00-83**), which has a sushi bar, blanket Wi-Fi, and family-friendly playpens; and **Castel Plage** (www.castelplage.com; ✆ **04-93-85-22-66**), a celebrity hangout in summer.

SCUBA DIVING   Of the many diving outfits in Nice harbor, **Nice Diving,** 13 quai des Deux Emmanuel (www.nicediving.com; ✆ **06-14-46-04-06**), offers bilingual instruction and *baptêmes* (dives for first-timers) around Nice and Cap Ferrat. A dive for experienced divers, equipment included, costs around 50€; appropriate diver's certification is required.

Shopping

CLOTHES   Nice's densest concentrations of fashionable French labels are clustered around **rue Masséna** and **avenue Jean-Médecin.** For more high-end couture, the streets around **place Magenta,** including **rue de Verdun, rue Paradis,** and **rue Alphonse Karr** are a credit card's worst nightmare. A shop of note is **Cotelac,** 12 rue Alphonse Karr (✆ **04-93-87-31-59**), which sells chic women's clothing. Men should try **Façonnable,** 7–9 rue Paradis (www.faconnable.com; ✆ **04-93-88-06-97**). This boutique is the original site of a chain with several hundred branches worldwide; the look is conservatively stylish. For more unusual apparel, **Lucien Chasseur,** 2 rue Bonaparte (✆ **04-93-55-52-14**), is the city's coolest spot for Italian-designed shoes, scarves, and soft leather satchels.

FOOD   The winding streets of Nice's Old Town are the best place to find local crafts, ceramics, gifts, and foodie purchases. If you're thinking of indulging in a Provençale *pique-nique,* **Nicola Alziari,** 14 rue St François de Paule (www.alziari.com.fr; ✆ **04-93-62-94-03**), will provide everything from olives, anchovies, and pistous to aiolis and tapenades. For an olive-oil tasting session—and the opportunity to buy the goods afterward—check out **Oliviera,** 2 rue Benoit Bunico (www.oliviera.com; ✆ **04-93-11-06-45**), run by the amiable Nadim Beyrouti. In the port, **Confiserie Florian,** 14 quai Papacino (www.confiserieflorian.com; ✆ **04-93-55-43-50**), has been candying fruit, chocolate-dipping roasted nuts, and crystalizing edible flowers since 1949.

SOUVENIRS The best selection of Provençal fabrics is at **Le Chandelier,** 7 rue de la Boucherie (② **04-93-85-85-19**), where you'll see designs by two of the region's best-known producers of cloth, Les Olivades and Valdrôme. Nearby at **Atelier des Cigales,** 13 rue du Collet (② **04-93-85-85-19**), expect top-class, hand-painted pottery and ceramics from across the province. For antiquarian books, contemporary art, kitsch, and comic books, wander north of place Garibaldi to **rue Delille,** just past the MAMAC modern art gallery. And for offbeat gifts, **Chambre Cinquante-Sept,** 16 rue Emmanuel Philibert (② **04-92-04-02-81**), stocks beautifully unique Art Deco *objets d'art.*

Nightlife

Nice has some of the most active nightlife and cultural offerings along the Riviera. Big evenings out usually begin at a cafe or bar, take in a restaurant, opera, or film, and finish in a club. The website **riviera.angloinfo.com** lists all the week's English-language movies in *version originale.*

The major cultural center on the Riviera is the **Opéra de Nice,** 4 rue St-François-de-Paule (www.opera-nice.org; ② **04-92-17-40-00**), built in 1885 by Charles Garnier, fabled architect of the Paris Opéra. It presents a full repertoire, with emphasis on serious, often large-scale operas, such as "Tristan and Isolde" and "La Boheme," as well as a *saison symphonique* dominated by the Orchestre Philharmonique de Nice. The opera hall is also the major venue for concerts and recitals. Tickets are available (to concerts, recitals, and full-blown operas) right up until the day of performance. You can show up at the box office (Mon–Thurs 9am–5:30pm; Fri until 7:45pm; Sat until 4:30pm) or buy tickets in advance online. Tickets run from 10€ to 80€.

Nice's most happening spots are the pedestrian-only streets around place Garibaldi and rue Bonaparte. Within the cool-kitsch decor of a former garage in the port area, talented staff serve up fruity cocktails and organic local wines at **Rosalina,** 16 rue Lascaris (② **04-93-89-34-96**). Around the corner, gay-friendly **Comptoir Central Électrique,** 10 rue Bonaparte (② **04-93-14-09-62**), is the neighborhood's epicenter of cool. Current gay-friendly hotspots include **Gossip,** 7 rue Bonaparte (② **04-83-45-72-15**), and seafront **G-Club,** 73 quai des Etats Unis (no phone).

The party spirit is best lapped up in the alfresco bars on the **cours Saleya.** Otherwise, head 1 block inland to **Wayne's Bar,** 15 rue de la Préfecture (www.waynes.fr; ② **04-93-13-46-99**), where dancing on the tables to raucous cover bands is the norm. For house tunes, nonstop dancing, and heaps of understated cool, head to **Bliss,** 12 rue de l'Abbaye (② **04-93-16-82-38**).

VILLEFRANCHE-SUR-MER ★★

935km (580 miles) S of Paris; 6.5km (4 miles) E of Nice

Just east of Nice, the coastal Lower Corniche sweeps inland to reveal Ville-franche, its medieval Old Town tumbling downhill into the shimmering sea. Paired with a dazzling sheltered bay set against picturesque Cap Ferrat

Villefranche, French Riviera.

beyond, it's little wonder than countless artists made this beachy getaway their home—or that it has served as the cinematic backdrop for numerous movies, including "Ronin" with Robert de Niro, "Dirty Rotten Scoundrels" with Steve Martin, and "Never Say Never Again" starring Sir Sean Connery.

Essentials

ARRIVING **Trains** arrive from all the Côte d'Azur's coastal resorts from Cannes to Monaco every 30 minutes or so. For rail schedules, visit www.voyages-sncf.com or call ⓒ **36-35. Ligne d'Azur** (www.lignes dazur.com; ⓒ **08-10-06-10-06**) maintains a **bus** service at 5- to 15-minute intervals aboard line no. 100 from Nice to Monte Carlo via Villefranche. One-way fares cost 1.50€. Buses deposit passengers just above the Old Town, almost directly opposite the tourist information office. Many visitors **drive** via the Basse Corniche (Lower Corniche).

VISITOR INFORMATION The **Office de Tourisme** is on Jardin François-Binon (www.villefranche-sur-mer.com; ⓒ **04-93-01-73-68**).

[FastFACTS] VILLEFRANCHE

ATMs/Banks **LCL Banque,** 6 av. du Maréchal Foch (ⓒ **04-93-76-24-01**).

Internet Access **Chez Net,** 5 place du Marché (www.cheznet.com; ⓒ **04-89-08-19-43**).

Mail & Postage **La Poste,** 6 av. Albert 1er (ⓒ **36-31**).

Pharmacies **Pharmacie Laurent,** 2 av. du Maréchal Foch (ⓒ **04-93-01-70-10**).

Where to Stay

Hotel Villa Patricia ★ This petite seaside hotel really does offer some of the Riviera's cheapest double rooms during the height of summer. A 5-minute amble from the water, it also boasts a shared garden sheltered by lemon trees. As one might expect for the price, some rooms are small, while others are oddly shaped, but all are stylish, smart, and exceptionally clean, and share a large lounge area complete with book swap, outdoor sofas, and a piano. It's a gentle 10-minute stroll from Villefranche, Beaulieu, and Cap Ferrat.

310 Avenue de l'Ange Gardien. www.hotel-patricia.riviera.fr. ℂ **04-93-01-06-70.** 10 units. 65€–93€ double; 100€–130€ triple; 89€–130€ suite. Free parking. Closed Dec–Jan. **Amenities:** Free Wi-Fi.

Hôtel Welcome ★ Villefranche's most prestigious hotel, the Welcome sits in the center of town and has been home to Riviera artists since the 1920s, including author and filmmaker Jean Cocteau (in room 22). Every one of the modern hotel's midsize-to-spacious rooms possesses a balcony and sea views. The on-site **wine bar** spills out onto the quay in warm weather. The hotel also rents out *Orphée,* its eight-person private sailboat, for daily cruises; prices from 770€ per half-day with crew.

3 quai Amiral Courbet. www.welcomehotel.com. ℂ **04-93-76-27-62.** 35 units. 179€–365€ double; 435€–537€ suite. Parking 45€. Closed mid-Nov to mid-Dec. **Amenities:** Bar; babysitting; room service; free Wi-Fi.

Where to Eat

Le Cosmo ★★ MEDITERRANEAN This friendly sidewalk cafe has been pulling in punters for a decade—and with good reason. Prices are reasonable, the creative menu is perfectly executed, and the setting is sublime: The restaurant's terraced seating overlooks Cocteau's Chapelle St-Pierre and the seafront beyond. Sample sautéed scallops with aubergine caviar, or *salade Cosmo,* topped with avocado, shrimp, grapefruit, and hearts of palm. Dozens of fantastical ice cream creations (think yogurt ice cream piled high with strawberries and raspberry puree, or a tower of praline ice cream, whipped cream, and chocolate sauce) are also on offer.

11 pl. Amélie Pollonais. www.restaurant-lecosmo.fr. ℂ **04-93-01-84-05.** Main courses 13€–26€. Daily 7:45am–2am.

Exploring Villefranche

Villefranche's long arc of golden sands, **plage des Marinières,** is the principal attraction for most visitors. From here, **quai Courbet** runs along the sea to the colorful Old Town past scores of bobbing boats; it's lined with waterside restaurants.

Old-town action revolves around **place Amélie Pollonnais,** a delightful square shaded by palms and spread with the tables of six easygoing restaurants. It's also the site of a Sunday antiques market, where people from across the Riviera come to root through vintage tourism posters, silverware, 1930s jewelry, and ex-hotel linens.

The painter, writer, filmmaker, and well-respected dilettante Jean Cocteau left a fine memorial to the town's inhabitants. He spent a year (1956–57) painting frescoes on the 14th-century walls of the Romanesque **Chapelle St-Pierre,** quai Courbet (ℂ **04-93-76-90-70**). He presented it to "the fishermen of Villefranche in homage to the Prince of Apostles, the patron of fishermen." In the apse is a depiction of the miracle of St. Peter walking on the water, not knowing that an angel supports him. Villefranche's busty local women, in their regional costumes, are honored on the left side of the narthex. Admission is 3€, free for children under 15. In spring and summer, it is open Wednesday to Monday 10am to noon and 3 to 7pm; fall and winter hours are Wednesday to Monday 10am to noon and 2 to 6pm. It's closed from mid-November to mid-December.

A short coastal path leads from the car park below place Amélie Pollonnais to the **16th-century citadelle.** This castle dominates the bay, and its ramparts and small interior museums (free) can be wandered around at leisure.

ST-JEAN-CAP-FERRAT & BEAULIEU-SUR-MER ★★

939km (582 miles) S of Paris; 9.5km (6 miles) E of Nice

Of all the oases along the Côte d'Azur, no other place has the snob appeal of Cap-Ferrat. It's a 15km (9¼-mile) promontory sprinkled with luxurious villas and outlined by sheltered bays, beaches, and sun-kissed coves. In the charming port of St-Jean, the harbor accommodates yachts, fishing boats, and a dozen low-key eateries.

Cradled on the mainland just east of Cap-Ferrat, the Belle Epoque resort of Beaulieu-sur-Mer has long attracted *bonnes vivantes* with its freshly renovated casino and fine restaurants.

Essentials

ARRIVING Trains connect Beaulieu with Nice, Monaco, and the rest of the Côte d'Azur every 30 minutes. Many visitors take a **taxi** to St-Jean from Beaulieu's rail station; alternatively, it's a 30-minute walk along Cap-Ferrat's coastal pathway. For **rail** information, visit www.voyages-sncf.com or call ✆ **36-35. Bus** line no. 100 from Nice to Monte Carlo passes through Beaulieu, while the hourly no. 81 connects Nice with St-Jean. One-way fares costs 1.50€. For bus information and schedules, contact **Ligne d'Azur** (www.lignesdazur.com; ✆ **08-10-06-10-06**). By **car** from Nice, take D6098 (the *basse corniche*) east.

VISITOR INFORMATION St-Jean's **Office de Tourisme** is on 59 av. Denis-Séméria (www.saintjeancapferrat-tourisme.fr; ✆ **04-93-76-08-90**). Beaulieu's **Office de Tourisme** is on place Georges Clémenceau (www.beaulieusurmer.fr; ✆ **04-93-01-02-21**).

[FastFACTS] ST-JEAN & BEAULIEU

ATMs/Banks **Banque Populaire Côte d'Azur,** 5 av. Claude Vignon, St-Jean 06230 (✆ **04-89-81-11-42**).

Mail & Postage **La Poste,** 51 av. Denis Séméria, St-Jean 06230 (✆ **36-31**).

Pharmacies **Pharmacie Pont Saint Jean,** 57 bd. Dominique Durandy, St-Jean (✆ **04-93-01-62-50**).

Where to Stay

Grand Hôtel du Cap-Ferrat ★★★   Put simply, this grande dame of a hotel is the greatest building on Europe's richest peninsula. It's sumptuous, sexy, and incredibly welcoming, even to non-guests who are invited to sip cocktails, enjoy the spa, or feast in such rarified surroundings. Set on 17 acres of tropical trees and manicured lawns, it has been the exclusive retreat of the international elite since 1908. And since 2015 it has been a member of the superlative Four Seasons family of hotels. The **Le Spa** wellness center spills outside into curtained cabanas, where massages and other treatments can be indulged in. Aside from the modernist guestrooms, the coolest place to hang out is the seaside **Club Dauphin** beach club (nonguests can gain access for 90€ per day). It is reached by a funicular rail pod that descends from the hotel. The children of many visiting celebrities, including the Kennedys and Paul McCartney, have learned to swim in the Olympic-size infinity pool. **Le Cap,** the hotel's acclaimed gourmet restaurant, is overseen by head chef Didier Aniès. His Michelin-starred cuisine is heavy on caviar, oysters, and luxurious French classics, while the wine list runs from rare local Bellet vintages to the esteemed Château d'Yquem.

71 bd. du Général-de-Gaulle, Cap Ferrat. www.fourseasons.com/capferrat. ✆ **04-93-76-50-50.** 73 units. 295€–1,120€ double; 715€–5,400€ suite. Closed Jan and Feb. Amenities: 3 restaurants; bar; babysitting; beach club; bikes; Olympic-size heated outdoor pool; room service; spa; tennis; free Wi-Fi.

Hôtel Brise Marine ★   An Italianate villa constructed in 1878, the Brise Marine is tucked into a quiet residential neighborhood south of St-Jean. Rooms are simply furnished and sunny, with enchanting sea views. Breakfast on the rose-twined terrace, and you can almost imagine you're aboard one of the luxury superyachts bobbing off nearby Paloma Plage.

58 av. Jean-Mermoz, St-Jean-Cap-Ferrat. www.hotel-brisemarine.com. ✆ **04-93-76-04-36.** 16 units. 160€–203€ double; 190€–233€ triple. Parking 15€. Closed Nov–Feb. **Amenities:** Bar; room service; free Wi-Fi.

Where to Eat

African Queen ★ FRENCH/INTERNATIONAL   A lively mix of yachties, celebrity patrons, and excellent cuisine makes this portside restaurant perennially popular. Wood-fired pizzas are superb; the finely chopped *salade Niçoise* is dressed at your table; the sole *meunière* a buttery classic. Service can be erratic, but both the menu (which included a new Japanese selection in 2015) and the atmosphere are a delight. Celebrity-spotting opportunities abound all summer long.

Port de Plaisance, Beaulieu-sur-Mer. www.africanqueen.fr. ✆ **04-93-01-10-85.** Reservations recommended. Pizzas 12€–29€; main courses 12€–80€. Daily noon–midnight. Closed some holidays.

Capitaine Cook ★ PROVENÇAL/SEAFOOD   Perhaps the peninsula's most beloved eatery, Capitaine Cook is run by husband-and-wife team Lionel and Nelly Pelletier. Dine outdoors on the leafy terrace or indoors within the ruggedly maritime dining room. The menu is particularly strong on hearty yet imaginative fish dishes, from stuffed sardines to salmon ravioli.

11 av. Jean-Mermoz, St-Jean-Cap-Ferrat. ℰ **04-93-76-02-66.** Reservations recommended. Main courses 18€–30€; fixed-price menu 27€–32€. Fri–Tues 12:30–2pm; Thurs–Tues 7:30–10:30pm. Closed mid-Nov to Dec.

Exploring St-Jean & Beaulieu

One way to enjoy the area's beautiful backdrop is to stroll the public pathway that links Beaulieu and St-Jean. It eventually circles the entire peninsula, winding past deserted coves and alongside the gardens of countless millionaire dwellings. The most scenic section runs from chic **plage de Paloma,** near the Cap-Ferrat's southernmost tip, to **pointe St-Hospice,** where a panoramic view of the Riviera landscape unfolds. Allow around 3 hours to hike from St-Jean to family-friendly **plage Passable,** on the northwestern "neck" of the peninsula. Just offshore is a vast cetacean sanctuary where **dolphins and whales** can be viewed via a guided tour (www.dauphin-mediterranee.com) for 48€ per person.

Villa Ephrussi de Rothschild ★★ HISTORIC HOME/MUSEUM The winter residence of Baronne Béatrice Ephrussi de Rothschild, this Italianate villa was completed in 1912 according to the finicky specifications of its ultra-rich owner. Today the pink edifice preserves an eclectic collection, gathered over her lifetime: 18th-century furniture, Tiepolo ceilings, tapestries from Gobelin, a games table gifted from Marie-Antoine (Ephrussi's hero) to a friend, and tiny seats for her beloved poodles. The nine themed gardens, from Florentine to Japanese, are a particular delight. An attractive tea salon overlooks the Bay of Villefranche.

Villa Ephrussi de Rothschild.

1 av. Ephrussi de Rothschild. www.villa-ephrussi.com. ℰ **04-93-01-33-09.** Admission 13€ adults, 10€ students and children 7–17, free for children 6 and under. July–Aug daily 10am–7pm; Mar–June and Sept–Oct daily 10am–6pm; Nov–Feb Mon–Fri 2–6pm, Sat–Sun 10am–6pm.

Villa Kérylos ★★ HISTORIC HOME/MUSEUM This replica ancient Greek residence, constructed between 1902 and 1908, was painstakingly designed by archaeologist and devoted Hellenophile Theodore Reinach. Both indoors and out, the villa is a fastidiously flawless copy of a 2nd-century Greek home. All period furniture was re-created using traditional Greek methods, while various rooms incorporated 20th-century conveniences, such as running water in the villa's *balaneion*, or thermal baths. The bucolic waterside gardens are dotted with olive and pomegranate trees and offer sweeping vistas over nearby Cap-Ferrat.

Impasse Gustave Eiffel. www.villa-kerylos.com. ℂ **04-93-01-01-44.** Admission 12€ adults, 9€ students and children 7–17, free for children 6 and under. July–Aug daily 10am–7pm; Mar–June and Sept–Oct daily 10am–6pm; Nov–Feb Mon–Fri 2–6pm, Sat–Sun 10am–6pm.

8 EZE & LA TURBIE ★★

942km (584 miles) S of Paris; 11km (6¾ miles) NE of Nice

The hamlets of Eze and La Turbie, 6.5km (4 miles) apart, are picture-perfect hill villages that literally cling to the mountains. Both have fortified medieval cores overlooking the coast, and both were built during the early Middle Ages to stave off raids from Saracen pirates. In Eze's case, it's now tour buses, not coastal raiders, that make daily invasions into town. Impossibly cute streets contain galleries, boutiques, and artisans' shops. La Turbie is much quieter, offering a welcome respite from the coast's summertime heat.

Essentials

ARRIVING Trains connect Eze-sur-Mer with Nice, Monaco, and the rest of the Côte d'Azur every 30 minutes. You may take a taxi from here up (1,400 ft.) to Eze; alternatively, bus no. 83 connects the rail station with the hilltop village. For rail information, visit www.voyages-sncf.com or call ℂ **36-35. Bus** line no. 82 runs between Nice and Eze around every 90 minutes, while five to seven daily buses (no. 116) connect Nice and La Turbie. Both journeys take 40 minutes. One-way fares cost 1.50€. For all bus information and schedules, contact **Ligne d'Azur** (www.lignesdazur.com; ℂ **08-10-06-10-06**). By **car** from Nice, take the spellbindingly pretty D6007 (the *moyenne corniche*) east.

VISITOR INFORMATION Eze's **Office de Tourisme** is on place du Général-de-Gaulle, Eze-Village (www.eze-tourisme.com; ℂ **04-93-41-26-00**). La Turbie's small **tourist information point** is at 2 place Detras, La Turbie (ℂ **04-93-41-21-15;** www.ville-la-turbie.fr).

[FastFACTS] EZE & LA TURBIE

ATMs/Banks   **Société Générale,** place de la Colette, Eze (ℂ **04-92-41-51-10**); **BNP Paribas,** 6 av Général de Gaulle, La Turbie (ℂ **08-20-82-00-01**).

Mail & Postage   **La Poste,** av. du Jardin Exotique, Eze; **La Poste,** place Neuve, La Turbie; both (ℂ **36-31**).

Pharmacies   **Pharmacie Lecoq,** place Colette, Eze (ℂ **04-93-41-06-17**); **Pharmacie de La Turbie,** 6 av Général de Gaulle, La Turbie (ℂ **04-93-41-16-50**).

Where to Stay

Château de la Chèvre d'Or ★★★   No hotel better sums up the glamour and grace of the French Riviera than La Chèvre d'Or. This resort hotel is built into and around the elegant hilltop town of Eze. Each sumptuously decorated suite is a grand apartment with a panoramic view of the coastline. It's a habitual favorite of royalty and A-listers, and recent makeovers have made it popular with vacationing families and young hipsters as well. The 38 terraced gardens drip down the hill towards the Mediterranean to ensure absolute privacy—indeed there's a ratio of one garden and three staff members to each room or suite. The best thing about La Chèvre d'Or? That would be the eponymous double-Michelin-starred **restaurant** overseen by top chef Ronan Kervaree (set menus 98€–230€). Experimental dishes include a vegan square decorated with an edible garden of herbs and flowers; San Remo shrimp wrapped in oyster-infused gossamer-thin pasta; and baby lamb shot through with parsley and violet.

Rue du Barri, Eze. www.chevredor.com. ℂ **04-92-10-66-66.** 37 units. 310€–640€ double; 760€–2,600€ suite. Parking 15€. Closed Dec–Feb. **Amenities:** 4 restaurants; bar; babysitting; exercise room; outdoor pool; room service; sauna; free Wi-Fi.

Where to Eat

Gascogne Café ★ FRENCH/ITALIAN   On the main road just outside of Eze's fortified Old Town, this bustling eatery is a friendly spot to sample authentic local fare. The menu ranges from traditional flavors (homemade lasagna, sea bass on a bed of ratatouille) to more creative offerings (Asian-style rolls stuffed with snails and garlic cream). Tasty pizzas are also available. The ambience is decidedly casual.

151 av. de Verdun, place de la Collette, Eze. www.gascogne-hotel-restaurant.fr. ℂ **04-93-41-18-50.** Main courses 12€–22€; fixed-price menus 17€–32€. Daily 12:30–3pm and 7:30–10pm.

Exploring Eze & La Turbie

Aside from its pretty lanes, the leading attraction in Eze is the **Jardin d'Eze ★**, 20 rue du Château (ℂ **04-93-41-10-30**). Here exotic plants are interspersed with feminine sculptures by Jean Philippe Richard, all perched atop the town at 1,400 feet. Admission is 6€ adults, 2.50€ students and ages 12 to 25, and free children 11 and under. In

Exotic cactus in the Jardin d'Eze.

The Riviera's Newest Cultural Attractions

In 2015 the latest of two astounding new cultural sights opened either side of Monaco. The largest is the **Cap Moderne** collection of art deco villas and dwellings, avenue de la Gare, Roquebrune-Cap-Martin (www.capmoderne.com; ✆ **06-48-72-90-53**), on the promontory of Cap Martin. Just below the peninsula's coastal path sit the historic houses of Irish designer Eileen Gray and Swiss architect Le Corbusier. Interestingly, the two artistic rivals had an unrequited love affair, which led the Swiss to build his La Cabanon and Unités de Camping beach cabins next door to Gray's Villa E-1027. Visits to this bucolic seaside site must be made by guided tour from Tuesday to Sunday at 10:30am or 2:30pm. Admission is 15€ adults, 10€ for visitors ages 8 to 17, free for children 7 and under.

On the western side of Monaco, again reachable by coastal trail, is the **Villa les Camélias,** 17 avenue Gramaglia, Cap d'Ail (www.villalescamelias.com; ✆ **04-93-98-36-57**). A local history museum, albeit one with astounding sea views and a private swimming pool, the villa charts the history of this Monaco suburb by way of photographs, handwritten notes from regular visitor Sir Winston Churchill, and even a calling card from a glamorous local bordello. It's open from Wednesday to Friday, and Sunday, from April to October 9:30am to 12:30pm and 2 to 6pm, and Sunday, Tuesday and Thursday, December to March 9.30am to noon and 1:30 to 4:30pm. Admission is 9€ adults, free for children 12 and under.

July and August, it's open daily 9am to 7:30pm; the rest of the year it opens daily at 9am and closes between 4 and 7pm, depending on the time of sunset.

Even higher than Eze is the heady village of La Turbie (the drive between the two settlements is an impressive series of mountain switchbacks). It boasts an impressive monument erected by Roman emperor Augustus in 6 B.C., the **Trophée des Alps (Trophy of the Alps)** ★. Still partially intact today, it was created to celebrate the subjugation of the French Alpine tribes by the Roman armies. The nearby **Musée du Trophée d'Auguste,** avenue Albert-1er (www.la-turbie.monuments-nationaux.fr; ✆ **04-93-41-20-84**), is an interactive mini-museum containing finds from digs nearby, a historical 3D film, and details about the monument's restoration. Both the ruins and the museum are open Tuesday to Sunday mid-May to mid-September 9:30am to 1pm and 2:30 to 6:30pm, and mid-September to mid-May 10am to 1:30pm and 2:30 to 5pm. Admission to both sites is 5.50€ adults, free children 18 and under.

MONACO ★★

939km (582 miles) S of Paris; 18km (11 miles) E of Nice

This sunny stretch of coast became the property of the Grimaldi clan in 1297, when one Francesco Grimaldi tricked his way into the fortress protecting the

Monaco's harbor with yacht's sailing at sunset.

harbor. The dynasty has maintained something resembling independence ever since. In recent decades the clan has turned Monaco into the world's chicest city-state with its own mini-airport (with direct helicopter links to Nice and St-Tropez, no less).

Hemmed in by France on three sides and the Mediterranean on the fourth, this feudal anomaly harbors the world's greatest number of billionaires per capita. And as almost everybody knows, the Monégasques do not pay taxes. Celebrity exiles—including tennis player Rafael Nadal and racing driver Lewis Hamilton—are attracted by the tax regime too. Nearly all of Monaco's revenue comes from banking, tourism, and gambling. Better still, in an astute feat of cunning, local residents aren't allowed to gamble away their inheritance, so visitors must bring a passport to play on the Principality's famed poker, roulette, and blackjack tables.

Monaco, or, more precisely, its capital of Monte Carlo, has for a century been a symbol of glamour. The 1956 marriage of Prince Rainier III to American actress Grace Kelly enhanced its status. She met the prince when she was in Cannes to promote "To Catch a Thief." Their daughter Caroline was born in 1957; a son, Albert, in 1958; and a second daughter, Stephanie, in 1965. The actress's life and times were recently relived on the silver screen in "Grace of Monaco." Starring Nicole Kidman as Grace Kelly, the movie opened at the 2014 Cannes Film Festival.

Prince Rainier was nicknamed the "Builder Prince" as he expanded the territory by building into the Mediterranean. Prince Albert took over from his late father in 2005 and burnishes his "Eco-Prince" credentials with pride. Newer, more environmentally conscious land-reclamation schemes near the Fairmont Hotel were announced in 2014, and work starts on this man-made yacht-lined peninsula soon. The Principality also has its own green car manufacturer, Venturi—although this marquee specializes in a typically Monégasque market for all-electric supercars. To confirm Albert's sustainable business leanings, Monaco's inaugural all-electric FormulaE Grand Prix took place before the prestigious Formula1 race in 2015.

Fortunately for the Grimaldi line, Albert married his girlfriend, South African swimmer Charlene Wittstock, in 2011, now Her Serene Highness The Princess of Monaco. Despite rumors of a pre-wedding fallout, the couple are idolized in the Principality, especially after the birth of their twins, Princess Gabriella and son Prince Jacques, in December 2014. The royal couple's official portrait has pride of place in every bar, hotel, and bakery in the land.

Essentials

ARRIVING   Monaco has rail, bus, highway—and helicopter—connections from other coastal cities, especially Nice. There are no border formalities when entering Monaco from France. The 19km (12 miles) **drive** from Nice takes around 30 minutes and runs along the N7 Moyenne Corniche. The pretty D6098 coast road takes a little longer. **Ligne d'Azur** (www.lignesdazur.com; ℂ **08-10-06-10-06**) runs a **bus** service at 15-minute intervals aboard line no. 100 from Nice to Monte Carlo. One-way bus transit from Nice costs 1.50€. **Trains** arrive every 30 minutes from Cannes, Nice, Menton, and Antibes. Monaco's underground railway station (*gare*) is on place St. Devote. A system of pedestrian tunnels, escalators, and elevators riddle the Principality, and such an underground walkway links the train station to Monte Carlo. The scheduled **chopper** service to Nice Airport costs 120€ via **Heli Air Monaco** (www.heliairmonaco.com; ℂ **92-05-00-50**). By **bus** it's just 20€ (www.nice airportxpress.com; ℂ **04-97-00-07-00**).

VISITOR INFORMATION   The **Direction du Tourisme et des Congrés** tourist office is at 2A bd. des Moulins (www.visitmonaco.com; ℂ **92-16-61-16**).

CITY LAYOUT   The second-smallest state in Europe (Vatican City is the tiniest), Monaco consists of four parts. The Old Town, **Monaco-Ville,** on a rocky promontory 60m (197 ft.) high is the seat of the Prince's Palace and the government building, as well as the Oceanographic Museum. To the west, **La Condamine** is at the foot of the Old Town, forming its ritzy harbor and port sector. Up from the port (Monaco is seriously steep) is **Monte Carlo,** the playground of royalty and celebrity, and the setting for the casino, the Tourist Office, and various luxurious hotels. The fourth part, **Fontvieille,** is a neat industrial suburb housing the Monaco Football club, which was purchased by Russian billionaire Dmitry Rybolovlev. Thanks to the Russian's financial backing, the soccer club was promoted to the French premier league in 2013, and topped the table several times in 2015.

SPECIAL EVENTS   Two of the most-watched **car-racing events** in the world are in January (**Le Rallye**) and May (**the Grand Prix**): See www.acm. mc and www.formula1monaco.com. The coolest place to watch both events is on the top deck of the **Yacht Club de Monaco,** a liner-shaped restaurant, bar, and club designed by Lord Norman Foster. The **Monte-Carlo Masters** ATP tennis tournament (www.monte-carlorolexmasters.com) takes place in April. The **Monte-Carlo International Fireworks Festival** lasts all summer long. The skies above the harbor are lit up several times a week as millions of euros go up in smoke, courtesy of those who can assuredly afford it.

[FastFACTS]
MONACO

ATMs/Banks Among many others, there are several banks along boulevard Albert 1er behind the Port of Monaco.

Internet Access **Bilig Café,** 11 rue Princesse Caroline (℃ **97-98-20-43**).

Mail & Postage **La Poste,** place de la Mairie in Monte-Carlo (℃ **36-31**).

Pharmacies **Pharmacie Internationale,** 22 rue Grimaldi (℃ **04-93-50-35-99**).

Earth Calling Monaco
To call Monaco from within France, dial 00 (the access code for all international long-distance calls from France); followed by the **country code, 377;** and then the eight-digit local phone number. (Don't dial 33; that's the country code for France.)

Getting Around

BY FOOT Aside from two very steep hills, the world's second-smallest country is **pedestrian-friendly.** Hardy local Jean-Marc Ferrie at **Monaco Rando** (www.monaco-rando.com; ℃ **06-30-12-57-03**) organizes **guided hikes** around his hometown from 10€ per person with an interpreter in-tow.

BY TAXI Taxis wait outside Monaco train station, or call ℃ **08-20-20-98-98.**

BY PUBLIC TRANSPORT CAM (www.cam.mc; ℃ **97-70-22-22**) runs buses inside the Principality. Lines nos. 1 and 2 link Monaco-Ville with the casino area. CAM's **solar-powered shuttle boat** hops between the banks of Monaco's port every 20 minutes. The ride is great for kids and connects the casino area with foot of Monaco-Ville. All CAM tickets cost 2€.

BY OPEN-TOP BUS **Monaco–Le Grand Tour** (www.monacolegrand tour.com; ℃ **97-70-26-36**) open-top minibuses allows visitors to hop-on and hop-off at the Principality's 12 main sights. Day passes cost 21€ adults; 8€ children between 4 and 11; free children under 4.

BY ELECTRIC CAR It may be the land of the gas-guzzling Grand Prix, but Monaco is a global pioneer in green technology and is justly proud of its eco-credentials. Join the club with a rented two-person **Renault Twizy** (a super-tiny electric car; 35€ for 2 hr.) on Monaco's new all-electric car sharing scheme **Mobee** (www.mobee-monaco.com; ℃ **97-70-22-22**). Reserving and picking-up your car using their innovative app is a cinch.

Where to Stay

Fairmont Monte Carlo ★★ The five-star hotel is easily Monaco's most fun. It combines fine-dining restaurants, a spa, and a rooftop pool with an unstuffy attitude; albeit one backed by a legion of ever-smiling, mostly Italian, staff. Of course, this vision of modern opulence is also one of the most valuable pieces of real estate on the Côte d'Azur. It drips into the Mediterranean from behind the Casino de Monte-Carlo—indeed, a private passageway runs to the casino's rear entrance—and guests may combine the endless breakfast with the best sea views in the Principality. Formula 1 fans should also note that the fastest park of the Monaco Grand Prix zips right beneath the basement, while the twisting Fairmont Hairpin sits just outside. The hotel also has a partnership with four local beach clubs, where families are dropped off with towels, mineral water, and sun spray, then picked up on demand. Diners are in for a treat too. Choose between bistro **Saphir,** Japanese atelier **Nobu,** and rooftop Italian restaurant **Horizonte.**

12 av. des Spélugues. www.fairmont.com/montecarlo. ✆ **93-50-65-00.** 602 units. 279€–879€ double; from 889€ suite. Parking 50€. **Amenities:** 2 restaurants; 2 bars; babysitting; concierge; health club; 1 outdoor pools; room service; spa; Wi-Fi (20€/day or free if you enroll in the Fairmont President Club at no charge at check-in).

Hôtel Ambassador ★   A 5-minute stroll from the main Monaco action, the Ambassador makes a bargain base from which to explore the Principality. Elegant guestrooms benefit from a recent style overhaul. Dimensions are tiny (but the entire country occupies less than 1 sq. mile, so little wonder). A buffet breakfast (included in the price) is offered next door in the cheap and tasty **P&P** restaurant and pizzeria.

10 avenue Prince Pierre, Monaco 98000. www.ambassadormonaco.com. ✆ **97-97-96-96.** 35 units. 137€–207€ double. Parking 18€. **Amenities:** Bar, free Wi-Fi.

Hôtel Hermitage ★★   Never has so much history and glamour been suffused into 280 effortlessly chic guest rooms. La Prairie products and free access to the **Thermes Marins spa** (p. 298) come as standard in them all. If that isn't enough, the Hôtel Hermitage boasts several sister hotels, including the five-star family friendly **Monte-Carlo Beach Hotel** (www.monte-carlo-beach.com; ✆ **93-28-66-66**), whose **Restaurant Elsa** received the region's first 100% organic certificate.

Square Beaumarchais, Monaco. www.hotelhermitagemontecarlo.com. ✆ **98-06-40-00.** 182 units. 413€–735€ double; from 805€ suite. Valet parking 40€. **Amenities:** restaurant; 3 bars; babysitting; concierge; exercise room; pool access; room service; sauna; Thermes Marins spa offering thalassotherapy; free Wi-Fi.

Where to Eat

Pinch yourself. This postcard-sized Principality boasts a total of eight Michelin stars, and includes the most highly rated eatery on the entire Mediterranean, Le Louis XV. For a bargain pizza simply dine at the cheap eateries that ring the harbor. After all, not everyone's a billionaire.

Bouchon ★ TRADITIONAL FRENCH   A refreshing new addition to the Principality's über-hip dining scene, Bouchon purveys classic bistro cuisine at distinctly un-Monaco prices. Art Deco *objets d'art* hand-selected from the flea markets of Paris and Nice set the scene. Breakfast kicks off with eggs and *viennoiseries* (delicious pastries that range from mini croissants to pan au chocolat). Lunch continues with salade Niçoise, *moules marinières* (creamy, garlicky mussels), and a daily specials board. Dinner is slightly grander, although dishes like *filet de boeuf* or seared tuna won't break the bank when ordered with a *pichet* (jug) of wine.

11 av. Princesse Grace. www.bouchon.mc. ☎ **97-77-08-80.** Main courses 13€–38€; fixed-price lunch 20€–22€. Daily 7:30am–11pm.

Café Llorca ★ MEDITERRANEAN   Super-chef Alain Llorca provided the very restaurant that Monaco lacked for so long: an affordable contemporary eatery overlooking the shimmering sea. Café Llorca is a bargain. Daily lunch mains at press time included crab spring rolls and Niçois beef stew (Mon), red mullet terrine and sautéed kidneys (Wed), and mackerel marinade and Provençal aioli (Fri). Call ahead for dinner—the establishment is often booked up for events.

11 av. Princesse Grace. www.cafellorca.mc. ☎ **99-99-29-29.** Main courses 16€–19€; fixed-price lunch 22€. Daily 11am–11pm.

Le Café de Paris ★ MODERN FRENCH   Pricey, pretentious, and ever-popular, this Parisian-style restaurant-cafe on place du Casino has a location to die for. The menu has taken on an even more classic edge under head chef Jean-Claude Brugel, who trained alongside several top Riviera chefs including Roger Vergé and Joël Garault. Simple starters like garlic escargot and croque monsieurs share the menu with more innovative mains like filet of plaice (a North Sea fish) with pumpkin purée or steak tartare. From October to March, a special seafood stall dispenses Oléron oysters, sea urchins, and platters of chilled crab to passersby.

Place du Casino. ☎ **98-06-76-23.** Reservations recommended. Main courses 17€–50€; fixed-price menu 35€. Daily 8am–2am.

Le Louis XV ★★★ MEDITERRANEAN   In the Hôtel de Paris, the Louis XV offers one of the finest dining experiences on the Riviera, and thus the world. Superstar chef Alain Ducasse oversees the refined but not overly adorned cuisine. The restaurant's head chef, Domique Lory, can be seen in Nice's market at dawn buying local cheeses or wandering through the corridors of the Hôtel de Paris carrying white truffles purchased from over the Italian border. Everything is light and attuned to the seasons, with intelligent, modern interpretations of Provençal and northern Italian dishes. You'll find chargrilled breast of baby pigeon with sautéed duck liver, and an ongoing specialty known as Provençal vegetables with crushed truffles. All is served under a magnificent frescoed ceiling, which includes the portraits of Louis XV's six mistresses.

In the Hôtel de Paris, place du Casino. ☎ **98-06-88-64.** Reservations recommended. Jacket and tie recommended for men. Main courses 74€–160€; fixed-price lunch 145€, dinner 230€–310€. Thurs–Mon 12:15–1:45pm and 8–9:45pm. Closed first 2 weeks Mar.

Exploring Monaco

Monaco's main sights—including its glamorous port, casino and hotels—are clustered around the pedestrianized Place du Casino Square. Its principal museums, including the Prince's Palace and Oceanographic Museum, are situated on the history-laden rock of Monaco-Ville.

Collection des Voitures Anciennes de S.A.S. le Prince de Monaco ★ MUSEUM Petrolheads, racing enthusiasts, and big kids alike will love the vintage car collection of Prince Rainier III. This private collection encompasses more than 100 vintage autos, including a locally built electric Venturi supercar and the bulletproof Lexus that served as the wedding car for Prince Albert and Charlene Wittstock. Other items include a Mercedes McLaren SLR and a classic Lamborghini Countach.

Les Terrasses de Fontvieille. www.palais.mc. ⓒ **92-05-28-56.** Admission 6.50€ adults, 3€ students and children 8–14, free for children 7 and under. Daily 10am–6pm.

Les Grands Appartements du Palais ★ PALACE The home of Monaco's royal family, the Palais du Prince dominates the Principality from the Rock. A tour of the Grands Appartements—with audio tour recorded by none other than Prince Albert himself—allows visitors to glimpse the Throne Room and artworks by Bruegel and Holbein. The palace was built in the 13th century, and some of it dates from the Renaissance. The ideal time to arrive is 11:55am, so you can watch the 10-minute **Relève de la Garde (Changing of the Guard).** Summer concerts by the **Monte-Carlo Philharmonic Orchestra** are held outside in the courtyard.

Place du Palais. www.palais.mc. ⓒ **93-25-18-31.** Admission 8€ adults, 4€ children 8–14, free for children 7 and under. Daily Apr–Oct 10am–6pm. Closed Nov–Mar.

Musée Océanographique de Monaco ★ AQUARIUM This mammoth oceanfront museum was founded by Albert I, great-grandfather of the present prince, in 1910. It's now a living, breathing science lesson covering the world's oceans by way of a Mediterranean aquarium, tropical tanks, and a shark reserve. A delight for budding marine scientists is the 18m-long (60-ft.) whale skeleton that washed up on a local beach a century ago. As compelling are the scientific specimens brought up from the ocean depths over the past 100 years.

Av. St-Martin. www.oceano.mc. ⓒ **93-15-36-00.** Admission 14€ adults, 7€ children 4–18, free for children 5 and under. Apr–June and Sept daily 10am–7pm; July–Aug daily 10am–8pm; Oct–Mar daily 10am–6pm.

Nouveau Musée National de Monaco ★★ ART MUSEUM Over the past decade Monaco has touted its cultural credentials to bring in a savvier, younger, and more artistically aware crowd. The Villa Sauber and Villa Paloma museums are two stunning art spaces set in palatial former homes across the city from one another. Both bring in global culture vultures by the score by way of contemporary-art exhibitions and shows covering sculpture, architecture, photography, and the glamorous history of the French Riviera. Since 2015 both offer free access on Sundays.

Villa Sauber, 17 av. Princess Grace; Villa Paloma, 56 bd. du Jardin Exotique. www.nmnm.mc. ⓒ **98-98-16-82.** Admission to both 6€ adults, free entrance for visitors 26 and under. June–Sept daily 11am–7pm. Oct–May daily 10am–6pm.

Opéra de Monte-Carlo ★ OPERA HOUSE Monaco takes music seriously. In 2015 Pharrell Williams and Lady Gaga played live to sell-out crowds. The Principality's lavish Opera House sits next to the casino, where its Salle Garnier hosts rock, pop, classical and opera events—and even hosted the wedding reception of Prince Albert and Charlene Wittstock in 2011. For big-hitting pop and DJ events, try the **Grimaldi Forum,** 10 av. Princesse-Grace (www.grimaldiforum.com; ✆ **99-99-20-00**).

Place du Casino. ✆ **98-06-28-28.** www.opera.mc. Year-round admission prices 10€–150€ adults, reduced entrance for visitors 26 and under.

Outdoor Activities

BEACHES   Just outside the border, on French soil, the **Monte-Carlo Beach Club** adjoins the **Monte-Carlo Beach Hotel,** 22 av. Princesse-Grace (www.monte-carlo-beach.com; ✆ **93-28-66-66**). It has an Olympic-sized swimming pool, a La Prairie spa, cabanas, a poolside fine dining restaurant called Le Deck, and a low-key Mediterranean restaurant with lunch buffet called La Vigie. Beach activities include donuts, jet skis, and parachute rides. As the temperature drops in late October, the beach closes for the winter. The admission charge of 60€ to 150€, depending on the season, grants you access to changing rooms, toilets, restaurants, and bar, along with use of a mattress for sunbathing. In 2015 its relaxed beach restaurant, **Elsa** (✆ **98-06-50-05**), was awarded a Michelin star for its all-organic cuisine.

All-Night Glamour

Museums are all well and good, but to survey the soul of Monaco you need a credit card, a suntan, and a late-morning wake-up call. Early-evening glamour revolves around the bars that surround the historic port. Here, locally based luxury yacht agencies like **Y.CO** (www.ycoyacht.com; ✆ **93-50-12-12**) charter 50m-long (262-ft.) sailing craft for around $100,000 per week. At sundown the action moves uphill to Casino Square, where **Buddha Bar** (✆ **98-06-19-19**) is bedecked with chinoiserie, Asian statues, and a raised DJ booth. For sheer class, the **Crystal Bar** (✆ **98-06-98-99**) inside the Hôtel Hermitage pulls out all the stops. Elegant dress, vintage Champagne, and the odd feather boa sets the scene until 1am. **Le Bar Américain** (✆ **98-06-38-38**), in the Hôtel de Paris, is far more raucous, with chillingly expensive cocktails and nightly jazz. Across place du Casino the timeless superclub **Jimmy'z**

(✆ **98-06-36-36**), open nightly 11pm to 5am, has attracted stars from Farrah Fawcett to George Clooney. But it's the mythical **Casino de Monte-Carlo** (www.montecarlocasinos.com; ✆ **98-06-21-21**) that lends the square its name. The casino's marble-floored Atrium is open—for free—to all comers from 2pm who wish to shoot slots or play blackjack in the hallowed Salle des Amériques or try their luck at roulette in the Salle Europe. For roulette, *trente et quarante,* and Texas Hold'em in the private areas of rococo Salon Touzet and Salon Médecin, gamers must pay a 10€ fee. Entrance to Les Salons Supers Privés is by invitation only (hey, they've got our number!) and requires smart dress and nerves of steel. Another great summer addition is the Casino de Monte-Carlo **alfresco** terrace. Here visitors may play roulette and poker overlooking the moonlit Mediterranean. Now *that's* glamorous.

If you insist on the likes of Hermès, Gucci, and Lanvin, you'll find them cheek by jowl near the Hôtel de Paris and the Casino de Monte-Carlo. But the prize for Monaco's hippest store goes to **Lull**, 29 rue de Millo (℡ **97-77-54-54**), awash in labels like Dries Van Noten and Raf Simons. Almost next door, **Une Femme à Suivre** (℡ **97-77-10-52**) sells French classics from the likes of Tara Jarman and Mariona Gen. The **Galeries du Métropole** is packed with high-fashion and specialty stores.

As well as Dunhill and Gant, try **McMarket** (℡ **97-77-12-12**). Serious labels in this fashion emporium include Balenciaga, Louboutin, and Jimmy Choo. **FNAC** (℡ **08-25-02-00-20**) is recommended for English-language novels, Monaco history books, and the latest electronics. For real-people shopping, stroll **rue Grimaldi**, the Principality's most commercial street, near the fruit, flower, and food market at **place des Armes,** which opens daily at 7:30am until noon.

CINEMA   From June to September, the **Monaco Open Air Cinema** (www. cinema2monaco.com) occupies an alfresco amphitheater below the Rock of Monaco. Nightly blockbuster screenings take place in English-language only at 10pm in June and July, and at 9pm in August and September. Tickets costs 11€, or 9€ for persons aged 20 or under.

SPA TREATMENTS   The century-old **Thermes Marins,** 2 av. de Monte-Carlo (www.thermesmarinsmontecarlo.com; ℡ **98-06-69-00**), reopened in 2015. Spread over four floors is a pool, Turkish *hammam* (steam bath), healthy restaurant, juice bar, tanning booths, fitness center, beauty center, and private treatment rooms. A day pass, giving access to the sauna, steam rooms, fitness facilities, and pools, is 100€. Therapies include an hour-long foot cocooning for 160€.

SWIMMING   Overlooking the yacht-studded harbor, the **Stade Nautique Rainier-III,** quai Albert-1er, at La Condamine (℡ **93-30-64-83**), a pool frequented by the Monégasques, was a gift from Prince Rainier to his subjects. A word of advice: Don't wear your baggy old bikini, as it is poseur central. It's open May to October daily 9am to 6pm (until 8pm June–Aug). Admission costs 5.60€ per person. Between November and March, it's an ice-skating rink.

TENNIS & SQUASH   The **Monte Carlo Country Club,** 155 av. Princesse-Grace, Roquebrune-Cap Martin, France (www.mccc.mc; ℡ **04-93-41-30-15**), has 21 clay and 2 concrete tennis courts. The 45€ fee provides access to a restaurant, health club with Jacuzzi and sauna, putting green, beach, squash courts, and well-maintained tennis courts. Guests of the hotels administered by the Société des Bains de Mer (Hôtel de Paris, Hermitage, Monte Carlo Bay, and Monte Carlo Beach Club) pay half-price. It's open daily 8am to 8 or 9pm, depending on the season.

PLANNING YOUR TRIP TO FRANCE

O f almost any destination in the world, flying into France is one of the most effortless undertakings in global travel. There are no shots to get and no particular safety precautions, and more and more French people now speak English. With your passport, airline or train ticket, and enough money, you just go. In the pages that follow, you'll find everything you need to know to plan your trip: finding the best airfare, deciding when to go, getting around the country, and much, much more.

GETTING THERE

By Plane

The two Paris airports—**Orly** (airport code: ORY) and **Charles de Gaulle** (airport code: CDG)—are about even in terms of convenience to the city's center. Orly, the older of the two, is 13km (8 miles) south of the center; Charles de Gaulle is 22km (14 miles) northeast. Air France serves Charles de Gaulle (Terminal 2C) from North America. U.S. carriers land at both airports—although note that both can be very busy depending on the season and security checks. Flight status and transport information for both airports can be found online (www.aeroportsdeparis.fr). If you're heading to the South of France, **Nice Côte d'Azur** (airport code: NCE; www.nice.aeroport.fr) is served by direct flights from New York, and most European cities.

Most airlines charge their lowest fares between November and mid-March. The shoulder season (Oct and mid-Mar to mid-June) is a bit more expensive, but we think it's the ideal time to visit France.

By Train

Paris is one of Europe's busiest rail junctions, with trains departing from its seven major stations every few minutes. If you are in the U.K., Germany, Holland, Italy, or Spain, our recommendation would be to travel to the country by train.

Eurostar (www.eurostar.com; © **800/387-6782** in the U.S.) links London directly with Paris Gare du Nord station from as little as $69 one-way; trip time just over 2 hours. It also runs direct seasonal routes to Disneyland Paris, Avignon, Aix-en-Provence, and, newly inaugurated in 2015, Marseille. Better still, trips from London can be booked online to any major station in France. For the best deals, book as tickets become available exactly 3 months in advance. Highly recommended is train and accommodation specialist **Railbookers** (www.railbookers.com; © **888/829-3040** in the U.S.). Their specialized teams can plan bespoke rail journeys throughout France. Start out from Paris and discover rural France and the Côte d'Azur, or tick off the essential European cities before a European Grand Tour.

By Car

The major highways into Paris are A1 from the north (Great Britain and Benelux); A13 from Rouen, Normandy, and northwest France; A11 from Nantes and the Loire valley; and the A6 from Lyon, Provence, the Riviera, and Italy.

By Boat from England

Ferries and hydrofoils operate day and night from the English channel ports to Normandy. The major routes include at least 12 trips a day between Dover or Folkestone and Calais or Boulogne. Ferries often drop passengers off by the rail junction of each port.

There are various operators of ferries across the channel depending on your destination. **P&O Ferries** (www.poferries.com; © **0800/130-0030** in the U.K.) operate car and passenger ferries between Dover, England, and Calais, France (more than 20 sailings a day; 90 min. each way). **Brittany Ferries** (www.brittanyferries.com; © **0871/244-0744**) operates ferry services from Portsmouth and Poole, England, to Cherbourg, Caen or Le Havre, France (one or two departures a day; 3–4 hr. each way). **DFDS Seaways** (www.dfds.co.uk; © **0844/576-8836** in the U.K.) operates two sailings per day between Portsmouth and Le Havre (4–8 hr. each way). It also sails up to 44 times daily between Dover and Calais (1½ hr.) and Dover and Dunkirk (2 hr.).

SPECIAL-INTEREST TRIPS & TOURS

Academic Trips & Language Classes

The **Alliance Française,** 101 bd. Raspail, Paris 75006 (www.alliancefr.org; © **01-42-84-90-00**), is a nonprofit French-language teaching organization with a network of 850 establishments in 136 countries. The school in Paris is open all year; week-long courses range from around 101€ to 253€.

Just outside Nice, the **Institut de Francais,** 23 av. Général-Leclerc, Villefranche-sur-Mer 06230 (www.institutdefrancais.com; © **04-93-01-88-44**), offers highly acclaimed month-long French immersion courses. Each day includes 8 hours of lessons, plus breakfast and lunch taken together with professors. Prices range from 2,990€ to 3,620€.

A clearinghouse for information on French-language schools is **Lingua Service Worldwide** (www.linguaserviceworldwide.com; ℭ **800/394-5327**). Its programs are available in many cities throughout France. Cost ranges from around $200 to close to $6,000 per week, depending on the city, the school, and accommodation.

Adventure Trips

LUXURY CRUISES   Dozens of major cruise lines call at Marseille, Nice, Villefranche, Monaco, and at many points between, plus along the Normandy Coast. Google each destination for a list of who goes where (it's a big list!) but the major players include **Princess** (www.msccruisesusa.com; ℭ **800/744-6237**) and **Celebrity** (www.celebritycruises.com; ℭ **302/341-0205**).

RIVER CRUISES   Before the advent of rail, many crops, building supplies, raw materials, and finished products were barged through France on a series of rivers, canals, and estuaries. Many of these waterways retain their old-fashioned locks and pumps, allowing shallow-draft boats easy access through idyllic countryside.

Go Barging (www.gobarging.com; ℭ **800/394-8630**) operates 6-night river cruises departing from Paris along the River Seine, as well as trips through the Loire Valley and Canal du Midi. Fares range start from 3,450€ per person (double occupancy) including all meals and drinks.

Viking River Cruises (www.vikingrivercruises.com; ℭ **855/707-4837**) leads 1-week tours from Paris through Normandy, with stops in Rouen, Giverny, and at the D-Day beaches. For double occupancy, prices start at $1,356.

Wellness Trips

For serious Provençal pampering just outside of Gordes, the five-star **Les Bories Hotel & Spa** (www.hotellesbories.com; ℭ **04-90-72-00-51**) offers 2- to 5-day treatment programs at their on-site spa, La Maison d'Ennea. Facials, massages, and wraps use locally sourced essential oils, such as lavender and sweet orange.

There are plenty of excellent **yoga** and **meditation** retreats dotted around the country. A few popular places include **Les Passesroses** (www.passesroses. com) northeast of Bordeaux, **Dévi Yoga Retreats** (www.deviyogaretreats. com) across the South of France, **Kaliyoga/France** (www.kaliyoga.com) in Provence's Luberon, and **LuxYoga** (www.luxyoga.com) on the French Riviera.

Food & Wine Trips

Established in 1895, **Le Cordon Bleu,** 8 rue Léon Delhomme, 75015 Paris (www.cordonbleu.edu; ℭ **01-53-68-22-50**), is the most famous French cooking school, where Julia Child learned to perfect her *pâté brisée* and *mousse au* *chocolat.* There are year-long courses that will prepare you to work among the masters of haute cuisine, but most visitors will opt for less intense (and less costly) experiences, ranging from 1-hour demonstration classes (from 48€) to 4-day workshops (from 990€).

Less formal but equally enjoyable are the cooking classes offered by **La Cuisine Paris** (www.lacuisineparis.com; 🕾 **01-40-51-78-18**), a friendly school set up by a Franco-American team. It offers small classes by professional chefs in both French and English, including the popular French Macaron Class. Food tours are also offered. Prices range from 65€ for 2 hours to 185€ for 5 hours.

Cook'n with Class (www.cooknwithclass.com; 🕾 **01-42-57-22-84**; Métro: Simplon or Jules Joffrin) offers a range of individual and small-group classes, the most popular of which is the Morning Market Class; it includes a walk to a local market. Set up by a French chef, all classes are taught in English by professionals. Prices range from 130€ for 3-hour classes to 195€ for 5-hour classes.

Run by longtime local resident, US-born and raised Preston Mohr, **Paris by the Glass** (www.parisbytheglass.com) offers wine tastings in Paris (from 85€ per person, 2-hr. session) as well as tasting excursions to Champagne (from 299€ per person, 12-hr. day trip) and the Loire (from 299€ per person, 11-hr. day trip). Groups are limited to six participants.

At Home with Patricia Wells (www.patriciawells.com) is a Paris- and Provence-based cooking school taught by Patricia Wells, cookbook author and famed former restaurant critic for the "International Herald Tribune." The extremely popular 5-day classes in Paris and Provence cost $5,500 (accommodations not included).

Les Petits Farcis (www.petitsfarcis.com), run by Cordon Bleu-trained Canadian chef Rosa Jackson, offers tours of Nice's colorful produce market, followed by daylong gourmet cooking sessions. Prices begin at 195€ per person and include a four-course lunch with wine.

Guided Tours

BIKE TOURS Some of the best cycling tours of France are offered by **VBT** (www.vbt.com; 🕾 **800/245-3868**), which offers trips in six of the most scenic parts of France. Rides range from a gentle peddle among the Loire's châteaux to a more challenging exploration of the D-Day beaches. Prices start at $3,995 per person, with airfare packages also available.

Cycling for Softies (www.cycling-for-softies.co.uk; 🕾 **44/161-248-8282**) is ideal for easygoing travelers with little cycling experience. Tours cover most of France. Prices vary according to type of tour (both self-guided and small groups are available); buffet breakfasts and gourmet dinners are included.

Fat Tire Bike Tours (www.fattirebiketours.com/paris; 🕾 **01-82-88-80-96**) offers a 3½-hour day or night tour of Paris by bike in English; adult tickets cost 32€. It also organizes popular cycling tours of Versailles and Giverny.

BUS TOURS   Most larger cities in France offer hop-on, hop-off bus tours, ideal for scoping out the lay of the land. See specific chapters for details.

CHAUFFEURED TOURS   **4 Roues Sous 1 Parapluie** (www.4roues-sous-1parapluie.com; $\textcircled{C}$ **01-58-59-27-82**) offers chauffeur-driven themed rides around Paris in its colorful fleet of Citroën 2CV, the tiny but classic French car described as "4 roues sous 1 parapluie" ("4 wheels under 1 umbrella"). Tours for three start at 20€ per person for 30 minutes and 71€ per person for a 1½-hour Paris movie tour. The fewer people in the car, the more expensive the tour per person.

SHOPPING TOURS   Paris is a dream come true for shopaholics. **Chic Shopping Paris** (www.chicshoppingparis.com; $\textcircled{C}$ **573/355-9777** in North America) offers tours in English designed to give visitors a behind-the-scenes shopping experience. Themed tours include Made in France and Arts and Antiques. All of the standard tours are 4 hours and start at 100€ per person.

WALKING TOURS & EXCURSIONS   Context Travel (www.context travel.com; $\textcircled{C}$ **800/691-6036**) organizes small-group and private walking tours led by scholars and experts in Paris. Day trips to various destinations such as Normandy, the Loire, and Chartres Tours are also offered, lasting from 2 hours to all day. Prices start at 70€per person.

GETTING AROUND

Within most major cities—including Paris, Marseille, and Nice—public transportation is efficient, comprehensive, and cheap. In smaller towns, such as Rouen, Arles, or Antibes, it's easy to navigate the city center on foot. See each chapter for specific details.

By Plane

Air France (www.airfrance.com; $\textcircled{C}$ **800/237-2747**) is the country's primary carrier, serving around 30 cities in France and 30 more destinations throughout Europe. Air travel time from Paris to almost anywhere in France is about 1 hour. **British Airways** (www.ba.com) links London with Paris, Marseille, and Nice. Low-cost airline **Easyjet** (www.easyjet.com) also links London with Paris, Marseille, and Nice.

By Car

The most charming châteaux and country hotels always seem to lie away from the main cities and train stations. Renting a car is a good way to travel around the French countryside, especially along the Normandy beaches, the Loire Valley, and in rural Provence.

RENTALS   To rent a car, you'll need to present a passport, a driver's license, and a credit card. You will also have to meet the company's minimum-age requirement; 21 or above at most rental agents. The biggest agencies have pickup spots all over France, including **Budget** (www.budget.com; $\textcircled{C}$ **800/472-3325** in the U.S. and Canada), **Hertz** (www.hertz.com; $\textcircled{C}$ **800/654-3001** in the

U.S. and Canada), and **Europcar** (www.europcar.com; ℭ **877/940-6900** in the U.S. and Canada).

Note: The best deals are always booked online, in advance. Though the rental company won't usually mind if you drive your car into, say, Germany, Switzerland, Italy, or Spain, it's often forbidden to transport your car by ferry, including across the Channel to England.

In France, **collision damage waiver (CDW)** is usually factored into the overall rate quoted, but you should always verify this before taking a car on the road. At most companies, the CDW provision won't protect you against theft, so if this is the case, ask about purchasing extra theft protection. Automatic transmission is a luxury in Europe. If you prefer it to stickshift, you must specifically request it—and you'll pay a little extra for it.

GASOLINE Known in France as *essence,* gas is expensive for those accustomed to North American prices, although the smaller cars common in Europe use far less gas. Depending on your car, you'll need either leaded *(avec plomb)* or unleaded *(sans plomb).*

Note: Sometimes you can drive for miles in rural France without encountering a gas station; don't let your tank get dangerously low.

DRIVING RULES Everyone in the car, in both the front and the back seats, must wear seat belts. Children 11 and under must ride in the back seat.

In France, you drive on the right. Drivers are supposed to yield to the car on their right, except where signs indicate otherwise, as at traffic circles.

If you violate the speed limit, expect a big fine. Limits are about 130kmph (81 mph) on expressways, about 110kmph (68 mph) on major national highways, and 90kmph (56 mph) on country roads. In towns, don't exceed 50kmph (31 mph).

Note: It's illegal to use a cellphone while you're driving in France; you will be ticketed if you're stopped.

MAPS While most Frenchmen are happy with Google Maps, traditional motorists opt for the large **Michelin maps** of the country and regions (www. viamichelin.com) on sale at all gas stations. Big travel-book stores in North America carry these maps as well. GPS navigation devices can be rented at most car-hire stations.

BREAKDOWNS/ASSISTANCE A breakdown is called *une panne* in France. Call the police at ℭ **17** (if calling from a landline) or ℭ **112** (if calling from a mobile phone) anywhere in France to be put in touch with the nearest garage. Most local garages offer towing.

By Train

The world's fastest trains—known as *Train à Grande Vitesse,* or TGVs—link some 50 French cities, allowing you to travel from Paris to just about anywhere else in the country within hours. With 32,000km (20,000 miles) of track and 3,000 stations, SNCF (French National Railroads; www.voyages-sncf.com, or call ℭ **36-35** in France) is fabled for its on-time performance and comfy trains. You can travel in first or second class by day and couchette by night. Most trains have light dining facilities.

For information or reservations, go online (www.voyages-sncf.com). You can also visit any local travel agency. If you have a chip credit card and know your PIN, you can use your card to buy your ticket at the easy-to-use *billet-teries* (ticket machines with an English-menu option) in every train station.

RAIL PASSES Rail passes as well as individual rail tickets are available from **Rail Europe** (www.raileurope.com; ✆ **800/622-8600** in the U.S.). Options include a 5-day rail pass usable for a 1-month period for $264. **Eurail** (www.eurail.com) offers regional rail passes throughout Europe, including a France-and-Italy combined pass for $447, allowing 6 days of first-class travel within a 2-month period.

By Bicycle

Over the past few years, most cities and towns throughout France have initiated bike-sharing schemes. You can register online or directly at one of the city's dozens of bike stands; in most cases, you'll need a credit card and a mobile phone. Average fees range from 1€ for 1 day to 7€ for a week and entitle you to use any of the city's hundreds of bikes for up to 30 minutes at a time. When you're finished, just slot the cycle back into any allocated bike stand around town. Among many others, Paris, Rouen, Caen, Avignon, Aix-en-Provence, Marseille, and Nice all offer city-wide bike-sharing. Monaco, being the showiest town in the South of France, introduced an all-electric bike-share scheme (as well as an all-electric car-share program) in 2015. See each chapter for specific details.

On Foot

France's ancient **Sentiers de Grande Randonnée** (www.grsentiers.org), or "GR" walking routes, link many of the country's prettiest towns. Close to 2 centuries old and stretching over 180,000km (112,000 miles), these footpaths ripple through vineyards and along the coastline, crisscrossing picturesque towns and mountain passes en route. Favorites include the GR6, from Bordeaux to the Alps via the Pont du Gard, the GR 223 past Normandy's beaches and Mont St-Michel, and the challenging GR20, a mountainous trail along Corsica's spine. A new section of the GR network, the GR 653A, connects the towns of Menton and Arles with the Santiago de Compostela pilgrim's route in Spain. Keep an eye out for the routes' red and white way-markings.

[Fast FACTS] FRANCE

Business Hours Business hours in France can be erratic. Most banks are open Monday through Friday from 9:30am to 4:30pm. Many, particularly in small towns, take a long lunch break. Hours are usually posted on the door. Most museums close 1 day a week (often Tues), and they're generally closed on national holidays. Usual hours are from 9:30am to 5pm. In Paris or other big French cities, stores are open from around 10am to 6 or 7pm, with or without a lunch break (up to 2 hr.). Some shops, delis, cafes, and newsstands open at 8am and close at 8 or 9pm.

Disabled Travelers

Facilities for travelers in France, and nearly all new or modern hotels, provide disabled access. The TGVs (high-speed trains) are wheelchair accessible; older trains have compartments for wheelchair boarding. If you visit the Paris tourist office website (www.paris info.com) and click on "Practical Paris," the section "Practical information for Disabled Visitors" includes links to a number of websites dedicated to travelers with disabilities. For disabled-access to Paris public transport, see www.infomobi.com. **Handiplage** (www.handiplage.fr) has a detailed map and breakdown of every French beach that offers accessible to disabled visitors.

Doctors

Doctors are listed in Pages Jaunes (Yellow Pages; www.pages jaunes.fr) under "Médecins: Médecins généralistes." The minimum fee for a consultation is about 23€—for this rate, look for a doctor who is described as "secteur 1." The higher the "secteur," the higher the fee. **SOS Médecins** (www.sosmede cins.fr; *C* **36-24**) can make house calls. See also "Emergencies" and "Health" later in this section.

Drinking Laws

As well as bars and restaurants, supermarkets and cafes sell alcoholic beverages. The legal drinking age is 18, but persons under that age can be served alcohol if accompanied by a parent or guardian. Drinking and driving is illegal, and incurs a heavy fine.

Drugstores

Spot French *pharmacies* by the green neon cross above the door. If your local pharmacy is closed, there should be a sign on the door indicating the nearest one open. Alternatively, **Pharmacies de Garde** (www.pharmaciesde garde.com; *C* **32-37**) can direct you to the nearest open pharmacy.

Electricity

Electricity in France runs on 220 volts AC (60 cycles). Adapters or transformers are needed to fit sockets, which you can buy in branches of Darty or FNAC.

Embassies & Consulates

If you have a passport, immigration, legal, or other problem, contact your consulate. Many are open Monday to Friday, approximately 10am to 5pm. However, call or check online before you visit to confirm.

Australian Embassy: 4 rue Jean-Rey, 15e (www.france. embassy.gov.au; *C* **01-40-59-33-00;** Métro: Bir Hakeim).

Canadian Embassy: 35 av. Montaigne, 8e (www.amb-canada.fr; *C* **01-44-43-29-00;** Métro: Franklin-D-Roosevelt or Alma-Marceau).

Irish Embassy: 4 rue Rude, 16e (www.embassyofireland. fr; *C* **01-44-17-67-00;** Métro: Argentine).

New Zealand Embassy: 7ter rue Léonard de Vinci, 16e (www.nzembassy.com/ france; *C* **01-45-01-43-43;** Métro: Victor Hugo).

British Embassy: 35 Rue du Faubourg St-Honoré, 8e (http://ukinfrance.fco.gov. uk; *C* **01-44-51-31-00;** Métro: Concorde or Madeleine).

United States Embassy: 2 av. Gabriel, 8e (http:// france.usembassy.gov; *C* **01-43-12-22-22;** Métro: Concorde).

Emergencies

In an emergency while at a hotel, contact the front desk. If the emergency involves theft, go to the police station in person. Otherwise, call *C* **112** from a cellphone. The fire brigade can be reached at *C* **18.** For an ambulance, call *C* **15.** For the police, call *C* **17.**

Etiquette & Customs

French value pleasantries and take manners seriously: Say "Bonjour, Madame/Monsieur" when entering an establishment and "Au revoir" when you depart. Always say "Pardon" when you accidentally bump into someone. With strangers, people who are older than you and professional contacts use *vous* rather than *tu* (*vous* is the polite form of the pronoun *you*).

Health

For travel abroad, non-E.U. nationals should consider buying medical travel insurance. For U.S. citizens, Medicare and Medicaid do not provide coverage for medical costs incurred abroad; check your health insurance before leaving home. U.K. nationals need a **European Health Insurance Card** (**EHIC;** www.ehic.org.uk) to receive free or reduced-cost medical care during a visit to a France.

If you take regular medication, pack it in its original pharmacy containers, along with a copy of your prescription

Holidays   Major holidays are New Year's Day (Jan 1), Easter Sunday and Monday (late Mar/Apr), Labor Day (May 1), VE Day (May 8), Ascension Thursday (40 days after Easter), Pentecost/Whit Sunday and Whit Monday (seventh Sun/Mon after Easter), Bastille Day (July 14), Assumption Day (Aug 15), All Saints Day (Nov 1), Armistice Day (Nov 11), and Christmas Day (Dec 25).

Hospitals   Dial 🕾 **15** for medical emergencies. In Paris, the **American Hospital,** 63 bd. Victor-Hugo, in the suburb of Neuilly-sur-Seine (www.american-hospital.org; 🕾 **01-46-41-25-25;** Métro: Pont-de-Levallois), operates a 24-hour, bilingual emergency service. For hospitals in other major French cities, see individual chapters.

Hotlines   **SOS Help** is a hotline for English-speaking callers in crisis (www.sos-helpline.org;

🕾 **01-46-21-46-46**). Open 3 to 11pm daily.

LGBT Travelers   France is one of the world's most tolerant countries toward gays and lesbians. Paris boasts a large gay population, with many clubs, restaurants, organizations, and services. For books, DVDs, and local information, visit Paris's best-stocked gay bookstore, **Les Mots à la Bouche,** 6 rue Ste-Croix-de-la-Bretonnerie, 4e (www.motsbouche.com; 🕾 **01-42-78-88-30;** Métro: Hôtel-de-Ville). Visit www.paris-gay.com, www.gayvox.fr, and www.gay-provence.org for updated listings about the gay and lesbian scene.

Mail   Most post offices in France are open Monday to Friday from 8am to 5pm and every Saturday from 8am to noon. A 24-hour post office is located in Paris at 52 rue du Louvre 1e (🕾 **36-31**). Allow 5 to 8 days to send or receive mail from home. Stamps are also sold in *tabacs* (tobacconists). For more information, see www.laposte.fr.

Mobile Phones   You can use your mobile phone in France, provided it is **GSM** (Global System for Mobile Communications) and triband or quad-band; just confirm with your operator before you leave.

Using your phone abroad can be expensive, so it's a good idea to get it "unlocked" before you leave. This means you can buy a French SIM card from one of the three main French providers, **Bouygues Télécom** (www.bouyguestelecom.fr), **Orange** (www.orange.fr), or **SFR** (www.sfr.fr). Or do like the locals do and use **Skype** (www.skype.com) for long-distance calls.

Money & Costs
Frommer's lists exact prices in the local currency. The currency conversions quoted here were correct at press time. However, rates fluctuate, so before departing, consult a currency exchange website such as www.oanda.com to check current rates.

It's always advisable to bring a mix of cash and credit cards on vacation. Before you leave home, exchange enough petty cash to cover airport incidentals, tipping, and transportation to your hotel. Alternatively, withdraw money upon arrival at an airport ATM. In many international destinations, ATMs offer the best exchange rates. Avoid exchanging money at commercial exchange bureaus and hotels, which often have the highest transaction fees and terrible exchange rates.

THE VALUE OF THE EURO VS. OTHER POPULAR CURRENCIES

Euro (€)	US$	C$	UK£	A$	NZ$
1	1.37	1.49	0.82	1.46	1.58

ATMs are widely available in France.

Newspapers The most popular French newspapers are **Le Monde** (www.lemonde.fr), **Le Figaro** (www.lefigaro.fr), and left-leaning **Libération** (www.liberation.fr).

The English-language **International New York Times** (http://international.nytimes.com), based in Paris and published Monday to Saturday, is distributed all over France.

Packing Tips Remember that the bulk of hotel rooms in France are small indeed. Try to adhere to the old traveling maxim, "pack half of what you think you need." You will *always* actually need far less than you imagine. And you can easily purchase any missing items—along with the copious souvenirs you'll pick up too—along the way.

Passports Citizens of the U.K., New Zealand, Australia, Canada, and the United States need a valid passport to enter France. The passport is valid for a stay of 90 days.

Police In an emergency, call ☎ **17** or **112** from a mobile or land-line phone anywhere in France.

Safety The most common menace, especially in large cities and on street markets, is the plague of *pickpockets*. Take precautions and be vigilant at all times: Don't take more money with you than necessary, keep your passport in a concealed pouch or leave it at your hotel, and ensure

that your bag is firmly closed at all times. In cafes, bars, and restaurants, it's best not to leave your bag under the table, on the back of your chair, or on an empty chair beside you. Keep it between your legs or on your lap. Never leave valuables or luggage in a car, and never travel with your car unlocked.

In general, Paris is a safe city and it is safe to use the Métro late at night, though it is always best to not draw attention to the fact you are foreign by speaking loudly in English. Use common sense when taking public transport at night.

Although there is a significant level of discrimination against West and North African immigrants, there has been almost no harassment of African-American tourists to Paris or France itself in recent decades. However. **S.O.S. Racisme,** 51 av. de Flandre, 19e (www.sos-racisme.org; ☎ **01-40-35-36-55**), offers legal advice to victims of prejudice and will even intervene to help with the police.

Female travelers should not expect any more hassle than in other major cities, and the same precautions apply. Avoid walking alone at night and never get into an unmarked taxi. If you are approached in the street or on public transportation, it's best to avoid entering into conversation, and walk into a well-lit, populated area.

Senior Travel Many discounts are available to men and women over 60. Senior

citizens do not get a discount for traveling on public transport in Paris, but national trains have senior discounts. Check out www.voyages-sncf.com for more information. Frommers.com offers more information and resources on travel for seniors.

Smoking Smoking is banned in all public places in France, including cafes, restaurants, and nightclubs. It's permitted on outdoor and semi-enclosed terraces.

Student Travel Student discounts are less common in France than other countries, but simply because young people under 26 are usually offered reduced rates. Be on the lookout for the **Ticket Jeunes Weekend** when using the Métro in Paris. It can be used on a Saturday, Sunday, or bank holiday, and provides unlimited travel in zones 1 to 3 for 3.85€. SNCF also offer discounts for under-26-year-olds traveling on national trains (www.voyages-sncf.com).

Taxes As a member of the European Union, France routinely imposes a value-added tax (VAT in English; TVA in French) on most goods. The standard VAT is 20%, and prices that include it are often marked TTC (*toutes taxes comprises*, "all taxes included"). If you're not an E.U. resident, you can get a VAT refund if you're spending less than 6 months in France, you purchase goods worth at least 175€ at a single shop on the same day, the goods fit into your luggage, and the shop offers *vente en détaxe* (duty-free sales or tax-free shopping). Give the shop your passport and ask for a *bordereau de détaxe* (export sales invoice). When you leave the country, you need to get all three pages of this invoice validated by France's Customs officials. They'll keep one sheet, and you must post the pink one back to the shop. Once the shop receives its stamped copy, it will send you a *virement* (fund transfer) using the payment method you requested. It may take several months. You can also opt to receive your VAT refund in cash at some airports for an additional fee.

Telephones Public phones can still be found in France. All require a phone card (known as a *télécarte*), which can be purchased at post offices or *tabacs*.

The country code for France is 33. To make a local or long-distance call within France, dial the person or place's 10-digit number. If you're calling from outside of France, drop the initial 0 (zero).

Mobile numbers begin with 06 or 07. Numbers beginning with 0-800,

0-804, 0-805, and 0-809 are free in France; other numbers beginning with 8 are not. Most four-digit numbers starting with 10, 30, and 31 are free of charge.

Time France is on Central European Time, which is 1 hour ahead of Greenwich Mean Time. French daylight saving time lasts from the last Sunday in March to the last Sunday in October, when clocks are set 1 hour ahead of the standard time. France uses the 24-hour clock (so 13h is 1pm, 14h15 is 2:15pm, and so on).

Tipping By law, all bills in **cafes, bars, and restaurants** say *service compris*, which means the service charge is included. However, it is customary to leave 1€ or 2€, depending on the quality of the service; in more upscale restaurants leave 5€ to 10€. **Taxi drivers** usually expect a 5% to 10% tip, or for the fare to be rounded up to the next euro. The French tip **hairdressers** around 10%, and if you go to the theater, you're expected to tip the **usher** about 2€.

Toilets If you're in dire need, duck into a cafe or brasserie to use the lavatory. It's customary to make

a small purchase if you do so. Paris is full of gray-colored automatic street toilets, some of which are free to use, and are washed and disinfected after each use. France still has some hole-in-the-ground squat toilets. Try not to lose your change down the pan!

Visas E.U. nationals don't need a visa to enter France. Nor do U.S., Canadian, Australian, New Zealand, or South African citizens for trips of up to 3 months. Nationals of other countries should make inquiries or look online at the nearest French embassy or consulate.

Visitor Information Before you go, your best source of information is the **French Government Tourist Office** (www.france tourism.com).

Water Drinking water is generally safe. If you ask for water in a restaurant, it'll be served bottled (for which you'll pay), unless you specifically request *une carafe d'eau* or *l'eau du robinet* (tap water). Your waiter may ask if you'd like your water *avec gas* (carbonated) or *sans gas* (without bubbles).

Accommodations

Restaurants

PHOTO CREDITS